EVIDENCES OF CHRISTIANITY

by

WILLIAM PALEY, D.D.

Based on Paley's Revised 1851 Edition

EVIDENCES OF CHRISTIANITY

by

WILLIAM PALEY, D.D.

Based on Paley's Revised 1851 Edition

EVIDENCES OF CHRISTIANITY by WILLIAM PALEY, D.D.

Based on Paley's Revised 1851 Edition

Published by Suzeteo Enterprises. Copyright 2012.

ISBN: 978-1-936830-42-8

THE HONOURABLE AND RIGHT REVEREND
JAMES YORK, D.D., LORD BISHOP OF ELY

My LORD,

When, five years ago, an important station in the University of Cambridge awaited your Lordship's disposal, you were pleased to offer it to me. The circumstances under which this offer was made demand a public acknowledgment. I had never seen your Lordship; I possessed no connection which could possibly recommend me to your favour; I was known to you only by my endeavour, in common with many others, to discharge my duty as a tutor in the University; and by some very imperfect, but certainly well-intended, and, as you thought, useful publications since. In an age by no means wanting in examples of honourable patronage, although this deserve not to be mentioned in respect of the object of your Lordship's choice, it is inferior to none in the purity and disinterestedness of the motives which suggested it.

How the following work may be received, I pretend not to foretell. My first prayer concerning it is, that it may do good to any: my second hope, that it may assist, what it hath always been my earnest wish to promote, the religious part of an academical education. If in this latter view it might seem, in any degree, to excuse your Lordship's judgment of its author, I shall be gratified by the reflection that, to a kindness flowing from public principles, I have made the best public return in my power.

In the mean time, and in every event, I rejoice in the opportunity here afforded me of testifying the sense I entertain of your Lordship's conduct, and of a notice which I regard as the most flattering distinction of my life.

I am, MY LORD, With sentiments of gratitude and respect, Your Lordship's faithful And most obliged servant,

WILLIAM PALEY.

CONTENTS
Preparatory Considerations—Of the antecedent Credibility of Miracles.

PART I.
OF THE DIRECT HISTORICAL EVIDENCE OF CHRISTIANITY, AND WHEREIN IT IS DISTINGUISHED FROM THE EVIDENCE ALLEGED FOR OTHER MIRACLES.

Proposition stated:

PROPOSITION I.
That there is satisfactory Evidence, that many professing to be original Witnesses of the Christian Miracles passed their Lives in Labours, Dangers, and Sufferings, voluntarily undergone in Attestation of the Accounts which they delivered, and solely in consequence of their Belief of those Accounts; and that they submitted, from the same Motives, to new Rules of Conduct.

OF THE DIRECT HISTORICAL EVIDENCE OF CHRISTIANITY, AND WHEREIN IT IS DISTINGUISHED FROM THE EVIDENCE ALLEGED FOR OTHER MIRACLES.

PROPOSITION II.

That there is not satisfactory Evidence, that Persons pretending to be original Witnesses of any other similar Miracles have acted in the same Manner, in Attestation of the Accounts which they delivered, and solely in consequence of their Belief of the Truth of those Accounts.

PART II.
OF THE AUXILIARY EVIDENCES OF CHRISTIANITY.

PART III
A BRIEF CONSIDERATION OF SOME POPULAR OBJECTIONS.

PREPARATORY CONSIDERATIONS.

I deem it unnecessary to prove that mankind stood in need of a revelation because I have met with no serious person who thinks that, even under the Christian revelation, we have too much light, or any degree of assurance which is superfluous. I desire, moreover, that in judging of Christianity, it may be remembered that the question lies between this religion and none: for, if the Christian religion be not credible, no one, with whom we have to do, will support the pretensions of any other.

Suppose, then, the world we live in to have had a Creator; suppose it to appear, from the predominant aim and tendency of the provisions and contrivances observable in the universe, that the Deity, when he formed it, consulted for the happiness of his sensitive creation; suppose the disposition which dictated this counsel to continue; suppose a part of the creation to have received faculties from their Maker, by which they are capable of rendering a moral obedience to his will, and of voluntarily pursuing any end for which he has designed them; suppose the Creator to intend for these, his rational and accountable agents, a second state of existence, in which their situation will be by their behaviour in the first state, by which suppose (and by no other) the objection to the divine government in not putting a difference between the good and the bad, and the inconsistency of this confusion with the care and benevolence discoverable in the works of the Deity is done away; suppose it to be of the utmost importance to the subjects of this dispensation to know what is intended for them, that is, suppose the knowledge of it to be highly conducive to the happiness of the species, a purpose which so many provisions of nature are calculated to promote: Suppose, nevertheless, almost the whole race, either by the imperfection of their faculties, the misfortune of their situation, or by the loss of some prior revelation, to want this knowledge, and not to be likely, without the aid of a new revelation, to attain it; under these circumstances, is it improbable that a revelation should be made? Is it incredible that God should interpose for such a purpose? Suppose him to design for mankind a future state; is it unlikely that he should acquaint him with it?

Now in what way can a revelation be made, but by miracles? In none which we are able to conceive. Consequently, in whatever degree it is probable, or not very improbable, that a revelation should be communicated to mankind at all: in the same degree is it probable, or not very improbable, that miracles should be wrought. Therefore, when miracles are related to have been wrought in the promulgating of a revelation manifestly wanted, and, if true, of inestimable value, the improbability which arises from the miraculous nature of the things

1

related is not greater than the original improbability that such a revelation should be imparted by God.

I wish it, however, to be correctly understood, in what manner, and to what extent, this argument is alleged. We do not assume the attributes of the Deity, or the existence of a future state, in order to prove the reality of miracles. That reality always must be proved by evidence. We assert only, that in miracles adduced in support of revelation there is not any such antecedent improbability as no testimony can surmount. And for the purpose of maintaining this assertion, we contend, that the incredibility of miracles related to have been wrought in attestation of a message from God, conveying intelligence of a future state of rewards and punishments, and teaching mankind how to prepare themselves for that state, is not in itself greater than the event, call it either probable or improbable, of the two following propositions being true: namely, first, that a future state of existence should be destined by God for his human creation; and, secondly, that, being so destined, he should acquaint them with it. It is not necessary for our purpose, that these propositions be capable of proof, or even that, by arguments drawn from the light of nature, they can be made out to be probable; it is enough that we are able to say concerning them, that they are not so violently improbable, so contradictory to what we already believe of the divine power and character, that either the propositions themselves, or facts strictly connected with the propositions (and therefore no further improbable than they are improbable), ought to be rejected at first sight, and to be rejected by whatever strength or complication of evidence they be attested.

This is the prejudication we would resist. For to this length does a modern objection to miracles go, viz., that no human testimony can in any case render them credible. I think the reflection above stated, that, if there be a revelation, there must be miracles, and that, under the circumstances in which the human species are placed, a revelation is not improbable, or not to any great degree, to be a fair answer to the whole objection.

But since it is an objection which stands in the very threshold our argument, and, if admitted, is a bar to every proof, and to all future reasoning upon the subject, it may be necessary, before we proceed further, to examine the principle upon which it professes to be founded; which principle is concisely this, That it is contrary to experience that a miracle should be true, but not contrary to experience that testimony should be false.

Now there appears a small ambiguity in the term "experience," and in the phrases, "contrary to experience," or "contradicting experience," which it may be necessary to remove in the first place. Strictly speaking, the narrative of a fact is then only contrary to experience, when the fact is related to have existed at a time and place, at which time and place we being present did not perceive it to exist; as if it should be asserted, that in a particular room, and at a particular hour of a certain day, a man was raised from the dead, in which room, and at the time specified, we, being present and looking on, perceived no such event to have taken place. Here the assertion is contrary to experience properly so called; and this is a contrariety which no evidence can surmount. It matters nothing, whether the fact be of a miraculous nature, or not. But although this be the experience, and the contrariety, which Archbishop Tillotson alleged in the quotation with which Mr. Hume opens his Essay, it is certainly not that experience, nor that contrariety, which Mr. Hume himself intended to object. And short of this I know no intelligible signification which can be affixed to the term "contrary to experience," but one, viz., that of not having ourselves experienced anything similar to the thing related, or such things not being generally experienced by others. I say "not generally" for to state concerning the fact in question, that no such thing was ever experienced, or that universal experience is against it, is to assume the subject of the controversy.

Now the improbability which arises from the want (for this properly is a want, not a contradiction) of experience, is only equal to the probability there is, that, if the thing were true, we should experience things similar to it, or that such things would be generally experienced. Suppose it then to be true that miracles were wrought on the first promulgation of Christianity, when nothing but miracles could decide its authority, is it certain that such miracles would be repeated so often, and in so many places, as to become objects of general experience? Is it a probability approaching to certainty? Is it a probability of any great strength or force? Is it such as no evidence can encounter? And yet this probability is the exact converse, and therefore the exact measure, of the improbability which arises from the want of experience, and which Mr. Hume represents as invincible by human testimony.

It is not like alleging a new law of nature, or a new experiment in natural philosophy; because, when these are related, it is expected that, under the same circumstances, the same effect will follow universally; and in proportion as this expectation is justly entertained, the want of a corresponding experience negatives the history. But to expect concerning a miracle, that it should succeed upon a repetition, is to expect that which would make it cease to be a miracle, which is contrary to its nature as such, and would totally destroy the use and purpose for which it was wrought.

The force of experience as an objection to miracles is founded in the presumption, either that the course of nature is invariable, or that, if it be ever varied, variations will be frequent and general. Has the necessity of this alternative been demonstrated? Permit us to call the course of nature the agency of an intelligent Being, and is there any good reason for judging this state of the case to be probable? Ought we not rather to expect that such a Being, on occasions of peculiar importance, may interrupt the order which he had appointed, yet, that such occasions should return seldom; that these interruptions consequently should be confined to the experience of a few; that the want of it, therefore, in many, should be matter neither of surprise nor objection?

But, as a continuation of the argument from experience, it is said that, when we advance accounts of miracles, we assign effects without causes, or we attribute effects to causes inadequate to the purpose, or to causes of the operation of which we have no experience of what causes, we may ask, and of what effects, does the objection speak? If it be answered that, when we ascribe the cure of the palsy to a touch, of blindness to the anointing of the eyes with clay, or the raising of the dead to a word, we lay ourselves open to this imputation; we reply that we ascribe no such effects to such causes. We perceive no virtue or energy in these things more than in other things of the same kind. They are merely signs to connect the miracle with its end. The effect we ascribe simply to the volition of Deity; of whose existence and power, not to say of whose Presence and agency, we have previous and independent proof. We have, therefore, all we seek for in the works of rational agents—a sufficient power and an adequate motive. In a word, once believe that there is a God, and miracles are not incredible.

Mr. Hume states the ease of miracles to be a contest of opposite improbabilities, that is to say, a question whether it be more improbable that the miracle should be true, or the testimony false: and this I think a fair account of the controversy. But herein I remark a want of argumentative justice, that, in describing the improbability of miracles, he suppresses all those circumstances of extenuation, which result from our knowledge of the existence, power, and disposition of the Deity; his concern in the creation, the end answered by the miracle, the importance of that end, and its subserviency to the plan pursued in the work of nature. As Mr. Hume has represented the question, miracles are alike incredible to him who is previously assured of the constant agency of a Divine Being, and to him who believes that no such Being exists in the universe. They are equally incredible, whether related to have been wrought upon occasion the most deserving, and for purposes the most beneficial, or for no assignable end whatever, or for an end confessedly trifling or pernicious. This surely cannot be a correct statement. In adjusting also the other side of the balance, the strength and weight of testimony, this author has provided an answer to every possible accumulation of historical proof by telling us that we are not obliged to explain how the story of the evidence arose. Now I think that we are obliged; not, perhaps, to show by positive accounts how it did, but by a probable hypothesis how it might so happen. The existence of the testimony is a phenomenon; the truth of the fact solves the phenomenon. If we reject this solution, we ought to have

4

some other to rest in; and none, even by our adversaries, can be admired, which is not inconsistent with the principles that regulate human affairs and human conduct at present, or which makes men then to have been a different kind of beings from what they are now.

But the short consideration which, independently of every other, convinces me that there is no solid foundation in Mr. Hume's conclusion, is the following. When a theorem is proposed to a mathematician, the first thing he does with it is to try it upon a simple case, and if it produce a false result, he is sure that there must be some mistake in the demonstration. Now to proceed in this way with what may be called Mr. Hume's theorem. If twelve men, whose probity and good sense I had long known, should seriously and circumstantially relate to me an account of a miracle wrought before their eyes, and in which it was impossible that they should be deceived: if the governor of the country, hearing a rumour of this account, should call these men into his presence, and offer them a short proposal, either to confess the imposture, or submit to be tied up to a gibbet; if they should refuse with one voice to acknowledge that there existed any falsehood or imposture in the case: if this threat were communicated to them separately, yet with no different effect; if it was at last executed; if I myself saw them, one after another, consenting to be racked, burnt, or strangled, rather than live up the truth of their account;— still if Mr. Hume's rule be my guide, I am not to believe them. Now I undertake to say that there exists not a sceptic in the world who would not believe them, or who would defend such incredulity.

Instances of spurious miracles supported by strong apparent testimony undoubtedly demand examination; Mr. Hume has endeavoured to fortify his argument by some examples of this kind. I hope in a proper place to show that none of them reach the strength or circumstances of the Christian evidence. In these, however, consists the weight of his objection; in the principle itself, I am persuaded, there is none.

PART I.

OF THE DIRECT HISTORICAL EVIDENCE OF CHRISTIANITY, AND WHEREIN IT IS DISTINGUISHED FROM THE EVIDENCE ALLEGED FOR OTHER MIRACLES.

The two propositions which I shall endeavour to establish are these:

I. That there is satisfactory evidence that many professing to be original witnesses of the Christian miracles passed their lives in labours, dangers, and sufferings, voluntarily undergone in attestation of the accounts which they delivered, and solely in consequence of their belief of those accounts; and that they also submitted, from the same motives, to new rules of conduct.

2. That there is not satisfactory evidence that persons professing to be original witnesses of other miracles, in their nature as certain as these are, have ever acted in the same manner, in attestation of the accounts which they delivered, and properly in consequence of their belief of those accounts.

The first of these prepositions, as it forms the argument will stand at the head of the following nine chapters.

CHAPTER I

There is satisfactory evidence that many, professing to be original witness of the Christian miracles, passed their lives in labours, dangers, and sufferings, voluntarily undergone in attestation of the accounts which they delivered, and solely in consequence of their of belief of those accounts; and that they also submitted, from the same motives, to new rules of conduct.

To support this proposition, two points are necessary to be made out: first, that the Founder of the institution, his associates and immediate followers, acted the part which the proposition imputes to them: secondly, that they did so in attestation of the miraculous history recorded in our Scriptures, and solely in consequence of their belief of the truth of this history.

Before we produce any particular testimony to the activity and sufferings which compose the subject of our first assertion, it will be proper to consider the degree of probability which the assertion derives from the nature of the case, that is, by inferences from those parts of the case which, in point of fact, are on all hands acknowledged.

First, then, the Christian Religion exists, and, therefore, by some means or other, was established. Now it either owes the principle of its establishment, i.e. its first publication, to the activity of the Person who was the founder of the institution, and of those who were joined with him in the undertaking, or we are driven upon the strange supposition, that, although they might lie by, others would take it up; although they were quiet and silent, other persons busied themselves in the success and propagation of their story. This is perfectly incredible. To me it appears little less than certain, that, if the first announcing of the religion by the Founder had not been followed up by the zeal and industry of his immediate disciples, the attempt must have expired in its birth. Then as to the kind and degree of exertion which was employed, and the mode of life to which these persons submitted, we reasonably suppose it to be like that which we observe in all others who voluntarily become missionaries of a new faith. Frequent, earnest, and laborious preaching, constantly conversing with religious persons upon religion, a sequestration from the common pleasures, engagements, and varieties of life, and an addiction to one serious object, compose the habits of such men. I do not say that this mode of life is without enjoyment, but I say that the enjoyment springs from sincerity. With a consciousness at the bottom of hollowness and falsehood, the fatigue and restraint would become insupportable. I am apt to believe that very few hypocrites engage in these undertakings; or, however, persist in them long. Ordinarily speaking, nothing can overcome the indolence of mankind, the love which is natural to most tempers of cheerful society and cheerful scenes, or the desire, which is common to all, of personal ease and freedom, but conviction.

Secondly, it is also highly probable, from the nature of the case, that the propagation of the new religion was attended with difficulty and danger. As addressed to the Jews, it was a system adverse, not only to their habitual opinions but to those opinions upon which their hopes, their partialities, their pride, their consolation, was founded. This people, with or without reason, had worked themselves into a persuasion, that some signal and greatly advantageous change was to be effected in the condition of their country, by the agency of a long-promised messenger from heaven.[1] The rulers of the Jews, their leading sect, their priesthood, had been the authors of this persuasion to the common people. So that it was not merely the conjecture of theoretical divines, or the secret expectation of a few recluse devotees, but it was become the popular hope and Passion, and, like all popular opinions, undoubting and impatient of contradiction. They clung to this hope under every misfortune of their country, and with more tenacity as their dangers and calamities increased. To find, therefore, that expectations so gratifying were to be worse than disappointed; that they were to end in the diffusion of a mild unambitious religion, which, instead of victories and triumphs, instead of exalting their nation and institution above the rest of the world, was to advance those whom they despised to an equality with themselves, in those very points of comparison in which they most valued their own distinction, could be no very pleasing discovery to a Jewish mind; nor could the messengers of such intelligence expect to be well received or easily credited. The doctrine was equally harsh and novel. The extending of the kingdom of God to those who did not conform to the law of Moses was a notion that had never before entered into the thoughts of a Jew.

The character of the new institution was, in other respects also, ungrateful to Jewish habits and principles. Their own religion was in a high degree technical. Even the enlightened Jew placed a great deal of stress upon the ceremonies of his law, saw in them a great deal of virtue and efficacy; the gross and vulgar had scarcely anything else; and the hypocritical and ostentatious magnified them above measure, as being the instruments of their own reputation and influence. The Christian scheme, without formally repealing the Levitical code, lowered its estimation extremely. In the place of strictness and zeal in performing the observances which that code prescribed, or which tradition had added to

---

[1] "Pererebuerat oriento toto vetus et contans opinio, esse in fatis, ut eo tempore Judaea profecti rerum potirsatur." Sueton. Vespasian. cap. 4—8.
"Pluribus persuasio inerat, antiquis sacerdotum literis contineri, eo ipso tempore fore, ut valesecret oriens, profectique Judaea rerum potirentur." Tacit. Hist. lib. v. cap. 9—13.

it, the new sect preached up faith, well-regulated affections, inward purity, and moral rectitude of disposition, as the true ground, on the part of the worshipper, of merit and acceptance with God. This, however rational it may appear, or recommending to us at present, did not by any means facilitate the plan then. On the contrary, to disparage those qualities which the highest characters in the country valued themselves most upon, was a sure way of making powerful enemies. As if the frustration of the national hope was not enough, the long-esteemed merit of ritual zeal and punctuality was to be decried, and that by Jews preaching to Jews.

The ruling party at Jerusalem had just before crucified the Founder of the religion. That is a fact which will not be disputed. They, therefore, who stood forth to preach the religion must necessarily reproach these rulers with an execution which they could not but represent as an unjust and cruel murder. This would not render their office more easy, or their situation more safe.

With regard to the interference of the Roman government which was then established in Judea, I should not expect, that, despising as it did the religion of the country, it would, if left to itself, animadvert, either with much vigilance or much severity, upon the schisms and controversies which arose within it. Yet there was that in Christianity which might easily afford a handle of accusation with a jealous government. The Christians avowed an unqualified obedience to a new master. They avowed also that he was the person who had been foretold to the Jews under the suspected title of King. The spiritual nature of this kingdom, the consistency of this obedience with civil subjection, were distinctions too refined to be entertained by a Roman president, who viewed the business at a great distance, or through the medium of very hostile representations. Our histories accordingly inform us, that this was the turn which the enemies of Jesus gave to his character and pretensions in their remonstrances with Pontius Pilate. And Justin Martyr, about a hundred years afterwards, complains that the same mistake prevailed in his time: "Ye, having heard that we are waiting for a kingdom, suppose without distinguishing that we mean a human kingdom, when in truth we speak of that which is with God."[2] And it was undoubtedly a natural source of calumny and misconstruction.

The preachers of Christianity had, therefore, to contend with prejudice backed by power. They had to come forward to a disappointed people, to a priesthood possessing a considerable share of municipal authority, and actuated by strong motives of opposition and resentment; and they had to do this under a foreign government, to whose favour they made no pretensions, and which was constantly surrounded by their

---

[2] Ap. Ima p. 16. Ed. Thirl.

enemies. The well-known, because the experienced, fate of reformers, whenever the reformation subverts some reigning opinion, and does not proceed upon a change that has already taken place in the sentiments of a country, will not allow, much less lead us to suppose that the first propagators of Christianity at Jerusalem and in Judea, under the difficulties and the enemies they had to contend with, and entirely destitute as they were of force, authority, or protection, could execute their mission with personal ease and safety.

Let us next inquire, what might reasonably be expected by the preachers of Christianity when they turned themselves to the heathen public. Now the first thing that strikes us is, that the religion they carried with them was exclusive. It denied without reserve the truth of every article of heathen mythology, the existence of every object of their worship. It accepted no compromise, it admitted no comprehension. It must prevail, if it prevailed at all, by the overthrow of every statue, altar, and temple in the world, It will not easily be credited, that a design, so bold as this was, could in any age be attempted to be carried into execution with impunity.

For it ought to be considered, that this was not setting forth, or magnifying the character and worship of some new competitor for a place in the Pantheon, whose pretensions might he discussed or asserted without questioning the reality of any others: it was pronouncing all other gods to be false, and all other worship vain. From the facility with which the polytheism of ancient nations admitted new objects of worship into the number of their acknowledged divinities, or the patience with which they might entertain proposals of this kind, we can argue nothing as to their toleration of a system, or of the publishers and active propagators of a system, which swept away the very foundation of the existing establishment. The one was nothing more than what it would be, in popish countries, to add a saint to the calendar; the other was to abolish and tread under foot the calendar itself.

Secondly, it ought also to be considered, that this was not the case of philosophers propounding in their books, or in their schools, doubts concerning the truth of the popular creed, or even avowing their disbelief of it. These philosophers did not go about from place to place to collect proselytes from amongst the common people; to form in the heart of the country societies professing their tenets; to provide for the order, instruction and permanency of these societies; nor did they enjoin their followers to withdraw themselves from the public worship of the temples, or refuse a compliance with rites instituted by the laws.[3] These things are

---

[3] The best of the ancient philosophers, Plato, Cicero, and Epictetus, allowed, or rather enjoined, men to worship the gods of the country, and in the established form. See passages to this purpose collected from their works by Dr. Clarke, Nat.

what the Christians did, and what the philosophers did not; and in these consisted the activity and danger of the enterprise.

Thirdly, it ought also to be considered, that this danger proceeded not merely from solemn acts and public resolutions of the state, but from sudden bursts of violence at particular places, from the licence of the populace, the rashness of some magistrates and negligence of others; from the influence and instigation of interested adversaries, and, in general, from the variety and warmth of opinion which an errand so novel and extraordinary could not fail of exciting. I can conceive that the teachers of Christianity might both fear and suffer much from these causes, without any general persecution being denounced against them by imperial authority. Some length of time, I should suppose, might pass, before the vast machine of the Roman empire would be put in motion, or its attention be obtained to religious controversy: but, during that time, a great deal of ill usage might be endured, by a set of friendless, unprotected travellers, telling men, wherever they came, that the religion of their ancestors, the religion in which they had been brought up, the religion of the state, and of the magistrate, the rites which they frequented, the pomp which they admired, was throughout a system of folly and delusion.

Nor do I think that the teachers of Christianity would find protection in that general disbelief of the popular theology, which is supposed to have prevailed amongst the intelligent part of the heathen public. It is by no means true that unbelievers are usually tolerant. They are not disposed (and why should they?) to endanger the present state of things, by suffering a religion of which they believe nothing to be disturbed by another of which they believe as little. They are ready themselves to conform to anything; and are, oftentimes, amongst the foremost to procure conformity from others, by any method which they think likely to be efficacious. When was ever a change of religion patronized by infidels? How little, not withstanding the reigning scepticism, and the magnified liberality of that age, the true principles of toleration were understood by the wisest men amongst them, may be gathered from two eminent and uncontested examples. The younger Pliny, polished as he was by all the literature of that soft and elegant period, could gravely pronounce this monstrous judgment:—"Those who persisted in declaring themselves Christians, I ordered to be led away to punishment, (i.e. to execution,) for I DID NOT DOUBT, whatever it was that they confessed, that contumacy and inflexible obstinacy ought to be punished." His master Trajan, a mild and accomplished prince, went, nevertheless, no further in his sentiments of moderation and equity than what appears in

---

and Rev. Rel. p. 180. ed. v—Except Socrates, they all thought it wiser to comply with the laws than to contend.

the following rescript:—"The Christians are not to be sought for; but if any are brought before you, and convicted, they are to be punished." And this direction he gives, after it had been reported to him by his own president, that, by the most strict examination, nothing could be discovered in the principles of these persons, but "a bad and excessive superstition," accompanied, it seems, with an oath or mutual federation, "to allow themselves in no crime or immoral conduct whatever." The truth is, the ancient heathens considered religion entirely as an affair of state, as much under the tuition of the magistrate as any other part of the police. The religion of that age was not merely allied to the state; it was incorporated into it. Many of its offices were administered by the magistrate. Its titles of pontiffs, augurs, and flamens, were borne by senators, consuls, and generals. Without discussing, therefore, the truth of the theology, they resented every affront put upon the established worship, as a direct opposition to the authority of government.

Add to which, that the religious systems of those times, however ill supported by evidence, had been long established. The ancient religion of a country has always many votaries, and sometimes not the fewer, because its origin is hidden in remoteness and obscurity. Men have a natural veneration for antiquity, especially in matters of religion. What Tacitus says of the Jewish was more applicable to the heathen establishment: "Hi ritus, quoquo modo inducti, antiquitate defenduntur." It was also a splendid and sumptuous worship. It had its priesthood, its endowments, its temples. Statuary, painting, architecture, and music, contributed their effect to its ornament and magnificence. It abounded in festival shows and solemnities, to which the common people are greatly addicted, and which were of a nature to engage them much more than anything of that sort among us. These things would retain great numbers on its side by the fascination of spectacle and pomp, as well as interest many in its preservation by the advantage which they drew from it. "It was moreover interwoven," as Mr. Gibbon rightly represents it, "with every circumstance of business or pleasure, of public or private life, with all the offices and amusements of society." On the due celebration also of its rites, the people were taught to believe, and did believe, that the prosperity of their country in a great measure depended.

I am willing to accept the account of the matter which is given by Mr. Gibbon: "The various modes of worship which prevailed in the Roman world were all considered by the people as equally true, by the philosopher as equally false, and by the magistrate as equally useful:" and I would ask from which of these three classes of men were the Christian missionaries to look for protection or impunity? Could they expect it from the people, "whose acknowledged confidence in the public religion" they subverted from its foundation? From the philosopher, who, "considering all religious as equally false," would of course rank theirs among the number, with the addition of regarding them as busy and troublesome zealots? Or from the magistrate, who, satisfied with the "utility" of the subsisting religion, would not be likely to countenance a spirit of proselytism and innovation:—a system which declared war against every other, and which, if it prevailed, must end in a total rupture of public opinion; an upstart religion, in a word, which was not content with its own authority, but must disgrace all the settled religions of the world? It was not to be imagined that he would endure with patience, that the religion of the emperor and of the state should be calumniated and borne down by a company of superstitious and despicable Jews.

Lastly; the nature of the case affords a strong proof, that the original teachers of Christianity, in consequence of their new profession, entered upon a new and singular course of life. We may be allowed to presume, that the institution which they preached to others, they conformed to in their own persons; because this is no more than what every teacher of a new religion both does, and must do, in order to obtain either proselytes or hearers. The change which this would produce was very considerable. It is a change which we do not easily estimate, because, ourselves and all about us being habituated to the institutions from our infancy, it is what we neither experience nor observe. After men became Christians, much of their time was spent in prayer and devotion, in religious meetings, in celebrating the Eucharist, in conferences, in exhortations, in preaching, in an affectionate intercourse with one another, and correspondence with other societies. Perhaps their mode of life, in its form and habit, was not very unlike the Unitas Fratrum, or the modern methodists. Think then what it was to become such at Corinth, at Ephesus, at Antioch, or even at Jerusalem. How new! How alien from all their former habits and ideas, and from those of everybody about them! What a revolution there must have been of opinions and prejudices to bring the matter to this!

We know what the precepts of the religion are; how pure, how benevolent, how disinterested a conduct they enjoin; and that this purity and benevolence are extended to the very thoughts and affections. We are not, perhaps, at liberty to take for granted that the lives of the preachers of Christianity were as perfect as their lessons; but we are entitled to contend, that the observable part of their behaviour must have agreed in a great measure with the duties which they taught. There was, therefore, (which is all that we assert,) a course of life pursued by them, different from that which they before led. And this is of great importance. Men are brought to anything almost sooner than to change their habit of life, especially when the change is either inconvenient, or made against the force of natural inclination, or with the loss of accustomed indulgences. It is the most difficult of all things to convert men from vicious habits to virtuous ones, as every one may judge from what he feels in himself, as well as from what he sees in others.[4] It is almost like making men over again.

Left then to myself, and without any more information than a knowledge of the existence of the religion, of the general story upon which it is founded, and that no act of power, force, and authority was concerned in its first success, I should conclude, from the very nature and exigency of the case, that the Author of the religion, during his life, and his immediate disciples after his death, exerted themselves in spreading and publishing the institution throughout the country in which it began, and into which it was first carried; that, in the prosecution of this purpose, they underwent the labours and troubles which we observe the propagators of new sects to undergo; that the attempt must necessarily have also been in a high degree dangerous; that, from the subject of the mission, compared with the fixed opinions and prejudices of those to whom the missionaries were to address themselves, they could hardly fail of encountering strong and frequent opposition; that, by the hand of government, as well as from the sudden fury and unbridled licence of the people, they would oftentimes experience injurious and cruel treatment; that, at any rate, they must have always had so much to fear for their personal safety, as to have passed their lives in a state of constant peril and anxiety; and lastly, that their mode of life and conduct, visibly at least, corresponded with the institution which they delivered, and, so far, was both new, and required continual self-denial.

---

[4] Hartley's Essays on Man, p. 190.

CHAPTER II.

There is satisfactory evidence that many, professing to be original witnesses of the Christian miracles, passed their lives in labours, dangers and sufferings, voluntarily undergone in attestation of the accounts which they delivered, and solely in consequence of their belief of those accounts; and that they also submitted, from the same motives, to new rules of conduct.

After thus considering what was likely to happen, we are next to inquire how the transaction is represented in the several accounts that have come down to us. And this inquiry is properly preceded by the other, forasmuch as the reception of these accounts may depend in part on the credibility of what they contain.

The obscure and distant view of Christianity, which some of the heathen writers of that age had gained, and which a few passage in their remaining works incidentally discover to us, offers itself to our notice in the first place: because, so far as this evidence goes, it is the concession of adversaries; the source from which it is drawn is unsuspected. Under this head, a quotation from Tacitus, well known to every scholar, must be inserted, as deserving particular attention. The reader will bear in mind that this passage was written about seventy years after Christ's death, and that it relates to transactions which took place about thirty years after that event— Speaking of the fire which happened at Rome in the time of Nero, and of the suspicions which were entertained that the emperor himself was concerned in causing it, the historian proceeds in his narrative and observations thus:—

"But neither these exertions, nor his largesses to the people, nor his offerings to the gods, did away the infamous imputation under which Nero lay, of having ordered the city to be set on fire. To put an end, therefore, to this report, he laid the guilt, and inflicted the most cruel punishments, upon a set of people, who were holden in abhorrence for their crimes, and called by the vulgar, Christians. The founder of that name was Christ, who suffered death in the reign of Tiberius, under his procurator, Pontius Pilate—This pernicious superstition, thus checked for a while, broke out again; and spread not only over Judea, where the evil originated, but through Rome also, whither everything bad upon the earth finds its way and is practised. Some who confessed their sect were first seized, and afterwards, by their information, a vast multitude were apprehended, who were convicted, not so much of the crime of burning Rome, as of hatred to mankind. Their sufferings at their execution were aggravated by insult and mockery; for some were disguised in the skins of wild beasts, and worried to death by dogs; some were crucified; and others were wrapped in pitched shirts,[1] and set on fire when the day closed, that they might serve as lights to illuminate the night. Nero lent his own gardens for these executions, and exhibited at the same time a mock Circensian entertainment; being a spectator of the whole, in the dress of a charioteer, sometimes mingling with the crowd on foot, and sometimes viewing the spectacle from his car. This conduct made the sufferers pitied; and though they were criminals, and deserving the severest punishments, yet they were considered as sacrificed, not so much out of a regard to the public good, as to gratify the cruelty of one man."

Our concern with this passage at present is only so far as it affords a presumption in support of the proposition which we maintain, concerning the activity and sufferings of the first teachers of Christianity. Now, considered in this view, it proves three things: 1st, that the Founder of the institution was put to death; 2dly, that in the same country in which he was put to death, the religion, after a short check, broke out again and spread; 3dly, that it so spread as that, within thirty-four years from the Author's death, a very great number of Christians (ingens eorum multitudo) were found at Rome. From which fact, the two following inferences may be fairly drawn: first, that if, in the space of thirty-four years from its commencement, the religion had spread throughout Judea, had extended itself to Rome, and there had numbered a great multitude of converts, the original teachers and missionaries of the institution could not have been idle; secondly, that when the Author of the undertaking was put to death as a malefactor for his attempt, the endeavours of his followers to establish his religion in the same country, amongst the same people, and in the same age, could not but be attended with danger.

Suetonius, a writer contemporary with Tacitus, describing the transactions of the same reign, uses these words: "*Affecti suppliciis Christiani genus hominum superstitionis novae et maleficae.*" (Suet. Nero. Cap. 16) "The Christians, a set of men of a new and mischievous (or magical) superstition, were punished."

Since it is not mentioned here that the burning of the city was the pretence of the punishment of the Christians, or that they were the Christians of Rome who alone suffered, it is probable that Suetonius refers to some more general persecution than the short and occasional one which Tacitus describes.

Juvenal, a writer of the same age with the two former, and intending, it should seem, to commemorate the cruelties exercised under Nero's government, has the following lines: (Sat. i. ver. 155)

"Pone Tigellinum, taeda lucebis in illa,

---

[1] This is rather a paraphrase, but is justified by what the Scholiast upon Juvenal says; "*Nero maleficos homines taeda et papyro et cera supervestiebat, et sic ad ignem admoveri jubebat.*" Lard. Jewish and Heath. Test. vol. i. p. 359.

16

Qua stantes ardent, qui fixo gutture fumant,
Et latum media sulcum deducit arena" (Forsan "deducis.")

"Describe Tigellinus (a creature of Nero), and you shall suffer the same punishment with those who stand burning in their own flame and smoke, their head being held up by a stake fixed to their chin, till they make a long stream of blood and melted sulphur on the ground."

If this passage were considered by itself, the subject of allusion might be doubtful; but, when connected with the testimony of Suetonius, as to the actual punishment of the Christians by Nero, and with the account given by Tacitus of the species of punishment which they were made to undergo, I think it sufficiently probable that these were the executions to which the poet refers.

These things, as has already been observed, took place within thirty-one years after Christ's death, that is, according to the course of nature, in the life-time, probably, of some of the apostles, and certainly in the life-time of those who were converted by the apostles, or who were converted in their time. If then the Founder of the religion was put to death in the execution of his design; if the first race of converts to the religion, many of them, suffered the greatest extremities for their profession; it is hardly credible, that those who came between the two, who were companions of the Author of the institution during his life, and the teachers and propagators of the institution after his death, could go about their undertaking with ease and safety.

The testimony of the younger Pliny belongs to a later period; for, although he was contemporary with Tacitus and Suetonius, yet his account does not, like theirs, go back to the transactions of Nero's reign, but is confined to the affairs of his own time. His celebrated letter to Trajan was written about seventy years after Christ's death; and the information to be drawn from it, so far as it is connected with our argument, relates principally to two points: first, to the number of Christians in Bithynia and Pontus, which was so considerable as to induce the governor of these provinces to speak of them in the following terms: "*Multi, omnis aetatis, utriusque sexus etiam;—neque enim civitates tantum, sed vicos etiam et agros, superstitionis istius contagio pervagata est.*" "There are many of every age and of both sexes;—nor has the contagion of this superstition seized cities only, but smaller towns also, and the open country." Great exertions must have been used by the preachers of Christianity to produce this state of things within this time. Secondly, to a point which has been already noticed, and, which I think of importance to be observed, namely, the sufferings to which Christians were exposed, without any public persecution being denounced against them by sovereign authority. For, from Pliny's doubt how he was to act, his silence concerning any subsisting law on the subject, his requesting the emperor's rescript, and the emperor, agreeably to his request, propounding a rule for his direction without reference to any prior rule, it may be inferred that there was, at that time, no public edict in force against the Christians. Yet from this same epistle of Pliny it appears "that accusations, trials, and examinations, were, and had been, going on against them in the provinces over which he presided; that schedules were delivered by anonymous informers, containing the names of persons who were suspected of holding or of favouring the religion; that, in consequence of these informations, many had been apprehended, of whom some boldly avowed their profession, and died in the cause; others denied that they were Christians; others, acknowledging that they had once been Christians, declared that they had long ceased to be such." All which demonstrates that the profession of Christianity was at that time (in that country at least) attended with fear and danger: and yet this took place without any edict from the Roman sovereign, commanding or authorizing the persecution of Christians. This observation is further confirmed by a rescript of Adrian to Minucius Fundanus, the proconsul of Asia (Lard. Heath. Test. vol. ii. p. 110): from which rescript it appears that the custom of the people of Asia was to proceed against the Christians with tumult and uproar. This disorderly practice, I say, is recognised in the edict, because the emperor enjoins, that, for the future, if the Christians were guilty, they should be legally brought to trial, and not be pursued by importunity and clamour.

Martial wrote a few years before the younger Pliny: and, as his manner was, made the suffering of the Christians the subject of his ridicule.

In matutina nuper spectatus arena
Mucius, imposuit qui sua membra focis,
Si patiens fortisque tibi durusque videtur,
Abderitanae pectora plebis habes;
Nam cum dicatur, tunica praesente molesta,
Ure manum: plus est dicere, Non facio.
Forsan "thure manum."

Nothing, however, could show the notoriety of the fact with more certainty than this does. Martial's testimony, as well indeed as Pliny's, goes also to another point, viz, that the deaths of these men were martyrdom in the strictest sense, that is to say, were so voluntary, that it was in their power, at the time of pronouncing the sentence, to have averted the execution, by consenting to join in heathen sacrifices.

The constancy, and by consequence the sufferings, of the Christians of this period, is also referred to by Epictetus, who imputes their intrepidity to madness, or to a kind of fashion or habit; and about fifty years afterwards, by Marcus Aurelius, who ascribes it to obstinacy. "Is it possible (Epictetus asks) that a man may arrive at this temper, and become indifferent to those things from madness or from habit, as the Galileans?" "Let this preparation of the mind (to die) arise from its own judgment, and not from obstinacy like the Christians." (Epict. I. iv. C. 7.) (Marc. Aur. Med. 1. xi. c. 3.)

CHAPTER III.

There is satisfactory evidence that many, professing to be original witnesses of the Christian miracles, passed there lives in labours, dangers, and sufferings, voluntarily undergone in attestation of the accounts which they delivered, and solely in consequence of their belief of those accounts; and that they also submitted, from the same motives, to new rules of conduct.

Of the primitive condition of Christianity, a distant only and general view can be acquired from heathen writers. It is in our own books that the detail and interior of the transaction must be sought for. And this is nothing different from what might be expected. Who would write a history of Christianity, but a Christian? Who was likely to record the travels, sufferings, labours, or successes of the apostles, but one of their own number, or of their followers? Now these books come up in their accounts to the full extent of the proposition which we maintain. We have four histories of Jesus Christ. We have a history taking up the narrative from his death, and carrying on an account of the propagation of the religion, and of some of the most eminent persons engaged in it, for a space of nearly thirty years. We have, what some may think still more original, a collection of letters, written by certain principal agents in the business upon the business, and in the midst of their concern and connection with it. And we have these writings severally attesting the point which we contend for, viz. the sufferings of the witnesses of the history, and attesting it in every variety of form in which it can be conceived to appear: directly and indirectly, expressly and incidentally, by assertion, recital, and allusion, by narratives of facts, and by arguments and discourses built upon these facts, either referring to them, or necessarily presupposing them.

I remark this variety, because, in examining ancient records, or indeed any species of testimony, it is, in my opinion, of the greatest importance to attend to the information or grounds of argument which are casually and undesignedly disclosed; forasmuch as this species of proof is, of all others, the least liable to be corrupted by fraud or misrepresentation.

I may be allowed therefore, in the inquiry which is now before us, to suggest some conclusions of this sort, as preparatory to more direct testimony.

1. Our books relate, that Jesus Christ, the founder of the religion, was, in consequence of his undertaking, put to death, as a malefactor, at Jerusalem. This point at least will be granted, because it is no more than what Tacitus has recorded. They then proceed to tell us that the religion was, notwithstanding, set forth at this same city of Jerusalem, propagated thence throughout Judea, and afterwards preached in other parts of the Roman Empire. These points also are fully confirmed by Tacitus, who

informs us that the religion, after a short check, broke out again in the country where it took its rise; that it not only spread throughout Judea, but had reached Rome, and that it had there great multitudes of converts: and all this within thirty years after its commencement. Now these facts afford a strong inference in behalf of the proposition which we maintain. What could the disciples of Christ expect for themselves when they saw their master put to death? Could they hope to escape the dangers in which he had perished? If they had persecuted me, they will also persecute you, was the warning of common sense. With this example before their eyes, they could not be without a full sense of the peril of their future enterprise.

2. Secondly, all the histories agree in representing Christ as foretelling the persecution of his followers:— "Then shall they deliver you up to be afflicted, and shall kill you, and ye shall be hated of all nations for my name's sake." (Matt. xxiv. 9.)

"When affliction or persecution ariseth for the word's sake, immediately they are offended." (Mark iv. 17. See also chap. x. 30.)

"They shall lay hands on you, and persecute you, delivering you up to the synagogues, and into prisons, being brought before kings and rulers for my name's sake:—and ye shall be betrayed both by parents and brethren, and kinsfolks and friends, and some of you shall they cause to be put to death." (Luke xxi. 12—16. See also chap. xi. 49.)

"The time cometh, that he that killed you will think that he doeth God service. And these things will they do unto you, because they have not known the Father, nor me. But these things have I told you, that when the time shall come, ye may remember that I told you of them." (John xvi. 4. See also chap. xv. 20; xvi. 33.)

I am not entitled to argue from these passages, that Christ actually did foretell these events, and that they did accordingly come to pass; because that would be at once to assume the truth of the religion: but I am entitled to contend that one side or other of the following disjunction is true; either that the Evangelists have delivered what Christ really spoke, and that the event corresponded with the prediction; or that they put the prediction into Christ's mouth, because at the time of writing the history, the event had turned out so to be: for, the only two remaining suppositions appear in the highest degree incredible; which are, either that Christ filled the minds of his followers with fears and apprehensions, without any reason or authority for what he said, and contrary to the truth of the case; or that, although Christ had never foretold any such thing, and the event would have contradicted him if he had, yet historians who lived in the age when the event was known, falsely, as well as officiously, ascribed these words to him.

3. Thirdly, these books abound with exhortations to patience, and with topics of comfort under distress.

"Who shall separate us from the love of Christ? Shall tribulation, or distress, or persecution, or famine, or nakedness, or peril, or sword? Nay, in all these things we are more than conquerors through Him that loved us." (Rom. viii. 35-37.)

"We are troubled on every side, yet not distressed; we are perplexed, but not in despair; persecuted, but not forsaken; cast down, but not destroyed; always bearing about in the body the dying of the Lord Jesus, that the life also of Jesus might be made manifest in our body;—knowing that he which raised up the Lord Jesus shall raise us up also by Jesus, and shall present us with you—For which cause we faint not; but, though our outward man perish, yet the inward man is renewed day by day. For our light affliction, which is but for a moment, worketh for us a far more exceeding and eternal weight of glory." (2 Cor. iv. 8, 9, 10, 14, 16, 17.)

"Take, my brethren, the prophets, who have spoken in the name of the Lord, for an example of suffering affliction, and of patience. Behold, we count them happy which endure. Ye have heard of the patience of Job, and have seen the end of the Lord; that the Lord is very pitiful, and of tender mercy." (James v. 10, 11.)

"Call to remembrance the former days, in which, after ye were illuminated, ye endured a great fight of afflictions partly whilst ye were made a gazing-stock both by reproaches and afflictions, and partly whilst ye became companions of them that were so used; for ye had compassion of me in my bonds, and took joyfully the spoiling of your goods, knowing in yourselves that ye have in heaven a better and an enduring substance. Cast not away, therefore, your confidence, which hath great recompense of reward; for ye have need of patience, that, after ye have done the will of God, ye might receive the promise." (Heb. x. 32-36.)

"So that we ourselves glory in you in the churches of God, for your patience and faith in all your persecutions and tribulations that ye endure. Which is a manifest token of the righteous judgment of God, that ye may be counted worthy of the kingdom for which ye also suffer." (2 Thess. i. 4, 5.)

"We rejoice in hope of the glory of God; and not only so, but we glory in tribulations also; knowing that tribulation worketh patience, and patience experience, and experience hope." (Rom. v. 3, 4.)

"Beloved, think it not strange concerning the fiery trial which is to try you, as though some strange thing happened unto you; but rejoice, inasmuch as ye are partakers of Christ's sufferings.—Wherefore let them that suffer according to the will of God commit the keeping of their souls to him in well doing, as unto a faithful Creator." (1 Pet. iv. 12, 13, 19.)

What could all these texts mean, if there was nothing in the circumstances of the times which required patience,—which called for the exercise of constancy and resolution? Or will it be pretended, that these exhortations (which, let it be observed, come not from one author, but from many) were put in merely to induce a belief in after-ages, that the Christians were exposed to dangers which they were not exposed to, or underwent sufferings which they did not undergo? If these books belong to the age to which they lay claim, and in which age, whether genuine or spurious, they certainly did appear, this supposition cannot be maintained for a moment; because I think it impossible to believe that passages, which must be deemed not only unintelligible, but false, by the persons into whose hands the books upon their publication were to come, should nevertheless be inserted, for the purpose of producing an effect upon remote generations. In forgeries which do not appear till many ages after that to which they pretend to belong, it is possible that some contrivance of that sort may take place; but in no others can it be attempted.

CHAPTER IV.

There is satisfactory evidence that many professing to be original witnesses of the Christian miracles, passed their lives in labours, dangers, and sufferings, voluntarily undergone in attestation of the accounts which they delivered, and solely in consequence of their belief of those accounts; and that they also submitted, from the same motives, to new rules of conduct.

The account of the treatment of the religion, and of the exertions of its first preachers, as stated in our Scriptures (not in a professed history of persecutions, or in the connected manner in which I am about to recite it, but dispersedly and occasionally, in the course of a mixed general history, which circumstance, alone negatives the supposition of any fraudulent design), is the following: "That the Founder of Christianity, from the commencement of his ministry to the time of his violent death, employed himself wholly in publishing the institution in Judea and Galilee; that, in order to assist him in this purpose, he made choice, out of the number of his followers, of twelve persons, who might accompany him as he travelled from place to place; that, except a short absence upon a journey in which he sent them two by two to announce his mission, and one of a few days, when they went before him to Jerusalem, these persons were steadily and constantly attending upon him; that they were with him at Jerusalem when he was apprehended and put to death; and that they were commissioned by him, when his own ministry was concluded, to publish his Gospel, and collect disciples to it from all countries of the world." The account then proceeds to state, "that a few days after his departure, these persons, with some of his relations, and some who had regularly frequented their society, assembled at Jerusalem; that, considering the office of preaching the religion as now devolved upon them, and one of their number having deserted the cause, and, repenting of his perfidy, having destroyed himself, they proceeded to elect another into his place, and that they were careful to make their election out of the number of those who had accompanied their master from the first to the last, in order, as they alleged, that he might be a witness, together with themselves, of the principal facts which they were about to produce and relate concerning him; (Acts i. 12, 22.) that they began their work at Jerusalem by publicly asserting that this Jesus, whom the rulers and inhabitants of that place had so lately crucified, was, in truth, the person in whom all their prophecies and long expectations terminated; that he had been sent amongst them by God; and that he was appointed by God the future judge of the human species; that all who were solicitous to secure to themselves happiness after death, ought to receive him as such, and to make profession of their belief, by being baptised in his name." (Acts xi.)

The history goes on to relate, "that considerable numbers accepted this proposal, and that they who did so formed amongst themselves a strict union and society; (Acts iv. 32.) that the attention of the Jewish government being soon drawn upon them, two of the principal persons of the twelve, and who also had lived most intimately and constantly with the Founder of the religion, were seized as they were discoursing to the people in the temple; that after being kept all night in prison, they were brought the next day before an assembly composed of the chief persons of the Jewish magistracy and priesthood; that this assembly, after some consultation, found nothing, at that time, better to be done towards suppressing the growth of the sect, than to threaten their prisoners with punishment if they persisted; that these men, after expressing, in decent but firm language, the obligation under which they considered themselves to be, to declare what they knew, 'to speak the things which they had seen and heard,' returned from the council, and reported what had passed to their companions; that this report, whilst it apprized them of the danger of their situation and undertaking, had no other effect upon their conduct than to produce in them a general resolution to persevere, and an earnest prayer to God to furnish them with assistance, and to inspire them with fortitude, proportioned to the increasing exigency of the service." (Acts iv.) A very short time after this, we read "that all the twelve apostles were seized and cast into prison; (Acts v. 18.) that, being brought a second time before the Jewish Sanhedrim, they were upbraided with their disobedience to the injunction which had been laid upon them, and beaten for their contumacy; that, being charged once more to desist, they were suffered to depart; that however they neither quitted Jerusalem, nor ceased from preaching, both daily in the temple, and from house to house (Acts v. 42.) and that the twelve considered themselves as so entirely and exclusively devoted to this office, that they now transferred what may be called the temporal affairs of the society to other hands."[1]

---

1 I do not know that it has ever been insinuated that the Christian mission, in the hands of the apostles, was a scheme for making a fortune, or for getting money. But it may nevertheless be fit to remark upon this passage of their history, how perfectly free they appear to have been from any pecuniary or interested views whatever. The most tempting opportunity which occurred of making gain of their converts, was by the custody and management of the public funds, when some of the richer members, intending to contribute their fortunes to the common support of the society, sold their possessions, and laid down the prices at the apostles' feet. Yet, so insensible or undesirous were they of the advantage which that confidence afforded, that we find they very soon disposed of the trust, by putting it into the hands, not of nominees of their own, but of stewards formally elected for the purpose by the society at large.

Hitherto the preachers of the new religion seem to have had the common people on their side; which is assigned as the reason why the Jewish rulers did not, at this time, think it prudent to proceed to greater extremities. It was not long, however, before the enemies of the institution found means to represent it to the people as tending to subvert their law, degrade their lawgiver, and dishonour their temple. (Acts vi. 12.) And these insinuations were dispersed with so much success as to induce the people to join with their superiors in the stoning of a very active member of the new community.

The death of this man was the signal of a general persecution, the activity of which may be judged of from one anecdote of the time:—"As for , he made havoc of the church, entering into every house, and taking men and women committed them to prison." (Acts viii. 3.) This persecution raged at Jerusalem with so much fury as to drive most of the new converts out of the place,[2] except the twelve apostles. The converts thus "scattered abroad," preached the religion wherever they came; and their preaching was, in effect, the preaching of the twelve; for it was so far carried on in concert and correspondence with them, that when they heard of the success of their emissaries in a particular country, they sent two of their number to the place, to complete and confirm the mission.

An event now took place, of great importance in the future history of the religion. The persecution which had begun at Jerusalem followed the Christians to other cities, (Acts ix.) in which the authority of the Jewish Sanhedrim over those of their own nation was allowed to be exercised. A young man, who had signalized himself by his hostility to the profession, and had procured a commission from the council at Jerusalem to seize any converted Jews whom he might find at Damascus, suddenly became a proselyte to the religion which he was going about to extirpate. The new convert not only shared, on this extraordinary change, the fate of his companions, but brought upon himself a double measure of enmity from the party which he had left. The Jews at Damascus, on his return to that city, watched the gates night and day, with so much diligence, that he escaped from their hands only by being let down in a basket by the wall.

We may add also, that this excess of generosity, which cast private property into the public stock, was so far from being required by the apostles, or imposed as a law of Christianity, that Peter reminds Ananias that he had been guilty, in his behaviour, of an officious and voluntary prevarication; "for whilst," says he, "thy estate remained unsold, was it not thine own? And after it was sold, was it not in thine own power?"

[2] Acts viii. I. "And they were all scattered abroad;" but the term "all" is not, I think, to be taken strictly as denoting more than the generality; in like manner as in Acts ix. 35: "And all that dwelt at Lydda and Saron saw him, and turned to the Lord."

Nor did he find himself in greater safety at Jerusalem, whither he immediately repaired. Attempts were there also soon set on foot to destroy him; from the danger of which he was preserved by being sent away to Cilicia, his native country.

For some reason not mentioned, perhaps not known, but probably connected with the civil history of the Jews, or with some danger[3] which engrossed the public attention, an intermission about this time took place in the sufferings of the Christians. This happened, at the most, only seven or eight, perhaps only three or four years after Christ's death, within which period, and notwithstanding that the late persecution occupied part of it, churches, or societies of believers, had been formed in all Judea, Galilee, and Samaria; for we read that the churches in these countries "had now rest and were edified, and, walking in the fear of the Lord, and in the comfort of the Holy Ghost, were multiplied." (Acts ix 31.) The original preachers of the religion did not remit their labours or activity during this season of quietness; for we find one, and he a very principal person among them, passing throughout all quarters. We find also those who had been before expelled from Jerusalem by the persecution which raged there, travelling as far as Poenice, Cyprus, and Antioch; (Acts xi. 19.) and lastly, we find Jerusalem again in the centre of the mission, the place whither the preachers returned from their several excursions, where they reported the conduct and effects of their ministry, where questions of public concern were canvassed and settled, whence directions were sought, and teachers sent forth.

The time of this tranquillity did not, however, continue long. Herod Agrippa, who had lately acceded to the government of Judea, "stretched forth his hand to vex certain of the church." (Acts xii. 1.) He began his cruelty by beheading one of the twelve original apostles, a kinsman and constant companion of the Founder of the religion. Perceiving that this execution gratified the Jews, he proceeded to seize, in order to put to death, another of the number,—and him, like the former, associated with Christ during his life, and eminently active in the service since his death. This man was, however, delivered from prison, as the account states miraculously, (Acts xii. 3—17.) and made his escape from Jerusalem.

These things are related, not in the general terms under which, in giving the outlines of the history, we have here mentioned them, but with the utmost particularity of names, persons, places, and circumstances; and, what is deserving of notice, without the smallest discoverable

---

[3] Dr. Lardner (in which he is followed also by Dr. Benson) ascribes the cessation of the persecution of the Christians to the attempt of Caligula to set up his own statue in the temple of Jerusalem, and to the consternation thereby excited in the minds of the Jewish people; which consternation for a season superseded every other contest.

propensity in the historian, to magnify the fortitude, or exaggerate the sufferings, of his party. When they fled for their lives, he tells us. When the churches had rest, he remarks it. When the people took their part, he does not leave it without notice. When the apostles were carried a second time before the Sanhedrim, he is careful to observe that they were brought without violence. When milder counsels were suggested, he gives us the author of the advice and the speech which contained it. When, in consequence of this advice, the rulers contented themselves with threatening the apostles, and commanding them to be beaten with stripes, without urging at that time the persecution further, the historian candidly and distinctly records their forbearance. When, therefore, in other instances, he states heavier persecutions, or actual martyrdoms, it is reasonable to believe that he states them because they were true, and not from any wish to aggravate, in his account, the sufferings which Christians sustained, or to extol, more than it deserved, their patience under them.

Our history now pursues a narrower path. Leaving the rest of the apostles, and the original associates of Christ, engaged in the propagation of the new faith, (and who there is not the least reason to believe abated in their diligence or courage,) the narrative proceeds with the separate memoirs of that eminent teacher, whose extraordinary and sudden conversion to the religion, and corresponding change of conduct, had before been circumstantially described. This person, in conjunction with another, who appeared among the earlier members of the society at Jerusalem, and amongst the immediate adherents of the twelve apostles, (Acts iv. 36.) set out from Antioch upon the express business of carrying the new religion through the various provinces of the Lesser Asia. (Acts xiii. 2.) During this expedition, we find that in almost every place to which they came, their persons were insulted, and their lives endangered. After being expelled from Antioch in Pisidia, they repaired to Iconium. (Acts xiii. 51.) At Iconium, an attempt was made to stone them; at Lystra, whither they fled from Iconium, one of them actually was stoned and drawn out of the city for dead. (Acts xiv. 19.) These two men, though not themselves original apostles, were acting in connection and conjunction with the original apostles; for, after the completion of their journey, being sent on a particular commission to Jerusalem, they there related to the apostles (Acts xv. 12—26.) and elders the events and success of their ministry, and were in return recommended by them to the churches, "as men who had hazarded their lives in the cause."

The treatment which they had experienced in the first progress did not deter them from preparing for a second. Upon a dispute, however, arising between them, but not connected with the common subject of their labours, they acted as wise and sincere men would act; they did not retire in disgust from the service in which they were engaged, but, each

27

devoting his endeavours to the advancement of the religion, they parted from one another, and set forward upon separate routes. The history goes along with one of them; and the second enterprise to him was attended with the same dangers and persecutions as both had met with in the first. The apostle's travels hitherto had been confined to Asia. He now crosses for the first time the Aegean sea, and carries with him, amongst others, the person whose accounts supply the information we are stating. (Acts xvi. 11.) The first place in Greece at which he appears to have stopped, was Philippi in Macedonia. Here himself and one of his companions were cruelly whipped, cast into prison, and kept there under the most rigorous custody, being thrust, whilst yet smarting with their wounds, into the inner dungeon, and their feet made fast in the stocks. (Acts xvi. 23, 24, 33.) Notwithstanding this unequivocal specimen of the usage which they had to look for in that country, they went forward in the execution of their errand. After passing through Amphipolis and Apollonia, they came to Thessalonica; in which city the house in which they lodged was assailed by a party of their enemies, in order to bring them out to the populace. And when, fortunately for their preservation, they were not found at home, the master of the house was dragged before the magistrate for admitting them within his doors. (Acts xvii. 1—5.) Their reception at the next city was something better: but neither had they continued long before their turbulent adversaries the Jews, excited against them such commotions amongst the inhabitants as obliged the apostle to make his escape by a private journey to Athens. (Acts xvii. 13.) The extremity of the progress was Corinth. His abode in this city, for some time, seems to have been without molestation. At length, however, the Jews found means to stir up an insurrection against him, and to bring him before the tribunal of the Roman president. (Acts xviii. 12.) It was to the contempt which that magistrate entertained for the Jews and their controversies, of which he accounted Christianity to be one, that our apostle owed his deliverance. (Acts xviii. 15.)

This indefatigable teacher, after leaving Corinth, returned by Ephesus into Syria; and again visited Jerusalem, and the society of Christians in that city, which, as hath been repeatedly observed, still continued the centre of the mission. (Acts xviii. 22.) It suited not, however, with the activity of his zeal to remain long at Jerusalem. We find him going thence to Antioch, and, after some stay there, traversing once more the northern provinces of Asia Minor. (Acts xviii. 23.) This progress ended at Ephesus: in which city, the apostle continued in the daily exercise of his ministry two years, and until his success, at length, excited the apprehensions of those who were interested in the support of the national worship. Their clamour produced a tumult, in which he had nearly lost his life. (Acts xix. 1, 9, 10.) Undismayed, however, by the dangers to which he saw himself exposed, he was driven from Ephesus only to renew his labours in

Greece. After passing over Macedonia, he thence proceeded to his former station at Corinth. (Acts xx. 1, 2.) When he had formed his design of returning by a direct course from Corinth into Syria, he was compelled by a conspiracy of the Jews, who were prepared to intercept him on his way, to trace back his steps through Macedonia to Philippi, and thence to take shipping into Asia. Along the coast of Asia, he pursued his voyage with all the expedition he could command, in order to reach Jerusalem against the feast of Pentecost. (Acts xx. 16.) His reception at Jerusalem was of a piece with the usage he had experienced from the Jews in other places. He had been only a few days in that city, when the populace, instigated by some of his old opponents in Asia, who attended this feast, seized him in the temple, forced him out of it, and were ready immediately to have destroyed him, had not the sudden presence of the Roman guard rescued him out of their hands. (Acts xxi. 27—33.) The officer, however, who had thus seasonably interposed, acted from his care of the public peace, with the preservation of which he was charged, and not from any favour to the apostle, or indeed any disposition to exercise either justice or humanity towards him; for he had no sooner secured his person in the fortress, than he was proceeding to examine him by torture. (Acts xxii 24.)

From this time to the conclusion of the history, the apostle remains in public custody of the Roman government. After escaping assassination by a fortunate discovery of the plot, and delivering himself from the influence of his enemies by an appeal to the audience of the emperor, (Acts xxv. 9, 11.) he was sent, but not until he had suffered two years' imprisonment, to Rome. (Acts xxiv. 27.) He reached Italy after a tedious voyage, and after encountering in his passage the perils of a desperate shipwreck. (Acts xxvii.) But although still a prisoner, and his fate still depending, neither the various and long-continued sufferings which he had undergone, nor the danger of his present situation, deterred him from persisting in preaching the religion: for the historian closes the account by telling us that, for two years, he received all that came unto him in his own hired house, where he was permitted to dwell with a soldier that guarded him, "preaching the kingdom of God, and teaching those things which concern the Lord Jesus Christ, with all confidence."

Now the historian, from whom we have drawn this account, in the part of his narrative which relates to Saint Paul, is supported by the strongest corroborating testimony that a history can receive. We are in possession of letters written by Saint Paul himself upon the subject of his ministry, and either written during the period which the history comprises, or, if written afterwards, reciting and referring to the transactions of that period. These letters, without borrowing from the history, or the history from them, unintentionally confirm the account which the history delivers, in a great variety of particulars. What belongs to our present purpose is the description exhibited of the apostle's sufferings: and the representation, given in our history, of the dangers and distresses which he underwent not only agrees in general with the language which he himself uses whenever he speaks of his life or ministry, but is also, in many instances, attested by a specific correspondency of time, place, and order of events. If the historian put down in his narrative, that at Philippi the apostle "was beaten with many stripes, cast into prison, and there treated with rigour and indignity;" (Acts xvi. 23, 24.) we find him, in a letter to a neighbouring church, (I Thess. ii. 2.) reminding his converts that, "after he had suffered before, and was shamefully entreated at Philippi, he was bold, nevertheless, to speak unto them (to whose city he next came) the Gospel of God." If the history relates that, (Acts xvii. 5.) at Thessalonica, the house in which the apostle was lodged, when he first came to that place, was assaulted by the populace, and the master of it dragged before the magistrate for admitting such a guest within his doors; the apostle, in his letter to the Christians of Thessalonica, calls to their remembrance "how they had received the Gospel in much affliction." (1 Thess. i. 6.) If the history deliver an account of an insurrection at Ephesus, which had nearly cost the apostle his life, we have the apostle himself, in a letter written a short time after his departure from that city, describing his despair, and returning thanks for his deliverance. (Acts xix. 2 Cor. i. 8—10.) If the history inform us, that the apostle was expelled from Antioch in Pisidia, attempted to be stoned at Iconium, and actually stoned at Lystra; there is preserved a letter from him to a favourite convert, whom, as the same history tells us, he first met with in these parts; in which letter he appeals to that disciple's knowledge "of the persecutions which befell him at Antioch, at Iconium, at Lystra." (Acts xiii. 50; xiv. 5, 19. 2 Tim. 10, 11.) If the history make the apostle, in his speech to the Ephesian elders, remind them, as one proof of the disinterestedness of his views, that, to their knowledge, he had supplied his own and the necessities of his companions by personal labour; (Acts xx. 34.) we find the same apostle, in a letter written during his residence at Ephesus, asserting of himself, "that even to that hour he laboured, working with his own hands." (1 Cor. iv 11, 12.)

These coincidences, together with many relative to other parts of the apostle's history, and all drawn from independent sources, not only confirm the truth of the account, in the particular points as to which they are observed, but add much to the credit of the narrative in all its parts; and support the author's profession of being a contemporary of the person whose history he writes, and, throughout a material portion of his narrative, a companion.

What the epistles of the apostles declare of the suffering state of Christianity the writings which remain of their companions and immediate followers expressly confirm.

Clement, who is honourably mentioned by Saint Paul in his epistle to the Philippians, (Philipp. iv. 3.) hath left us his attestation to this point, in the following words: "Let us take (says he) the examples of our own age. Through zeal and envy, the most faithful and righteous pillars of the church have been persecuted even to the most grievous deaths. Let us set before our eyes the holy apostles. Peter, by unjust envy, underwent not one or two, but many sufferings; till at last, being martyred, he went to the place of glory that was due unto him. For the same cause did Paul, in like manner, receive the reward of his patience. Seven times he was in bonds; he was whipped, was stoned; he preached both in the East and in the West, leaving behind him the glorious report of his faith; and so having taught the whole world righteousness, and for that end travelled even unto the utmost bounds of the West, he at last suffered martyrdom by the command of the governors, and departed out of the world, and went unto his holy place, being become a most eminent pattern of patience unto all ages. To these holy apostles were joined a very great number of others, who, having through envy undergone, in like manner, many pains and torments, have left a glorious example to us. For this, not only men, but women, have been persecuted; and, having suffered very grievous and cruel punishments, have finished the course of their faith with firmness." (Clem. ad Cor. c. v. vi. Abp. Wake's Trans.)

Hermas, saluted by Saint Paul in his epistle to the Romans, in a piece very little connected with historical recitals, thus speaks: "Such as have believed and suffered death for the name of Christ, and have endured with a ready mind, and have given up their lives with all their hearts." (Shepherd of Hermas, c. xxviii.)

Polycarp, the disciple of John (though all that remains of his works be a very short epistle), has not left this subject unnoticed. "I exhort (says he) all of you, that ye obey the word of righteousness, and exercise all patience, which ye have seen set forth before your eyes, not only in the blessed Ignatius, and Lorimus, and Rufus, but in others among yourselves, and in Paul himself and the rest of the apostles; being confident in this, that all these have not run in vain, but in faith and righteousness; and are gone to the place that was due to them from the Lord, with whom also they suffered. For they loved not this present world, but him who died, and was raised again by God for us." (Pol. ad Phil c. ix.)

Ignatius, the contemporary of Polycarp, recognises the same topic, briefly indeed, but positively and precisely. "For this cause, (i.e. having felt and handled Christ's body at his resurrection, and being convinced, as Ignatius expresses it, both by his flesh and spirit,) they (i.e. Peter, and those who were present with Peter at Christ's appearance) despised death, and were found to be above it." (19. Ep. Smyr. c. iii.)

Would the reader know what a persecution in those days was, I would refer him to a circular letter, written by the church of Smyrna soon after the death of Polycarp, who it will be remembered, had lived with Saint John; and which letter is entitled a relation of that bishop's martyrdom. "The sufferings (say they) of all the other martyrs were blessed and generous, which they underwent according to the will of God. For so it becomes us, who are more religious than others, to ascribe the power and ordering of all things unto Him. And, indeed, who can choose but admire the greatness of their minds, and that admirable patience and love of their Master, which then appeared in them? Who, when they were so flayed with whipping that the frame and structure of their bodies were laid open to their very inward veins and arteries, nevertheless endured it. In like manner, those who were condemned to the beasts, and kept a long time in prison, underwent many cruel torments, being forced to lie upon sharp spikes laid under their bodies, and tormented with divers other sorts of punishments; that so, if it were possible, the tyrant, by the length of their sufferings, might have brought them to deny Christ." (Rel. Mor. Pol. c. ii.)

CHAPTER V.

There is satisfactory evidence that many, professing to be original witnesses of the Christian miracles, passed their lives in labours, dangers, and sufferings, voluntarily undergone in attestation of the accounts which they delivered, and solely in consequence of their belief of those accounts; and that they also submitted, from the same motives, to new rules of conduct.

On the history, of which the last chapter contains an abstract, there are a few observations which it may be proper to make, by way of applying its testimony to the particular propositions for which we contend.

I. Although our Scripture history leaves the general account of the apostles in an early part of the narrative, and proceeds with the separate account of one particular apostle, yet the information which it delivers so far extends to the rest, as it shows the nature of the service. When we see one apostle suffering persecution in the discharge of this commission, we shall not believe, without evidence, that the same office could, at the same time, be attended with ease and safety to others. And this fair and reasonable inference is confirmed by the direct attestation of the letters, to which we have so often referred. The writer of these letters not only alludes, in numerous passages, to his own sufferings, but speaks of the rest of the apostles as enduring like sufferings with himself. "I think that God hath set forth us the apostles last, as it were, appointed to death; for we are made a spectacle unto the world, and to angels, and to men; even unto this present hour, we both hunger and thirst, and are naked, and are buffeted, and have no certain dwelling-place; and labour, working with our own hands: being reviled, we bless; being persecuted, we suffer it; being defamed, we entreat: we are made as the filth of the earth, and as the offscouring of all things unto this day." (I Cor. iv. 9, et seq.) Add to which, that in the short account that is given of the other apostles in the former part of the history, and within the short period which that account comprises, we find, first, two of them seized, imprisoned, brought before the Sanhedrim, and threatened with further punishment; (Acts iv. 3, 21.) then, the whole number imprisoned and beaten; (Acts v. 18, 40.) soon afterwards, one of their adherents stoned to death, and so hot a persecution raised against the sect as to drive most of them out of the place; a short time only succeeding, before one of the twelve was beheaded, and another sentenced to the same fate; and all this passing in the single city of Jerusalem, and within ten years after the Founder's death, and the commencement of the institution.

II. We take no credit at present for the miraculous part of the narrative, nor do we insist upon the correctness of single passages of it. If the whole story be not a novel, a romance; the whole action a dream; if

Peter, and James, and Paul, and the rest of the apostles mentioned in the account, be not all imaginary persons; if their letters be not all forgeries, and, what is more, forgeries of names and characters which never existed; then is there evidence in our hands sufficient to support the only fact we contend for (and which, I repeat again, is, in itself, highly probable), that the original followers of Jesus Christ exerted great endeavours to propagate his religion, and underwent great labours, dangers, and sufferings, in consequence of their undertaking.

III. The general reality of the apostolic history is strongly confirmed by the consideration, that it, in truth, does no more than assign adequate causes for effects which certainly were produced; and describe consequences naturally resulting from situations which certainly existed. The effects were certainly there, of which this history sets forth the cause, and origin, and progress. It is acknowledged on all hands, because it is recorded by other testimony than that of the Christians themselves, that the religion began to prevail at that time, and in that country. It is very difficult to conceive how it could begin without the exertions of the Founder and his followers, in propagating the new persuasion. The history now in our hands describes these exertions, the persons employed, the means and endeavours made use of, and the labours undertaken in the prosecution of this purpose. Again, the treatment which the history represents the first propagators of the religion to have experienced was no other than what naturally resulted from the situation in which they were confessedly placed. It is admitted that the religion was adverse, in great degree, to the reigning opinions, and to the hopes and wishes of the nation to which it was first introduced; and that it overthrew, so far as it was received, the established theology and worship of every other country. We cannot feel much reluctance in believing that when the messengers of such a system went about not only publishing their opinions, but collecting proselytes, and forming regular societies of proselytes, they should meet with opposition in their attempts, or that this opposition should sometimes proceed to fatal extremities. Our history details examples of this opposition, and of the sufferings and dangers which the emissaries of the religion underwent, perfectly agreeable to what might reasonably be expected, from the nature of their undertaking, compared with the character of the age and country in which it was carried on.

IV. The records before us supply evidence of what formed another member of our general proposition, and what, as hath already been observed, is highly probable, and almost a necessary consequence of their new profession, viz., that, together with activity and courage in propagating the religion, the primitive followers of Jesus assumed, upon their conversion, a new and peculiar course of private life. Immediately after their Master was withdrawn from them, we hear of their "continuing with one accord in prayer and supplication;" (Acts i. 14.) of their "continuing daily with one accord in the temple" (Acts ii. 46.) Of "many being gathered together praying." (Acts xii. 12.) We know that strict instructions were laid upon the converts by their teachers. Wherever they came, the first word of their preaching was, "Repent!" We know that these injunctions obliged them to refrain from many species of licentiousness, which were not, at that time, reputed criminal. We know the rules of purity, and the maxims of benevolence, which Christians read in their books; concerning which rules it is enough to observe, that, if they were, I will not say completely obeyed, but in any degree regarded, they could produce a system of conduct, and, what is more difficult to preserve, a disposition of mind, and a regulation of affections, different from anything to which they had hitherto been accustomed, and different from what they would see in others. The change and distinction of manners, which resulted from their new character, is perpetually referred to in the letters of their teachers. "And you hath he quickened, who were dead in trespasses and sins, wherein in times past ye walked, according to the course of this world, according to the prince of the power of the air, the Spirit that now worketh in the children of disobedience; among whom also we all had our conversation in times past, in the lusts of our flesh, fulfilling the desires of the flesh, and of the mind, and were by nature the children of wrath, even as others." (Eph. ii 1-3. See also Tit. iii. 3.)—"For the time past of our life may suffice us to have wrought the will of the Gentiles, when we walked in lasciviousness, lusts, excess of wine, revellings, banquetings, and abominable idolatries; wherein they think it strange that ye run not with them to the same excess of riot." (1 Pet. iv. 3, 4.) Saint Paul, in his first letter to the Corinthians, after enumerating, as his manner was, a catalogue of vicious characters, adds, "Such were some of you; but ye are washed, but ye are sanctified." (1 Cor. vi. 11.) In like manner, and alluding to the same change of practices and sentiments, he asked the Roman Christians, "what fruit they had in those things, whereof they are now ashamed?" (Rom. vi. 21.) The phrases which the same writer employs to describe the moral condition of Christians, compared with their condition before they became Christians, such as "newness of life," being "freed from sin," being "dead to sin;" "the destruction of the body of sin, that, for the future, they should not serve sin;" "children of light and of the day," as opposed to "children of darkness and of the night;" "not sleeping as others;" imply, at least, a new system of obligation, and, probably, a new series of conduct, commencing with their conversion.

The testimony which Pliny bears to the behaviour of the new sect in his time, and which testimony comes not more than fifty years after that of St. Paul, is very applicable to the subject under consideration. The character which this writer gives of the Christians of that age, and which was drawn from a pretty accurate inquiry, because he considered their

35

moral principles as the point in which the magistrate was interested, is as follows:—He tells the emperor, "that some of those who had relinquished the society, or who, to save themselves, pretended that they had relinquished it, affirmed that they were wont to meet together on a stated day, before it was light, and sang among themselves alternately a hymn to Christ as a God; and to bind themselves by an oath, not to the commission of any wickedness, but that they would not be guilty of theft, or robbery, or adultery; that they would never falsify their word, or deny a pledge committed to them, when called upon to return it." This proves that a morality, more pure and strict than was ordinary, prevailed at that time in Christian societies. And to me it appears, that we are authorised to carry his testimony back to the age of the apostles; because it is not probable that the immediate hearers and disciples of Christ were more relaxed than their successors in Pliny's time, or the missionaries of the religion than those whom they taught.

CHAPTER VI.

There is satisfactory evidence that many professing to be original witnesses of the Christian miracles, passed their lives in labours, dangers, and sufferings, voluntarily undergone in attestation of the accounts which they delivered, and solely in consequence of their belief of those accounts; and that they also submitted, from the same motives, to new rules of conduct.

When we consider, first, the prevalency of the religion at this hour; secondly, the only credible account which can be given of its origin, viz. the activity of the Founder and his associates; thirdly, the opposition which that activity must naturally have excited; fourthly, the fate of the Founder of the religion, attested by heathen writers, as well as our own; fifthly, the testimony of the same writers to the sufferings of Christians, either contemporary with, or immediately succeeding, the original settlers of the institution; sixthly, predictions of the suffering of his followers ascribed to the Founder of the religion, which ascription alone proves, either that such predictions were delivered and fulfilled, or that the writers of Christ's life were induced by the event to attribute such predictions to him; seventhly, letters now in our possession, written by some of the principal agents in the transaction, referring expressly to extreme labours, dangers, and sufferings, sustained by themselves and their companions; lastly, a history purporting to be written by a fellow-traveller of one of the new teachers, and, by its unsophisticated correspondency with letters of that person still extant, proving itself to be written by some one well acquainted with the subject of the narrative, which history contains accounts of travels, persecutions, and martyrdoms, answering to what the former reasons lead us to expect: when we lay together these considerations, which taken separately are, I think correctly such as I have stated them in the preceding chapters, there cannot much doubt remain upon our minds but that a number of persons at that time appeared in the world, publicly advancing an extraordinary story, and for the sake of propagating the belief of that story, voluntarily incurring great personal dangers, traversing seas and kingdoms, exerting great industry, and sustaining great extremities of ill usage and persecution. It is also proved that the same persons, in consequence of their persuasion, or pretended persuasion, of the truth of what they asserted, entered upon a course of life in many respects new and singular.

From the clear and acknowledged parts of the case, I think it to be likewise in the highest degree probable, that the story for which these persons voluntarily exposed themselves to the fatigues and hardships which they endured was a miraculous story; I mean, that they pretended to miraculous evidence of some kind or other. They had nothing else to stand upon. The designation of the person, that is to say, that Jesus of

Nazareth, rather than any other person, was the Messiah, and as such the subject of their ministry, could only be founded upon supernatural tokens attributed to him. Here were no victories, no conquests, no revolutions, no surprising elevation of fortune, no achievements of valour, of strength, or of policy, to appeal to; no discoveries in any art or science, no great efforts of genius or learning to produce. A Galilean peasant was announced to the world as a divine lawgiver. A young man of mean condition, of a private and simple life, and who had wrought no deliverance for the Jewish nation, was declared to be their Messiah. This, without ascribing to him at the same time some proofs of his mission, (and what other but supernatural proofs could there be?) was too absurd a claim to be either imagined, or attempted, or credited. In whatever degree, or in whatever part, the religion was argumentative, when it came to the question, "Is the carpenter's son of Nazareth the person whom we are to receive and obey?" there was nothing but the miracles attributed to him by which his pretensions could be maintained for a moment. Every controversy and every question must presuppose these: for, however such controversies, when they did arise, might and naturally would, be discussed upon their own grounds of argumentation, without citing the miraculous evidence which had been asserted to attend the Founder of the religion (which would have been to enter upon another, and a more general question), yet we are to bear in mind, that without previously supposing the existence or the pretence of such evidence, there could have been no place for the discussion of the argument at all. Thus, for example, whether the prophecies, which the Jews interpreted to belong to the Messiah, were or were not applicable to the history of Jesus of Nazareth, was a natural subject of debate in those times; and the debate would proceed without recurring at every turn to his miracles, because it set out with supposing these; inasmuch as without miraculous marks and tokens (real or pretended), or without some such great change effected by his means in the public condition of the country, as might have satisfied the then received interpretation of these prophecies, I do not see how the question could ever have been entertained. Apollos, we read, "mightily convinced the Jews, showing by the Scriptures that Jesus was Christ;" (Acts xviii. 28.) but unless Jesus had exhibited some distinction of his person, some proof of supernatural power, the argument from the old Scriptures could have had no place. It had nothing to attach upon. A young man calling himself the Son of God, gathering a crowd about him, and delivering to them lectures of morality, could not have excited so much as a doubt among the Jews, whether he was the object in whom a long series of ancient prophecies terminated, from the completion of which they had formed such magnificent expectations, and expectations of a nature so opposite to what appeared; I mean no such doubt could exist when they had the whole case before them, when they saw him put to death for his officiousness, and when by his death the evidence concerning him was closed. Again, the effect of the Messiah's coming, supposing Jesus to have been he, upon Jews, upon Gentiles, upon their relation to each other, upon their acceptance with God, upon their duties and their expectations; his nature, authority, office, and agency; were likely to become subjects of much consideration with the early votaries of the religion, and to occupy their attention and writings. I should not however expect, that in these disquisitions, whether preserved in the form of letters, speeches, or set treatises, frequent or very direct mention of his miracles would occur. Still, miraculous evidence lay at the bottom of the argument. In the primary question, miraculous pretensions and miraculous pretensions alone, were what they had to rely upon.

That the original story was miraculous, is very fairly also inferred from the miraculous powers which were laid claim to by the Christians of succeeding ages. If the accounts of these miracles be true, it was a continuation of the same powers; if they be false, it was an imitation, I will not say of what had been wrought, but of what had been reported to have been wrought, by those who preceded them. That imitation should follow reality, fiction should be grafted upon truth; that, if miracles were performed at first, miracles should be pretended afterwards; agrees so well with the ordinary course of human affairs, that we can have no great difficulty in believing it. The contrary supposition is very improbable, namely, that miracles should be pretended to by the followers of the apostles and first emissaries of the religion, when none were pretended to, either in their own persons or that of their Master, by these apostles and emissaries themselves.

CHAPTER VII.

There is satisfactory evidence that many, professing to be original witnesses of the Christian miracles, passed their lives in labours, dangers, and sufferings, voluntarily undergone in attestation of the accounts which they delivered, and solely in consequence of their belief of those accounts; and that they also submitted, from the same motives, to new rules of conduct.

It being then once proved, that the first propagators of the Christian institution did exert activity, and subject themselves to great dangers and sufferings, in consequence and for the sake of an extraordinary and, I think, we may say, of a miraculous story of some kind or other; the next great question is, whether the account, which our Scriptures contain, be that story; that which these men delivered, and for which they acted and suffered as they did? This question is, in effect, no other than whether the story which Christians have now be the story which Christians had then? And of this the following proofs may be deduced from general considerations, and from considerations prior to any inquiry into the particular reasons and testimonies by which the authority of our histories is supported.

In the first place, there exists no trace or vestige of any other story. It is not, like the death of Cyrus the Great, a competition between opposite accounts, or between the credit of different historians. There is not a document, or scrap of account, either contemporary with the commencement of Christianity, or extant within many ages afar that commencement, which assigns a history substantially different from ours. The remote, brief, and incidental notices of the affair which are found in heathen writers, so far as they do go, go along with us. They bear testimony to these facts—that the institution originated from Jesus; that the Founder was put to death, as a malefactor, at Jerusalem, by the authority of the Roman governor, Pontius Pilate; that the religion nevertheless spread in that city, and throughout Judea; and that it was propagated thence to distant countries; that the converts were numerous; that they suffered great hardships and injuries for their profession; and that all this took place in the age of the world which our books have assigned. They go on, further, to describe the manners of Christians in terms perfectly conformable to the accounts extant in our books; that they were wont to assemble on a certain day; that they sang hymns to Christ as to a God; that they bound themselves by an oath not to commit any crime, but to abstain from theft and adultery, to adhere strictly to their promises, and not to deny money deposited in their hands;[1] that they worshipped

---

[1] See Pliny's Letter—Bonnet, in his lively way of expressing himself, says,— "Comparing Pliny's Letter with the account of the Acts, it seems to me that I had

him who was crucified in Palestine; that this their first lawgiver had taught them that they were all brethren; that they had a great contempt for the things of this world, and looked upon them as common; that they flew to one another's relief; that they cherished strong hopes of immortality; that they despised death, and surrendered themselves to sufferings.[2]

This is the account of writers who viewed the subject at a great distance; who were uninformed and uninterested about it. It bears the characters of such an account upon the face of it, because it describes effects, namely the appearance in the world of a new religion, and the conversion of great multitudes to it, without descending, in the smallest degree, to the detail of the transaction upon which it was founded, the interior of the institution, the evidence or arguments offered by those who drew over others to it. Yet still here is no contradiction of our story; no other or different story set up against it: but so far a confirmation of it as that, in the general points on which the heathen account touches, it agrees with that which we find in our own books.

The same may be observed of the very few Jewish writers of that and the adjoining period, which have come down to us. Whatever they omit, or whatever difficulties we may find in explaining the omission, they advance no other history of the transaction than that which we acknowledge. Josephus, who wrote his Antiquities, or History of the Jews, about sixty years after the commencement of Christianity, in a passage generally admitted as genuine, makes mention of John under the name of John the Baptist; that he was a preacher of virtue; that he baptized his proselytes; that he was well received by the people; that he was imprisoned and put to death by Herod; and that Herod lived in a criminal cohabitation with Herodias, his brother's wife. (Antiq. I. xviii. cap. v. sect. 1, 2.) In another passage allowed by many, although not without considerable question being moved about it, we hear of "James, the brother of him who was called Jesus, and of his being put to death." (Antiq. I. xx. cap. ix. sect. 1.) In a third passage, extant in every copy that remains of Josephus's history, but the authenticity of which has

---

not taken up another author, but that I was still reading the historian of that extraordinary society." This is strong; but there is undoubtedly an affinity, and all the affinity that could be expected.

[2] "It is incredible, what expedition they use when any of their friends are known to be in trouble. In a word, they spare nothing upon such an occasion;—for these miserable men have no doubt they shall be immortal and live for ever; therefore they contemn death, and many surrender themselves to sufferings. Moreover, their first lawgiver has taught them that they are all brethren, when once they have turned and renounced the gods of the Greeks, and worship this Master of theirs who was crucified, and engage to live according to his laws. They have also a sovereign contempt for all the things of this world, and look upon them as common." Lucian, de Morte Peregrini, t. i. p. 565, ed. Graev.

nevertheless been long disputed, we have an explicit testimony to the substance of our history in these words:—"At that time lived Jesus, a wise man, if he may be called a man, for he performed many wonderful works. He was a teacher of such men as received the truth with pleasure. He drew over to him many Jews and Gentiles. This was the Christ; and when Pilate, at the instigation of the chief men among us had condemned him to the cross, they who before had conceived an affection for him did not cease to adhere to him; for, on the third day, he appeared to them alive again, the divine prophets having foretold these and many wonderful things concerning him. And the sect of the Christians, so called from him, subsists to this time." (Antiq. I. xviii. cap. iii. sect 3.) Whatever become of the controversy concerning the genuineness of this passage; whether Josephus go the whole length of our history, which, if the passage be sincere, he does; or whether he proceed only a very little way with us, which, if the passage be rejected, we confess to be the case; still what we asserted is true, that he gives no other or different history of the subject from ours, no other or different account of the origin of the institution. And I think also that it may with great reason be contended, either that the passage is genuine, or that the silence of Josephus was designed. For, although we should lay aside the authority of our own books entirely, yet when Tacitus, who wrote not twenty, perhaps not ten, years after Josephus, in his account of a period in which Josephus was nearly thirty years of age, tells us, that a vast multitude of Christians were condemned at Rome; that they derived their denomination from Christ, who, in the reign of Tiberius, was put to death, as a criminal, by the procurator, Pontius Pilate; that the superstition had spread not only over Judea, the source of the evil but it had reached Rome also:—when Suetonius, an historian contemporary with Tacitus, relates that, in the time of Claudius, the Jews were making disturbances at Rome, Christus being their leader: and that, during the reign of Nero, the Christians were punished; under both which emperors Josephus lived: when Pliny, who wrote his celebrated epistle not more than thirty years after the publication of Josephus's history, found the Christians in such numbers in the province of Bithynia as to draw from him a complaint that the contagion had seized cities, towns, and villages, and had so seized them as to produce a general desertion of the public rites; and when, as has already been observed, there is no reason for imagining that the Christians were more numerous in Bithynia than in many other parts of the Roman empire; it cannot, I should suppose, after this, be believed, that the religion, and the transaction upon which it was founded, were too obscure to engage the attention of Josephus, or to obtain a place in his history. Perhaps he did not know how to represent the business, and disposed of his difficulties by passing it over in silence. Eusebius wrote the life of Constantine, yet omits entirely the most remarkable circumstance in that life, the death of his son Crispus; undoubtedly for the reason here given. The reserve of Josephus upon the subject of Christianity appears also in his passing over the banishment of the Jews by Claudius, which Suetonius, we have seen, has recorded with an express reference to Christ. This is at least as remarkable as his silence about the infants of Bethlehem.[3] Be, however, the fact, or the cause of the omission in Josephus,[4] what it may, no other or different history on the subject has been given by him, or is pretended to have been given.

But further; the whole series of Christian writers, from the first age of the institution down to the present, in their discussions, apologies, arguments, and controversies, proceed upon the general story which our Scriptures contain, and upon no other. The main facts, the principal agents, are alike in all. This argument will appear to be of great force, when it is known that we are able to trace back the series of writers to a contact with the historical books of the New Testament, and to the age of the first emissaries of the religion, and to deduce it, by an unbroken continuation, from that end of the train to the present.

The remaining letters of the apostles, (and what more original than their letters can we have?) though written without the remotest design of transmitting the history of Christ, or of Christianity, to future ages, or even of making it known to their contemporaries, incidentally disclose to us the following circumstances:—Christ's descent and family; his innocence; the meekness and gentleness of his character (a recognition which goes to the whole Gospel history); his exalted nature; his circumcision; his transfiguration; his life of opposition and suffering; his patience and resignation; the appointment of the Eucharist, and the manner of it; his agony; his confession before Pontius Pilate; his stripes, crucifixion, and burial; his resurrection; his appearance after it, first to Peter, then to the rest of the apostles; his ascension into heaven; and his designation to be the future judge of mankind; the stated residence of the apostles at Jerusalem; the working of miracles by the first preachers of the

---

[3] Michaelis has computed, and, as it should seem, fairly enough; that probably not more than twenty children perished by this cruel precaution. Michaelis's Introduction to the New Testament, translated by Marsh; vol. i. c. ii. sect. 11.

[4] There is no notice taken of Christianity in the Mishna, a collection of Jewish traditions compiled about the year 180; although it contains a Tract "De cultu peregrino," of strange or idolatrous worship; yet it cannot be disputed but that Christianity was perfectly well known in the world at this time. There is extremely little notice of the subject in the Jerusalem Talmud, compiled about the year 300, and not much more in the Babylonish Talmud, of the year 500; although both these works are of a religions nature, and although, when the first was compiled, Christianity was on the point of becoming the religion of the state, and, when the latter was published, had been so for 200 years.

Gospel, who were also the hearers of Christ;[5] the successful propagation of the religion; the persecution of its followers; the miraculous conversion of Paul; miracles wrought by himself, and alleged in his controversies with his adversaries, and in letters to the persons amongst whom they were wrought; finally, that MIRACLES were the signs of an apostle.[6]

In an epistle bearing the name of Barnabas, the companion of Paul, probably genuine, certainly belonging to that age, we have the sufferings of Christ, his choice of apostles and their number, his passion, the scarlet robe, the vinegar and gall, the mocking and piercing, the casting lots for his coat, (Ep. Bar. c. vii.) his resurrection on the eighth, (i.e. the first day of the week,[Ep. Bar. c. vi.]) and the commemorative distinction of that day, his manifestation after his resurrection, and, lastly, his ascension. We have also his miracles generally but positively referred to in the following words:—"Finally, teaching the people of Israel, and doing many wonders and signs among them, he preached to them, and showed the exceeding great love which he bare towards them." (Ep. Bar. c. v.)

In an epistle of Clement, a hearer of St. Paul, although written for a purpose remotely connected with the Christian history, we have the resurrection of Christ, and the subsequent mission of the apostles, recorded in these satisfactory terms: "The apostles have preached to us from our Lord Jesus Christ from God:—For, having received their command, and being thoroughly assured by the resurrection of our Lord Jesus Christ, they went abroad, publishing that the kingdom of God was at hand." (Ep. Clem. Rom. c. xlii.) We find noticed, also, the humility, yet the power of Christ, (Ep. Clem. Rom. c. xvi.) his descent from Abraham—his crucifixion. We have Peter and Paul represented as faithful and righteous pillars of the church; the numerous sufferings of Peter; the bonds, stripes, and stoning of Paul, and more particularly his extensive and unwearied travels.

---

[5] Heb. ii. 3. "How shall we escape, if we neglect so great salvation, which, at the first, began to be spoken by the Lord, and was confirmed unto us by them that heard him, God also be bearing them witness, both with signs and wonders, and with divers miracles, and gifts of the Holy Ghost?" I allege this epistle without hesitation; for, whatever doubts may have been raised about its author, there can be none concerning the age in which it was written. No epistle in the collection carries about it more indubitable marks of antiquity than this does. It speaks for instance, throughout, of the temple as then standing and of the worship of the temple as then subsisting.—Heb. viii. 4: "For, if he were on earth, he should not be a priest, seeing there are priests that offer according to the law."—Again, Heb. xiii. 10: "We have an altar whereof they have no right to eat which serve the tabernacle."

[6] Truly the signs of as apostle were wraught among you in all patience, in signs, and wonders, and mighty deeds.' 2 Cor. xii. 12.

In an epistle of Polycarp, a disciple of St. John, though only a brief hortatory letter, we have the humility, patience, sufferings, resurrection, and ascension of Christ, together with the apostolic character of St. Paul, distinctly recognised. (Pol. Ep. Ad Phil. C. v. viii. ii. iii.) Of this same father we are also assured, by Irenaeus, that he (Irenaeus) had heard him relate, "what he had received from eye-witnesses concerning the Lord, both concerning his miracles and his doctrine." (Ir. ad Flor. 1 ap. Euseb. 1. v. c. 20.)

In the remaining works of Ignatius, the contemporary of Polycarp, larger than those of Polycarp, (yet, like those of Polycarp, treating of subjects in nowise leading to any recital of the Christian history,) the occasional allusions are proportionably more numerous. The descent of Christ from David, his mother Mary, his miraculous conception, the star at his birth, his baptism by John, the reason assigned for it, his appeal to the prophets, the ointment poured on his head, his sufferings under Pontius Pilate and Herod the tetrarch, his resurrection, the Lord's day called and kept in commemoration of it, and the Eucharist, in both its Parts,—are unequivocally referred to. Upon the resurrection, this writer is even circumstantial. He mentions the apostles' eating and drinking with Christ after he had risen, their feeling and their handling him; from which last circumstance Ignatius raises this just reflection;—"They believed, being convinced both by his flesh and spirit; for this cause, they despised death, and were found to be above it." (Ad Smyr. c. iii.)

Quadratus, of the same age with Ignatius, has left us the following noble testimony:—"The works of our Saviour were always conspicuous, for they were real; both those that were healed, and those that were raised from the dead; who were seen not only when they were healed or raised, but for a long time afterwards; not only whilst he dwelled on this earth, but also after his departure, and for a good while after it, insomuch that some of them have reached to our times." (Ap. Euseb. H. E. 1. iv. c. 3.)

Justin Martyr came little more than thirty years after Quadratus. From Justin's works, which are still extant, might be collected a tolerably complete account of Christ's life, in all points agreeing with that which is delivered in our Scriptures; taken indeed, in a great measure, from those Scriptures, but still proving that this account, and no other, was the account known and extant in that age. The miracles in particular, which form the part of Christ's history most material to be traced, stand fully and distinctly recognised in the following passage:—"He healed those who had been blind, and deaf, and lame from their birth; causing, by his word, one to leap, another to hear, and a third to see: and, by raising the dead, and making them to live, he induced, by his works, the men of that age to know him." (Just. Dial. cum Tryph. p. 288, ed. Thirl.)

It is unnecessary to carry these citations lower, because the history, after this time, occurs in ancient Christian writings as familiarly as it is wont to do in modern sermons;—occurs always the same in substance, and always that which our evangelists represent.

This is not only true of those writings of Christians which are genuine, and of acknowledged authority; but it is, in a great measure, true of all their ancient writings which remain; although some of these may have been erroneously ascribed to authors to whom they did not belong, or may contain false accounts, or may appear to be undeserving of credit, or never indeed to have obtained any. Whatever fables they have mixed with the narrative, they preserve the material parts, the leading facts, as we have them; and, so far as they do this, although they be evidence of nothing else, they are evidence that these points were fixed, were received and acknowledged by all Christians in the ages in which the books were written. At least, it may be asserted, that, in the places where we were most likely to meet with such things, if such things had existed, no reliques appear of any story substantially different from the present, as the cause, or as the pretence, of the institution.

Now that the original story, the story delivered by the first preachers of the institution, should have died away so entirely as to have left no record or memorial of its existence, although so many records and memorials of the time and transaction remain; and that another story should have stepped into its place, and gained exclusive possession of the belief of all who professed, themselves disciples of the institution, is beyond any example of the corruption of even oral tradition, and still less consistent with the experience of written history: and this improbability, which is very great, is rendered still greater by the reflection, that no such change as the oblivion of one story, and the substitution of another, took place in any future period of the Christian aera. Christianity hath travelled through dark and turbulent ages; nevertheless it came out of the cloud and the storm, such, in substance, as it entered in. Many additions were made to the primitive history, and these entitled to different degrees of credit; many doctrinal errors also were from time to time grafted into the public creed; but still the original story remained, and remained the same. In all its principal parts, it has been fixed from the beginning.

Thirdly: The religious rites and usages that prevailed amongst the early disciples of Christianity were such as belonged to, and sprung out of, the narrative now in our hands; which accordancy shows, that it was the narrative upon which these persons acted, and which they had received from their teachers. Our account makes the Founder of the religion direct that his disciples should be baptized: we know that the first Christians were baptized, Our account makes him direct that they should hold religious assemblies: we find that they did hold religious assemblies. Our accounts make the apostles assemble upon a stated day of the week: we find, and that from information perfectly independent of our accounts, that the Christians of the first century did observe stated days of assembling. Our histories record the institution of the rite which we call the Lord's Supper, and a command to repeat it in perpetual succession: we find, amongst the early Christians, the celebration of this rite universal. And, indeed, we find concurring in all the above-mentioned observances, Christian societies of many different nations and languages, removed from one another by a great distance of place and dissimilitude of situation. It is also extremely material to remark, that there is no room for insinuating that our books were fabricated with a studious accommodation to the usages which obtained at the time they were written; that the authors of the books found the usages established, and framed the story to account for their original. The Scripture accounts, especially of the Lord's Supper, are too short and cursory, not to say too obscure, and in this view, deficient, to allow a place for any such suspicion.[7]

Amongst the proofs of the truth of our proposition, viz. That the story which we have now is, in substance, the story which the Christians had then, or, in other words, that the accounts in our Gospels are, as to their principal parts, at least, the accounts which the apostles and original teachers of the religion delivered, one arises from observing, that it appears by the Gospels themselves that the story was public at the time; that the Christian community was already in possession of the substance and principal parts of the narrative. The Gospels were not the original cause of the Christian history being believed, but were themselves among the consequences of that belief. This is expressly affirmed by Saint Luke, in his brief, but, as I think, very important and instructive preface:— "Forasmuch (says the evangelist) as many have taken in hand to set forth in order a declaration of those things which are most surely believed amongst us, even as they delivered them unto us, which, from the beginning, were eye-witnesses and ministers of the word; it seemed good to me also, having had perfect understanding of all things from the very first, to write unto thee in order, most excellent Theophilus, that thou mightest know the certainty of those things wherein thou hast been instructed."—This short introduction testifies, that the substance of the history which the evangelist was about to write was already believed by Christians; that it was believed upon the declarations of eye-witnesses and ministers of the word; that it formed the account of their religion in which Christians were instructed; that the office which the historian proposed to himself was to trace each particular to its origin, and to fix the certainty of many things which the reader had before heard of. In Saint John's Gospel

---

[7] The reader who is conversant in these researches, by comparing the short Scripture accounts of the Christian rites above-mentioned with the minute and circumstantial directions contained in the pretended apostolical constitutions, will see the force of this observation; the difference between truth and forgery.

the same point appears hence, that there are some principal facts to which the historian refers, but which he does not relate. A remarkable instance of this kind is the ascension, which is not mentioned by St. John in its place, at the conclusion of his history, but which is plainly referred to in the following words of the sixth chapter; "What and if ye shall see the Son of man ascend up where he was before?" (Also John iii. 31; and xvi. 28.) And still more positively in the words which Christ, according to our evangelist, spoke to Mary after his resurrection, "Touch me not, for I am not yet ascended to my Father: but go unto my brethren, and say unto them, I ascend unto my Father and your Father, unto my God and your God." (John xx. 17.) This can only be accounted for by the supposition that St. John wrote under a sense of the notoriety of Christ's ascension, among those by whom his book was likely to be read. The same account must also be given of Saint Matthew's omission of the same important fact. The thing was very well known, and it did not occur to the historian that it was necessary to add any particulars concerning it. It agrees also with this solution, and with no other, that neither Matthew nor John disposes of the person of our Lord in any manner whatever. Other intimations in St. John's Gospel of the then general notoriety of the story are the following: His manner of introducing his narrative (ch. i. ver. 15.)—"John bare witness of him, and cried, saying" evidently presupposes that his readers knew who John was. His rapid parenthetical reference to John's imprisonment, "for John was not yet cast into prison," (John iii, 24.) could only come from a writer whose mind was in the habit of considering John's imprisonment as perfectly notorious. The description of Andrew by the addition "Simon Peter's brother," (John i. 40.) takes it for granted, that Simon Peter was well known. His name had not been mentioned before. The evangelist's noticing the prevailing misconstruction of a discourse, (John xxi. 24.) which Christ held with the beloved disciple, proves that the characters and the discourse were already public. And the observation which these instances afford is of equal validity for the purpose of the present argument, whoever were the authors of the histories.

These four circumstances:—first, the recognition of the account in its principal parts by a series of succeeding writers; secondly, the total absence of any account of the origin of the religion substantially different from ours; thirdly, the early and extensive prevalence of rites and institutions, which resulted from our account; fourthly, our account bearing in its construction proof that it is an account of facts which were known and believed at the time, are sufficient, I conceive, to support an assurance, that the story which we have now is, in general, the story which Christians had at the beginning. I say in general; by which term I mean, that it is the same in its texture, and in its principal facts. For instance, I make no doubt, for the reasons above stated, but that the resurrection of the Founder of the religion was always a part of the Christian story. Nor can a doubt of this remain upon the mind of any one who reflects that the resurrection is, in some form or other, asserted, referred to, or assumed, in every Christian writing, of every description which hath come down to us.

And if our evidence stopped here, we should have a strong case to offer: for we should have to allege, that in the reign of Tiberius Caesar, a certain number of persons set about an attempt of establishing a new religion in the world: in the prosecution of which purpose, they voluntarily encountered great dangers, undertook great labours, sustained great sufferings, all for a miraculous story, which they published wherever they came; and that the resurrection of a dead man, whom during his life they had followed and accompanied, was a constant part of this story. I know nothing in the above statement which can, with any appearance of reason, be disputed; and I know nothing, in the history of the human species, similar to it.

CHAPTER VIII.

There is satisfactory evidence that many, professing to be original witnesses of the Christian miracles, passed their lives in labours, dangers, and sufferings, voluntarily undergone in attestation of the accounts which they delivered, and solely in consequence of their belief of those accounts; and that they also submitted, from the same motives, to new rules of conduct.

That the story which we have now is, in the main, the story which the apostles published, is, I think, nearly certain, from the considerations which have been proposed. But whether, when we come to the particulars, and the detail of the narrative, the historical books of the New Testament be deserving of credit as histories, so that a fact ought to be accounted true, because it is found in them; or whether they are entitled to be considered as representing the accounts which, true or false, the apostles published; whether their authority, in either of these views, can be trusted to, is a point which necessarily depends upon what we know of the books, and of their authors.

Now, in treating of this part of our argument, the first and most material observation upon the subject is, that such was the situation of the authors to whom the four Gospels are ascribed, that, if any one of the four be genuine, it is sufficient for our purpose. The received author of the first was an original apostle and emissary of the religion. The received author of the second was an inhabitant of Jerusalem, at the time, to whose house the apostles were wont to resort, and himself an attendant upon one of the most eminent of that number. The received author of the third was a stated companion and fellow-traveller of the most active of all the teachers of the religion, and, in the course of his travels, frequently in the society of the original apostles. The received author of the fourth, as well as of the first, was one of these apostles. No stronger evidence of the truth of a history can arise from the situation of the historian than what is here offered. The authors of all the histories lived at the time and upon the spot. The authors of two of the histories were present at many of the scenes which they describe; eye-witnesses of the facts, ear-witnesses of the discourses; writing from personal knowledge and recollection; and, what strengthens their testimony, writing upon a subject in which their minds were deeply engaged, and in which, as they must have been very frequently repeating the accounts to others, the passages of the history would be kept continually alive in their memory. Whoever reads the Gospels (and they ought to be read for this particular purpose) will find in them not merely a general affirmation of miraculous powers, but detailed circumstantial accounts of miracles, with specifications of time, place, and persons; and these accounts many and various. In the Gospels, therefore, which bear the names of Matthew and John, these narratives, if they really proceeded from these men, must either be true as far as the fidelity of human recollection is usually to be depended upon, that is, must be true in substance and in their principal parts, (which is sufficient for the purpose of proving a supernatural agency,) or they must be wilful and mediated falsehoods. Yet the writers who fabricated and uttered these falsehoods, if they be such, are of the number of those who, unless the whole contexture of the Christian story be a dream, sacrificed their ease and safety in the cause, and for a purpose the most inconsistent that is possible with dishonest intentions. They were villains for no end but to teach honesty, and martyrs without the least prospect of honour or advantage.

The Gospels which bear the names of Mark and Luke, although not the narratives of eye-witnesses, are, if genuine, removed from that only by one degree. They are the narratives of contemporary writers, or writers themselves mixing with the business; one of the two probably living in the place which was the principal scene of action; both living in habits of society and correspondence with those who had been present at the transactions which they relate. The latter of them accordingly tells us (and with apparent sincerity, because he tells it without pretending to personal knowledge, and without claiming for his work greater authority than belonged to it) that the things which were believed amount Christians came from those who from the beginning were eye-witnesses and ministers of the word; that he had traced accounts up to their source; and that he was prepared to instruct his reader in the certainty of the things which he related.[1] Very few histories lie so close to their facts; very few historians are so nearly connected with the subject of their narrative, or possess such means of authentic information, as these.

The situation of the writers applies to the truth of the facts which they record. But at present we use their testimony to a point somewhat short of this, namely, that the facts recorded in the Gospels, whether true or false, are the facts, and the sort of facts which the original preachers of the religion allege. Strictly speaking, I am concerned only to show, that what the Gospels contain is the same as what the apostles preached. Now, how stands the proof of this point? A set of men went about the world, publishing a story composed of miraculous accounts, (for miraculous from the very nature and exigency of the case they must have been,) and upon the strength of these accounts called upon mankind to quit the religions in which they had been educated, and to take up, thenceforth, a

---

[1] Why should not the candid and modest preface of this historian be believed, as well as that which Dion Cassius prefixes to his Life of Commodus? "These things and the following I write, not from the report of others, but from my own knowledge and observation." I see no reason to doubt but that both passages describe truly enough the situation of the authors.

new system of opinions, and new rules of action. What is more in attestation of these accounts, that is, in support of an institution of which these accounts were the foundation, is, that the same men voluntarily exposed themselves to harassing and perpetual labours, dangers, and sufferings. We want to know what these accounts were. We have the particulars, i.e. many particulars, from two of their own number. We have them from an attendant of one of the number, and who, there is reason to believe, was an inhabitant of Jerusalem at the time. We have them from a fourth writer, who accompanied the most laborious missionary of the institution in his travels; who, in the course of these travels, was frequently brought into the society of the rest; and who, let it be observed, begins his narrative by telling us that he is about to relate the things which had been delivered by those who were ministers of the word, and eye-witnesses of the facts. I do not know what information can be more satisfactory than this. We may, perhaps, perceive the force and value of it more sensibly if we reflect how requiring we should have been if we had wanted it. Supposing it to be sufficiently proved, that the religion now professed among us owed its original to the preaching and ministry of a number of men, who, about eighteen centuries ago, set forth in the world a new system of religious opinions, founded upon certain extraordinary things which they related of a wonderful person who had appeared in Judea; suppose it to be also sufficiently proved, that, in the course and prosecution of their ministry, these men had subjected themselves to extreme hardships, fatigue, and peril; but suppose the accounts which they published had not been committed to writing till some ages after their times, or at least that no histories but what had been composed some ages afterwards had reached our hands; we should have said, and with reason, that we were willing to believe these under the circumstances in which they delivered their testimony, but that we did not, at this day, know with sufficient evidence what their testimony was. Had we received the particulars of it from any of their own number, from any of those who lived and conversed with them, from any of their hearers, or even from any of their contemporaries, we should have had something to rely upon. Now, if our books be genuine, we have all these. We have the very species of information which, as it appears to me, our imagination would have carved out for us, if it had been wanting.

But I have said that if any one of the four Gospels be genuine, we have not only direct historical testimony to the point we contend for, but testimony which, so far as that point is concerned, cannot reasonably be rejected. If the first Gospel was really written by Matthew, we have the narrative of one of the number, from which to judge what were the miracles, and the kind of miracles, which the apostles attributed to Jesus. Although, for argument's sake, and only for argument's sake, we should allow that this Gospel had been erroneously ascribed to Matthew; yet, if the Gospel of St. John be genuine, the observation holds with no less strength. Again, although the Gospels both of Matthew and John could be supposed to be spurious, yet, if the Gospel of Saint Luke were truly the composition of that person, or of any person, be his name what it might, who was actually in the situation in which the author of that Gospel professes himself to have been, or if the Gospel which bear the name of Mark really proceeded from him; we still, even upon the lowest supposition, possess the accounts of one writer at least, who was not only contemporary with the apostles, but associated with them in their ministry; which authority seems sufficient, when the question is simply what it was which these apostles advanced.

I think it material to have this well noticed. The New Testament contains a great number of distinct writings, the genuineness of any one of which is almost sufficient to prove the truth of the religion: it contains, however, four distinct histories, the genuineness of any one of which is perfectly sufficient.

If, therefore, we must be considered as encountering the risk of error in assigning the authors of our books, we are entitled to the advantage of so many separate probabilities. And although it should appear that some of the evangelists had seen and used each other's works, this discovery, whist it subtracts indeed from their characters as testimonies strictly independent, diminishes, I conceive, little either their separate authority, (by which I mean the authority of any one that is genuine,) or their mutual confirmation. For, let the most disadvantageous supposition possible be made concerning them; let it be allowed, what I should have no great difficulty in admitting, that Mark compiled his history almost entirely from those of Matthew and Luke; and let it also for a moment be supposed that were not, in fact, written by Matthew and Luke; yet, if it be true that Mark, a contemporary of the apostles, living, in habits of society with the apostles, a fellow-traveller and fellow-labourer with some of them; if, I say, it be true, that this person made the compilation, it follows, that the writings from which he made it existed in the time of the apostles, and not only so, but that they were then in such esteem and credit, that a companion of the apostles formed a history out of them. Let the Gospel of Mark be called an epitome of that of Matthew; if a person in the situation in which Mark is described to have been actually made the epitome, it affords the strongest possible attestation to the character of the original.

Again, parallelisms in sentences, in word, and in the order of words, have been traced out between the Gospel of Matthew and that of Luke; which concurrence cannot easily be explained, otherwise than by supposing, either that Luke had consulted Matthew's history, or, what appears to me in nowise incredible, that minutes of some of Christ's discourses, as well as brief memoirs of some passages of his life, had been committed to writing at the time; and that such written accounts had by both authors been occasionally admitted into their histories. Either supposition is perfectly consistent with the acknowledged formation of St. Luke's narrative, who professes not to write as an eye-witness, but to have investigated the original of every account which he delivers: in other words, to have collected them from such documents and testimonies as he, who had the best opportunities of making inquiries, judged to be authentic. Therefore, allowing that this writer also, in some instances, borrowed from the Gospel which we call Matthew's and once more allowing for the sake of stating the argument, that that Gospel was not the production of the author to whom we ascribe it; yet still we have in St. Luke's Gospel a history given by a writer immediately connected with the transaction with the witnesses of it with the persons engaged in it, and composed from materials which that person, thus situated, deemed to be safe source of intelligence; in other words, whatever supposition be made concerning any or all the other Gospels, if Saint Luke's Gospel be genuine, we have in it a credible evidence of the point which we maintain. The Gospel according to Saint John appears to be, and is on all hands allowed to be, an independent testimony, strictly and properly so called. Notwithstanding therefore, any connexion or supposed connexion, between one of the Gospels, I again repeat what I before said, that if any one of the four be genuine, we have, in that one, strong reason, from the character and situation of the writer, to believe that we possess the accounts which the original emissaries of the religion delivered.

Secondly: In treating of the written evidences of Christianity, next to their separate, we are to consider their aggregate authority. Now, there is in the evangelic history a cumulation of testimony which belongs hardly to any other history, but which our habitual mode of reading the Scriptures sometimes causes us to overlook. When a passage, in any wise relating to the history of Christ is read to us out of the epistle of Clemens Romanus, the epistles of Ignatius, of Polycarp, or from any other writing of that age, we are immediately sensible of the confirmation which it affords to the Scripture account. Here is a new witness. Now, if we had been accustomed to read the Gospel of Matthew alone, and had known that of Luke only as the generality of Christians know the writings of the apostolical fathers, that is, had known that such a writing was extant and acknowledged; when we came, for the first time, to look into what it contained, and found many of the facts which Matthew recorded, recorded also there, many other facts of a similar nature added, and throughout the whole work the same general series of transactions stated, and the same general character of the person who was the subject of the history preserved, I apprehend that we should feel our minds strongly impressed by this discovery of fresh evidence. We should feel a renewal of the same sentiment in first reading the Gospel of Saint John. That of Saint Mark perhaps would strike us as an abridgment of the history with which we were already acquainted; but we should naturally reflect, that if that history was abridged by such a person as Mark, or by any person of so early an age, it afforded one of the highest possible attestations to the value of the work. This successive disclosure of proof would leave us assured, that there must have been at least some reality in a story which not one, but many, had taken in hand to commit to writing. The very existence of four separate histories would satisfy us that the subject had a foundation; and when, amidst the variety which the different information of the different writers had supplied to their accounts, or which their different choice and judgment in selecting their materials had produced, we observed many facts to stand the same in all; of these facts, at least, we should conclude, that they were fixed in their credit and publicity. If, after this, we should come to the knowledge of a distinct history, and that also of the same age with the rest, taking up the subject where the others had left it, and carrying on a narrative of the effects produced in the world by the extraordinary causes of which we had already been informed, and which effects subsist at this day, we should think the reality of the original story in no little degree established by this supplement. If subsequent inquiries should bring to our knowledge, one after another, letters written by some of the principal agents in the business, upon the business, and during the time of their activity and concern in it, assuming all along and recognising the original story, agitating the questions that arose out of it, pressing the obligations which resulted from it, giving advice and directions to these who acted upon it; I conceive that we should find, in every one of these, a still further support to the conclusion we had formed. At present, the weight of this successive confirmation is, in a great measure; unperceived by us. The evidence does not appear to us what it is; for, being from our infancy accustomed to regard the New Testament as one book, we see in it only one testimony. The whole occurs to us as a single evidence; and its different parts not as distinct attestations, but as different portions only of the same. Yet in this conception of the subject we are certainly mistaken; for the very discrepancies among the several documents which form our volume prove, if all other proof were wanting, that in their original composition they were separate, and most of them independent productions.

If we dispose our ideas in a different order, the matter stands thus:— Whilst the transaction was recent, and the original witnesses were at hand to relate it; and whilst the apostles were busied in preaching and travelling, in collecting disciples, in forming and regulating societies of converts, in supporting themselves against opposition; whilst they exercised their ministry under the harassings of frequent persecutions, and in a state of almost continual alarm, it is not probable that, in this engaged, anxious, and unsettled condition of life, they would think immediately of writing histories for the information of the public or of posterity.[2] But it is very probable, that emergencies might draw from some of them occasional letters upon the subject of their mission, to converts, or to societies of converts, with which they were connected; or that they might address written discourses and exhortations to the disciples of the institution at large, which would be received and read with a respect proportioned to the character of the writer. Accounts in the mean time would get abroad of the extraordinary things that had been passing, written with different degrees of information and correctness. The extension of the Christian society, which could no longer be instructed: by a personal intercourse with the apostles, and the possible circulation of imperfect or erroneous narratives, would soon teach some amongst them the expediency of sending forth authentic memoirs of the life and doctrine of their Master. When accounts appeared authorised by the name, and credit, and situation of the writers, recommended or recognised by the apostles and first preachers of the religion, or found to coincide with what the apostles and first preachers of the religion had taught, other accounts would fall into disuse and neglect; whilst these, maintaining their reputation (as, if genuine and well founded, they would do) under the test of time, inquiry, and contradiction, might be expected to make their way into the hands of Christians of all countries of the world.

This seems the natural progress of the business; and with this the records in our possession, and the evidence concerning them correspond. We have remaining, in the first place, many letters of the kind above described, which have been preserved with a care and fidelity answering to the respect with which we may suppose that such letters would be received. But as these letters were not written to prove the truth of the Christian religion, in the sense in which we regard that question; nor to convey information of facts, of which those to whom the letters were written had been previously informed; we are not to look in them for anything more than incidental allusions to the Christian history. We are able, however, to gather from these documents various particular attestations which have been already enumerated; and this is a species of written evidence, as far as it goes, in the highest degree satisfactory, and in point of time perhaps the first. But for our more circumstantial information, we have, in the next place, five direct histories, bearing the names of persons acquainted, by their situation, with the truth of what they relate, and three of them purporting, in the very body of the

---

[2] This thought occurred to Eusebius: "Nor were the apostles of Christ greatly concerned about the writing of books, being engaged in a more excellent ministry which is above all human power." Eccles. Hist. 1. iii. c. 24.—The same consideration accounts also for the paucity of Christian writings in the first century of its aera.

narrative, to be written by such persons; of which books we know, that some were in the hands of those who were contemporaries of the apostles, and that, in the age immediately posterior to that, they were in the hands, we may say, of every one, and received by Christians with so much respect and deference, as to be constantly quoted and referred to by them, without any doubt of the truth of their accounts. They were treated as such histories, proceeding from such authorities, might expect to be treated. In the preface to one of our histories, we have intimations left us of the existence of some ancient accounts which are now lost. There is nothing in this circumstance that can surprise us. It was to be expected, from the magnitude and novelty of the occasion, that such accounts would swarm. When better accounts came forth, these died away. Our present histories superseded others. They soon acquired a character and established a reputation which does not appear to have belonged to any other: that, at least, can be proved concerning them which cannot be proved concerning any other.

But to return to the point which led to these reflections. By considering our records in either of the two views in which we have represented them, we shall perceive that we possess a connection of proofs, and not a naked or solitary testimony; and that the written evidence is of such a kind, and comes to us in such a state, as the natural order and progress of things, in the infancy of the institution, might be expected to produce.

Thirdly: The genuineness of the historical books of the New Testament is undoubtedly a point of importance, because the strength of their evidence is augmented by our knowledge of the situation of their authors, their relation to the subject, and the part which they sustained in the transaction; and the testimonies which we are able to produce compose a firm ground of persuasion, that the Gospels were written by the persons whose names they bear. Nevertheless, I must be allowed to state, that to the argument which I am endeavouring to maintain, this point is not essential; I mean, so essential as that the fate of the argument depends upon it. The question before us is, whether the Gospels exhibit the story which the apostles and first emissaries of the religion published, and for which they acted and suffered in the manner in which, for some miraculous story or other, they did act and suffer. Now let us suppose that we possess no other information concerning these books than that they were written by early disciples of Christianity; that they were known and read during the time, or near the time, of the original apostles of the religion; that by Christians whom the apostles instructed, by societies of Christians which the apostles founded, these books were received, (by which term "received" I mean that they were believed to contain authentic accounts of the transactions upon which the religion rested, and accounts which were accordingly used, repeated, and relied upon,) this reception would be a valid proof that these books, whoever were the authors of them, must have accorded with what the apostles taught. A reception by the first race of Christians, is evidence that they agreed with what the first teachers of the religion delivered. In particular, if they had not agreed with what the apostles themselves preached, how could they have gained credit in churches and societies which the apostles established?

Now the fact of their early existence, and not only of their existence, but their reputation, is made out by some ancient testimonies which do not happen to specify the names of the writers: add to which, what hath been already hinted, that two out of the four Gospels contain averments in the body of the history, which, though they do not disclose the names, fix the time and situation of the authors, viz., that one was written by an eye-witness of the sufferings of Christ, the other by a contemporary of the apostles. In the Gospel of St. John (xix. 35), describing the crucifixion, with the particular circumstance of piercing Christ's side with a spear, the historian adds, as for himself, "and he that saw it bare record, and his record is true, and he knoweth that he saith true, that ye might believe." Again (xxi. 24), after relating a conversation which passed between Peter and "the disciple," as it is there expressed, "whom Jesus loved," it is added, "this is the disciple which testifieth of these things, and wrote these things." This testimony, let it be remarked, is not the less worthy of regard, because it is, in one view, imperfect. The name is not mentioned; which, if a fraudulent purpose had been intended, would have been done. The third of our present Gospels purports to have been written by the person who wrote the Acts of the Apostles; in which latter history, or rather latter part of the same history, the author, by using in various places the first person plural, declares himself to have been a contemporary of all, and a companion of one, of the original preachers of the religion.

CHAPTER IX.

There is satisfactory evidence that many, professing to be original witnesses of the Christian miracles, passed their lives in labours, dangers, and sufferings, voluntarily undergone in attestation of the accounts which they delivered, and solely in consequence of their belief of those accounts; and that they also submitted, from the same motives, to new rules of conduct.

OF THE AUTHENTICITY OF THE SCRIPTURES.

Not forgetting, therefore, what credit is due to the evangelical history, supposing even any one of the four Gospels to be genuine; what credit is due to the Gospels, even supposing nothing to be known concerning them but that they were written by early disciples of the religion, and received with deference by early Christian churches; more especially not forgetting what credit is due to the New Testament in its capacity of cumulative evidence; we now proceed to state the proper and distinct proofs, which show not only the general value of these records, but their specific authority, and the high probability there is that they actually came from the persons whose names they bear.

There are, however, a few preliminary reflections, by which we may draw up with more regularity to the propositions upon which the close and particular discussion of the subject depends. Of which nature are the following:

I. We are able to produce a great number of ancient manuscripts, found in many different countries, and in countries widely distant from each other, all of them anterior to the art of printing, some Certainly seven or eight hundred years old, and some which have been preserved probably above a thousand years.[1] We have also many ancient versions of these books, and some of them into languages which are not at present, nor for many ages have been, spoken in any part of the world. The existence of these manuscripts and versions proves that the Scriptures were not the production of any modern contrivance. It does away also the uncertainty which hangs over such publications as the works, real or pretended, of Ossian and Rowley, in which the editors are challenged to produce their manuscripts and to show where they obtained their copies. The number of manuscripts, far exceeding those of any other book, and their wide dispersion, afford an argument, in some measure to the senses, that the Scriptures anciently, in like manner as at this day, were more read and sought after than any other books, and that also in many different

---

[1] The Alexandrian manuscript, now in the British Museum, was written probably in the fourth or fifth century.

countries. The greatest part of spurious Christian writings are utterly lost, the rest preserved by some single manuscript. There is weight also in Dr. Bentley's observation, that the New Testament has suffered less injury by the errors of transcribers than the works of any profane author of the same size and antiquity; that is, there never was any writing, in the preservation and purity of which the world was so interested or so careful.

II. An argument of great weight with those who are judges of the proofs upon which it is founded, and capable, through their testimony, of being addressed to every understanding, is that which arises from the style and language of the New Testament. It is just such a language as might be expected from the apostles, from persons of their age and in their situation, and from no other persons. It is the style neither of classic authors, nor of the ancient Christian fathers, but Greek coming from men of Hebrew origin; abounding, that is, with Hebraic and Syriac idioms, such as would naturally be found in the writings of men who used a language spoken indeed where they lived, but not the common dialect of the country. This happy peculiarity is a strong proof of the genuineness of these writings: for who should forge them? The Christian fathers were for the most part totally ignorant of Hebrew, and therefore were not likely to insert Hebraisms and Syriasms into their writings. The few who had a knowledge of the Hebrew, as Justin Martyr, Origen, and Epiphanius, wrote in a language which hears no resemblance to that of the New Testament. The Nazarenes, who understood Hebrew, used chiefly, perhaps almost entirely, the Gospel of Saint Matthew, and therefore cannot be suspected of forging the rest of the sacred writings. The argument, at any rate, proves the antiquity of these books; that they belonged to the age of the apostles; that they could be composed, indeed, in no other.[2]

III. Why should we question the genuineness of these books? Is it for that they contain accounts of supernatural events? I apprehend that this, at the bottom, is the real, though secret, cause of our hesitation about them: for had the writings inscribed with the names of Matthew and John related nothing but ordinary history, there would have been no more doubt whether these writings were theirs than there is concerning the acknowledged works of Josephus or Philo; that is, there would have been no doubt at all. Now it ought to be considered that this reason, however it may apply to the credit which is given to a writer's judgment or veracity, affects the question of genuineness very indirectly. The works of Bede exhibit many wonderful relations: but who, for that reason, doubts that they were written by Bede? The same of a multitude of other authors. To which may be added that we ask no more for our books than what we

---

[2] See this argument stated more at large in Michaelis's Introduction, (Marsh's translation,) vol. i. c. ii. sect. 10, from which these observations are taken.

allow to other books in some sort similar to ours: we do not deny the genuineness of the Koran; we admit that the history of Apollonius Tyanaeus, purporting to be written by Philostratus, was really written by Philostratus.

IV. If it had been an easy thing in the early times of the institution to have forged Christian writings, and to have obtained currency and reception to the forgeries, we should have had many appearing in the name of Christ himself. No writings would have been received with so much avidity and respect as these: consequently none afforded so great a temptation to forgery. Yet have we heard but of one attempt of this sort, deserving of the smallest notice, that in a piece of a very few lines, and so far from succeeding, I mean, from obtaining acceptance and reputation, or an acceptance an reputation in anywise similar to that which can be proved to have attended the books of the New Testament, that it is not so much as mentioned by any writer of the first three centuries. The learned reader need not be informed that I mean the epistle of Christ to Abgarus, king of Edessa, found at present in the work of Eusebius,[3] as a piece acknowledged by him, though not without considerable doubt whether the whole passage be not an interpolation, as it is most certain, that, after the publication of Eusebius's work, this epistle was universally rejected.

V. If the ascription of the Gospels to their respective authors had been arbitrary or conjectural, they would have been ascribed to more eminent men. This observation holds concerning the first three Gospels, the reputed authors of which were enabled, by their situation, to obtain true intelligence, and were likely to deliver an honest account of what they knew, but were persons not distinguished in the history by extraordinary marks of notice or commendation. Of the apostles, I hardly know any one of whom less is said than of Matthew, or of whom the little that is said is less calculated to magnify his character. Of Mark, nothing is said in the Gospels; and what is said of any person of that name in the Acts, and in the epistles, in no part bestows praise or eminence upon him. The name of Luke is mentioned only in St Paul's epistles,[4] and that very transiently. The judgment, therefore, which assigned these writings to these authors

---

[3] Hist. Eccl. lib. i. c. 15. + Augustin, A.D. 895 (De Consens. Evan. c. 34), had heard that the Pagans pretended to be possessed of an epistle of Christ to Peter and Paul; but he had never seen it, and appears to doubt of the existence of any such piece either genuine or spurious. No other ancient writer mentions it. He also, and he alone, notices, and that in order to condemn it, an epistle ascribed to Christ by the Manichees, A.D. 270, and a short hymn attributed to him by the Priscillianists, A.D. 378 (cont. Faust. Man. Lib xxviii, c,4). The lateness of the writer who notices these things, the manner in which he notices them, and above all, the silence of every preceding writer, render them unworthy on of consideration.

[4] Col. iv. 14. 2Tim. iv. 11. Philem. 24. + Lardner, Cred. vol. viii. P.291, et seq.

proceeded, it may be presumed, upon proper knowledge and evidence, and not upon a voluntary choice of names.

VI. Christian writers and Christian churches appear to have soon arrived at a very general agreement upon the subject, and that without the interposition of any public authority. When the diversity of opinion which prevailed, and prevails among Christians in other points, is considered, their concurrence in the canon of Scripture is remarkable, and of great weight, especially as it seems to have been the result of private and free inquiry. We have no knowledge of any interference of authority in the question before the council of Laodicea in the year 363. Probably the decree of this council rather declared than regulated the public judgment, or, more properly speaking, the judgment of some neighbouring churches; the council itself consisting of no more than thirty or forty bishops of Lydia and the adjoining countries.+ Nor does its authority seem to have extended further; for we find numerous Christian writers, after this time, discussing the question, "What books were entitled to be received as Scripture," with great freedom, upon proper grounds of evidence, and without any reference to the decision at Laodicea.

These considerations are not to be neglected: but of an argument concerning the genuineness of ancient writings, the substance, undoubtedly, and strength, is ancient testimony.

This testimony it is necessary to exhibit somewhat in detail; for when Christian advocates merely tell us that we have the same reason for believing the Gospels to be written by the evangelists whose names they bear as we have for believing the Commentaries to be Caesar's, the Aeneid Virgil's, or the Orations Cicero's, they content themselves with an imperfect representation. They state nothing more than what is true, but they do not state the truth correctly. In the number, variety, and early date of our testimonies, we far exceed all other ancient books. For one which the most celebrated work of the most celebrated Greek or Roman writer can allege, we produce many. But then it is more requisite in our books than in theirs to separate and distinguish them from spurious competitors. The result, I am convinced, will be satisfactory to every fair inquirer: but this circumstance renders an inquiry necessary.

In a work, however, like the present, there is a difficulty in finding a place for evidence of this kind. To pursue the details of proof throughout, would be to transcribe a great part of Dr. Lardner's eleven octavo volumes: to leave the argument without proofs is to leave it without effect; for the persuasion produced by this species of evidence depends upon a view and induction of the particulars which compose it.

The method which I propose to myself is, first, to place before the reader, in one view, the propositions which comprise the several heads of our testimony, and afterwards to repeat the same propositions in so many distinct sections, with the necessary authorities subjoined to each.[5]

The following, then, are the allegations upon the subject which are capable of being established by proof:—

I. That the historical books of the New Testament, meaning thereby the four Gospels and the Acts of the Apostles, are quoted, or alluded to, by a series of Christian writers, beginning with those who were contemporary with the apostles, or who immediately followed them, and proceeding in close and regular succession from their time to the present.

II. That when they are quoted, or alluded to, they are quoted or alluded to with peculiar respect, as books 'sui generis'; as possessing an authority which belonged to no other books, and as conclusive in all questions and controversies amongst Christians.

III. That they were, in very early times, collected into a distinct volume.

IV. That they were distinguished by appropriate names and titles of respect.

V. That they were publicly read and expounded in the religious assemblies of the early Christians.

VI. That commentaries were written upon them, harmonies formed out of them, different copies carefully collated, and versions of them made into different languages.

VII. That they were received by Christians of different sects, by many heretics as well as Catholics, and usually appealed to by both sides in the controversies which arose in those days.

VIII. That the four Gospels, the Acts of the Apostles, thirteen Epistles of Saint Paul, the first epistle of John, and the first of-Peter, were received without doubt by those who doubted concerning the other books which are included in our present canon.

IX. That the Gospels were attacked by the early adversaries of Christianity, as books containing the accounts upon which the religion was founded.

X. That formal catalogues of authentic Scriptures were published; in all which our present sacred histories were included.

XI. That these propositions cannot be affirmed of any other books claiming to be books of Scripture; by which are meant those books which are commonly called apocryphal books of the New Testament.

---

[5] The reader, when he has the propositions before him, will observe that the argument, if he should omit the sections, proceeds connectedly from this point.

SECTION I.

The historical books of the New Testament, meaning thereby the four Gospels and the Acts of the Apostles, are quoted, or alluded to, by a series of Christian writers, beginning with those who were contemporary with the apostles, or who immediately followed them, and proceeding in close and regular succession from their time to the present.

The medium of proof stated in this proposition is, of all others, the most unquestionable, the least liable to any practices of fraud, and is not diminished by the lapse of ages. Bishop Burnet, in the History of his Own Times, inserts various extracts from Lord Clarendon's History. One such insertion is a proof that Lord Clarendon's History was extant at the time when Bishop Burnet wrote, that it had been read by Bishop Burnet, that it was received by Bishop Burnet as a work of Lord Clarendon, and also regarded by him as an authentic account of the transactions which it relates; and it will be a proof of these points a thousand years hence, or as long as the books exist. Quintilian having quoted as Cicero's, (Quint. lib. xl. c. l.) that well known trait of dissembled vanity:—"Si quid est in me ingenii, Judices, quod sentio quam sit exiguum;"—the quotation would be strong evidence, were there any doubt, that the oration, which opens with this address, actually came from Cicero's pen. These instances, however simple, may serve to point out to a reader who is little accustomed to such researches the nature and value of the argument.

The testimonies which we have to bring forward under this proposition are the following:—

I. There is extant an epistle ascribed to Barnabas,[6] the companion of Paul. It is quoted as the epistle of Barnabas, by Clement of Alexandria, A.D. CXCIV; by Origen, A.D. CCXXX. It is mentioned by Eusebius, A.D. CCCXV, and by Jerome, A.D. CCCXCII, as an ancient work in their time, bearing the name of Barnabas, and as well known and read amongst Christians, though not accounted a part of Scripture. It purports to have been written soon after the destruction of Jerusalem, during the calamities which followed that disaster; and it bears the character of the age to which it professes to belong.

In this epistle appears the following remarkable passage:—"Let us, therefore, beware lest it come upon us, as it is written; There are many called, few chosen." From the expression, "as it is written," we infer with certainty, that at the time when the author of this epistle lived, there was a book extant, well known to Christians, and of authority amongst them, containing these words:—"Many are called, few chosen." Such a book is

---

[6] Lardner, Cred. edit. 1755, vol. i. p. 23, et seq. The reader will observe from the references, that the materials of these sections are almost entirely extracted from Dr. Lardner's work; my office consisted in arrangement and selection.

our present Gospel of Saint Matthew, in which this text is twice found, (Matt xx. 16; xxii. 14.) and is found in no other book now known. There is a further observation to be made upon the terms of the quotation. The writer of the epistle was a Jew. The phrase "it is written" was the very form in which the Jews quoted their Scriptures. It is not probable, therefore, that he would have used this phrase, and without qualification, of any book but what had acquired a kind of Scriptural authority. If the passage remarked in this ancient writing had been found in one of Saint Paul's Epistles, it would have been esteemed by every one a high testimony to Saint Matthew's Gospel. It ought, therefore, to be remembered, that the writing in which it is found was probably by very few years posterior to those of Saint Paul.

Beside this passage, there are also in the epistle before us several others, in which the sentiment is the same with what we meet with in Saint Matthew's Gospel, and two or three in which we recognize the same words. In particular, the author of the epistle repeats the precept, "Give to every one that asketh thee;" (Matt. v. 42.) and saith that Christ chose as his apostles, who were to preach the Gospel, men who were great sinners, that he might show that he came "not to call the righteous, but sinners to repentance." (Matt. Ix. 13.)

II. We are in possession of an epistle written by Clement, bishop of Rome, (Lardner, Cred. vol. p. 62, et seq.) whom ancient writers, without any doubt or scruple, assert to have been the Clement whom Saint Paul mentions, Phil. iv. 3; "with Clement also, and other my fellow-labourers, whose names are in the book of life." This epistle is spoken of by the ancients as an epistle acknowledged by all; and, as Irenaeus well represents its value, "written by Clement, who had seen the blessed apostles, and conversed with them; who had the preaching of the apostles still sounding in his ears, and their traditions before his eyes." It is addressed to the church of Corinth; and what alone may seem almost decisive of its authenticity, Dionysius, bishop of Corinth, about the year 170, i.e. about eighty or ninety years after the epistle was written, bears witness, "that it had been wont to be read in that church from ancient times."

This epistle affords, amongst others, the following valuable passages:—"Especially remembering the words of the Lord Jesus, which he spake teaching gentleness and long-suffering: for thus he said:[7] Be ye merciful, that ye may obtain mercy; forgive, that it my be forgiven unto

---

[7] "Blessed are the merciful, for they shall obtain mercy." Matt. v. 7.—"Forgive, and ye shall be forgiven; give, and it shall be given unto you." Luke vi. 37, 38.—"Judge not, that ye be not judged; for with what judgment ye judge, ye shall be judged; and with what measure ye mete, it shall be measured to you again." Matt. vii. 1, 2.

you; as you do, so shall it be done unto you; as you give, so shall it be given unto you; as ye judge, so shall ye be judged; as ye show kindness, so shall kindness be shown unto you; with what measure ye mete, with the same shall it be measured to you. By this command, and by these rules, let us establish ourselves, that we may always walk obediently to his holy words."

Again; "Remember the words of the Lord Jesus, for he said, Woe to that man by whom offences come; it were better for him that he had not been born, than that he should offend one of my elect; it were better for him that a millstone should be tied about his neck, and that he should be drowned in the sea, than that he should offend one of my little ones."[8]

In both these passages we perceive the high respect paid to the words of Christ as recorded by the evangelists; "Remember the words of the Lord Jesus;—by this command, and by these rules, let us establish ourselves, that we may always walk obediently to his holy words." We perceive also in Clement a total unconsciousness of doubt whether these were the real words of Christ, which are read as such in the Gospels. This observation indeed belongs to the whole series of testimony, and especially to the most ancient part of it. Whenever anything now read in the Gospels is met with in an early Christian writing, it is always observed to stand there as acknowledged truth, i.e. to be introduced without hesitation, doubt, or apology. It is to be observed also, that, as this epistle was written in the name of the church of Rome, and addressed to the church of Corinth, it ought to be taken as exhibiting the judgment not only of Clement, who drew up the letter, but of these churches themselves, at least as to the authority of the books referred to.

It may be said that, as Clement has not used words of quotation, it is not certain that he refers to any book whatever. The words of Christ which he has put down, he might himself have heard from the apostles, or might have received through the ordinary medium of oral tradition. This has been said: but that no such inference can be drawn from the absence of words of quotation, is proved by the three following considerations:—First, that Clement, in the very same manner, namely, without any mark of reference, uses a passage now found in the epistle to the Romans; (Rom. i. 29.) which passage, from the peculiarity of the words which compose it, and from their order, it is manifest that he must have taken from the book. The same remark may be repeated of some very singular

---

[8] Matt. xviii. 6. "But whoso shall offend one of these little ones which believe in me, it were better for him that a mill-stone were hanged about his neck, and that he were cast into the sea." The latter part of the passage in Clement agrees exactly with Luke xvii. 2; "It were better for him that a mill-stone were hanged about his neck, and he cast into the sea, than that he should offend one of these little ones."

sentiments in the Epistle to the Hebrews. Secondly, that there are many sentences of Saint Paul's First Epistle to the Corinthians standing in Clement's epistle without any sign of quotation, which yet certainly are quotations; because it appears that Clement had Saint Paul's epistle before him, inasmuch as in one place he mentions it in terms too express to leave us in any doubt:—"Take into your hands the epistle of the blessed apostle Paul." Thirdly, that this method of adopting words of Scripture without reference or acknowledgment was, as will appear in the sequel, a method in general use amongst the most ancient Christian writers.—These analogies not only repel the objection, but cast the presumption on the other side, and afford a considerable degree of positive proof, that the words in question have been borrowed from the places of Scripture in which we now find them. But take it if you will the other way, that Clement had heard these words from the apostles or first teachers of Christianity; with respect to the precise point of our argument, viz. that the Scriptures contain what the apostles taught, this supposition may serve almost as well.

III. Near the conclusion of the epistle to the Romans, Saint Paul, amongst others, sends the following salutation: "Salute Asyncritus, Phlegon, Hermas, Patrobas, Hermes, and the brethren which are with them." Of Hermas, who appears in this catalogue of Roman Christians as contemporary with Saint Paul, a book bearing the name, and it is most probably rightly, is still remaining. It is called the Shepherd, (Lardner, Cred. vol. i. p. 111.) or pastor of Hermas. Its antiquity is incontestable, from the quotations of it in Irenaeus, A.D. 178; Clement of Alexandria, A.D. 194; Tertullian, A.D. 200; Origen, A.D. 230. The notes of time extant in the epistle itself agree with its title, and with the testimonies concerning it, for it purports to have been written during the life-time of Clement.

In this place are tacit allusions to Saint Matthew's, Saint Luke's, and Saint John's Gospels; that is to say, there are applications of thoughts and expressions found in these Gospels, without citing the place or writer from which they were taken. In this form appear in Hermas the confessing and denying of Christ; (Matt. x. :i2, 33, or, Luke xli. 8, 9.) the parable of the seed sown (Matt. xiii. 3, or, Luke viii. 5); the comparison of Christ's disciples to little children; the saying "he that putteth away his wife, and marrieth another, committeth adultery" (Luke xvi. 18.); The singular expression, "having received all power from his Father," in probable allusion to Matt. xxviii. 18; and Christ being the "gate," or only way of coming "to God," in plain allusion to John xiv. 6; x. 7, 9. There is also a probable allusion to Acts v. 32.

This piece is the representation of a vision, and has by many been accounted a weak and fanciful performance. I therefore observe, that the character of the writing has little to do with the purpose for which we adduce it. It is the age in which it was composed that gives the value to its testimony.

IV. Ignatius, as it is testified by ancient Christian writers, became bishop of Antioch about thirty-seven years after Christ's ascension; and, therefore, from his time, and place, and station, it is probable that he had known and conversed with many of the apostles. Epistles of Ignatius are referred to by Polycarp, his contemporary. Passages found in the epistles now extant under his name are quoted by Irenaeus, A.D. 178; by Origen, A.D. 230; and the occasion of writing the epistles is given at large by Eusebius and Jerome. What are called the smaller epistles of Ignatius are generally deemed to be those which were read by Irenaeus, Origen, and Eusebius (Lardner, Cred. vol. i. p. 147.).

In these epistles are various undoubted allusions to the Gospels of Saint Matthew and Saint John; yet so far of the same form with those in the preceding articles, that, like them, they are not accompanied with marks of quotation.

Of these allusions the following are clear specimens:

Matt.[9]: "Christ was baptized of John, that all righteousness might be fulfilled by him." "Be ye wise as serpents in all things, and harmless as a dove."

John[10]: "Yet the Spirit is not deceived, being from God: for it knows whence it comes and whither it goes." "He (Christ) is the door of the Father, by which enter in Abraham and Isaac, and Jacob, and the apostles, and the church."

As to the manner of quotation, this is observable;—Ignatius, in one place, speaks of St. Paul in terms of high respect, and quotes his Epistle to the Ephesians by name; yet, in several other places, he borrows words and sentiments from the same epistle without mentioning it; which shows that this was his general manner of using and applying writings then extant, and then of high authority.

V. Polycarp (Lardner, Cred. vol. i. 192.) had been taught by the apostles; had conversed with many who had seen Christ; was also by the apostles appointed bishop of Smyrna. This testimony concerning Polycarp is given by Irenaeus, who in his youth had seen him:—"I can tell the place," saith Irenaeus, "in which the blessed Polycarp sat and taught, and his going out and coming in, and the manner of his life, and the form of his person, and the discourses he made to the people, and how he related

---

[9] Chap. iii. 15. "For thus it becometh us to fulfil all righteousness." Chap. x. 16. "Be ye therefore wise as serpents, and harmless as doves."

[10] Chap. iii. 8. "The wind bloweth where it listeth and thou hearest the sound thereof, but canst not tell whence it cometh, and whither it goeth; so is everyone that is born of the Spirit." Chap. x. 9. "I am the door; by me if any man enter in he shall be saved."

his conversation with John, and others who had seen the Lord, and how he related their sayings, and what he had heard concerning the Lord, both concerning his miracles and his doctrine, as he had received them from the eyewitnesses of the word of life: all which Polycarp related agreeable to the Scriptures."

Of Polycarp, whose proximity to the age and country and persons of the apostles is thus attested, we have one undoubted epistle remaining. And this, though a short letter, contains nearly forty clear allusions to books of the New Testament; which is strong evidence of the respect which Christians of that age bore for these books.

Amongst these, although the writings of St. Paul are more frequently used by Polycarp than any other parts of Scripture, there are copious allusions to the Gospel of St. Matthew, some to passages found in the Gospels both of Matthew and Luke, and some which more nearly resemble the words in Luke.

I select the following as fixing the authority of the Lord's prayer, and the use of it amongst the primitive Christians: "If therefore we pray the Lord, that he will forgive us, we ought also to forgive."

"With supplication beseeching the all-seeing God not to lead us into temptation."

And the following, for the sake of repeating an observation already made, that words of our Lord found in our Gospels were at this early day quoted as spoken by him; and not only so, but quoted with so little question or consciousness of doubt about their being really his words, as not even to mention, much less to canvass, the authority from which they were taken:

"But remembering what the Lord said, teaching, Judge not, that ye be not judged; forgive, and ye shall be forgiven; be ye merciful, that ye may obtain mercy; with what measure ye mete, it shall be measured to you again." (Matt. vii. 1, 2; v. 7; Luke vi. 37, 38.)

Supposing Polycarp to have had these words from the books in which we now find them, it is manifest that these books were considered by him, and, as he thought, considered by his readers, us authentic accounts of Christ's discourses; and that that point was incontestible [sic].

The following is a decisive, though what we call a tacit reference to St. Peter's speech in the Acts of the Apostles:—"whom God hath raised, having loosed the pains of death." (Acts ii. 24.)

VI. Papias, (Lardner, Cred. vol. i. p. 239.) a hearer of John, and companion of Polycarp, as Irenaeus attests, and of that age, as all agree, in a passage quoted by Eusebius, from a work now lost, expressly ascribes the respective Gospels to Matthew and Mark; and in a manner which proves that these Gospels must have publicly borne the names of these authors at that time, and probably long before; for Papias does not say that one Gospel was written by Matthew, and another by Mark; but, assuming this as perfectly well known, he tells us from what materials Mark collected his account, viz. from Peter's preaching, and in what language Matthew wrote, viz. in Hebrew. Whether Papias was well informed in this statement, or not; to the point for which I produce this testimony, namely, that these books bore these names at this time, his authority is complete.

The writers hitherto alleged had all lived and conversed with some of the apostles. The works of theirs which remain are in general very short pieces, yet rendered extremely valuable by their antiquity; and none, short as they are, but what contain some important testimony to our historical Scriptures.[11]

VII. Not long after these, that is, not much more than twenty years after the last, follows Justin Martyr (Lardner, Cred. vol. i. p. 258.). His remaining works are much larger than any that have yet been noticed. Although the nature of his two principal writings, one of which was addressed to heathens, and the other was a conference with a Jew, did not lead him to such frequent appeals to Christian books as would have appeared in a discourse intended for Christian readers; we nevertheless reckon up in them between twenty and thirty quotations of the Gospels and Acts of the Apostles, certain, distinct, and copious: if each verse be counted separately, a much greater number; if each expression, a very great one.[12]

We meet with quotations of three of the Gospels within the compass of half a page: "And in other words he says, Depart from me into outer darkness, which the Father hath prepared for Satan and his angels," (which is from Matthew xxv. 41.) "And again he said, in other words, I give unto you power to tread upon serpents and scorpions, and venomous beasts, and upon all the power of the enemy." (This from Luke x. 19.) "And before he was crucified, he said, The Son of Man must suffer many things, and be rejected of the Scribes and Pharisees, and be crucified, and rise again the third day." (This from Mark viii. 31.)

---

[11] That the quotations are more thinly strewn in these than in the writings of the next and of succeeding ages, is in a good measure accounted for by the observation, that the Scriptures of the New Testament had not yet, nor by their recency hardly could have, become a general part of Christian education; read as the Old Testament was by Jews and Christians from their childhood, and thereby intimately mixing, as that had long done, with all their religious ideas, and with their language upon religious subjects. In process of time, and as soon perhaps as could be expected, this came to be the case. And then we perceive the effect, in a proportionably greater frequency, as well as copiousness of allusion.—Mich. Introd. c. ii. sect. vi.

[12] "He cites our present canon, and particularly our four Gospels, continually, I dare say, above two hundred times." Jones's New and Full Method. Append. vol. i. p. 589, ed. 1726.

In another place Justin quotes a passage in the history of Christ's birth, as delivered by Matthew and John, and fortifies his quotation by this remarkable testimony: "As they have taught, who have written the history of all things concerning our Saviour Jesus Christ; and we believe them." Quotations are also found from the Gospel of Saint John. What moreover seems extremely material to be observed is, that in all Justin's works, from which might be extracted almost a complete life of Christ, there are but two instances in which he refers to anything as said or done by Christ, which is not related concerning him in our present Gospels: which shows, that these Gospels, and these, we may say, alone, were the authorities from which the Christians of that day drew the information upon which they depended. One of these instances is of a saying of Christ, not met with in any book now extant.[13]

The other of a circumstance in Christ's baptism, namely, a fiery or luminous appearance upon the water, which, according to Epiphanius, is noticed in the Gospel of the Hebrews: and which might be true: but which, whether true or false, is mentioned by Justin, with a plain mark of diminution when compared with what he quotes as resting upon Scripture authority. The reader will advert to this distinction: "and then, when Jesus came to the river Jordan, where John was baptizing, as Jesus descended into the water, a fire also was kindled in Jordan: and when he came up out of the water, (the apostles of this our Christ have written), that the Holy Ghost lighted upon him as a dove."

All the references in Justin are made without mentioning the author; which proves that these books were perfectly notorious, and that there were no other accounts of Christ then extant, or, at least, no other so received and credited as to make it necessary to distinguish these from the rest.

But although Justin mentions not the author's name, he calls the books, "Memoirs composed by the Apostles;" "Memoirs composed by the Apostles and their Companions;" which descriptions, the latter especially,

---

[13] "Wherefore also our Lord Jesus Christ has said, In whatsoever I shall find you, in the same I will also judge you." Possibly Justin designed not to quote any text, but to represent the sense of many of our Lord's sayings. Fabrieius has observed, that this saying has been quoted by many writers, and that Justin is the only one who ascribes it to our Lord, and that perhaps by a slip of his memory. Words resembling these are read repeatedly in Ezekiel; "I will judge them according to their ways;" (chap. vii. 3; xxxiii. 20.) It is remarkable that Justin had just before expressly quoted Ezekiel. Mr. Jones upon this circumstance founded a conjecture, that Justin wrote only "the Lord hath said," intending to quote the words of God, or rather the sense of those words in Ezekiel; and that some transcriber, imagining these to be the words of Christ, inserted in his copy the addition "Jesus Christ." Vol. 1. p. 539.

exactly suit with the titles which the Gospels and Acts of the Apostles now bear.

VIII. Hegesippus (Lardner, Cred. vol. i. p. 314.) came about thirty years after Justin. His testimony is remarkable only for this particular; that he relates of himself that, travelling from Palestine to Rome, he visited, on his journey, many bishops; and that, "in every succession, and in every city, the same doctrine is taught, which the Law and the Prophets, and the Lord teacheth." This is an important attestation, from good authority, and of high antiquity. It is generally understood that by the word "Lord," Hegesippus intended some writing or writings, containing the teaching of Christ; in which sense alone the term combines with the other term "Law and Prophets," which denote writings; and together with them admit of the verb "teacheth" in the present tense. Then, that these writings were some or all of the books of the New Testament, is rendered probable from hence, that in the fragments of his works, which are preserved in Eusebius, and in a writer of the ninth century, enough, though it be little, is left to show, that Hegesippus expressed divers thing in the style of the Gospels, and of the Acts of the Apostles; that he referred to the history in the second chapter of Matthew, and recited a text of that Gospel as spoken by our Lord.

IX. At this time, viz. about the year 170, the churches of Lyons and Vienne, in France, sent a relation of the sufferings of their martyrs to the churches of Asia and Phrygia. (Lardner, Cred. vol. i. p. 332.) The epistle is preserved entire by Eusebius. And what carries in some measure the testimony of these churches to a higher age, is, that they had now for their bishop, Pothinus, who was ninety years old, and whose early life consequently must have immediately joined on with the times of the apostles. In this epistle are exact references to the Gospels of Luke and John, and to the Acts of the Apostles; the form of reference the same as in all the preceding articles. That from Saint John is in these words: "Then was fulfilled that which was spoken by the Lord, that whosoever killeth you, will think that he doeth God service." (John xvi. 2.)

X. The evidence now opens upon us full and clear. Irenaeus (Lardner, vol. i. p. 344.) succeeded Pothinus as bishop of Lyons. In his youth he had been a disciple of Polycarp, who was a disciple of John. In the time in which he lived, he was distant not much more than a century from the publication of the Gospels; in his instruction only by one step separated from the persons of the apostles. He asserts of himself and his contemporaries, that they were able to reckon up, in all the principal churches, the succession of bishops from the first. (Adv. Haeres. 1. iii. c. 3.) I remark these particulars concerning Irenaeus with more formality than usual, because the testimony which this writer affords to the historical books of the New Testament, to their authority, and to the titles which they bear, is express, positive, and exclusive. One principal passage, in which this testimony is contained, opens with a precise assertion of the point which we have laid down as the foundation of our argument, viz., that the story which the Gospels exhibit is the story which the apostles told. "We have not received," saith Irenaeus, "the knowledge of the way of our salvation by any others than those by whom the Gospel has been brought to us. Which Gospel they first preached, and afterwards, by the will of God, committed to writing, that it might be for time to come the foundation and pillar of our faith.—For after that our Lord arose from the dead, and they (the apostles) were endowed from above with the power of the Holy Ghost coming down upon them, they received a perfect knowledge of all things. They then went forth to all the ends of the earth, declaring to men the Message of heavenly peace, having all of them, and every one, alike the Gospel of God. Matthew then, among the Jews, wrote a Gospel in their own language, while Peter and Paul were preaching the Gospel at Rome, and founding a church there: and after their exit, Mark also, the disciple and interpreter of Peter, delivered to us in writing the things that had been preached by Peter and Luke, the companion of Paul, put down in a book the Gospel preached by him (Paul). Afterwards John, the disciple of the Lord, who also leaned upon his breast, he likewise published a Gospel while he dwelt at Ephesus in Asia." If any modern divine should write a book upon the genuineness of the Gospels, he could not assert it more expressly, or state their original more distinctly, than Irenaeus hath done within little more than a hundred years after they were published.

The correspondency, in the days of Irenaeus, of the oral and written tradition, and the deduction of the oral tradition through various channels from the age of the apostles, which was then lately passed, and, by consequence, the probability that the books truly delivered what the apostles taught, is inferred also with strict regularity from another passage of his works. "The tradition of the apostles," this father saith, "hath spread itself over the whole universe; and all they who search after the sources of truth will find this tradition to be held sacred in every church, We might enumerate all those who have been appointed bishops to these churches by the apostles, and all their successors, up to our days. It is by this uninterrupted succession that we have received the tradition which actually exists in the church, as also the doctrines of truth, as it was preached by the apostles." (Iren. in Haer. I. iii. c. 3.) The reader will observe upon this, that the same Irenaeus, who is now stating the strength and uniformity of the tradition, we have before seen recognizing, in the fullest manner, the authority of the written records; from which we are entitled to conclude, that they were then conformable to each other.

I have said that the testimony of Irenaeus in favour of our Gospels is exclusive of all others. I allude to a remarkable passage in his works, in which, for some reasons sufficiently fanciful, he endeavours to show that there could he neither more nor fewer Gospels than four. With his argument we have no concern. The position itself proves that four, and only four, Gospels were at that time publicly read and acknowledged. That these were our Gospels, and in the state in which we now have them, is shown from many other places of this writer beside that which we have already alleged. He mentions how Matthew begins his Gospel, bow Mark begins and ends his, and their supposed reasons for so doing. He enumerates at length the several passages of Christ's history in Luke, which are not found in any of the other evangelists. He states the particular design with which Saint John composed his Gospel, and accounts for the doctrinal declarations which precede the narrative.

To the book of the Acts of the Apostles, its author, and credit, the testimony of Irenaeus is no less explicit. Referring to the account of Saint Paul's conversion and vocation, in the ninth chapter of that book, "Nor can they," says he, meaning the parties with whom he argues, "show that he is not to be credited, who has related to us the truth with the greatest exactness." In another place, he has actually collected the several texts, in which the writer of the history is represented as accompanying Saint Paul; which leads him to deliver a summary of almost the whole of the last twelve chapters of the book.

In an author thus abounding with references and allusions to the Scriptures, there is not one to any apocryphal Christian writing whatever. This is a broad line of distinction between our sacred books and the pretensions of all others.

The force of the testimony of the period which we have considered is greatly strengthened by the observation, that it is the testimony, and the concurring testimony, of writers who lived in countries remote from one another. Clement flourished at Rome, Ignatius at Antioch, Polycarp at Smyrna, Justin Martyr in Syria, and Irenaeus in France.

XI. Omitting Athenagoras and Theophilus, who lived about this time; (Lardner, vol. i. p. 400 & 422.) in the remaining works of the former of whom are clear references to Mark and Luke; and in the works of the latter, who was bishop of Antioch, the sixth in succession from the apostles, evident allusions to Matthew and John, and probable allusions to Luke (which, considering the nature of the compositions, that they were addressed to heathen readers, is as much as could be expected); observing also, that the works of two learned Christian writers of the same age, Miltiades and Pantaenus, (Lardner, vol. i. p.413, 450.) are now lost: of which Miltiades Eusebius records, that his writings "were monuments of zeal for the Divine Oracles;" and which Pantaenus, as Jerome testifies, was a man of prudence and learning, both in the Divine Scriptures and secular literature, and had left many commentaries upon the Holy Scriptures then extant. Passing by these without further remark, we come to one of the most voluminous of ancient Christian writers, Clement of

Alexandria (Lardner, vol. ii. p. 469.). Clement followed Irenaeus at the distance of only sixteen years, and therefore may be said to maintain the series of testimony in an uninterrupted continuation.

In certain of Clement's works, now lost, but of which various parts are recited by Eusebius, there is given a distinct account of the order in which the four Gospels were written. The Gospels which contain the genealogies were (he says) written first; Mark's next, at the instance of Peter's followers; and John's the last; and this account he tells us that he had received from presbyters of more ancient times. This testimony proves the following points; that these Gospels were the histories of Christ then publicly received and relied upon; and that the dates, occasions, and circumstances, of their publication were at that time subjects of attention and inquiry amongst Christians. In the works of Clement which remain, the four Gospels are repeatedly quoted by the names of their authors, and the Acts of the Apostles is expressly ascribed to Luke. In one place, after mentioning a particular circumstance, he adds these remarkable words: "We have not this passage in the four Gospels delivered to us, but in that according to the Egyptians;" which puts a marked distinction between the four Gospels and all other histories, or pretended histories, of Christ. In another part of his works, the perfect confidence with which he received the Gospels is signified by him in these words: "That this is true appears from hence, that it is written in the Gospel according to Saint Luke;" and again, "I need not use many words, but only to allege the evangelic voice of the Lord." His quotations are numerous. The sayings of Christ, of which he alleges many, are all taken from our Gospels; the single exception to this observation appearing to be a loose quotation of a passage in Saint Matthew's Gospel.[14]

XII. In the age in which they lived, (Lardner, vol. ii. p. 561.) Tertullian joins on with Clement. The number of the Gospels then received, the names of the evangelists, and their proper descriptions, are exhibited by this writer in one short sentence:—"Among the apostles John and Matthew teach us the faith; among apostolical men, Luke and Mark refresh it." The next passage to be taken from Tertullian affords as complete an attestation to the authenticity of our books as can be well imagined. After enumerating the churches which had been founded by Paul at Corinth, in Galatia, at Philippi, Thessalonica, and Ephesus; the

---

[14] "Ask great things and the small shall be added unto you." Clement rather chose to expound the words of Matthew (chap. vi. 33), than literally to cite them; and this is most undeniably proved by another place in the same Clement, where he both produces the text and these words am an exposition:—"Seek ye first the kingdom of heaven and its righteousness, for these are the great things; but the small things, and things relating to this life, shall be added unto you." Jones's New and Full Method, vol. i. p. 553.

church of Rome established by Peter and Paul, and other churches derived from John; he proceeds thus:—"I say, then, that with them, but not with them only which are apostolical, but with all who have fellowship with them in the same faith, is that Gospel of Luke received from its first publication, which we so zealously maintain:" and presently afterwards adds, "The same authority of the apostolical churches will support the other Gospels which we have from them and according to them, I mean John's and Matthew's; although that likewise which Mark published may be said to be Peter's, whose interpreter Mark was." In another place Tertullian affirms, that the three other Gospels were in the hands of the churches from the beginning, as well as Luke's. This noble testimony fixes the universality with which the Gospels were received and their antiquity; that they were in the hands of all, and had been so from the first. And this evidence appears not more than one hundred and fifty years after the publication of the books. The reader must be given to understand that, when Tertullian speaks of maintaining or defending (tuendi) the Gospel of Saint Luke, he only means maintaining or defending the integrity of the copies of Luke received by Christian churches, in opposition to certain curtailed copies used by Marcion, against whom he writes.

This author frequently cites the Acts of the Apostles under that title, once calls it Luke's Commentary, and observes how Saint Paul's epistles confirm it.

After this general evidence, it is unnecessary to add particular quotations. These, however, are so numerous and ample as to have led Dr. Lardner to observe, "that there are more and larger quotations of the small volume of the New Testament in this one Christian author, than there are of all the works of Cicero in writers of all characters for several ages." (Lardner, vol ii. p. 647.)

Tertullian quotes no Christian writing as of equal authority with the Scriptures, and no spurious books at all; a broad line of distinction, we may once more observe, between our sacred books and all others.

We may again likewise remark the wide extent through which the reputation of the Gospels, and of the Acts of the Apostles had spread, and the perfect consent, in this point, of distant and independent societies. It is now only about one hundred and fifty years since Christ was crucified; and within this period, to say nothing of the apostolical fathers who have been noticed already, we have Justin Martyr at Neapolis, Theophilus at Antioch, Irenaeus in France, Clement at Alexandria, Tertullian at Carthage, quoting the same books of historical Scriptures, and I may say, quoting these alone.

XIII. An interval of only thirty years, and that occupied by no small number of Christian writers, (Minucius Felix, Apollonius, Caius, Asterius Urbanus Alexander bishop of Jerusalem, Hippolytus, Ammonius Julius

Africanus) whose works only remain in fragments and quotations, and in every one of which is some reference or other to the Gospels (and in one of them, Hippolytus, as preserved in Theodoret, is an abstract of the whole Gospel history), brings us to a name of great celebrity in Christian antiquity, Origen (Lardner, vol. iii. p. 234.) of Alexandria, who in the quantity of his writings exceeded the most laborious of the Greek and Latin authors. Nothing can be more peremptory upon the subject now under consideration, and, from a writer of his learning and information, more satisfactory, than the declaration of Origen, preserved, in an extract from his works, by Eusebius; "That the four Gospels alone are received without dispute by the whole church of God under heaven:" to which declaration is immediately subjoined a brief history of the respective authors to whom they were then, as they are now, ascribed. The language holden concerning the Gospels, throughout the works of Origen which remain, entirely corresponds with the testimony here cited. His attestation to the Acts of the Apostles is no less Positive: "And Luke also once more sounds the trumpet, relating the acts of the apostles." The universality with which the Scriptures were then read is well signified by this writer in a passage in which he has occasion to observe against Celsus, "That it is not in any private books, or such as are read by a few only, and those studious persons, but in books read by everybody, That it is written, The invisible things of God from the creation of the world are clearly seen, being understood by things that are made." It is to no purpose to single out quotations of Scripture from such a writer as this. We might as well make a selection of the quotations of Scripture in Dr. Clarke's Sermons. They are so thickly sown in the works of Origen, that Dr. Mill says, "If we had all his works remaining, we should have before us almost the whole text of the Bible." (Mill, Proleg. esp. vi. p. 66.)

Origen notices, in order to censure, certain apocryphal Gospels. He also uses four writings of this sort; that is, throughout his large works he once or twice, at the most, quotes each of the four; but always with some mark, either of direct reprobation or of caution to his readers, manifestly esteeming them of little or no authority.

XIV. Gregory, bishop of Neocaesaea, and Dionysius of Alexandria, were scholars of Origen. Their testimony, therefore, though full and particular, may be reckoned a repetition only of his. The series, however, of evidence is continued by Cyprian, bishop of Carthage, who flourished within twenty years after Origen. "The church," said this father, "is watered, like Paradise, by four rivers, that is, by four Gospels." The Acts of the Apostles is also frequently quoted by Cyprian under that name, and under the name of the "Divine Scriptures." In his various writings are such constant and copious citations of Scripture, as to place this part of the testimony beyond controversy. Nor is there, in the works of this eminent African bishop, one quotation of a spurious or apocryphal Christian writing.

XV. Passing over a crowd[15] of writers following Cyprian at different distances, but all within forty years of his time; and who all, in the perfect remains of their works, either cite the historical Scriptures of the New Testament, or speak of them in terms of profound respect: I single out Victorin, bishop of Pettaw, in Germany, merely on account of the remoteness of his situation from that of Origen and Cyprian, who were Africans; by which circumstance his testimony, taken in conjunction with theirs, proves that the Scripture histories, and the same histories, were known and received from one side of the Christian world to the other. This bishop (Lardner, vol. v. p. 214.) lived about the year 290: and in a commentary upon this text of the Revelation, "The first was like a lion, the second was like a calf, the third like a man, and the fourth like a flying eagle," he makes out that by the four creatures are intended the four Gospels; and, to show the propriety of the symbols, he recites the subject with which each evangelist opens his history. The explication is fanciful, but the testimony positive. He also expressly cites the Acts of the Apostles.

XVI. Arnobius and Lactantius (Lardner, vol. viii. p. 43, 201.), about the year 300, composed formal arguments upon the credibility of the Christian religion. As these arguments were addressed to Gentiles, the authors abstain from quoting Christian books by name, one of them giving this very reason for his reserve; but when they came to state, for the information of their readers, the outlines of Christ's history, it is apparent that they draw their accounts from our Gospels, and from no other sources; for these statements exhibit a summary of almost everything which is related of Christ's actions and miracles by the four evangelists. Arnobius vindicates, without mentioning their names, the credit of these historians; observing that they were eye-witnesses of the facts which they relate, and that their ignorance of the arts of composition was rather a confirmation of their testimony, than an objection to it. Lactantius also argues in defence of the religion, from the consistency, simplicity, disinterestedness, and sufferings of the Christian historians, meaning by that term our evangelists.

XVII. We close the series of testimonies with that of Eusebius, (Lardner, vol. viii. p. 33.) bishop of Caesarea who flourished in the year 315, contemporary with, or posterior only by fifteen years to, the authors last cited. This voluminous writer, and most diligent collector of the writings of others, beside a variety of large works, composed a history of

---

[15] Novatus, Rome, A.D. 251; Dionysius, Rome, A.D. 259; Commodian, A.D. 270; Anatolius, Laodicea, A.D. 270; Theognostus A.D. 282; Methodius Lycia, A.D. 290; Phileas, Egypt, A.D. 296.

the affairs of Christianity from its origin to his own time. His testimony to the Scriptures is the testimony of a man much conversant in the works of Christian authors, written during the first three centuries of its era, and who had read many which are now lost. In a passage of his Evangelical Demonstration, Eusebius remarks, with great nicety, the delicacy of two of the evangelists, in their manner of noticing any circumstance which regarded themselves; and of Mark, as writing under Peter's direction, in the circumstances which regarded him. The illustration of this remark leads him to bring together long quotations from each of the evangelists: and the whole passage is a proof that Eusebius, and the Christians of those days, not only read the Gospels, but studied them with attention and exactness. In a passage of his ecclesiastical History, he treats, in form, and at large, of the occasions of writing the four Gospels, and of the order in which they were written. The title of the chapter is, "Of the Order of the Gospels;" and it begins thus: "Let us observe the writings of this apostle John, which are not contradicted by any: and, first of all, must be mentioned, as acknowledged by all, the Gospel according to him, well-known to all the churches under heaven; and that it has been justly placed by the ancients the fourth in order, and after the other three, may be made evident in this manner."—Eusebius then proceeds to show that John wrote the last of the four, and that his Gospel was intended to supply the omissions of the others; especially in the part of our Lord's ministry which took place before the imprisonment of John the Baptist. He observes, "that the apostles of Christ were not studious of the ornaments of composition, nor indeed forward to write at all, being wholly occupied with their ministry."

This learned author makes no use at all of Christian writings, forged with the names of Christ's apostle, or their companions. We close this branch of our evidence here, because, after Eusebius, there is no room for any question upon the subject; the works of Christian writers being as full of texts of Scripture, and of references to Scripture, as the discourses of modern divines. Future testimonies to the books of Scripture could only prove that they never lost their character or authority.

SECTION II.

When the Scriptures are quoted, or alluded to, they are quoted with peculiar respect, as books sui generis; as possessing an authority which belonged to no other books, and as conclusive in all questions and controversies amongst Christians.

Beside the general strain of reference and quotation, which uniformly and strongly indicates this distinction, the following may be regarded as specific testimonies:

I. Theophilus, (Lardner, Cred. part ii. vol. i. p. 429.) bishop of Antioch, the sixth in succession from the apostles, and who flourished little more than a century after the books of the New Testament were written, having occasion to quote one of our Gospels, writes thus: "These things the Holy Scriptures teach us, and all who were moved by the Holy Spirit, among whom John says, In the beginning was the Word, and the Word was with God." Again: "Concerning the righteousness which the law teaches, the like things are to be found in the prophets and the Gospels, because that all, being inspired, spoke by one and the same Spirit of God." (Lardner, Cred. part ii. vol. i. p. 448.) No words can testify more strongly than these do, the high and peculiar respect in which these books were holden.

II. A writer against Artemon, (Lardner, Cred. part ii. vol. iii. p. 40.) who may be supposed to come about one hundred and fifty-eight years after the publication of the Scripture, in a passage quoted by Eusebius, uses these expressions: "Possibly what they (our adversaries) say, might have been credited, if first of all the Divine Scriptures did not contradict them; and then the writings of certain brethren more ancient than the times of Victor." The brethren mentioned by name are Justin, Miltiades, Tatian, Clement, Irenaeus, Melito, with a general appeal to many more not named. This passage proves, first, that there was at that time a collection called Divine Scriptures; secondly, that these Scriptures were esteemed of higher authority than the writings of the most early and celebrated Christians.

III. In a piece ascribed to Hippolytus, (Lardner, Cred. vol. iii. p. 112.) who lived near the same time, the author professes, in giving his correspondent instruction in the things about which he inquires, "to draw out of the sacred-fountain, and to set before him from the Sacred Scriptures what may afford him satisfaction." He then quotes immediately Paul's epistles to Timothy, and afterwards many books of the New Testament. This preface to the quotations carries in it a marked distinction between the Scriptures and other books.

IV. "Our assertions and discourses," saith Origen, (Lardner, Cred. vol. iii. pp. 287-289.) "are unworthy of credit; we must receive the Scriptures as witnesses." After treating of the duty of prayer, he proceeds with his argument thus: "What we have said, may be proved from the Divine Scriptures." In his books against Celsus we find this passage: "That our religion teaches us to seek after wisdom, shall be shown, both out of the ancient Jewish Scriptures which we also use, and out of those written since Jesus, which are believed in the churches to be divine." These expressions afford abundant evidence of the peculiar and exclusive authority which the Scriptures possessed.

V. Cyprian, bishop of Carthage, (Lardner, Cred. vol. vi. p. 840.) whose age lies close to that of Origen, earnestly exhorts Christian teachers, in all doubtful cases, "to go back to the fountain; and, if the truth has in any case been shaken, to recur to the Gospels and apostolic writings."—"The precepts of the Gospel," says he in another place, "are nothing less than authoritative divine lessons, the foundations of our hope, the supports of our faith, the guides of our way, the safeguards of our course to heaven."

VI. Novatus, (Lardner, Cred. vol. v. p. 102.) a Roman contemporary with Cyprian, appeals to the Scriptures, as the authority by which all errors were to be repelled, and disputes decided. "That Christ is not only man, but God also, is proved by the sacred authority of the Divine Writings."—"The Divine Scripture easily detects and confutes the frauds of heretics."—"It is not by the fault of the heavenly Scriptures, which never deceive." Stronger assertions than these could not be used.

VII. At the distance of twenty years from the writer last cited, Anatolius (Lardner, Cred. vol. v. p. 146.), a learned Alexandrian, and bishop of Laedicea, speaking of the rule for keeping Easter, a question at that day agitated with much earnestness, says of those whom he opposed, "They can by no means prove their point by the authority of the Divine Scripture."

VIII. The Arians, who sprung up about fifty years after this, argued strenuously against the use of the words consubstantial, and essence, and like phrases; "because they were not in Scripture." (Lardner, Cred. vol. vii. pp. 283-284.) And in the same strain one of their advocates opens a conference with Augustine, after the following manner: "If you say what is reasonable, I must submit. If you allege anything from the Divine Scriptures which are common to both, I must hear. But unscriptural expressions (quae extra Scripturam sunt) deserve no regard."

Athanasius, the great antagonist of Arianism, after having enumerated the books of the Old and New Testament, adds, "These are the fountain of salvation, that he who thirsts may be satisfied with the oracles contained in them. In these alone the doctrine of salvation is proclaimed. Let no man add to them, or take anything from them." (Lardner, Cred. vol. xii. p. 182.)

IX. Cyril, bishop of Jerusalem (Lardner, Cred. vol. viii. p. 276.), who wrote about twenty years after the appearance of Arianism, uses these remarkable words: "Concerning the divine and holy mysteries of faith, not the least article ought to be delivered without the Divine Scriptures." We are assured that Cyril's Scriptures were the same as ours, for he has left us a catalogue of the books included under that name.

X. Epiphanius, (Lardner, Cred. vol. viii. p. 314.) twenty years after Cyril, challenges the Arians, and the followers of Origen, "to produce any passage of the Old and New Testament favouring their sentiments."

XI. Poebadius, a Gallic bishop, who lived about thirty years after the council of Nice, testifies, that "the bishops of that council first consulted the sacred volumes, and then declared their faith." (Lardner, Cred. vol. ix. p. 52.)

XII. Basil, bishop of Caesarea, in Cappadocia, contemporary with Epiphanius, says, that "hearers instructed in the Scriptures ought to examine what is said by their teachers, and to embrace what is agreeable to the Scriptures, and to reject what is otherwise." (Lardner, Cred. vol. ix. p. 124.)

XIII. Ephraim, the Syrian, a celebrated writer of the same times, bears this conclusive testimony to the proposition which forms the subject of our present chapter: "the truth written in the Sacred Volume of the Gospel is a perfect rule. Nothing can be taken from it nor added to it, without great guilt." (Lardner, Cred. vol. ix. p. 202.)

XIV. If we add Jerome to these, it is only for the evidence which he affords of the judgment of preceding ages. Jerome observes, concerning the quotations of ancient Christian writers, that is, of writers who were ancient in the year 400, that they made a distinction between books; some they quoted as of authority, and others not: which observation relates to the books of Scripture, compared with other writings, apocryphal or heathen. (Lardner, Cred. vol. x. pp. 123-124.)

SECTION III.

The Scriptures were in very early times collected into a distinct volume.

Ignatius, who was bishop of Antioch within forty years after the Ascension, and who had lived and conversed with the apostles, speaks of the Gospel and of the apostles in terms which render it very probable that he meant by the Gospel the book or volume of the Gospels, and by the apostles the book or volume of their Epistles. His words in one place are, (Lardner, Cred. part ii. vol. i. p. 180.) "Fleeing to the Gospel as the flesh of Jesus, and to the apostles as the presbytery of the church;" that is, as Le Clere interprets them, "in order to understand the will of God, he fled to the Gospels, which he believed no less than if Christ in the flesh had been speaking to him; and to the writings of the apostles, whom he esteemed as the presbytery of the whole Christian church." It must be observed, that about eighty years after this we have direct proof, in the writings of Clement of Alexandria, (Lardner, Cred. part ii. vol. ii. p. 516.) that these two names, "Gospel," and "Apostles," were the names by which the writings of the New Testament, and the division of these writings, were usually expressed.

Another passage from Ignatius is the following:—"But the Gospel has somewhat in it more excellent, the appearance of our Lord Jesus Christ, his passion and resurrection." (Lardner, Cred. part ii. vol. ii. p. 182.)

And a third: "Ye ought to hearken to the Prophets, but especially to the gospel, in which the passion has been manifested to us, and the resurrection perfected." In this last passage, the Prophets and the Gospel are put in conjunction; and as Ignatius undoubtedly meant by the prophets a collection of writings, it is probable that he meant the same by the Gospel, the two terms standing in evident parallelism with each other.

This interpretation of the word "Gospel," in the passages above quoted from Ignatius, is confirmed by a piece of nearly equal antiquity, the relation of the martyrdom of Polycarp by the church of Smyrna. "All things," say they, "that went before, were done, that the Lord might show us a martyrdom according to the Gospel, for he expected to be delivered up as the Lord also did." (Ignat. Ep. c.i.) And in another place, "We do not commend those who offer themselves, forasmuch as the Gospel, teaches us no such thing." (Ignat. Ep. c. iv.) In both these places, what is called the Gospel seems to be the history of Jesus Christ, and of his doctrine.

If this be the true sense of the passages, they are not only evidences of our proposition, by strong and very ancient proofs of the high esteem in which the books of the New Testament were holden.

II. Eusebius relates, that Quadratus and some others, who were the immediate successors of the apostles, travelling abroad to preach Christ, carried the Gospels with them, and delivered them to their converts. The words of Eusebius are: "Then travelling abroad, they performed the work of evangelists, being ambitious to preach Christ, and deliver the Scripture of the divine Gospels." (Lardner, Cred. part ii. vol. i. p. 236.) Eusebius had before him the writings both of Quadratus himself, and of many others of that age, which are now lost. It is reasonable, therefore to believe that he had good grounds for his assertion. What is thus recorded of the Gospels took place within sixty, or at the most seventy, years after they were published: and it is evident that they must, before this time (and, it is probable, long before this time), have been in general use and in high esteem in the churches planted by the apostles, inasmuch as they were now, we find, collected into a volume: and the immediate successors of the apostles, they who preached the religion of Christ to those who had not already heard it, carried the volume with them, and delivered it to their converts.

III. Irenaeus, in the year 178, (Lardner, Cred. part ii. vol. i. p. 383.) puts the evangelic and apostolic writings in connexion with the Law and the Prophets, manifestly intending by the one a code or collection of Christian sacred writings, as the other expressed the code or collection of Jewish sacred writings. And,

IV. Melito, at this time bishop of Sardis, writing to one Onesimus, tells his correspondent, (Lardner, Cred. vol. i. p. 331.) that he had procured an accurate account of the books of the Old Testament. The occurrence in this message of the term Old Testament has been brought to prove, and it certainly does prove, that there was then a volume or collection of writings called the New Testament.

V. In the time of Clement of Alexandria, about fifteen years after the last quoted testimony, it is apparent that the Christian Scriptures were divided into two parts, under the general titles of the Gospels and Apostles; and that both these were regarded as of the highest authority. One out of many expressions of Clement, alluding to this distribution, is the following: "There is a consent and harmony between the Law and the Prophets, the Apostles and the Gospel." (Lardner, Cred. vol. ii. p. 516.)

VI. The same division, "Prophets, Gospels, and Apostles," appears in Tertullian, the contemporary of Clement. The collection of the Gospels is likewise called by this writer the "Evangelic Instrument;" the whole volume the "New Testament;" and the two parts, the "Gospels and Apostles." (Lardner, Cred. vol. ii. pp. 631,574 & 632.)

VII. From many writers also of the third century, and especially from
Cyprian, who lived in the middle of it, it is collected that the
Christian Scriptures were divided into two cedes or volumes, one called
the "Gospels or Scriptures of the Lord," the other the "Apostles, or
Epistles of the Apostles" (Lardner, Cred. vol. iv. p. 846.)

VIII. Eusebius, as we have already seen, takes some pains to show that the Gospel of Saint John had been justly placed by the ancients, "the fourth in order, and after the other three." (Lardner, Cred. vol. viii. p. 90.) These are the terms of his proposition: and the very introduction of such an argument proves incontestably, that the four Gospels had been collected into a volume, to the exclusion of every other: that their order in the volume had been adjusted with much consideration; and that this had been done by those who were called ancients in the time of Eusebius.

In the Diocletian persecution, in the year 303, the Scriptures were sought out and burnt:(Lardner, Cred. vol. vii. pp. 214 et seq.) many suffered death rather than deliver them up; and those who betrayed them to the persecutors were accounted as lapsed and apostate. On the other hand, Constantine, after his conversion, gave directions for multiplying copies of the Divine Oracles, and for magnificently adorning them at the expense of the imperial treasury. (Lardner, Cred. vol. vii. p. 432.) What the Christians of that age so richly embellished in their prosperity, and, which is more, so tenaciously preserved under persecution, was the very volume of the New Testament which we now read.

SECTION IV.

Our present Sacred Writings were soon distinguished by appropriate names and titles of respect.

Polycarp. "I trust that ye are well exercised in the Holy Scriptures;—as in these Scriptures it is said, Be ye angry and sin not, and let not the sun go down upon your wrath." (Lardner, Cred. vol. i. p. 203.) This passage is extremely important; because it proves that, in the time of Polycarp, who had lived with the apostles, there were Christian writings distinguished by the name of "Holy Scriptures," or Sacred Writings. Moreover, the text quoted by Polycarp is a text found in the collection at this day. What also the same Polycarp hath elsewhere quoted in the same manner, may be considered as proved to belong to the collection; and this comprehends Saint Matthew's and, probably, Saint Luke's Gospel, the Acts of the Apostles, ten epistles of Paul, the First Epistle of Peter, and the First of John. (Lardner, Cred. vol. i. p. 223.) In another place, Polycarp has these words: "Whoever perverts the Oracles of the Lord to his own lusts, and says there is neither resurrection nor judgment, he is the first born of Satan." (Lardner, Cred. vol. i. p. 223.)—It does not appear what else Polycarp could mean by the "Oracles of the Lord," but those same "Holy Scriptures," or Sacred Writings, of which he had spoken before.

II. Justin Martyr, whose apology was written about thirty years after Polycarp's epistle, expressly cites some of our present histories under the title of Gospel, and that not as a name by him first ascribed to them, but as the name by which they were generally known in his time. His words are these:—"For the apostles in the memoirs composed by them, which are called Gospels, have thus delivered it, that Jesus commanded them to take bread, and give thanks." (Lardner, Cred. vol. i. p. 271.) There exists no doubt, but that, by the memoirs above-mentioned, Justin meant our present historical Scriptures; for throughout his works he quotes these and no others.

III. Dionysius, bishop of Corinth, who came thirty years after Justin, in a passage preserved in Eusebius (for his works are lost), speaks "of the Scriptures of the Lord." (Lardner, Cred. vol. i. p. 298.)

IV. And at the same time, or very nearly so, by Irenaeus, bishop of Lyons in France, (The reader will observe the remoteness of these two writers in country and situation) they are called "Divine Scriptures,"—"Divine Oracles,"—"Scriptures of the Lord,"—"Evangelic and Apostolic writings." (Lardner, Cred. vol. i. p. 343, et seq.) The quotations of Irenaeus prove decidedly, that our present Gospels, and these alone, together with the Acts of the Apostles, were the historical books comprehended by him under these appellations.

V. Saint Matthew's Gospel is quoted by Theophilus, bishop of Antioch,

contemporary with Irenaeus, under the title of the "Evangelic voice;" (Lardner, Cred. vol. i. p. 427.) and the copious works of Clement of Alexandria, published within fifteen years of the same time, ascribe

85

to the books of the New Testament the various titles of "Sacred Books,"—"Divine Scriptures,"—"Divinely inspired Scriptures,"—"Scriptures of the Lord,"—"the true Evangelical Canon." (Lardner, Cred. vol. ii. p. 515.)

VI. Tertullian, who joins on with Clement, beside adopting most of the names and epithets above noticed, calls the Gospels "our Digesta," in allusion, as it should seem, to some collection of Roman laws then extant. (Lardner, Cred. vol. ii. p. 630.)

VII. By Origen, who came thirty years after Tertullian, the same, and other no less strong titles, are applied to the Christian Scriptures: and, in addition thereunto, this writer frequently speaks of the "Old and New Testament,"—"the Ancient and New Scriptures,"—"the Ancient and New Oracles." (Lardner, Cred. vol. iii. p. 230.)

VIII. In Cyprian, who was not twenty years later, they are "Books of the
Spirit,"—"Divine Fountains,"—"Fountains of the Divine Fulness." (Lardner, Cred. vol. iv. p. 844.)

The expressions we have thus quoted are evidences of high and peculiar respect. They all occur within two centuries from the publication of the books. Some of them commence with the companions of the apostles; and they increase in number and variety, through a series of writers touching upon one another, and deduced from the first age of the religion.

SECTION V.

Our Scriptures were publicly read and expounded in the religious assemblies of the early Christians. Justin MARTYR, who wrote in the year 140, which was seventy or eighty years after some, and less, probably, after others of the Gospels were published, giving, in his first apology an account, to the Emperor, of the Christian worship has this remarkable passage:

"The Memoirs of the Apostles, or the Writings of the Prophets, are read according as the time allows: and, when the reader has ended, the president makes a discourse, exhorting to the imitation of so excellent things." (Lardner, Cred. vol. i. p. 273.)

A few short observations will show the value of this testimony.

1. The "Memoirs of the Apostles," Justin in another place expressly tells us, are what are called "Gospels:" and that they were the Gospels which we now use, is made certain by Justin's numerous quotations of them, and his silence about any others.

2. Justin describes the general usage of the Christian church.

3. Justin does not speak of it as recent or newly instituted, but in the terms in which men speak of established customs.

II. Tertullian, who followed Justin at the distance of about fifty years, in his account of the religious assemblies of Christians as they were conducted in his time, says, "We come together to recollect the Divine Scriptures; we nourish our faith, raise our hope, confirm our trust, by the Sacred Word." (Lardner, Cred. vol. ii. p. 628.)

III. Eusebius records of Origen, and cites for his authority the letters of bishops contemporary with Origen, that when he went into Palestine about the year 216, which was only sixteen years after the date of Tertullian's testimony, he was desired by the bishops of that country to discourse and expound the Scriptures publicly in the church, though he was not yet ordained a presbyter. (Lardner, Cred. vol. iii. p. 68.) This anecdote recognises the usage, not only of reading, but of expounding the Scriptures; and both as subsisting in full force. Origen also himself bears witness to the same practice: "This," says he, "we do, when the Scriptures are read in the church, and when the discourse for explication is delivered to the people." (Lardner, Cred. vol. iii. p. 302.) And what is a still more ample testimony, many homilies of his upon the Scriptures of the New Testament, delivered by him in the assemblies of the church, are still extant.

IV. Cyprian, whose age was not twenty years lower than that of Origen, gives his people an account of having ordained two persons, who were before confessors, to be readers; and what they were to read appears by the reason which he gives for his choice; "Nothing," says Cyprian, "can be more fit than that he who has made a glorious confession of the Lord should read publicly in the church; that he who has shown himself willing to die a martyr should read the Gospel of Christ by which martyrs are made." (Lardner, Cred. vol. iv. p. 842.)

V. Intimations of the same custom may be traced in a great number of writers in the beginning and throughout the whole of the fourth century. Of these testimonies I will only use one, as being, of itself, express and full. Augustine, who appeared near the conclusion of the century, displays the benefit of the Christian religion on this very account, the public reading of the Scriptures in the churches, "where," says he, "is a consequence of all sorts of people of both sexes; and where they hear how they ought to live well in this world, that they may deserve to live happily and eternally in another." And this custom he declares to be universal: "The canonical books of Scripture being read every where, the miracles therein recorded are well known to all people." (Lardner, Cred. vol. x. p. 276, et seq.)

It does not appear that any books, other than our present Scriptures were thus publicly read, except that the epistle of Clement was read in the church of Corinth, to which it had been addressed, and in some others; and that the Shepherd of Hermas was read in many churches. Nor does it subtract much from the value of the argument, that these two writings partly come within it, because we allow them to be the genuine writings of apostolical men. There is not the least evidence, that any other Gospel than the four which we receive was ever admitted to this distinction.

SECTION VI.

Commentaries were anciently written upon the Scriptures; harmonies formed out of them; different copies carefully collated; and versions made of them into different languages.

No greater proof can be given of the esteem in which these books were holden by the ancient Christians, or of the sense then entertained of their value and importance, than the industry bestowed upon them. And it ought to be observed that the value and importance of these books consisted entirely in their genuineness and truth. There was nothing in them, as works of taste or as compositions, which could have induced any one to have written a note upon them. Moreover, it shows that they were even then considered as ancient books. Men do not write comments upon publications of their own times: therefore the testimonies cited under this head afford an evidence which carries up the evangelic writings much beyond the age of the testimonies themselves, and to that of their reputed authors.

I. Tatian, a follower of Justin Martyr, and who flourished about the year 170, composed a harmony, or collation of the Gospels, which he called Diatessaron, of the four. The title, as well as the work, is remarkable; because it shows that then, as now, there were four, and only four, Gospels in general use with Christians. And this was little more than a hundred years after the publication of some of them. (Lardner, Cred. vol. i. p. 307.)

II. Pantaenus, of the Alexandrian school, a man of great reputation and learning, who came twenty years after Tatian, wrote many commentaries upon the Holy Scriptures, which, as Jerome testifies, were extant in his time. (Lardner, Cred. vol. i. p. 455.)

III. Clement of Alexandria wrote short explications of many books of the
Old and New Testament. (Lardner, Cred. vol. ii. p. 462.)

IV. Tertullian appeals from the authority of a later version, then in use, to the authentic Greek. (Lardner, Cred. vol. ii. p. 638.)

V. An anonymous author, quoted by Eusebius, and who appears to have written about the year 212, appeals to the ancient copies of the Scriptures, in refutation of some corrupt readings alleged by the followers of Artemon. (Lardner, Cred. vol. iii. p. 46.)

VI. The same Eusebius, mentioning by name several writers of the church who lived at this time, and concerning whom he says, "There still remain divers monuments of the laudable industry of those ancient and ecclesiastical men," (i.e. of Christian writers who were considered as ancient in the year 300,) adds, "There are, besides, treatises of many others, whose names we have not been able to learn, orthodox and ecclesiastical men, as the interpretations of the Divine Scriptures given by each of them show." (Lardner, Cred. vol. ii. p. 551.)

VII. The last five testimonies may be referred to the year 200; immediately after which, a period of thirty years gives us Julius Africanus, who wrote an epistle upon the apparent difference in the genealogies in Matthew and Luke, which he endeavours to reconcile by the distinction of natural and legal descent, and conducts his hypothesis with great industry through the whole series of generations. (Lardner, Cred. vol. iii. p. 170.)

Ammonius, a learned Alexandrian, who composed, as Tatian had done, a harmony of the four Gospels, which proves, as Tatian's work did, that there were four Gospels, and no more, at this time in use in the church. It affords also on instance of the zeal of Christians for those writings, and of their solicitude about them. (Lardner, Cred. vol. iii. p. 122.)

And, above both these, Origen, who wrote commentaries, or homilies, upon most of the books included in the New Testament, and upon no other books but these. In particular, he wrote upon Saint John's Gospel, very largely upon Saint Matthew's, and commentaries, or homilies, upon the Acts of the Apostles. (Lardner, Cred. vol. iii. pp. 352, 192, 202 & 245.)

VIII. In addition to these, the third century likewise contains— Dionysius of Alexandria, a very learned man, who compared, with great accuracy, the accounts in the four Gospels of the time of Christ's resurrection, adding a reflection which showed his opinion of their authority: "Let us not think that the evangelists disagree or contradict each other, although there be some small difference; but let us honestly and faithfully endeavour to reconcile what we read." (Lardner, Cred. vol. iv. p. 166.)

Victorin, bishop of Pettaw, in Germany, who wrote comments upon Saint

Matthew's Gospel. (Lardner, Cred. vol. iv. p. 195.)

Lucian, a presbyter of Antioch; and Hesychius, an Egyptian bishop, who put forth editions of the New Testament.

IX. The fourth century supplies a catalogue[16] of fourteen writers, who expended their labours upon the books of the New Testament, and whose

---

[16] Eusebius ...... A.D. 315
Juvencus, Spain 330
Theodore, Thrace 334
Hilary, Poletiers 340

works or names are come down to our times; amongst which number it may be sufficient, for the purpose of showing the sentiments and studies of learned Christians of that age, to notice the following:

Eusebius, in the very beginning of the century, wrote expressly upon the discrepancies observable in the Gospels, and likewise a treatise, in which he pointed out what things are related by four, what by three, what by two, and what by one evangelist. (Lardner, Cred. vol. viii. p. 46.) This author also testifies what is certainly a material piece of evidence, "that the writings of the apostles had obtained such an esteem as to be translated into every language both of Greeks and Barbarians, and to be diligently studied by all nations." (Lardner, Cred. vol. viii. p. 201.) This testimony was given about the year 300; how long before that date these translations were made does not appear.

Damasus, bishop of Rome, corresponded with Saint Jerome upon the exposition of difficult texts of Scripture; and, in a letter still remaining, desires Jerome to give him a clear explanation of the word Hosanna, found in the New Testament; "He (Damasus) having met with very different interpretations of it in the Greek and Latin commentaries of Catholic writers which he had read." (Lardner, Cred. vol. ix. P. 108) This last clause shows the number and variety of commentaries then extant.

Gregory of Nyssen, at one time, appeals to the most exact copies of Saint Mark's Gospel; at another time, compares together, and proposes to reconcile, the several accounts of the Resurrection given by the four Evangelists; which limitation proves that there were no other histories of Christ deemed authentic beside these, or included in the same character with these. This writer observes, acutely enough, that "the disposition of the clothes in the sepulchre, the napkin that was about our Saviour's head, not lying with the linen clothes, but wrapped together in a place by itself, did not bespeak the terror and hurry of thieves, and therefore refutes the story of the body being stolen." (Lardner, Cred. vol. ix. p. 163.)

Ambrose, bishop of Milan, remarked various readings in the Latin copies of the New Testament, and appeals to the original Greek;

And Jerome, towards the conclusion of this century, put forth an edition of the New Testament in Latin, corrected, at least as to the Gospels, by Greek copies, and "those (he says) ancient."

Lastly, Chrysostom, it is well known, delivered and published a great many homilies, or sermons, upon the Gospels and the Acts of the Apostles.

It is needless to bring down this article lower, but it is of importance to add, that there is no example of Christian writers of the first three centuries composing comments upon any other books than those which are found in the New Testament, except the single one of Clement of Alexandria commenting upon a book called the Revelation of Peter.

Of the ancient versions of the New Testament, one of the most valuable is the Syriac. Syriac was the language of Palestine when Christianity was there first established. And although the books of Scripture were written in Greek, for the purpose of a more extended circulation than within the precincts of Judea, yet it is probable that they would soon be translated into the vulgar language of the country where the religion first prevailed. Accordingly, a Syriac translation is now extant, all along, so far as it appears, used by the inhabitants of Syria, bearing many internal marks of high antiquity, supported in its pretensions by the uniform tradition of the East, and confirmed by the discovery of many very ancient manuscripts in the libraries of Europe, It is about 200 years since a bishop of Antioch sent a copy of this translation into Europe to be printed; and this seems to be the first time that the translation became generally known to these parts of the world. The bishop of Antioch's Testament was found to contain all our books, except the second epistle of Peter, the second and third of John, and the Revelation; which books, however, have since been discovered in that language in some ancient manuscripts of Europe. But in this collection, no other book, besides what is in ours, appears ever to have had a place. And, which is very worthy of observation, the text, though preserved in a remote country, and without communication with ours, differs from ours very little, and in nothing that is important (Jones on the Canon, vol. i.e. 14.).

SECTION VII.

Our Scriptures were received by ancient Christians of different sects and persuasions, but many Heretics as well as Catholics, and were usually appealed to by both sides in the controversies which arose in those days.

The three most ancient topics of controversy amongst Christians were, the authority of the Jewish constitution, the origin of evil, and the nature of Christ. Upon the first of these we find, in very early times, one class of heretics rejecting the Old Testament entirely; another contending for the obligation of its law, in all its parts, throughout its whole extent, and over every one who sought acceptance with God. Upon the two latter subjects, a natural, perhaps, and venial, but a fruitless, eager, and impatient curiosity, prompted by the philosophy and by the scholastic habits of the age, which carried men much into bold hypotheses and conjectural solutions, raised, amongst some who professed Christianity, very wild and unfounded opinions. I think there is no reason to believe that the number of these bore any considerable proportion to the body of the Christian church; and, amidst the disputes which such opinions necessarily occasioned, it is a great satisfaction to perceive what, in a vast plurality of instances, we do perceive, all sides recurring to the same Scriptures.

[17]I. Basilides lived near the age of the apostles, about the year 120, or, perhaps, sooner. (Lardner, vol. ix. p. 271.) He rejected the Jewish institution, not as spurious, but as proceeding from a being inferior to the true God; and in other respects advanced a scheme of theology widely different from the general doctrine of the Christian church, and which, as it gained over some disciples, was warmly opposed by Christian writers of the second and third century. In these writings there is positive evidence that Basilides received the Gospel of Matthew; and there is no sufficient proof that he rejected any of the other three: on the contrary, it appears that he wrote a commentary upon the Gospel, so copious as to be divided into twenty-four books. (Lardner, vol. ix. ed. 1788, p. 305, 306.)

II. The Valentinians appeared about the same time. Their heresy consisted in certain notions concerning angelic natures, which can hardly be rendered intelligible to a modern reader. They seem, however, to have acquired as much importance as any of the separatists of that early age. Of this sect, Irenaeus, who wrote A.D. 172, expressly records that they endeavoured to fetch arguments for their opinions from the evangelic and apostolic writings. Heracleon, one of the most celebrated of the sect, and who lived probably so early as the year 125, wrote commentaries upon Luke and John. Some observations also of his upon Matthew are preserved by Origen. Nor is there any reason to doubt that he received the whole New Testament. (Lardner, vol. ix. ed. 1788, pp. 350-351; vol. i. p. 383; vol. ix. ed. 1788, p. 352-353.)

III. The Carpocratians were also an early heresy, little, if at all, later than the two preceding. Some of their opinions resembled what we at this day mean by Socinianism. With respect to the Scriptures, they are specifically charged, by Irenaeus and by Epiphanius, with endeavouring

---

[17] The materials of the former part of this section are taken from Dr. Lardner's History of the Heretics of the first two centuries, published since his death, with additions, by the Rev. Mr. Hogg, of Exeter, and inserted into the ninth volume of his works, of the edition of 1778.

to pervert a passage in Matthew, which amounts to a positive proof that they received that Gospel. Negatively, they are not accused, by their adversaries, of rejecting any part of the New Testament. (Lardner, vol. ix. ed. 1788, pp. 309 & 318.)

IV. The Sethians, A.D. 150; the Montanists, A.D. 156; the Marcosigns, A.D. 160; Hermogenes, A.D. 180; Praxias, A.D. 196; Artemon, A.D. 200; Theodotus, A.D. 200; all included under the denomination of heretics, and all engaged in controversies with Catholic Christians, received the Scriptures of the New Testament. (Lardner, vol. ix. ed. 1788, pp. 455, 482, 348, 473, 433, 466.)

V. Tatian, who lived in the year 172, went into many extravagant opinions, was the founder of a sect called Encratites, and was deeply involved in disputes with the Christians of that age; yet Tatian so received the four Gospels as to compose a harmony from them.

VI. From a writer quoted by Eusebius, of about the year 200, it is apparent that they who at that time contended for the mere humanity of Christ, argued from the Scriptures; for they are accused by this writer of making alterations in their copies in order to favour their opinions. (Lardner, vol. iii. P. 46.)

VII. Origen's sentiments excited great controversies,—the bishops of Rome and Alexandria, and many others, condemning, the bishops of the east espousing them; yet there is not the smallest question but that both the advocates and adversaries of these opinions acknowledged the same authority of Scripture. In his time, which the reader will remember was about one hundred and fifty years after the Scriptures were published, many dissensions subsisted amongst Christians, with which they were reproached by Celsus; yet Origen, who has recorded this accusation without contradicting it, nevertheless testifies, that the four Gospels were received without dispute, by the whole church of God under heaven. (Lardner, vol. iv. ed. 1788, p. 642.)

VIII. Paul of Samosata, about thirty years after Origen, so distinguished himself in the controversy concerning the nature of Christ as to be the subject of two councils or synods, assembled at Antioch, upon his opinions. Yet he is not charged by his adversaries with rejecting any book of the New Testament. On the contrary, Epiphanius, who wrote a history of heretics a hundred years afterwards, says, that Paul endeavoured to support his doctrine by texts of Scripture. And Vincentius Lirinensis, A.D. 434, speaking of Paul and other heretics of the same age, has these words: "Here, perhaps, some one may ask whether heretics also urge the testimony of Scripture. They urge it, indeed, explicitly and vehemently; for you may see them flying through every book of the sacred law." (Lardner, vol. ix. p. 158.)

IX. A controversy at the same time existed with the Noetians or Sabellians, who seem to have gone into the opposite extreme from that of

Paul of Samosata and his followers. Yet according to the express testimony of Epiphanius, Sabellius received all the Scriptures. And with both sects Catholic writers constantly allege the Scriptures, and reply to the arguments which their opponents drew from particular texts.

We have here, therefore, a proof, that parties who were the most opposite and irreconcilable to one another acknowledged the authority of Scripture with equal deference.

X. And as a general testimony to the same point, may be produced what was said by one of the bishops of the council of Carthage, which was holden a little before this time:—"I am of opinion that blasphemous and wicked heretics, who pervert the sacred and adorable words of the Scripture, should be execrated." Undoubtedly, what they perverted they received. (Lardner, vol. ix. p. 839.)

XI. The Millennium, Novatianism, the baptism of heretics, the keeping of Easter, engaged also the attention and divided the opinions of Christians, at and before that time (and, by the way, it may be observed, that such disputes, though on some accounts to be blamed, showed how much men were in earnest upon the subject.); yet every one appealed for the grounds of his opinion to Scripture authority. Dionysius of Alexandria, who flourished A.D. 247, describing a conference or public disputation, with the Millennarians of Egypt, confesses of them, though their adversary, "that they embrace whatever could be made out by good arguments, from the Holy Scriptures." (Lardner, vol. iv. p. 666.) Novatus, A.D. 251, distinguished by some rigid sentiments concerning the reception of those who had lapsed, and the founder of a numerous sect, in his few remaining works quotes the Gospel with the same respect as other Christians did; and concerning his followers, the testimony of Socrates, who wrote about the year 440, is positive, viz. "That in the disputes between the Catholics and them, each side endeavoured to support itself by the authority of the Divine Scriptures" (Lardner, vol. v. p. 105.)

XII. The Donatists, who sprung up in the year 328, used the same Scriptures as we do. "Produce," saith Augustine, "some proof from the Scriptures, whose authority is common to us both" (Lardner, vol. vii. p. 243.)

XIII. It is perfectly notorious, that in the Arian controversy, which arose soon after the year 300, both sides appealed to the same Scriptures, and with equal professions of deference and regard. The Arians, in their council of Antioch, A.D. 341, pronounce that "if any one, contrary to the sound doctrine of the Scriptures, say, that the Son is a creature, as one of the creatures, let him be an anathema." (Lardner, vol. vii. p. 277.) They and the Athanasians mutually accuse each other of using unscriptural phrases; which was a mutual acknowledgment of the conclusive authority of Scripture.

XIV. The Priscillianists, A.D. 378, the Pelagians, A.D. 405 received the same Scriptures as we do. (Lardner, vol. ix. p. 325; vol. xi p. 52.)

XV. The testimony of Chrysostom, who lived near the year 400, is so positive in affirmation of the proposition which we maintain, that it may form a proper conclusion of the argument. "The general reception of the Gospels is a proof that their history is true and consistent; for, since the writing of the Gospels, many heresies have arisen, holding opinions contrary to what is contained in them, who yet receive the Gospels either entire or in part." (Lardner, vol. x. p. 316.) I am not moved by what may seem a deduction from Chrysostom's testimony, the words, "entire or in part;" for if all the parts which were ever questioned in our Gospels were given up, it would not affect the miraculous origin of the religion in the smallest degree: e.g.

Cerinthus is said by Epiphanius to have received the Gospel of Matthew, but not entire. What the omissions were does not appear. The common opinion, that he rejected the first two chapters, seems to have been a mistake. (Lardner, vol. ix. ed. 1788, p. 322.) It is agreed, however, by all who have given any account of Cerinthus, that he taught that the Holy Ghost (whether he meant by that name a person or a power) descended upon Jesus at his baptism; that Jesus from this time performed many miracles, and that he appeared after his death. He must have retained therefore the essential parts of the history.

Of all the ancient heretics, the most extraordinary was Marcion. (Lardner, vol. ix. sect. ii. c. x. Also Michael vol. i. c. i. sect. xviii.) One of his tenets was the rejection of the Old Testament, as proceeding from an inferior and imperfect Deity; and in pursuance of this hypothesis, he erased from the New, and that, as it should seem, without entering into any critical reasons, every passage which recognised the Jewish Scriptures. He spared not a text which contradicted his opinion. It is reasonable to believe that Marcion treated books as he treated texts: yet this rash and wild controversialist published a recension, or chastised edition of Saint Luke's Gospel, containing the leading facts, and all which is necessary to authenticate the religion. This example affords proof that there were always some points, and those the main points, which neither wildness nor rashness, neither the fury of opposition nor the intemperance of controversy, would venture to call in question. There is no reason to believe that Marcion, though full of resentment against the Catholic Christians, ever charged them with forging their books. "The Gospel of Saint Matthew, the Epistle to the Hebrews, with those of Saint Peter and Saint James, as well as the Old Testament in general" he said, "were writings not for Christians but for Jews." This declaration shows the ground upon which Marcion proceeded in his mutilation of the Scriptures, viz., his dislike of the passages or the books. Marcion flourished about the year 130.[18]

Dr. Lardner, in his General Review, sums up this head of evidence in the following words:—"Noitus, Paul of Samosata, Sabellius, Marcelins, Photinus, the Novatiana, Donatists, Manicheans (This must be with an exception, however, of Faustus, who lived so late us the year 354), Priscillianists, beside Artemon, the Audians, the Arians, and divers others, all received most of all the same books of the New Testament which the Catholics received; and agreed in a like respect for them as written by apostles, or their disciples and companions." (Lardner, vol. iii. p. 12.—Dr. Lardner's future inquiries supplied him with many other instances.)

SECTION VIII.

The four Gospels, the Acts of the Apostles, thirteen Epistles of Saint Paul the First Epistle of John, and the First of Peter, were received without doubt by those who doubted concerning the other books which are included in our present Canon.

I state this proposition, because, if made out, it shows that the authenticity of their books was a subject amongst the early Christians of consideration and inquiry; and that, where there was cause of doubt, they did doubt; a circumstance which strengthens very much their testimony to such books as were received by them with full acquiescence.

I. Jerome, in his account of Caius, who was probably a presbyter of Rome, and who flourished near the year 200, records of him, that, reckoning up only thirteen epistles of Paul, he says the fourteenth, which is inscribed to the Hebrews, is not his: and then Jerome adds, "With the Romans to this day it is not looked upon as Paul's." This agrees in the main with the account given by Eusebius of the same ancient author and his work; except that Eusebius delivers his own remark in more guarded terms: "And indeed to this very time, by some of the Romans, this epistle is not thought to be the apostle's." (Lardner, vol. iii. p. 240.)

II. Origen, about twenty years after Caius, quoting the Epistle to the Hebrews, observes that some might dispute the authority of that epistle; and therefore proceeds to quote to the same point, as undoubted books of Scripture, the Gospel of Saint Matthew, the Acts of the Apostles, and Paul's First Epistle to the Thessalonians. (Lardner, vol. iii. p. 246.) and in another place, this author speaks of the Epistle to the Hebrews thus: "The account come down to us is various; some saying that Clement who was bishop of Rome, wrote this epistle; others, that it was Luke, the same who wrote the Gospel and the Acts." Speaking also, in the same paragraph, of

---

[18] I have transcribed this sentence from Michaelis (p. 38), who has not, however, referred to the authority upon which he attributes these words to Marcion.

Peter, "Peter," says he, "has left one epistle, acknowledged; let it be granted likewise that he wrote a second, for it is doubted of." And of John, "He has also left one epistle, of a very few lines; grant also a second and a third, for all do not allow them to be genuine." Now let it be noted, that Origen, who thus discriminates, and thus confesses his own doubts and the doubts which subsisted in his time, expressly witnesses concerning the four Gospels, "that they alone are received without dispute by the whole church of God under heaven." (Lardner, vol. iii. p. 234.)

III. Dionysius of Alexandria, in the year 247, doubts concerning the Book of Revelation, whether it was written by Saint John; states the grounds of his doubt, represents the diversity of opinion concerning it, in his own time, and before his time. (Lardner, vol. iv. p. 670.) Yet the same Dionysius uses and collates the four Gospels in a manner which shows that he entertained not the smallest suspicion of their authority, and in a manner also which shows that they, and they alone, were received as authentic histories of Christ. (Lardner, vol. iv. p. 661.)

IV. But this section may be said to have been framed on purpose to introduce to the reader two remarkable passages extant in Eusebius's Ecclesiastical History. The first passage opens with these words:—"Let us observe the writings of the apostle John which are uncontradicted: and first of all must be mentioned, as acknowledged of all, the Gospel according to him, well known to all the churches under heaven." The author then proceeds to relate the occasions of writing the Gospels, and the reasons for placing Saint John's the last, manifestly speaking of all the four as parallel in their authority, and in the certainty of their original. (Lardner, vol. viii. p. 90.) The second passage is taken from a chapter, the title of which is, "Of the Scriptures universally acknowledged, and of those that are not such." Eusebius begins his enumeration in the following manner:—"In the first place are to be ranked the sacred four Gospels; then the book of the Acts of the Apostles; after that are to be reckoned the Epistles of Paul. In the next place, that called the First Epistle of John, and the Epistle of Peter, are to be esteemed authentic. After this is to be placed, if it be thought fit, the Revelation of John, about which we shall observe the different opinions at proper seasons. Of the controverted, but yet well known or approved by the most, are, that called the Epistle of James, and that of Jude, and the Second of Peter, and the Second and Third of John, whether they are written by the evangelist, or another of the same name." (Lardner, vol. viii. p. 39.) He then proceeds to reckon up five others, not in our canon, which he calls in one place spurious, in another controverted, meaning, as appears to me, nearly the same thing by these two words.[19]

---

[19] That Eusebius could not intend, by the word rendered 'spurious' what we at present mean by it, is evident from a clause in this very chapter where, speaking

It is manifest from this passage, that the four Gospels, and the Acts of the Apostles (the parts of Scripture with which our concern principally lies), were acknowledged without dispute, even by those who raised objections, or entertained doubts, about some other parts of the same collection. But the passage proves something more than this. The author was extremely conversant in the writings of Christians which had been published from the commencement of the institution to his own time: and it was from these writings that he drew his knowledge of the character and reception of the books in question. That Eusebius recurred to this medium of information, and that he had examined with attention this species of proof, is shown, first, by a passage in the very chapter we are quoting, in which, speaking of the books which he calls spurious, "None," he says, "of the ecclesiastical writers, in the succession of the apostles, have vouchsafed to make any mention of them in their writings;" and, secondly, by another passage of the same work, wherein, speaking of the First Epistle of Peter, "This," he says, "the presbyters of ancient times have quoted in their writings as undoubtedly genuine;" (Lardner, vol. viii. p. 99.) and then, speaking of some other writings bearing the name of Peter, "We know," he says, "that they have not been delivered down to us in the number of Catholic writings, forasmuch as no ecclesiastical writer of the ancients, or of our times, has made use of testimonies out of them." "But in the progress of this history," the author proceeds, "we shall make it our business to show, together with the successions from the apostles, what ecclesiastical writers, in every age, have used such writings as these which are contradicted, and what they have said with regard to the Scriptures received in the New Testament, and acknowledged by all, and with regard to those which are not such." (Lardner, vol. viii. p. 111)

After this it is reasonable to believe that when Eusebius states the four Gospels, and the Acts of the Apostles, as uncontradicted, uncontested, and acknowledged by all; and when he places them in opposition, not only to those which were spurious, in our sense of that term, but to those which were controverted, and even to those which were well known and approved by many, yet doubted of by some; he represents not only the sense of his own age, but the result of the evidence which the writings of prior ages, from the apostles' time to his own, had furnished to his inquiries. The opinion of Eusebius and his contemporaries appears to have been founded upon the testimony of writers whom they then called ancient: and we may observe, that such of the works of these writers as have come down to our times entirely confirm the judgment, and support the distinction which Eusebius proposes. The books which he calls "books

---

of the Gospels of Peter, and Thomas and Matthias, and some others, he says, "They the are not so much as to be reckoned among the spurious, but are altogether absurd and impious." (Lardner, vol. viii. p. 99.)

universally acknowledged" are in fact used and quoted in time remaining works of Christian writers, during the 250 years between the apostles' time and that of Eusebius, much more frequently than, and in a different manner from, those the authority of which, he tells us, was disputed.

SECTION IX.

Our historical Scriptures were attacked by the early adversaries of Christianity, as containing the accounts upon which the Religion was founded.

Near the middle of the second century, Celsus, a heathen philosopher, wrote a professed treatise against Christianity. To this treatise Origen, who came about fifty years after him, published an answer, in which he frequently recites his adversary's words and arguments. The work of Celsus is lost; but that of Origen remains. Origen appears to have given us the words of Celsus, where he professes to give them, very faithfully; and amongst other reasons for thinking so, this is one, that the objection, as stated by him from Celsus, is sometimes stronger than his own answer. I think it also probable that Origen, in his answer, has retailed a large portion of the work of Celsus:

"That it may not be suspected," he says, "that we pass by any chapters because we have no answers at hand, I have thought it best, according to my ability, to confute everything proposed by him, not so much observing the natural order of things, as the order which he has taken himself." (Orig. cont. Cels. I. i. sect. 41.)

Celsus wrote about one hundred years after the Gospels were published; and therefore any notices of these books from him are extremely important for their antiquity. They are, however, rendered more so by the character of the author; for the reception, credit, and notoriety of these books must have been well established amongst Christians, to have made them subjects of animadversion and opposition by strangers and by enemies. It evinces the truth of what Chrysostom, two centuries afterwards, observed, that "the Gospels, when written, were not hidden in a corner or buried in obscurity, but they were made known to all the world, before enemies as well as others, even as they are now." (In Matt. Hom. I. 7.)

1. Celsus, or the Jew whom he personates, uses these words:—"I could say many things concerning the affairs of Jesus, and those, too, different from those written by the disciples of Jesus; but I purposely omit them." (Lardner, Jewish and Heathen Test. vol. ii. p. 274.) Upon this passage it has been rightly observed, that it is not easy to believe, that if Celsus could have contradicted the disciples upon good evidence in any material point, he would have omitted to do so, and that the assertion is, what Origen calls it, a mere oratorical flourish.

It is sufficient, however, to prove that, in the time of Celsus, there were books well known, and allowed to be written by the disciples of Jesus, which books contained a history of him. By the term disciples, Celsus does not mean the followers of Jesus in general; for them he calls Christians, or believers, or the like; but those who had been taught by Jesus himself, i.e. his apostles and companions.

2. In another passage, Celsus accuses the Christians of altering the Gospel. (Lardner, Jewish and Heathen Test. Vol. ii. p. 275.) The accusation refers to some variations in the readings of particular passages: for Celsus goes on to object, that when they are pressed hard, and one reading has been confuted, they disown that, and fly to another. We cannot perceive from Origen, that Celsus specified any particular instances, and without such specification the charge is of no value. But the true conclusion to be drawn from it is, that there were in the hands of the Christians histories which were even then of some standing: for various readings and corruptions do not take place in recent productions.

The former quotation, the reader will remember, proves that these books were composed by the disciples of Jesus, strictly so called; the present quotation shows, that though objections were taken by the adversaries of the religion to the integrity of these books, none were made to their genuineness.

3. In a third passage, the Jew whom Celsus introduces shuts up an argument in this manner:—"these things then we have alleged to you out of your own writings, not needing any other weapons." (Lardner, vol. ii. p. 276.) It is manifest that this boast proceeds upon the supposition that the books over which the writer affects to triumph possessed an authority by which Christians confessed themselves to be bound.

4. That the books to which Celsus refers were no other than our present Gospels, is made out by his allusions to various passages still found in these Gospels. Celsus takes notice of the genealogies, which fixes two of these Gospels; of the precepts, Resist not him that injures you, and if a man strike thee on the one cheek, offer to him the other also; of the woes denounced by Christ; of his predictions; of his saying, That it is impossible to serve two masters; (Lardner, vol. ii. pp. 276-277.) Of the purple robe, the crown of thorns, and the reed in his hand; of the blood that flowed from the body of Jesus upon the cross, which circumstance is recorded by John alone; and (what is instar omnium for the purpose for which we produce it) of the difference in the accounts given of the resurrection by the evangelists, some mentioning two angels at the sepulchre, ethers only one. (Lardner, vol. ii. pp. 280, 281, & 283.)

It is extremely material to remark, that Celsus not only perpetually referred to the accounts of Christ contained in the four Gospels, but that he referred to no other accounts; that he founded none of his objections to Christianity upon any thing delivered in spurious Gospels. (The particulars, of which the above are only a few, are well collected by Mr. Bryant, p. 140.)

II. What Celsus was in the second century, Porphyry became in the third. His work, which was a large and formal treatise against the Christian religion, is not extant. We must be content, therefore, to gather his objections from Christian writers, who have noticed in order to answer them; and enough remains of this species of information to prove completely, that Porphyry's animadversions were directed against the contents of our present Gospels, and of the Acts of the Apostles; Porphyry considering that to overthrow them was to overthrow the religion. Thus he objects to the repetition of a generation in Saint Matthew's genealogy; to Matthew's call; to the quotation of a text from Isaiah, which is found in a psalm ascribed to Asaph; to the calling of the lake of Tiberius a sea; to the expression of Saint Matthew, "the abomination of desolation;" to the variation in Matthew and Mark upon the text, "the voice of one crying in the wilderness," Matthew citing it from Isaias, Mark from the Prophets; to John's application of the term "Word;" to Christ's change of intention about going up to the feast of Tabernacles (John vii. 8); to the judgment denounced by Saint Peter upon Ananias and Sapphira, which he calls an "imprecation of death." (Jewish and Heathen Test. Vol. iii. p. 166, et seq.)

The instances here alleged serve, in some measure, to show the nature of Porphyry's objections, and prove that Porphyry had read the Gospels with that sort of attention which a writer would employ who regarded them as the depositaries of the religion which he attacked. Besides these specifications, there exists, in the writings of ancient Christians, general evidence that the places of Scripture upon which Porphyry had remarked were very numerous.

In some of the above-cited examples, Porphyry, speaking of Saint Matthew, calls him your Evangelist; he also uses the term evangelists in the plural number. What was said of Celsus is true likewise of Porphyry, that it does not appear that he considered any history of Christ except these as having authority with Christians.

III. A third great writer against the Christian religion was the emperor Julian, whose work was composed about a century after that of Porphyry.

In various long extracts, transcribed from this work by Cyril and Jerome, it appears, (Jewish and Heathen Test. vol. iv. p. 77, et seq.) that Julian noticed by name Matthew and Luke, in the difference between their genealogies of Christ that he objected to Matthew's application of the prophecy, "Out of Egypt have I called my son" (ii. 15), and to that of "A virgin shall conceive" (i. 23); that he recited sayings of Christ, and various passages of his history, in the very words of the evangelists; in particular, that Jesus healed lame and blind people, and exorcised demoniacs in the villages of Bethsaida and Bethany; that he alleged that none of Christ's disciples ascribed to him the creation of the world, except John; that neither Paul, nor Matthew, nor Luke, nor Mark, have dared to call Jesus God; that John wrote later than the other evangelists, and at a time when a great number of men in the cities of Greece and Italy were converted; that he alludes to the conversion of Cornelius and of Sergius Paulus, to Peter's vision, to the circular letter sent by the apostles and elders at Jerusalem, which are all recorded in the Acts of the Apostles: by which quoting of the four Gospels and the Acts of the Apostles, and by quoting no other, Julian shows that these were the historical books, and the only historical books, received by Christians as of authority, and as the authentic memoirs of Jesus Christ, of his apostles, and of the doctrines taught by them. But Julian's testimony does something more than represent the judgment of the Christian church in his time. It discovers also his own. He himself expressly states the early date of these records; he calls them by the names which they now bear. He all along supposes, he nowhere attempts to question, their genuineness.

The argument in favour of the books of the New Testament, drawn from the notice taken of their contents by the early writers against the religion, is very considerable. It proves that the accounts which Christians had then were the accounts which we have now; that our present Scriptures were theirs. It proves, moreover, that neither Celsus in the second, Porphyry in the third, nor Julian in the fourth century, suspected the authenticity of these books, or ever insinuated that Christians were mistaken in the authors to whom they ascribed them. Not one of them expressed an opinion upon this subject different from that which was holden by Christians. And when we consider how much it would have availed them to have cast a doubt upon this point, if they could; and how ready they showed themselves to be to take every advantage in their power; and that they were all men of learning and inquiry: their concession, or rather their suffrage, upon the subject is extremely valuable.

In the case of Porphyry, it is made still stronger, by the consideration that he did in fact support himself by this species of objection when he saw any room for it, or when his acuteness could supply any pretence for alleging it. The prophecy of Daniel he attacked upon this very ground of spuriousness, insisting that it was written after the time of Antiochus Epiphanes, and maintains his charge of forgery by some far-fetched indeed, but very subtle criticisms. Concerning the writings of the New Testament, no trace of this suspicion is anywhere to be found in him. (Michaelis's Introduction to the New Testament, vol. i. p. 43. Marsh's Translation.)

SECTION X.

Formal catalogues of authentic Scriptures were published, in all which our present sacred histories were included.

This species of evidence comes later than the rest; as it was not natural that catalogues of any particular class of books should be put forth until Christian writings became numerous; or until some writings showed themselves, claiming titles which did not belong to them, and thereby rendering it necessary to separate books of authority from others. But, when it does appear, it is extremely satisfactory; the catalogues, though numerous, and made in countries at a wide distance from one another, differing very little, differing in nothing which is material, and all containing the four Gospels. To this last article there is no exception.

I. In the writings of Origen which remain, and in some extracts preserved by Eusebius, from works of his which are now lost, there are enumerations of the books of Scriptures, in which the Four Gospels and the Acts of the Apostles are distinctly and honourably specified, and in which no books appear beside what are now received. The reader, by this time, will easily recollect that the date of Origen's works is A.D. 230. (Lardner, Cred. vol. iii. p. 234, et seq.; vol. viii. p. 196.)

II. Athanasius, about a century afterwards, delivered a catalogue of the books of the New Testament in form, containing our Scriptures and no others; of which he says, "In these alone the doctrine of Religion is taught; let no man add to them, or take anything from them." (Lardner, Cred. vol. ii. p. 223.)

III. About twenty years after Athanasius, Cyril, bishop of Jerusalem, set forth a catalogue of the books of Scripture, publicly read at that time in the church of Jerusalem, exactly the same as ours, except that the "Revelation" is omitted. (Lardner, Cred. vol. ii. p. 270.)

IV. And fifteen years after Cyril, the council of Laodicea delivered an authoritative catalogue of canonical Scripture, like Cyril's, the same as ours with the omission of the "Revelation."

V. Catalogues now became frequent. Within thirty years after the last date, that is, from the year 363 to near the conclusion of the fourth century, we have catalogues by Epiphanius, (Lardner, Cred. vol. ii. p. 368.) by Gregory Nazianzen, by Philaster, bishop of Breseia in Italy, (Lardner, Cred. vol. ix. p. 132 & 373.) by Amphilochius, bishop of Iconium; all, as they are sometimes called, clean catalogues (that is, they admit no books into the number beside what we now receive); and all, for every purpose of historic evidence, the same as ours. (Epiphanius omits the Acts of the Apostles. This must have been an accidental mistake, either in him or in some copyist of his work; for he elsewhere expressly refers to this book, and ascribes it to Luke.)

VI. Within the same period Jerome, the most learned Christian writer of his age, delivered a catalogue of the hooks of the New Testament, recognising every book now received, with the intimation of a doubt concerning the Epistle to the Hebrews alone, and taking not the least notice of any book which is not now received. (Lardner, Cred. vol. x. p. 77.)

VII. Contemporary with Jerome, who lived in Palestine, was St. Augustine, in Africa, who published likewise a catalogue, without joining to the Scriptures, as books of authority, any other ecclesiastical writing whatever, and without omitting one which we at this day acknowledge. (Lardner, Cred. vol. x. p. 213.)

VIII. And with these concurs another contemporary writer, Rufen, presbyter of Aquileia, whose catalogue, like theirs, is perfect and unmixed, and concludes with these remarkable words: "These are the volumes which the fathers have included in the canon, and out of which they would have us prove the doctrine of our faith." (Lardner, Cred. vol. x. p. 187.)

SECTION XI.

These propositions cannot be predicated of any of those books which are commonly called Apocryphal Books of the New Testament.

I do not know that the objection taken from apocryphal writings is at present much relied upon by scholars. But there are many, who, hearing that various Gospels existed in ancient times under the names of the apostles, may have taken up a notion, that the selection of our present Gospels from the rest was rather an arbitrary or accidental choice, than founded in any clear and certain cause of preference. To these it may be very useful to know the truth of the case. I observe, therefore:—

I. That, beside our Gospels and the Acts of the Apostles, no Christian history, claiming to be written by an apostle or apostolical man, is quoted within three hundred years after the birth of Christ, by any writer now extant or known; or, if quoted, is not quoted but with marks of censure and rejection.

I have not advanced this assertion without inquiry; and I doubt not but that the passages cited by Mr. Jones and Dr. Lardner, under the several titles which the apocryphal books bear; or a reference to the places where they are mentioned as collected in a very accurate table, published in the year 1773, by the Rev. J. Atkinson, will make out the truth of the proposition to the satisfaction of every fair and competent judgment. If there be any book which may seem to form an exception to the observation, it is a Hebrew Gospel, which was circulated under the various titles of, the Gospel according to the Hebrews, the Gospel of the Nazarenes, of the Ebionites, sometimes called of the Twelve, by some

104

ascribed to St Matthew. This Gospel is once, and only once, cited by Clemeus Alexandrinus, who lived, the reader will remember, in the latter part of the second century, and which same Clement quotes one or other of our four Gospels in almost every page of his work. It is also twice mentioned by Origen, A.D. 230; and both times with marks of diminution and discredit. And this is the ground upon which the exception stands. But what is still more material to observe is, that this Gospel, in the main, agreed with our present Gospel of Saint Matthew. (In applying to this Gospel what Jerome in the latter end of the fourth century has mentioned of a Hebrew Gospel, I think it probable that we sometimes confound it with a Hebrew copy of St. Matthew's Gospel, whether an original or version, which was then extant.)

Now if, with this account of the apocryphal Gospels, we compare what we have read concerning the canonical Scriptures in the preceding sections; or even recollect that general but well-founded assertion of Dr. Lardner, "That in the remaining works of Irenaeus, Clement of Alexandria, and Tertullian, who all lived in the first two centuries, there are more and larger quotations of the small volume of the New Testament than of all the works of Cicero, by writers of all characters, for several ages;" (Lardner, Cred. vol. xii. p. 53.) and if to this we add that, notwithstanding the loss of many works of the primitive times of Christianity, we have, within the above-mentioned period, the remains of Christian writers who lived in Palestine, Syria, Asia Minor, Egypt, the part of Africa that used the Latin tongue, in Crete, Greece, Italy, and Gaul, in all which remains references are found to our evangelists; I apprehend that we shall perceive a clear and broad line of division between those writings and all others pretending to similar authority.

II. But beside certain histories which assumed the names of apostles, and which were forgeries properly so called, there were some other Christian writings, in the whole or in part of an historical nature, which, though not forgeries, are denominated apocryphal, as being of uncertain or of no authority.

Of this second class of writings, I have found only two which are noticed by any author of the first three centuries without express terms of condemnation: and these are, the one a book entitled the Preaching of Peter, quoted repeatedly by Clemens Alexandrinus, A.D. 196; the other a book entitled the Revelation of Peter, upon which the above-mentioned Clemens Alexandrinus is said by Eusebius to have written notes; and which is twice cited in a work still extant, ascribed to the same author.

I conceive, therefore, that the proposition we have before advanced, even after it hath been subjected to every exception of every kind that can be alleged, separates, by a wide interval, our historical Scriptures from all other writings which profess to give an account of the same subject.

We may be permitted however to add,—

1. That there is no evidence that any spurious or apocryphal books whatever existed in the first century of the Christian era, in which century all our historical books are proved to have been extant. "There are no quotations of any such books in the apostolical fathers, by whom I mean Barnabas, Clement of Rome, Hermas, Ignatius, and Polycarp, whose writings reach from about the year of our Lord 70 to the year 108 (and some of whom have quoted each and every one of our historical Scriptures): I say this," adds Dr. Lardner, "because I think it has been proved." (Lardner, Cred. vol. xii. p. 158.)

2. These apocryphal writings were not read in the churches of Christians;

3. Were not admitted into their volume;

4. Do not appear in their catalogues;

5. Were not noticed by their adversaries;

6. Were not alleged by different parties, as of authority in their controversies;

7. Were not the subjects, amongst them, of commentaries, versions, collections, expositions.

Finally; beside the silence of three centuries, or evidence within that time of their rejection, they were, with a consent nearly universal, reprobated by Christian writers of succeeding ages.

Although it be made out by these observations that the books in question never obtained any degree of credit and notoriety which can place them in competition with our Scriptures; yet it appears from the writings of the fourth century, that many such existed in that century, and in the century preceding it. It may be difficult at this distance of time to account for their origin.

Perhaps the most probable explication is, that they were in general composed with a design of making a profit by the sale. Whatever treated of the subject would find purchasers. It was an advantage taken of the pious curiosity of unlearned Christians. With a view to the same purpose, there were many of them adapted to the particular opinions of particular sects, which would naturally promote their circulation amongst the favourers of those opinions. After all, they were probably much more obscure than we imagine. Except the Gospel according to the Hebrews, there is none of which we hear more than the Gospel of the Egyptians; yet there is good reason to believe that Clement, a presbyter of Alexandria in Egypt, A.D. 184, and a man of almost universal reading, had never seen it. (Jones, vol. i. p. 243.) A Gospel according to Peter was another of the most ancient books of this kind; yet Serapion, bishop of Antioch, A.D. 200, had not read it, when he heard of such a book being in the hands of the Christians of Rhossus in Cillcia; and speaks of obtaining a sight of this Gospel from some sectaries who used it. (Lardner, Cred. vol. ii. p. 557.) Even of the Gospel of the Hebrews, which confessedly stands at the head of the catalogue, Jerome, at the end of the fourth century, was glad to procure a copy by the favour of the Nazarenes of Berea. Nothing of this sort ever happened, or could have happened, concerning our Gospels.

One thing is observable of all the apocryphal Christian writings, viz. that they proceed upon the same fundamental history of Christ and his apostles as that which is disclosed in our Scriptures. The mission of Christ, his power of working miracles, his communication of that power to the apostles, his passion, death, and resurrection, are assumed or asserted by every one of them. The names under which some of them came forth are the names of men of eminence in our histories. What these books give are not contradictions, but unauthorised additions. The principal facts are supposed, the principal agents the same; which shows that these points were too much fixed to be altered or disputed.

If there be any book of this description which appears to have imposed upon some considerable number of learned Christians, it is the Sibylline oracles; but when we reflect upon the circumstances which facilitated that imposture, we shall cease to wonder either at the attempt or its success. It was at that time universally understood that such a prophetic writing existed. Its contents were kept secret. This situation afforded to some one a hint, as well as an opportunity, to give out a writing under this name, favourable to the already established persuasion of Christians, and which writing, by the aid and recommendation of these circumstances, would in some degree, it is probable, be received. Of the ancient forgery we know but little; what is now produced could not, in my opinion, have imposed upon any one. It is nothing else than the Gospel history woven into verse; perhaps was at first rather a fiction than a forgery; an exercise of ingenuity, more than an attempt to deceive.

CHAPTER X.

RECAPITULATION.

The reader will now be pleased to recollect, that the two points which form the subject of our present discussion are, first, that the Founder of Christianity, his associates, and immediate followers, passed their lives in labours, dangers, and sufferings; secondly, that they did so in attestation of the miraculous history recorded in our Scriptures, and solely in consequence of their belief of the truth of that history.

The argument, by which these two propositions have been maintained by us, stands thus:

No historical fact, I apprehend, is more certain, than that the original propagators of Christianity voluntarily subjected themselves to lives of fatigue, danger, and suffering, in the prosecution of their undertaking. The nature of the undertaking; the character of the persons employed in it; the opposition of their tenets to the fixed opinions and expectations of the country in which they first advanced them; their undissembled condemnation of the religion of all other countries; their total want of power, authority, or force—render it in the highest degree probable that this must have been the case. The probability is increased by what we know of the fate of the Founder of the institution, who was put to death for his attempt; and by what we also know of the cruel treatment of the converts to the institution, within thirty years after its commencement: both which points are attested by heathen writers, and, being once admitted, leave it very incredible that the primitive emissaries of the religion, who exercised their ministry, first, amongst the people who had destroyed their Master, and, afterwards, amongst those who persecuted their converts, should themselves escape with impunity, or pursue their purpose in ease and safety. This probability, thus sustained by foreign testimony, is advanced, I think, to historical certainty, by the evidence of our own books; by the accounts of a writer who was the companion of the persons whose sufferings he relates; by the letters of the persons themselves by predictions of persecutions ascribed to the Founder of the religion, which predictions would not have been inserted in his history, much less have been studiously dwelt upon, if they had not accorded with the event, and which, even if falsely ascribed to him, could only have been so ascribed, because the event suggested them; lastly, by incessant exhortations to fortitude and patience, and by an earnestness, repetition, and urgency upon the subject, which were unlikely to have appeared if there had not been, at the time, some extraordinary call for the exercise of these virtues.

It is made out also, I think, with sufficient evidence, that both the teachers and converts of the religion, in consequence of their new profession, took up a new course of life and behaviour.

The next great question is, what they did this FOR. That it was for a miraculous story of some kind or other, is to my apprehension extremely manifest; because, as to the fundamental article, the designation of the person, viz. that this particular person, Jesus of Nazareth, ought to be received as the Messiah, or as a messenger from God, they neither had, nor could have, anything but miracles to stand upon. That the exertions and sufferings of the apostles were for the story which we have now, is proved by the consideration that this story is transmitted to us by two of their own number, and by two others personally connected with them; that the particularity of the narrative proves that the writers claimed to possess circumstantial information, that from their situation they had full opportunity of acquiring such information, that they certainly, at least, knew what their colleagues, their companions, their masters taught; that each of these books contains enough to prove the truth of the religion; that if any one of them therefore be genuine, it is sufficient; that the genuineness, however, of all of them is made out, as well by the general arguments which evince the genuineness of the most undisputed remains of antiquity, as also by peculiar and specific proofs, viz. by citations from them in writings belonging to a period immediately contiguous to that in which they were published; by the distinguished regard paid by early Christians to the authority of these books; (which regard was manifested by their collecting of them into a volume, appropriating to that volume titles of peculiar respect, translating them into various languages, digesting them into harmonies, writing commentaries upon them, and, still more conspicuously, by the reading of them in their public assemblies in all parts of the world) by an universal agreement with respect to these books, whilst doubts were entertained concerning some others; by contending sects appealing to them; by the early adversaries of the religion not disputing their genuineness, but, on the contrary, treating them as the depositaries of the history upon which the religion was founded; by many formal catalogues of these, as of certain and authoritative writings, published in different and distant parts of the Christian world; lastly, by the absence or defect of the above-cited topics of evidence, when applied to any other histories of the same subject.

These are strong arguments to prove that the books actually proceeded from the authors whose names they bear (and have always borne, for there is not a particle of evidence to show that they ever went under any other); but the strict genuineness of the books is perhaps more than is necessary to the support of our proposition. For even supposing that, by reason of the silence of antiquity, or the loss of records, we knew not who were the writers of the four Gospels, yet the fact that they were received as authentic accounts of the transaction upon which the religion rested, and were received as such by Christians at or near the age of the apostles, by those whom the apostles had taught, and by societies which the apostles had founded; this fact, I say, connected with the consideration that they are corroborative of each other's testimony, and that they are further corroborated by another contemporary history taking up the story where they had left it, and, in a narrative built upon that story, accounting for the rise and production of changes in the world, the effects of which subsist at this day; connected, moreover, with the confirmation which they receive from letters written by the apostles themselves, which both assume the same general story, and, as often as occasions lead them to do so, allude to particular parts of it; and connected also with the reflection, that if the apostles delivered any different story it is lost; (the present and no other being referred to by a series of Christian writers, down from their age to our own; being like-wise recognised in a variety of institutions, which prevailed early and universally, amongst the disciples of the religion;) and that so great a change as the oblivion of one story and the substitution of another, under such circumstances, could not have taken place: this evidence would be deemed, I apprehend, sufficient to prove concerning these books, that, whoever were the authors of them, they exhibit the story which the apostles told, and for which, consequently, they acted and they suffered.

If it be so, the religion must be true. These men could not be deceivers. By only not bearing testimony, they might have avoided all these sufferings, and have lived quietly. Would men in such circumstances pretend to have seen what they never saw; assert facts which they had no knowledge of; go about lying to teach virtue; and, though not only convinced of Christ's being an impostor, but having seen the success of his imposture in his crucifixion, yet persist in carrying it on; and so persist, as to bring upon themselves for nothing, and with a full knowledge of the consequence, enmity and hatred, danger and death?

OF THE DIRECT HISTORICAL EVIDENCE OF CHRISTIANITY.

PROPOSITION II.

CHAPTER I.

Our first proposition was, That there is satisfactory evidence that many pretending to be original witnesses of the Christian miracles, passed their lives in labours, dangers, and sufferings, voluntarily undertaken and undergone in attestation of the accounts which they delivered, and solely in consequence of their belief of the truth of those accounts; and that they also submitted, from the same motives, to new rules of conduct.

Our second proposition, and which now remains to be treated of, is, That there is NOT satisfactory evidence, that persons pretending to be original witnesses of any other similar miracles have acted in the same manner, in attestation of the accounts which they delivered, and solely in consequence of their belief of the truth of those accounts.

I enter upon this part of my argument, by declaring how far my belief in miraculous accounts goes. If the reformers in the time of Wickliffe, or of Luther; or those of England in the time of Henry the Eighth, or of Queen Mary; or the founders of our religious sects since, such as were Mr. Whitfield and Mr. Wesley in our times—had undergone the life of toil and exertion, of danger and sufferings, which we know that many of them did undergo, for a miraculous story; that is to say, if they had founded their public ministry upon the allegation of miracles wrought within their own knowledge, and upon narratives which could not be resolved into delusion or mistake; and if it had appeared that their conduct really had its origin in these accounts, I should have believed them. Or, to borrow an instance which will be familiar to every one of my readers, if the late Mr. Howard had undertaken his labours and journeys in attestation, and in consequence of a clear and sensible miracle, I should have believed him also. Or, to represent the same thing under a third supposition; if Socrates had professed to perform public miracles at Athens; if the friends of Socrates, Phaedo, Cebes, Crito, and Simmias, together with Plato, and many of his followers, relying upon the attestations which these miracles afforded to his pretensions, had, at the hazard of their lives, and the certain expense of their ease and tranquillity, gone about Greece, after his death, to publish and propagate his doctrines: and if these things had come to our knowledge, in the same way as that in which the life of Socrates is now transmitted to us through the hands of his companions and disciples, that is, by writings received without doubt as theirs, from the age in which they were published to the present, I should have believed this likewise. And my belief would, in each case, be much strengthened, if the subject of the mission were of importance to the conduct and happiness of human life; if it testified anything which it behoved mankind to know from such authority; if the nature of what it delivered required the sort of proof which it alleged; if the occasion was adequate to the interposition, the end worthy of the means. In the last ease, my faith would be much confirmed if the effects of the transaction remained; more especially if a change had been wrought, at the time, in the opinion and conduct of such numbers as to lay the foundation of an institution, and of a system of doctrines, which had since overspread the greatest part of the civilized world. I should have believed, I say, the testimony in these cases; yet none of them do more than come up to the apostolic history.

If any one choose to call assent to its evidence credulity, it is at least incumbent upon him to produce examples in which the same evidence hath turned out to be fallacious. And this contains the precise question which we are now to agitate.

In stating the comparison between our evidence, and what our adversaries may bring into competition with ours, we will divide the distinctions which we wish to propose into two kinds,—those which relate to the proof, and those which relate to the miracles. Under the former head we may lay out of the case:—

I. Such accounts of supernatural events as are found only in histories by some ages posterior to the transaction; and of which it is evident that the historian could know little more than his reader. Ours is contemporary history. This difference alone removes out of our way the miraculous history of Pythagoras, who lived five hundred years before the Christian era, written by Porphyry and Jamblicus, who lived three hundred years after that era; the prodigies of Livy's history; the fables of the heroic ages; the whole of the Greek and Roman, as well as of the Gothic mythology; a great part of the legendary history of Popish saints, the very best attested of which is extracted from the certificates that are exhibited during the process of their canonization, a ceremony which seldom takes place till a century after their deaths. It applies also with considerable force to the miracles of Apollonius Tyaneus, which are contained in a solitary history of his life, published by Philostratus above a hundred years after his death; and in which, whether Philostratus had any prior account to guide him, depends upon his single unsupported assertion. Also to some of the miracles of the third century, especially to one extraordinary instance, the account of Gregory, bishop of Neocesarea, called Thaumaturgus, delivered in the writings of Gregory of Nyssen, who lived one hundred and thirty years after the subject of his panegyric.

The value of this circumstance is shown to have been accurately exemplified in the history of Ignatius Loyola, founder of the order of Jesuits. (Douglas's Criterion of Miracles, p. 74.) His life, written by a companion of his, and by one of the order, was published about fifteen years after his death. In which life, the author, so far from ascribing any

112

miracles to Ignatius, industriously states the reasons why he was not invested with any such power. The life was republished fifteen years afterwards, with the addition of many circumstances which were the fruit, the author says, of further inquiry, and of diligent examination; but still with a total silence about miracles. When Ignatius had been dead nearly sixty years, the Jesuits, conceiving a wish to have the founder of their order placed in the Roman calendar, began, as it should seem, for the first time, to attribute to him a catalogue of miracles which could not then be distinctly disproved; and which there was, in those who governed the church, a strong disposition to admit upon the slenderest proofs.

II. We may lay out of the case accounts published in one country, of what passed in a distant country, without any proof that such accounts were known or received at home. In the case of Christianity, Judea, which was the scene of the transaction, was the centre of the mission. The story was published in the place in which it was acted. The church of Christ was first planted at Jerusalem itself. With that church others corresponded. From thence the primitive teachers of the institution went forth; thither they assembled. The church of Jerusalem, and the several churches of Judea, subsisted from the beginning, and for many ages; received also the same books and the same accounts as other churches did. (The succession of many eminent bishops of Jerusalem in the first three centuries is distinctly preserved; as Alexander, A.D. 212, who succeeded Narcissus, then 116 years old.)

This distinction disposes, amongst others, of the above-mentioned miracles of Apollonius Tyaneus, most of which are related to have been performed in India; no evidence remaining that either the miracles ascribed to him, or the history of those miracles, were ever heard of in India. Those of Francis Xavier, the Indian missionary, with many others of the Romish breviary, are liable to the same objection, viz. that the accounts of them were published at a vast distance from the supposed scene of the wonders. (Douglas's Crit. p. 84.)

III. We lay out of the case transient rumours. Upon the first publication of an extraordinary account, or even of an article of ordinary intelligence, no one who is not personally acquainted with the transaction can know whether it be true or false, because any man may publish any story. It is in the future confirmation, or contradiction, of the account; in its permanency, or its disappearance; its dying away into silence, or its increasing in notoriety; its being followed up by subsequent accounts, and being repeated in different and independent accounts—that solid truth is distinguished from fugitive lies. This distinction is altogether on the side of Christianity. The story did not drop. On the contrary, it was succeeded by a train of action and events dependent upon it. The accounts which we have in our hands were composed after the first reports must have subsided. They were followed by a train of writings upon the subject. The historical testimonies of the transaction were many and various, and connected with letters, discourses, controversies, apologies, successively produced by the same transaction.

IV. We may lay out of the case what I call naked history. It has been said, that if the prodigies of the Jewish history had been found only in fragments of Manetho, or Berosus, we should have paid no regard to them: and I am willing to admit this. If we knew nothing of the fact, but from the fragment; if we possessed no proof that these accounts had been credited and acted upon, from times, probably, as ancient as the accounts themselves; if we had no visible effects connected with the history, no subsequent or collateral testimony to confirm it; under these circumstances I think that it would be undeserving of credit. But this certainly is not our case. In appreciating the evidence of Christianity, the books are to be combined with the institution; with the prevalency of the religion at this day; with the time and place of its origin, which are acknowledged points; with the circumstances of its rise and progress, as collected from external history; with the fact of our present books being received by the votaries of the institution from the beginning; with that of other books coming after these, filled with accounts of effects and consequences resulting from the transaction, or referring to the transaction, or built upon it; lastly, with the consideration of the number and variety of the books themselves, the different writers from which they proceed, the different views with which they were written, so disagreeing as to repel the suspicion of confederacy, so agreeing as to show that they were founded in a common original, i.e. in a story substantially the same. Whether this proof be satisfactory or not, it is properly a cumulation of evidence, by no means a naked or solitary record.

V. A mark of historical truth, although only a certain way, and to a certain degree, is particularity in names, dates, places, circumstances, and in the order of events preceding or following the transaction: of which kind, for instance, is the particularity in the description of St. Paul's voyage and shipwreck, in the 27th chapter of the Acts, which no man, I think, can read without being convinced that the writer was there; and also in the account of the cure and examination of the blind man in the 9th chapter of St. John's Gospel, which bears every mark of personal knowledge on the part of the historian. (Both these chapters ought to be read for the sake of this very observation.) I do not deny that fiction has often the particularity of truth; but then it is of studied and elaborate fiction, or of a formal attempt to deceive, that we observe this. Since, however, experience proves that particularity is not confined to truth, I have stated that it is a proof of truth only to a certain extent, i.e. it reduces the question to this, whether we can depend or not upon the probity of the relater? which is a considerable advance in our present argument; for an express attempt to deceive, in which case alone particularity can appear without truth, is charged upon the evangelists by few. If the historian acknowledge himself to have received his intelligence from others, the particularity of the narrative shows, prima facie, the accuracy of his inquiries, and the fulness of his information. This remark belongs to St. Luke's history. Of the particularity which we allege, many examples may be found in all the Gospels. And it is very difficult to conceive that such numerous particularities as are almost everywhere to be met with in the Scriptures should be raised out of nothing, or be spun out of the imagination without any fact to go upon.[1]

It is to be remarked, however, that this particularity is only to be looked for in direct history. It is not natural in references or allusions, which yet, in other respects, often afford, as far as they go, the most unsuspicious evidence.

VI. We lay out of the case such stories of supernatural events as require, on the part of the hearer, nothing more than an otiose assent; stories upon which nothing depends, in which no interest is involved, nothing is to be done or changed in consequence of believing them. Such stories are credited, if the careless assent that is given to them deserve that name, more by the indolence of the hearer, than by his judgment: or, though not much credited, are passed from one to another without inquiry or resistance. To this case, and to this case alone, belongs what is called the love of the marvellous. I have never known it carry men further. Men do not suffer persecution from the love of the marvellous. Of the indifferent nature we are speaking of are most vulgar errors and popular superstition: most, for instance, of the current reports of apparitions. Nothing depends upon their being true or false. But not, surely, of this kind were the alleged miracles of Christ and his apostles. They decided, if true, the most important question upon which the human mind can fix its anxiety. They claimed to regulate the opinions of mankind upon subjects in which they are not only deeply concerned, but usually refractory and obstinate. Men could not be utterly careless in such a case as this. If a Jew took up the story, he found his darling partiality to his own nation and law wounded; if a Gentile, he found his idolatry and polytheism reprobated and

---

[1] "There is always some truth where there are considerable particularities related, and they always seem to bear some proportion to one another. Thus, there is a great want of the particulars of time, place, and persons in Manetho's account of the Egyptian Dynasties, Etesias's of the Assyrian Kings, and those which the technical chronologers have given of the ancient kingdoms of Greece; and, agreeably thereto, the accounts have much fiction and falsehood, with some truth: whereas Thucydides's History of the Peloponnesian War, and Caesar's of the War in Gaul, in both which the particulars of time, place, and persons are mentioned, are universally esteemed true to a great degree of exactness." Hartley, vol. ii. p. 109.

condemned. Whoever entertained the account, whether Jew or Gentile, could not avoid the following reflection:—"If these things be true, I must give up the opinions and principles in which I have been brought up, the religion in which my fathers lived and died." It is not conceivable that a man should do this upon any idle report or frivolous account, or, indeed, without being fully satisfied and convinced of the truth and credibility of the narrative to which he trusted. But it did not stop at opinions. They who believed Christianity acted upon it. Many made it the express business of their lives to publish the intelligence. It was required of those who admitted that intelligence to change forthwith their conduct and their principles, to take up a different course of life, to part with their habits and gratifications, and begin a new set of rules and system of behaviour. The apostles, at least, were interested not to sacrifice their ease, their fortunes, and their lives for an idle tale; multitudes beside them were induced, by the same tale, to encounter opposition, danger, and sufferings.

If it be said, that the mere promise of a future state would do all this; I answer, that the mere promise of a future state, without any evidence to give credit or assurance to it, would do nothing. A few wandering fishermen talking of a resurrection of the dead could produce no effect. If it be further said that men easily believe what they anxiously desire; I again answer that in my opinion, the very contrary of this is nearer to the truth. Anxiety of desire, earnestness of expectation, the vastness of an event, rather causes men to disbelieve, to doubt, to dread a fallacy, to distrust, and to examine. When our Lord's resurrection was first reported to the apostles, they did not believe, we are told, for joy. This was natural, and is agreeable to experience.

VII. We have laid out of the case those accounts which require no more than a simple assent; and we now also lay out of the case those which come merely in affirmance of opinions already formed. This last circumstance is of the utmost importance to notice well. It has long been observed, that Popish miracles happen in Popish countries; that they make no converts; which proves that stories are accepted when they fall in with principles already fixed, with the public sentiments, or with the sentiments of a party already engaged on the side the miracle supports, which would not be attempted to be produced in the face of enemies, in opposition to reigning tenets or favourite prejudices, or when, if they be believed, the belief must draw men away from their preconceived and habitual opinions, from their modes of life and rules of action. In the former case, men may not only receive a miraculous account, but may both act and suffer on the side, and, in the cause, which the miracle supports, yet not act or suffer for the miracle, but in pursuance of a prior persuasion. The miracle, like any other argument which only confirms what was before believed, is admitted with little examination. In the moral, as in the natural world, it is change which requires a cause. Men are easily fortified in their old opinions, driven from them with great difficulty. Now how does this apply to the Christian history? The miracles there recorded were wrought in the midst of enemies, under a government, a priesthood, and a magistracy decidedly and vehemently adverse to them, and to the pretensions which they supported. They were Protestant miracles in a Popish country; they were Popish miracles in the midst of Protestants. They produced a change; they established a society upon the spot, adhering to the belief of them; they made converts; and those who were converted gave up to the testimony their most fixed opinions and most favourite prejudices. They who acted and suffered in the cause acted and suffered for the miracles: for there was no anterior persuasion to induce them, no prior reverence, prejudice, or partiality to take hold of Jesus had not one follower when he set up his claim. His miracles gave birth to his sect. No part of this description belongs to the ordinary evidence of Heathen or Popish miracles. Even most of the miracles alleged to have been performed by Christians, in the second and third century of its era, want this confirmation. It constitutes indeed a line of partition between the origin and the progress of Christianity. Frauds and fallacies might mix themselves with the progress, which could not possibly take place in the commencement of the religion; at least, according to any laws of human conduct that we are acquainted with. What should suggest to the first propagators of Christianity, especially to fishermen, tax-gatherers, and husbandmen, such a thought as that of changing the religion of the world; what could bear them through the difficulties in which the attempt engaged them; what could procure any degree of success to the attempt? are questions which apply, with great force, to the setting out of the institution—with less, to every future stage of it.

To hear some men talk, one would suppose the setting up a religion by miracles to be a thing of every day's experience: whereas the whole current of history is against it. Hath any founder of a new sect amongst Christians pretended to miraculous powers, and succeeded by his pretensions? "Were these powers claimed or exercised by the founders of the sects of the Waldenses and Albigenses? Did Wickliffe in England pretend to it? Did Huss or Jerome in Bohemia? Did Luther in Germany, Zuinglius in Switzerland, Calvin in France, or any of the reformers advance this plea?" (Campbell on Miracles, p. 120, ed. 1766.) The French prophets, in the beginning of the present century, (the eighteenth) ventured to allege miraculous evidence, and immediately ruined their cause by their temerity. "Concerning the religion of ancient Rome, of Turkey, of Siam, of China, a single miracle cannot be named that was ever offered as a test of any of those religions before their establishment." (Adams on Mir. p. 75.)

We may add to what has been observed of the distinction which we are considering, that, where miracles are alleged merely in affirmance of a prior opinion, they who believe the doctrine may sometimes propagate a belief of the miracles which they do not themselves entertain. This is the case of what are called pious frauds; but it is a case, I apprehend, which takes place solely in support of a persuasion already established. At least it does not hold of the apostolical history. If the apostles did not believe the miracles, they did not believe the religion; and without this belief, where was the piety, what place was there for anything which could bear the name or colour of piety, in publishing and attesting miracles in its behalf? If it be said that many promote the belief of revelation, and of any accounts which favour that belief, because they think them, whether well or ill founded, of public and political utility; I answer, that if a character exist which can with less justice than another be ascribed to the founders of the Christian religion, it is that of politicians, or of men capable of entertaining political views. The truth is, that there is no assignable character which will account for the conduct of the apostles, supposing their story to be false. If bad men, what could have induced them to take such pains to promote virtue? If good men, they would not have gone about the country with a string of lies in their mouths.

In appreciating the credit of any miraculous story, these are distinctions which relate to the evidence. There are other distinctions, of great moment in the question, which relate to the miracles themselves. Of which latter kind the following ought carefully to be retained.

I. It is not necessary to admit as a miracle what can be resolved into a false perception. Of this nature was the demon of Socrates; the visions of Saint Anthony, and of many others; the vision which Lord Herbert of Cherbury describes himself to have seen; Colonel Gardiner's vision, as related in his life, written by Dr. Doddridge. All these may be accounted for by a momentary insanity; for the characteristic symptom of human madness is the rising up in the mind of images not distinguishable by the patient from impressions upon the senses. (Batty on Lunacy.) The cases, however, in which the possibility of this delusion exists are divided from the cases in which it does not exist by many, and those not obscure marks. They are, for the most part, cases of visions or voices. The object is hardly ever touched. The vision submits not to be handled. One sense does not confirm another. They are likewise almost always cases of a solitary witness. It is in the highest degree improbable, and I know not, indeed, whether it hath ever been the fact, that the same derangement of the mental organs should seize different persons at the same time; a derangement, I mean, so much the same, as to represent to their imagination the same objects. Lastly, these are always cases of momentary miracles; by which term I mean to denote miracles of which the whole existence is of short duration, in contradistinction to miracles which are attended with permanent effects. The appearance of a spectre, the hearing of a supernatural sound, is a momentary miracle. The sensible proof is gone when the apparition or sound is over. But if a person born blind be restored to sight, a notorious cripple to the use of his limbs, or a dead man to life, here is a permanent effect produced by supernatural means. The change indeed was instantaneous, but the proof continues. The subject of the miracle remains. The man cured or restored is there: his former condition was known, and his present condition may be examined. This can by no possibility be resolved into false perception: and of this kind are by far the greater part of the miracles recorded in the New Testament. When Lazarus was raised from the dead, he did not merely move, and speak, and die again; or come out of the grave, and vanish away. He returned to his home and family, and there continued; for we find him some time afterwards in the same town, sitting at table with Jesus and his sisters; visited by great multitudes of the Jews as a subject of curiosity; giving, by his presence, so much uneasiness to the Jewish rulers as to beget in them a design of destroying him. (John xii. 1, 2, 9, 10.) No delusion can account for this. The French prophets in England, some time since, gave out that one of their teachers would come to life again; but their enthusiasm never made them believe that they actually saw him alive. The blind man whose restoration to sight at Jerusalem is recorded in the ninth chapter of Saint John's Gospel did not quit the place or conceal himself from inquiry. On the contrary, he was forthcoming, to answer the call, to satisfy the scrutiny, and to sustain the browbeating of Christ's angry and powerful enemies. When the cripple at the gate of the temple was suddenly cured by Peter, (Acts iii. 2.) he did not immediately relapse into his former lameness, or disappear out of the city; but boldly and honestly produced himself along with the apostles, when they were brought the next day before the Jewish council. (Acts iv. 14.) Here, though the miracle was sudden, the proof was permanent. The lameness had been notorious, the cure continued. This, therefore, could not be the effect of any momentary delirium, either in the subject or in the witnesses of the transaction. It is the same with the greatest number of the Scripture miracles. There are other cases of a mixed nature, in which, although the principal miracle be momentary, some circumstance combined with it is permanent. Of this kind is the history of Saint Paul's conversion. (Acts ix.) The sudden light and sound, the vision and the voice upon the road to Damascus, were momentary: but Paul's blindness for three days in consequence of what had happened; the communication made to Ananias in another place, and by a vision independent of the former; Ananias finding out Paul in consequence of intelligence so received, and finding him in the condition described, and Paul's recovery of his sight upon Ananias laying his hands upon him; are circumstances which take the transaction, and the principal miracle as included in it, entirely out of the case of momentary miracles, or of such as may be accounted for by false perceptions. Exactly the same thing may be observed of Peter's vision preparatory to the call of Cornelius, and of its connexion with what was imparted in a distant place to Cornelius himself, and with the message despatched by Cornelius to Peter. The vision might be a dream; the message could not. Either communication taken separately, might be a delusion; the concurrence of the two was impossible to happen without a supernatural cause.

Beside the risk of delusion which attaches upon momentary miracles, there is also much more room for imposture. The account cannot be examined at the moment: and when that is also a moment of hurry and confusion, it may not be difficult for men of influence to gain credit to any story which they may wish to have believed. This is precisely the case of one of the best attested of the miracles of Old Rome, the appearance of Castor and Pollux in the battle fought by Posthumius with the Latins at the lake Regillus. There is no doubt but that Posthumius, after the battle, spread the report of such an appearance. No person could deny it whilst it was said to last. No person, perhaps, had any inclination to dispute it afterwards; or, if they had, could say with positiveness what was or what was not seen by some or other of the army, in the dismay and amidst the tumult of a battle.

In assigning false perceptions as the origin to which some miraculous accounts may be referred, I have not mentioned claims to inspiration, illuminations, secret notices or directions, internal sensations, or consciousnesses of being acted upon by spiritual influences, good or bad, because these, appealing to no external proof, however convincing they may be to the persons themselves, form no part of what can be accounted miraculous evidence. Their own credibility stands upon their alliance with other miracles. The discussion, therefore, of all such pretensions may be omitted.

II. It is not necessary to bring into the comparison what may be called tentative miracles; that is, where, out of a great number of trials, some succeed; and in the accounts of which, although the narrative of the successful cases be alone preserved, and that of the unsuccessful cases sunk, yet enough is stated to show that the cases produced are only a few out of many in which the same means have been employed. This observation bears with considerable force upon the ancient oracles and auguries, in which a single coincidence of the event with the prediction is talked of and magnified, whilst failures are forgotten, or suppressed, or accounted for. It is also applicable to the cures wrought by relics, and at the tombs of saints. The boasted efficacy of the king's touch, upon which Mr. Hume lays some stress, falls under the same description. Nothing is alleged concerning it which is not alleged of various nostrums, namely, out of many thousands who have used them, certified proofs of a few who have recovered after them. No solution of this sort is applicable to the miracles of the Gospel. There is nothing in the narrative which can induce, or even allow, us to believe, that Christ attempted cures in many instances, and succeeded in a few; or that he ever made the attempt in vain. He did not profess to heal everywhere all that were sick; on the contrary, he told the Jews, evidently meaning to represent his own case, that, "although many widows were in Israel in the days of Elias, when the heaven was shut up three years and six months, when great famine was throughout all the land, yet unto none of them was Elias sent, save unto Sarepta, a city of Sidon, unto a woman that was a widow:" and that "many lepers were in Israel in the time of Eliseus the prophet, and none of them was cleansed saving Naaman the Syrian." (Luke iv. 25.) By which examples he gave them to understand, that it was not the nature of a Divine interposition, or necessary to its purpose, to be general; still less to answer every challenge that might be made, which would teach men to put their faith upon these experiments. Christ never pronounced the word, but the effect followed.[2]

It was not a thousand sick that received his benediction, and a few that were benefited; a single paralytic is let down in his bed at Jesus's feet, in the midst of a surrounding multitude; Jesus bid him walk, and he did so. (Mark ii. 3.) A man with a withered hand is in the synagogue; Jesus bid him stretch forth his hand in the presence of the assembly, and it was "restored whole like the other." (Matt. xii. 10.) There was nothing tentative in these cures; nothing that can be explained by the power of accident.

We may observe, also, that many of the cures which Christ wrought, such as that of a person blind from his birth; also many miracles besides cures, as raising the dead, walking upon the sea, feeding a great multitude with a few loaves and fishes, are of a nature which does not in anywise admit of the supposition of a fortunate experiment.

III. We may dismiss from the question all accounts in which, allowing the phenomenon to be real, the fact to be true, it still remains doubtful whether a miracle were wrought. This is the case with the ancient history of what is called the thundering legion, of the extraordinary circumstances which obstructed the rebuilding of the temple at Jerusalem by Julian; the circling of the flames and fragrant smell at the martyrdom of Polycarp; the sudden shower that extinguished the fire into which the Scriptures were thrown in the Diocletian persecution; Constantine's dream; his inscribing in consequence of it the cross upon his standard and the shields of his soldiers; his victory, and the escape of the standard-bearer; perhaps, also, the imagined appearance of the cross in the heavens, though this last

---

[2] One, and only one, instance may be produced in which the disciples of Christ do seem to have attempted a cure, and not to have been able to perform it. The story is very ingenuously related by three of the evangelists. (Matt. xvii. 14. Mark ix. 14. Luke ix. 33.) The patient was afterwards healed by Christ himself; and the whole transaction seems to have been intended, as it was well suited, to display the superiority of Christ above all who performed miracles in his name, a distinction which, during his presence in the world, it might be necessary to inculcate by some such proof as this.

circumstance is very deficient in historical evidence. It is also the case with the modern annual exhibition of the liquefaction of the blood of Saint Januarius at Naples. It is a doubt, likewise, which ought to be excluded by very special circumstances from those narratives which relate to the supernatural cure of hypochondriacal and nervous complaints, and of all diseases which are much affected by the imagination. The miracles of the second and third century are, usually, healing the sick and casting out evil spirits, miracles in which there is room for some error and deception. We hear nothing of causing the blind to see, the lame to walk, the deaf to hear, the lepers to be cleansed. (Jortin's Remarks, vol. ii. p. 51.) There are also instances in Christian writers of reputed miracles, which were natural operations, though not known to be such at the time; as that of articulate speech after the loss of a great part of the tongue.

IV. To the same head of objection, nearly, may also be referred accounts in which the variation of a small circumstance may have transformed some extraordinary appearance, or some critical coincidence of events, into a miracle; stories, in a word, which may be resolved into exaggeration. The miracles of the Gospel can by no possibility be explained away in this manner. Total fiction will account for anything; but no stretch of exaggeration that has any parallel in other histories, no force of fancy upon real circumstances, could produce the narratives which we now have. The feeding of the five thousand with a few loaves and fishes surpasses all bounds of exaggeration. The raising of Lazarus, of the widow's son at Nain, as well as many of the cures which Christ wrought, come not within the compass of misrepresentation. I mean that it is impossible to assign any position of circumstances however peculiar, any accidental effects however extraordinary, any natural singularity, which could supply an origin or foundation to these accounts.

Having thus enumerated several exceptions which may justly be taken to relations of miracles, it is necessary, when we read the Scriptures, to bear in our minds this general remark; that although there be miracles recorded in the New Testament, which fall within some or other of the exceptions here assigned, yet that they are united with others, to which none of the same exceptions extend, and that their credibility stands upon this union. Thus the visions and revelations which Saint Paul asserts to have been imparted to him may not, in their separate evidence, be distinguishable from the visions and revelations which many others have alleged. But here is the difference. Saint Paul's pretensions were attested by external miracles wrought by himself, and by miracles wrought in the cause to which these visions relate; or, to speak more properly, the same historical authority which informs us of one informs us of the other. This is not ordinarily true of the visions of enthusiasts, or even of the accounts in which they are contained. Again, some of Christ's own miracles were momentary; as the transfiguration, the appearance and voice from Heaven at his baptism, a voice from the clouds on one occasion afterwards (John xii. 28), and some others. It is not denied, that the distinction which we have proposed concerning miracles of this species applies, in diminution of the force of the evidence, as much to these instances as to others. But this is the case not with all the miracles ascribed to Christ, nor with the greatest part, nor with many. Whatever force therefore there may be in the objection, we have numerous miracles which are free from it; and even those to which it is applicable are little affected by it in their credit, because there are few who, admitting the rest, will reject them. If there be miracles of the New Testament which come within any of the other heads into which we have distributed the objections, the same remark must be repeated. And this is one way in which the unexampled number and variety of the miracles ascribed to Christ strengthen the credibility of Christianity. For it precludes any solution, or conjecture about a solution, which imagination, or even which experience might suggest, concerning some particular miracles, if considered independently of others. The miracles of Christ were of various kinds,[3] and performed in great varieties of situation, form, and manner; at Jerusalem, the metropolis of the Jewish nation and religion; in different parts of Judea and Galilee; in cities and villages; in synagogues, in private houses; in the street, in highways; with preparation, as in the case of Lazarus; by accident, as in the case of the widow's son of Nain; when attended by multitudes, and when alone with the patient; in the midst of his disciples, and in the presence of his enemies; with the common people around him, and before Scribes and Pharisees, and rulers of the synagogues.

I apprehend that, when we remove from the comparison the cases which are fairly disposed of by the observations that have been stated, many cases will not remain. To those which do remain, we apply this final distinction; "that there is not satisfactory evidence that persons pretending to be original witnesses of the miracles passed their lives in labours, dangers, and sufferings, voluntarily undertaken and undergone in attestation of the accounts which they delivered, and properly in consequence of their belief of the truth of those accounts."

---

[3] Not only healing every species of disease, but turning water into wine (John ii.); feeding multitudes with a few loaves and fishes (Matt. xiv. 15; Mark vi. 35; Luke ix. 12; John vi. 5); walking on the sea (Matt. xiv. 25); calming a storm (Matt. viii. 26; Luke viii. 24); a celestial voice at his baptism, and miraculous appearance (Matt. iii. 16; afterwards John xii. 28); his transfiguration (Matt. xvii. 18; Mark ix. 2; Luke ix. 28; 2 Peter i. 16, 17); raising the dead in three distinct instances (Matt. ix. 18; Mark v. 22; Luke vii. 14; viii. 41; John xi.).

CHAPTER II.

But they with whom we argue have undoubtedly a right to select their own examples. The instances with which Mr. Hume has chosen to confront the miracles of the New Testament, and which, therefore, we are entitled to regard as the strongest which the history of the world could supply to the inquiries of a very acute and learned adversary, are the three following:

I. The cure of a blind and of a lame man of Alexandria, by the emperor Vespasian, as related by Tacitus;

II. The restoration of the limb of an attendant in a Spanish church, as told by Cardinal de Retz; and,

III. The cures said to be performed at the tomb of the abbe Paris in the early part of the eighteenth century.

I. The narrative of Tacitus is delivered in these terms: "One of the common people of Alexandria, known to be diseased in his eyes, by the admonition of the god Serapis, whom that superstitious nation worship above all other gods, prostrated himself before the emperor, earnestly imploring from him a remedy for his blindness, and entreating that he would deign to anoint with his spittle his cheeks and the balls of his eyes. Another, diseased in his hand, requested, by the admonition of the same god, that he might be touched by the foot of the emperor. Vespasian at first derided and despised their application; afterwards, when they continued to urge their petitions, he sometimes appeared to dread the imputation of vanity; at other times, by the earnest supplication of the patients, and the persuasion of his flatterers, to be induced to hope for success. At length he commanded an inquiry to be made by the physicians, whether such a blindness and debility were vincible by human aid. The report of the physicians contained various points: that in the one, the power of vision was not destroyed, but would return if the obstacles were removed; that in the other, the diseased joints might be restored, if a healing power were applied; that it was, perhaps, agreeable to the gods to do this; that the emperor was elected by divine assistance; lastly, that the credit of the success would be the emperor's, the ridicule of the disappointment would fall upon the patients. Vespasian believing that everything was in the power of his fortune, and that nothing was any longer incredible, whilst the multitude which stood by eagerly expected the event, with a countenance expressive of joy, executed what he was desired to do. Immediately the hand was restored to its use, and light returned to the blind man. They who were present relate both these cures, even at this time, when there is nothing to be gained by lying." (Tacit. Hist. lib. iv.)

Now, though Tacitus wrote this account twenty-seven years after the miracle is said to have been performed, and wrote at Rome of what passed at Alexandria, and wrote also from report; and although it does not appear that he had examined the story or that he believed it, (but rather the contrary,) yet I think his testimony sufficient to prove that such a transaction took place: by which I mean, that the two men in question did apply to Vespasian; that Vespasian did touch the diseased in the manner related; and that a cure was reported to have followed the operation. But the affair labours under a strong and just suspicion, that the whole of it was a concerted imposture brought about by collusion between the patients, the physician, and the emperor. This solution is probable, because there was everything to suggest, and everything to facilitate such a scheme. The miracle was calculated to confer honour upon the emperor, and upon the god Serapis. It was achieved in the midst of the emperor's flatterers and followers; in a city and amongst a populace before-hand devoted to his interest, and to the worship of the god: where it would have been treason and blasphemy together to have contradicted the fame of the cure, or even to have questioned it. And what is very observable in the account is, that the report of the physicians is just such a report as would have been made of a case in which no external marks of the disease existed, and which, consequently, was capable of being easily counterfeited; viz. that in the first of the patients the organs of vision were not destroyed, that the weakness of the second was in his joints. The strongest circumstance in Tacitus's narration is, that the first patient was "notus tabe oculorum," remarked or notorious for the disease in his eyes. But this was a circumstance which might have found its way into the story in its progress from a distant country, and during an interval of thirty years; or it might be true that the malady of the eyes was notorious, yet that the nature and degree of the disease had never been ascertained; a case by no means uncommon. The emperor's reserve was easily affected: or it is possible he might not be in the secret. There does not seem to be much weight in the observation of Tacitus, that they who were present continued even then to relate the story when there was nothing to be gained by the lie. It only proves that those who had told the story for many years persisted in it. The state of mind of the witnesses and spectators at the time is the point to be attended to. Still less is there of pertinency in Mr. Hume's eulogium on the cautious and penetrating genius of the historian; for it does not appear that the historian believed it. The terms in which he speaks of Serapis, the deity to whose interposition the miracle was attributed, scarcely suffer us to suppose that Tacitus thought the miracle to be real: "by the admonition of the god Serapis, whom that superstitious nation (dedita superstitionibus gens) worship above all other gods." To have brought this supposed miracle within the limits of comparison with the miracles of Christ, it ought to have appeared that a person of a low and private station, in the midst of enemies, with the whole power of the country opposing him, with every one around him prejudiced or interested against his claims and character, pretended to perform these cures, and required the spectators, upon the strength of what they saw, to give up their firmest hopes and opinions, and follow him through a life of trial and danger; that many were so moved as to obey his call, at the expense both of every notion in which they had been brought up, and of their ease, safety, and reputation; and that by these beginnings a change was produced in the world, the effects of which remain to this day: a case, both in its circumstances and consequences, very unlike anything we find in Tacitus's relation.

II. The story taken from the Memoirs of Cardinal de Retz, which is the second example alleged by Mr. Hume, is this: "In the church of Saragossa in Spain, the canons showed me a man whose business it was to light the lamps; telling me, that he had been several years at the gate with one leg only. I saw him with two." (Liv. iv. A.D. 1654.)

It is stated by Mr. Hume, that the cardinal who relates this story did not believe it; and it nowhere appears that he either examined the limb, or asked the patient, or indeed any one, a single question about the matter. An artificial leg, wrought with art, would be sufficient, in a place where no such contrivance had ever before been heard of, to give origin and currency to the report. The ecclesiastics of the place would, it is probable, favour the story, inasmuch as it advanced the honour of their image and church. And if they patronized it, no other person at Saragossa, in the middle of the last century, would care to dispute it. The story likewise coincided not less with the wishes and preconceptions of the people than with the interests of their ecclesiastical rulers: so that there was prejudice backed by authority, and both operating upon extreme ignorance, to account for the success of the imposture. If, as I have suggested, the contrivance of an artificial limb was then new, it would not occur to the cardinal himself to suspect it; especially under the carelessness of mind with which he heard the tale, and the little inclination he felt to scrutinize or expose its fallacy.

III. The miracles related to have been wrought at the tomb of the abbe Paris admit in general of this solution. The patients who frequented the tomb were so affected by their devotion, their expectation, the place, the solemnity, and, above all, by the sympathy of the surrounding multitude, that many of them were thrown into violent convulsions, which convulsions, in certain instances, produced a removal of disorder, depending upon obstruction. We shall, at this day, have the less difficulty in admitting the above account, because it is the very same thing as hath lately been experienced in the operations of animal magnetism: and the report of the French physicians upon that mysterious remedy is very applicable to the present consideration, viz. that the pretenders to the art, by working upon the imaginations of their patients, were frequently able to produce convulsions; that convulsions so produced are amongst the most powerful, but, at the same time, most uncertain and unmanageable applications to the human frame which can be employed.

Circumstances which indicate this explication, in the case of the Parisian miracles, are the following:

1. They were tentative. Out of many thousand sick, infirm, and diseased persons who resorted to the tomb, the professed history of the miracles contains only nine cures.

2. The convulsions at the tomb are admitted.

3. The diseases were, for the most part, of that sort which depends upon inaction and obstruction, as dropsies, palsies, and some tumours.

4. The cures were gradual; some patients attending many days, some several weeks, and some several months.

5. The cures were many of them incomplete.

6. Others were temporary. (The reader will find these particulars verified in the detail, by the accurate inquiries of the present bishop of Sarum, in his Criterion of Miracles, p. 132, et seq.)

So that all the wonder we are called upon to account for is, that out of an almost innumerable multitude which resorted to the tomb for the cure of their complaints, and many of whom were there agitated by strong convulsions, a very small proportion experienced a beneficial change in their constitution, especially in the action of the nerves and glands.

Some of the cases alleged do not require that we should have recourse to this solution. The first case in the catalogue is scarcely distinguishable from the progress of a natural recovery. It was that of a young man who laboured under an inflammation of one eye, and had lost the sight of the other. The inflamed eye was relieved, but the blindness of the other remained. The inflammation had before been abated by medicine; and the young man, at the time of his attendance at the tomb, was using a lotion of laudanum. And, what is a still more material part of the case, the inflammation, after some interval, returned. Another case was that of a young man who had lost his sight by the puncture of an awl, and the discharge of the aqueous humour through the wound. The sight, which had been gradually returning, was much improved during his visit to the tomb, that is, probably in the same degree in which the discharged humour was replaced by fresh secretions. And it is observable, that these two are the only cases which, from their nature, should seem unlikely to be affected by convulsions.

In one material respect I allow that the Parisian miracles were different from those related by Tacitus, and from the Spanish miracle of the cardinal de Retz. They had not, like them, all the power and all the prejudice of the country on their side to begin with. They were alleged by one party against another, by the Jansenists against the Jesuits. These were of course opposed and examined by their adversaries. The consequence of which examination was that many falsehoods were detected, that with something really extraordinary much fraud appeared to be mixed. And if some of the cases upon which designed misrepresentation could not be charged were not at the time satisfactorily accounted for, it was because the efficacy of strong spasmodic affections was not then sufficiently known. Finally, the cause of Jansenism did not rise by the miracles, but sunk, although the miracles had the anterior persuasion of all the numerous adherents of that cause to set out with.

These, let us remember, are the strongest examples which the history of ages supplies. In none of them was the miracle unequivocal; by none of them were established prejudices and persuasions overthrown; of none of them did the credit make its way, in opposition to authority and power; by none of them were many induced to commit themselves, and that in contradiction to prior opinions, to a life of mortification, danger, and sufferings; none were called upon to attest them at the expense of their fortunes and safety.[1]

---

[1] It may be thought that the historian of the Parisian miracles, M. Montgeron, forms an exception to this last assertion. He presented his book (with a suspicion, as it should seem, of the danger of what he was doing) to the king; and was shortly afterwards committed to prison; from which he never came out. Had the miracles been unequivocal, and had M. Montgeron been originally convinced by them, I should have allowed this exception. It would have stood, I think, alone in the argument of our adversaries. But, beside what has been observed of the dubious nature of the miracles, the account which M. Montgeron has himself left of his conversion shows both the state of his mind and that his persuasion was not built upon external miracles.—"Scarcely had he entered the churchyard when he was struck," he tells us, "with awe and reverence, having never before heard prayers pronounced with so much ardour and transport as he observed amongst the supplicants at the tomb. Upon this, throwing himself on his knees, resting his elbows on the tombstone and covering his face with his hands, he spake the following prayer. O thou, by whose intercession so many miracles are said to be performed, if it be true that a part of thee surviveth the grave, and that thou hast influence with the Almighty, have pity on the darkness of my understanding, and through his mercy obtain the removal of it." Having prayed thus, "many thoughts," as he sayeth, "began to open themselves to his mind; and so profound was his attention that he continued on his knees four hours, not in the least disturbed by the vast crowd of surrounding supplicants. During this time, all the arguments which he ever heard or read in favour of Christianity occurred to him with so much force, and seemed so strong and convincing, that he went home fully satisfied of the truth of religion in general, and of the holiness and power of that person who," as he supposed, "had engaged the Divine Goodness to enlighten his understanding so suddenly." (Douglas's Crit of Mir. p. 214.)

PART II.

OF THE AUXILIARY EVIDENCES OF CHRISTIANITY

CHAPTER I.

PROPHECY.

Isaiah iii. 13; liii. "Behold, my servant shall deal prudently; he shall be exalted and extolled, and be very high. As many were astonished at thee; his visage was so marred more than any man, and his form more than the sons of men: so shall he sprinkle many nations; the kings shall shut their mouths at him: for that which had not been told them shall they see; and that which they had not heard shall they consider. Who hath believed our report? and to whom is the arm of the Lord revealed? For he shall grow up before him as a tender plant, and as a root out of a dry ground: he hath no form nor comeliness; and when we shall see him, there is no beauty that we should desire him. He is despised and rejected of men, a man of sorrows, and acquainted with grief: and we hid, as it were, our faces from him: he was despised, and we esteemed him not. Surely he hath borne our griefs, and carried our sorrows: yet we did esteem him stricken, smitten of God, and afflicted. But he was wounded for our transgressions, he was bruised for our iniquities, the chastisement of our peace was upon him; and with his stripes we are healed. All we like sheep have gone astray; we have turned every one to his own way; and the Lord hath laid on him the iniquity of us all. He was oppressed, and he was afflicted, yet he opened not his mouth: he is brought as a lamb to the slaughter, and as a sheep before her shearers is dumb, so he opened not his mouth. He was taken from prison and from judgment; and who shall declare his generation? for he was cut off out of the land of the living: for the transgression of my people was he stricken. And he made his grave with the wicked, and with the rich in his death; because he had done no violence, neither was any deceit in his mouth. Yet it pleased the Lord to bruise him; he hath put him to grief. When thou shalt make his soul an offering for sin, he shall see his seed, he shall prolong his days, and the pleasure of the Lord shall prosper in his hand. He shall see of the travail of his soul, and shall be satisfied: by his knowledge shall my righteous servant justify many; for he shall bear their iniquities. Therefore will I divide him a portion with the great, and he shall divide the spoil with the strong; because he hath poured out his soul unto death; and he was numbered with the transgressors, and he bare the sin of many, and made intercession for the transgressors."

These words are extant in a book purporting to contain the predictions of a writer who lived seven centuries before the Christian era.

That material part of every argument from prophecy, namely, that the words alleged were actually spoken or written before the fact to which they are applied took place, or could by any natural means be foreseen, is, in the present instance, incontestable. The record comes out of the custody of adversaries. The Jews, as an ancient father well observed, are our librarians. The passage is in their copies as well as in ours. With many attempts to explain it away, none has ever been made by them to discredit its authenticity.

And what adds to the force of the quotation is, that it is taken from a writing declaredly prophetic; a writing professing to describe such future transactions and changes in the world as were connected with the fate and interests of the Jewish nation. It is not a passage in an historical or devotional composition, which, because it turns out to be applicable to some future events, or to some future situation of affairs, is presumed to have been oracular. The words of Isaiah were delivered by him in a prophetic character, with the solemnity belonging to that character: and what he so delivered was all along understood by the Jewish reader to refer to something that was to take place after the time of the author. The public sentiments of the Jews concerning the design of Isaiah's writings are set forth in the book of Ecclesiasticus:[1] "He saw by an excellent spirit what should come to pass at the last, and he comforted them that mourned in Sion. He showed what should come to pass for ever, and secret things or ever they came."

It is also an advantage which this prophecy possesses, that it is intermixed with no other subject. It is entire, separate, and uninterruptedly directed to one scene of things.

The application of the prophecy to the evangelic history is plain and appropriate. Here is no double sense; no figurative language but what is sufficiently intelligible to every reader of every country. The obscurities (by which I mean the expressions that require a knowledge of local diction, and of local allusion) are few, and not of great importance. Nor have I found that varieties of reading, or a different construing of the original, produce any material alteration in the sense of the prophecy. Compare the common translation with that of Bishop Lowth, and the difference is not considerable. So far as they do differ, Bishop Lowth's corrections, which are the faithful result of an accurate examination, bring the description nearer to the New Testament history than it was before. In the fourth verse of the fifty-third chapter, what our bible renders "stricken" he translates "judicially stricken:" and in the eighth verse, the clause "he was taken from prison and from judgment," the bishop gives "by an oppressive judgment he was taken off." The next words to these, "who shall declare his generation?" are much cleared up in their meaning

---

[1] Chap. xlviii. ver. 24.

by the bishop's version; "his manner of life who would declare?" i.e. who would stand forth in his defence? The former part of the ninth verse, "and he made his grave with the wicked, and with the rich in his death," which inverts the circumstances of Christ's passion, the bishop brings out in an order perfectly agreeable to the event; "and his grave was appointed with the wicked, but with the rich man was his tomb." The words in the eleventh verse, "by his knowledge shall my righteous servant justify many," are, in the bishop's version, "by the knowledge of him shall my righteous servant justify many."

It is natural to inquire what turn the Jews themselves give to this prophecy.[2] There is good proof that the ancient Rabbins explained it of their expected Messiah:[3] but their modern expositors concur, I think, in representing it as a description of the calamitous state, and intended restoration, of the Jewish people, who are here, as they say, exhibited under the character of a single person. I have not discovered that their exposition rests upon any critical arguments, or upon these in any other than in a very minute degree.

The clause in the ninth verse, which we render "for the transgression of my people was he stricken," and in the margin, "was the stroke upon him," the Jews read "for the transgression of my people was the stroke upon them." And what they allege in support of the alteration amounts only to this, that the Hebrew pronoun is capable of a plural as well as of a singular signification; that is to say, is capable of their construction as well as ours.[4] And this is all the variation contended for; the rest of the

---

[2] "Vaticinium hoc Esaiae est carnificina Rabbinorum, de quo aliqui Judaei mihi confessi sunt, Rabbinos suos ex propheticis scripturis facile se extricare potuisse, modo; Esaias tacuisset." Hulse, Theol. Jud. P. 318, quoted by Poole, in loc.

[3] Hulse, Theol. Jud. p. 430.

[4] Bishop Lowth adopts in this place the reading of the seventy, which gives smitten to death, "for the transgression of my people was he smitten to death." The addition of the words "to death" makes an end of the Jewish interpretation of the clause. And the authority upon which this reading (though not given by the present Hebrew text) is adopted, Dr. Kennicot has set forth by an argument not only so cogent, but so clear and popular, that I beg leave to transcribe the substance of it into this note:—"Origen, after having quoted at large this prophecy concerning the Messiah, tells us that, having once made use of this passage, in a dispute against some that were accounted wise amongst the Jews, one of them replied that the words did not mean one man, but one people, the Jews, who were smitten of God, and dispersed among the Gentiles for their conversion; that he then urged many parts of this prophecy to show the absurdity of this interpretation, and that he seemed to press them the hardest by this sentence,—'for the transgression of my people was he smitten to death.'" Now as Origen, the author of the Hexapla, must have understood Hebrew, we cannot suppose that he would have urged this last text as so decisive, if the Greek

prophecy they read as we do. The probability, therefore, of their exposition is a subject of which we are as capable of judging as themselves. This judgment is open indeed to the good sense of every attentive reader. The application which the Jews contend for appears to me to labour under insuperable difficulties; in particular, it may be demanded of them to explain in whose name or person, if the Jewish people he the sufferer, does the prophet speak, when he says, "He hath borne our griefs, and carried our sorrows, yet we did esteem him stricken, smitten of God, and afflicted; but he was wounded for our transgressions, he was bruised for our iniquities, the chastisement of our peace was upon him, and with his stripes we are healed." Again, the description in the seventh verse, "he was oppressed and he was afflicted, yet he opened not his mouth; he is brought as a lamb to the slaughter, and as a sheep before her shearers is dumb, so he opened not his mouth," quadrates with no part of the Jewish history with which we are acquainted. The mention of the "grave" and the "tomb," in the ninth verse, is not very applicable to the fortunes of a nation; and still less so is the conclusion of the prophecy in the twelfth verse, which expressly represents the sufferings as voluntary, and the sufferer as interceding for the offenders; "because he hath poured out his soul unto death, and he was numbered with the transgressors, and he bare the sin of many, and made intercession for the transgressors."

There are other prophecies of the Old Testament, interpreted by Christians to relate to the Gospel history, which are deserving both of great regard and of a very attentive consideration: but I content myself with stating the above, as well because I think it the clearest and the strongest of all, as because most of the rest, in order that their value might be represented with any tolerable degree of fidelity, require a discussion unsuitable to the limits and nature of this work. The reader will find them disposed in order, and distinctly explained, in Bishop Chandler's treatise

---

version had not agreed here with the Hebrew text; nor that these wise Jews would have been at all distressed by this quotation, unless the Hebrew text had read agreeably to the words "to death," on which the argument principally depended; for by quoting it immediately, they would have triumphed over him, and reprobated his Greek version. This, whenever they could do it was their constant practice in their disputes with the Christians. Origen himself, who laboriously compared the Hebrew text with the Septuagint, has recorded the necessity of arguing with the Jews from such passages only as were in the Septuagint agreeable to the Hebrew. Wherefore, as Origen had carefully compared the Greek version of the Septuagint with the Hebrew text; and as he puzzled and confounded the learned Jews, by urging upon them the reading "to death" in this place; it seems almost impossible not to conclude, both from Origen's argument and the silence of his Jewish adversaries, that the Hebrew text at that time actually had the word agreeably to the version of the seventy. Lowth's Isaiah, p. 242.

on the subject; and he will bear in mind, what has been often, and, I think, truly, urged by the advocates of Christianity, that there is no other eminent person to the history of whose life so many circumstances can be made to apply. They who object that much has been done by the power of chance, the ingenuity of accommodation, and the industry of research, ought to try whether the same, or anything like it, could be done, if Mahomet, or any other person, were proposed as the subject of Jewish prophecy.

II. A second head of argument from prophecy is founded upon our Lord's predictions concerning the destruction of Jerusalem, recorded by three out of the four evangelists.

Luke xxi. 5-25. "And as some spake of the temple, how it was adorned with goodly stones and gifts, he said, As for these things which ye behold, the days will come in which there shall not be left one stone upon another, that shall not be thrown down. And they asked him, saying, Master, but when shall these things be? and what sign will there be when these things shall come to pass? And he said, Take heed that ye be not deceived; for many shall come in my name, saying, I am Christ; and the time draweth near; go ye not therefore after them. But when ye shall hear of wars and commotions, be not terrified: for these things must first come to pass; but the end is not by-and-by. Then said he unto them, Nation shall rise against nation, and kingdom against kingdom; and great earth-quakes shall be in divers places, and famines and pestilences; and fearful sights, and great signs shall there be from heaven. But before all these, they shall lay their hands on you, and persecute you, delivering you up to the synagogues, and into prisons, being brought before kings and rulers for my name's sake. And it shall turn to you for a testimony. Settle it therefore in your hearts not to meditate before what ye shall answer: for I will give you a mouth and wisdom, which all your adversaries shall not be able to gainsay nor resist. And ye shall be betrayed both by parents, and brethren, and kinsfolk, and friends; and some of you shall they cause to be put to death. And ye shall be hated of all men for my name's sake. But there shall not an hair of your head perish. In your patience possess ye your souls. And when ye shall see Jerusalem compassed with armies, then know that the desolation thereof is nigh. Then let them which are in Judea flee to the mountains; and let them which are in the midst of it depart out; and let not them that are in the countries enter thereinto. For these be the days of vengeance, that all things which are written may be fulfilled. But woe unto them that are with child and to them that give suck in those days: for there shall be great distress in the land, and wrath upon this people. And they shall fall by the edge of the sword, and shall be led away captive into all nations: and Jerusalem shall be trodden down by the Gentiles, until the times of the Gentiles be fulfilled."

In terms nearly similar, this discourse is related in the twenty-fourth chapter of Matthew and the thirteenth of Mark. The prospect of the same evils drew from our Saviour, on another occasion, the following affecting expressions of concern, which are preserved by St. Luke (xix. 41—44): "And when he was come near, he beheld the city and wept over it, saying, If thou hadst known, even thou, at least in this thy day, the things which belong unto thy peace! but now they are hid from thine eyes. For the day shall come upon thee, that thine enemies shall cast a trench about thee, and compass thee round and keep thee in on every side, and shall lay thee even with the ground, and thy children within thee; and they shall not leave in thee one stone upon another; because thou knowest not the time of thy visitation"—These passages are direct and explicit predictions. References to the same event, some plain, some parabolical, or otherwise figurative, are found in divers other discourses of our Lord. (Matt. xxi. 33-46; xxii. 1-7. Mark xii. 1-12. Luke xiii. 1-9; xx. 9-20; xxi. 5-13.)

The general agreement of the description with the event, viz. with the ruin of the Jewish nation, and the capture of Jerusalem under Vespasian, thirty-six years after Christ's death, is most evident; and the accordancy in various articles of detail and circumstances has been shown by many learned writers. It is also an advantage to the inquiry, and to the argument built upon it, that we have received a copious account of the transaction from Josephus, a Jewish and contemporary historian. This part of the case is perfectly free from doubt. The only question which, in my opinion, can be raised upon the subject is, whether the prophecy was really delivered before the event? I shall apply, therefore, my observations to this point solely.

1. The judgment of antiquity, though varying in the precise year of the publication of the three Gospels, concurs in assigning them a date prior to the destruction of Jerusalem. (Lardner, vol. xiii.)

2. This judgment is confirmed by a strong probability arising from the course of human life. The destruction of Jerusalem took place in the seventieth year after the birth of Christ. The three evangelists, one of whom was his immediate companion, and the other two associated with his companions, were, it is probable, not much younger than he was. They must, consequently, have been far advanced in life when Jerusalem was taken; and no reason has been given why they should defer writing their histories so long.

3. (Le Clerc, Diss. III. de Quat. Evang. num. vii. p. 541.) If the evangelists, at the time of writing the Gospels, had known of the destruction of Jerusalem, by which catastrophe the prophecies were plainly fulfilled, it is most probable that, in recording the predictions, they would have dropped some word or other about the completion; in like manner as Luke, after relating the denunciation of a dearth by Agabus, adds, "which came to pass in the days of Claudius Caesar;" (Acts xi. 28.)

whereas the prophecies are given distinctly in one chapter of each of the first three Gospels, and referred to in several different passages of each, and in none of all these places does there appear the smallest intimation that the things spoken of had come to pass. I do admit that it would have been the part of an impostor, who wished his readers to believe that this book was written before the event, when in truth it was written after it, to have suppressed any such intimation carefully. But this was not the character of the authors of the Gospel. Cunning was no quality of theirs. Of all writers in the world, they thought the least of providing against objections. Moreover, there is no clause in any one of them that makes a profession of their having written prior to the Jewish wars, which a fraudulent purpose would have led them to pretend. They have done neither one thing nor the other; they have neither inserted any words which might signify to the reader that their accounts were written before the destruction of Jerusalem, which a sophist would have done; nor have they dropped a hint of the completion of the prophecies recorded by them, which an undesigning writer, writing after the event, could hardly, on some or other of the many occasions that presented themselves, have missed of doing.

4. The admonitions[5] which Christ is represented to have given to his followers to save themselves by flight are not easily accounted for on the supposition of the prophecy being fabricated after the event. Either the Christians, when the siege approached, did make their escape from Jerusalem, or they did not: if they did, they must have had the prophecy amongst them: if they did not know of any such prediction at the time of the siege, if they did not take notice of any such warning, it was an improbable fiction, in a writer publishing his work near to that time (which, on any, even the lowest and most disadvantageous supposition, was the case with the gospels now in our hands), and addressing his work to Jews and to Jewish converts (which Matthew certainly did), to state that the followers of Christ had received admonition of which they made no use when the occasion arrived, and of which experience then recent proved that those who were most concerned to know and regard them were ignorant or negligent. Even if the prophecies came to the hands of the evangelists through no better vehicle than tradition, it must have been

---

[5] "When ye shall see Jerusalem compassed with armies, then know that the desolation thereof is nigh; then let them which are in Judea flee to the mountains; then let them which are in the midst of it depart out, and let not them that are in the countries enter thereinto."—Luke xxi. 20, 21. "When ye shall see Jerusalem compassed with armies, then let them which be in Judea flee unto the mountains; let him which is on the house-top not come down to take anything out of his house; neither let him which is in the field return back to take his clothes."— Matt. xiv. 18.

by a tradition which subsisted prior to the event. And to suppose that without any authority whatever, without so much as even any tradition to guide them, they had forged these passages, is to impute to them a degree of fraud and imposture from every appearance of which their compositions are as far removed as possible.

5. I think that, if the prophecies had been composed after the event, there would have been more specification. The names or descriptions of the enemy, the general, the emperor, would have been found in them. The designation of the time would have been more determinate. And I am fortified in this opinion by observing that the counterfeited prophecies of the Sibylline oracles, of the twelve patriarchs, and, I am inclined to believe, most others of the kind, are mere transcripts of the history, moulded into a prophetic form.

It is objected that the prophecy of the destruction of Jerusalem is mixed or connected with expressions which relate to the final judgment of the world; and so connected as to lead an ordinary reader to expect that these two events would not be far distant from each other. To which I answer, that the objection does not concern our present argument. If our Saviour actually foretold the destruction of Jerusalem, it is sufficient; even although we should allow that the narration of the prophecy had combined what had been said by him on kindred subjects, without accurately preserving the order, or always noticing the transition of the discourse.

CHAPTER II.

THE MORALITY OF THE GOSPEL.

Is stating the morality of the Gospel as an argument of its truth, I am willing to admit two points; first, that the teaching of morality was not the primary design of the mission; secondly, that morality, neither in the Gospel, nor in any other book, can be a subject, properly speaking, of discovery.

If I were to describe in a very few words the scope of Christianity as a revelation,[1] I should say that it was to influence the conduct of human life, by establishing the proof of a future state of reward and punishment,—"to bring life and immortality to light." The direct object, therefore, of the design is, to supply motives, and not rules; sanctions, and not precepts. And these were what mankind stood most in need of. The members of civilised society can, in all ordinary cases, judge tolerably well how they ought to act: but without a future state, or, which is the same thing, without credited evidence of that state, they want a motive to their duty; they want at least strength of motive sufficient to bear up against the force of passion, and the temptation of present advantage. Their rules want authority. The most important service that can be rendered to human life, and that consequently which one might expect beforehand would be the great end and office of a revelation from God, is to convey to the world authorised assurances of the reality of a future existence. And although in doing this, or by the ministry of the same person by whom this is done, moral precepts or examples, or illustrations of moral precepts, may be occasionally given and be highly valuable, yet still they do not form the original purpose of the mission.

Secondly; morality, neither in the Gospel nor in any other book, can be a subject of discovery, properly so called. By which proposition I mean that there cannot, in morality, be anything similar to what are called

---

[1] Great and inestimably beneficial effects may accrue from the mission of Christ, and especially from his death, which do not belong to Christianity as a revelation: that is, they might have existed, and they might have been accomplished, though we had never, in this life, been made acquainted with them. These effects may be very extensive; they may be interesting even to other orders of intelligent beings. I think it is a general opinion, and one to which I have long come, that the beneficial effects of Christ's death extend to the whole human species. It was the redemption of the world. "He is the propitiation for our sins, and not for ours only, but for the whole world;" 1 John ii. 2. Probably the future happiness, perhaps the future existence of the species, and more gracious terms of acceptance extended to all, might depend upon it or be procured by it. Now these effects, whatever they be, do not belong to Christianity as a revelation; because they exist with respect to those to whom it is not revealed.

discoveries in natural philosophy, in the arts of life, and in some sciences; as the system of the universe, the circulation of the blood, the polarity of the magnet, the laws of gravitation, alphabetical writing, decimal arithmetic, and some other things of the same sort; facts, or proofs, or contrivances, before totally unknown and unthought of. Whoever, therefore, expects in reading the New Testament to be struck with discoveries in morals in the manner in which his mind was affected when he first came to the knowledge of the discoveries above mentioned: or rather in the manner in which the world was affected by them, when they were first published; expects what, as I apprehend, the nature of the subject renders it impossible that he should meet with. And the foundation of my opinion is this, that the qualities of actions depend entirely upon their effects, which effects must all along have been the subject of human experience.

When it is once settled, no matter upon what principle, that to do good is virtue, the rest is calculation. But since the calculation cannot be instituted concerning each particular action, we establish intermediate rules; by which proceeding, the business of morality is much facilitated, for then it is concerning our rules alone that we need inquire, whether in their tendency they be beneficial; concerning our actions, we have only to ask whether they be agreeable to the rules. We refer actions to rules, and rules to public happiness. Now, in the formation of these rules, there is no place for discovery, properly so called, but there is ample room for the exercise of wisdom, judgment, and prudence.

As I wish to deliver argument rather than panegyric, I shall treat of the morality of the Gospel in subjection to these observations. And after all, I think it such a morality as, considering from whom it came, is most extraordinary; and such as, without allowing some degree of reality to the character and pretensions of the religion, it is difficult to account for: or, to place the argument a little lower in the scale, it is such a morality as completely repels the supposition of its being the tradition of a barbarous age or of a barbarous people, of the religion being founded in folly, or of its being the production of craft; and it repels also, in a great degree, the supposition of its having been the effusion of an enthusiastic mind.

The division under which the subject may be most conveniently treated is that of the things taught, and the manner of teaching.

Under the first head, I should willingly, if the limits and nature of my work admitted of it, transcribe into this chapter the whole of what has been said upon the morality of the Gospel by the author of The Internal Evidence of Christianity; because it perfectly agrees with my own opinion, and because it is impossible to say the same things so well. This acute observer of human nature, and, as I believe, sincere convert to Christianity, appears to me to have made out satisfactorily the two following positions, viz.—

I. That the Gospel omits some qualifies which have usually engaged the praises and admiration of mankind, but which, in reality, and in their general effects, have been Prejudicial to human happiness.

II. That the Gospel has brought forward some virtues which possess the highest intrinsic value, but which have commonly been overlooked and contemned.

The first of these propositions he exemplifies in the instances of friendship, patriotism, active courage; in the sense in which these qualities are usually understood, and in the conduct which they often produce.

The second, in the instances of passive courage or endurance of sufferings, patience under affronts and injuries, humility, irresistance, placability.

The truth is, there are two opposite descriptions of character under which mankind may generally be classed. The one possesses rigour, firmness, resolution; is daring and active, quick in its sensibilities, jealous of its fame, eager in its attachments, inflexible in its purpose, violent in its resentments.

The other meek, yielding, complying, forgiving; not prompt to act, but willing to suffer; silent and gentle under rudeness and insult, suing for reconciliation where others would demand satisfaction, giving way to the pushes of impudence, conceding and indulgent to the prejudices, the wrong-headedness, the intractability of those with whom it has to deal.

The former of these characters is, and ever hath been, the favourite of the world. It is the character of great men. There is a dignity in it which universally commands respect.

The latter is poor-spirited, tame, and abject. Yet so it hath happened, that with the Founder of Christianity this latter is the subject of his commendation, his precepts, his example; and that the former is so in no part of its composition. This, and nothing else, is the character designed in the following remarkable passages: "Resist not evil: but whosoever shall smite thee on the right cheek, turn to him the other also; and if any man will sue thee at the law, and take away thy coat, let him have thy cloak also: and whosoever shall compel thee to go a mile, go with him twain: love your enemies, bless them that curse you, do good to them that hate you, and pray for them which despitefully use you and persecute you." This certainly is not commonplace morality. It is very original. It shows at least (and it is for this purpose we produce it) that no two things can be more different than the Heroic and the Christian characters.

Now the author to whom I refer has not only marked this difference more strongly than any preceding writer, but has proved, in contradiction to first impressions, to popular opinion, to the encomiums of orators and poets, and even to the suffrages of historians and moralists, that the latter character possesses the most of true worth, both as being most difficult either to be acquired or sustained, and as contributing most to the happiness and tranquillity of social life. The state of his argument is as follows:

I. If this disposition were universal, the case is clear; the world would be a society of friends. Whereas, if the other disposition were universal, it would produce a scene of universal contention. The world could not hold a generation of such men.

II. If, what is the fact, the disposition be partial; if a few be actuated by it, amongst a multitude who are not; in whatever degree it does prevail, in the same proportion it prevents, allays, and terminates quarrels, the great disturbers of human happiness, and the great sources of human misery, so far as man's happiness and misery depend upon man. Without this disposition enmities must not only be frequent, but, once begun, must be eternal: for, each retaliation being a fresh injury, and consequently requiring a fresh satisfaction, no period can be assigned to the reciprocation of affronts, and to the progress of hatred, but that which closes the lives, or at least the intercourse, of the parties.

I would only add to these observations, that although the former of the two characters above described may be occasionally useful; although, perhaps, a great general, or a great statesman, may be formed by it, and these may be instruments of important benefits to mankind, yet is this nothing more than what is true of many qualities which are acknowledged to be vicious. Envy is a quality of this sort: I know not a stronger stimulus to exertion; many a scholar, many an artist, many a soldier, has been produced by it; nevertheless, since in its general effects it is noxious, it is properly condemned, certainly is not praised, by sober moralists.

It was a portion of the same character as that we are defending, or rather of his love of the same character, which our Saviour displayed in his repeated correction of the ambition of his disciples; his frequent admonitions that greatness with them was to consist in humility; his censure of that love of distinction and greediness of superiority which the chief persons amongst his countrymen were wont, on all occasions, great and little, to betray. "They (the Scribes and Pharisees) love the uppermost rooms at feasts, and the chief seats in the synagogues, and greetings in the markets, and to be called of men Rabbi, Rabbi. But be not ye called Rabbi, for one is your Master, even Christ, and all ye are brethren: and call no man your father upon the earth, for one is your father, which is in heaven; neither be ye called master, for one is your Master, even Christ; but he that is greatest among you shall be your servant; and whosoever shall exalt himself shall be abased, and he that shall humble himself shall be exalted." (Matt. xxiii. 6. See also Mark xii. 39; Luke xx. 46; xiv. 7.) I make no further remark upon these passages (because they are, in truth, only a repetition of the doctrine, different expressions of the principle, which we have already stated), except that some of the passages, especially our Lord's advice to the guests at an entertainment, (Luke iv.

7.) seem to extend the rule to what we call manners; which was both regular in point of consistency, and not so much beneath the dignity of our Lord's mission as may at first sight be supposed, for bad manners are bad morals.

It is sufficiently apparent that the precepts we have tired, or rather the disposition which these precepts inculcate, relate to personal conduct from personal motives; to cases in which men act from impulse, for themselves and from themselves. When it comes to be considered what is necessary to be done for the sake of the public, and out of a regard to the general welfare (which consideration, for the most part, ought exclusively to govern the duties of men in public stations), it comes to a case to which the rules do not belong. This distinction is plain; and if it were less so the consequence would not be much felt: for it is very seldom that in time intercourse of private life men act with public views. The personal motives from which they do act the rule regulates.

The preference of time patient to the heroic cheer, which we have here noticed, and which the reader will find explained at large in the work to which we have referred him, is a peculiarity in the Christian institution, which I propose as an argument of wisdom, very much beyond the situation and natural character of the person who delivered it.

II. A second argument, drawn from the morality of the New Testament, is the stress which is laid by our Saviour upon the regulation of the thoughts; and I place this consideration next to the other because they are connected. The other related to the malicious passions; this to the voluptuous. Together, they comprehend the whole character.

"Out of the heart proceed evil thoughts, murders, adulteries, fornications," &c. "These are the things which defile a man." (Matt. xv. 19.)

"Wo unto you, Scribes and Pharisees, hypocrites! for ye make clean the outside of the cup and of the platter, but within they are full of extortion and excess.—Ye are like unto whited sepulchres, which indeed appear beautiful outward, but are within full of dead men's bones, and of all uncleanness; even so ye also outwardly appear righteous unto men, but within ye are full of hypocrisy and iniquity" (Matt. xxiii. 25, 27)

And more particularly that strong expression, (Matt. v. 28.) "Whosoever looketh on a woman to lust after her, hath committed adultery with her already in his heart."

There can be no doubt with any reflecting mind but that the propensities of our nature must be subject to regulation; but the question is, where the check ought to be placed, upon the thought, or only upon the action? In this question our Saviour, in the texts here quoted, has pronounced a decisive judgment. He makes the control of thought essential. Internal purity with him is everything. Now I contend that this is the only discipline which can succeed; in other words, that a moral system which prohibits actions, but leaves the thoughts at liberty, will be ineffectual, and is therefore unwise. I know not how to go about the proof of a point which depends upon experience, and upon a knowledge of the human constitution, better than by citing the judgment of persons who appear to have given great attention to the subject, and to be well qualified to form a true opinion about it. Boerhaave, speaking of this very declaration of our Saviour, "Whosoever looketh on a woman to lust after her, hath already committed adultery with her in his heart," and understanding it, as we do, to contain an injunction to lay the check upon the thoughts, was wont to say that "our Saviour knew mankind better than Socrates." Hailer, who has recorded this saying of Boerhaave, adds to it the following remarks of his own:—(Letters to his Daughter.) "It did not escape the observation of our Saviour that the rejection of any evil thoughts was the best defence against vice: for when a debauched person fills his imagination with impure pictures, the licentious ideas which he recalls fail not to stimulate his desires with a degree of violence which he cannot resist. This will be followed by gratification, unless some external obstacle should prevent him from the commission of a sin which he had internally resolved on." "Every moment of time," says our author, "that is spent in meditations upon sin increases the power of the dangerous object which has possessed our imagination." I suppose these reflections will be generally assented to.

III. Thirdly, had a teacher of morality been asked concerning a general principle of conduct, and for a short rule of life; and had he instructed the person who consulted him, "constantly to refer his actions to what he believed to be the will of his Creator, and constantly to have in view not his own interest and gratification alone, but the happiness and comfort of those about him," he would have been thought, I doubt not, in any age of the world, and in any, even the most improved state of morals, to have delivered a judicious answer; because, by the first direction, he suggested the only motive which acts steadily and uniformly, in sight and out of sight, in familiar occurrences and under pressing temptations; and in the second he corrected what of all tendencies in the human character stands most in need of correction, selfishness, or a contempt of other men's conveniency and satisfaction. In estimating the value of a moral rule, we are to have regard not only to the particular duty, but the general spirit; not only to what it directs us to do, but to the character which a compliance with its direction is likely to form in us. So, in the present instance, the rule here recited will never fail to make him who obeys it considerate not only of the rights, but of the feelings of other men, bodily and mental, in great matters and in small; of the ease, the accommodation, the self-complacency of all with whom he has any concern, especially of all who are in his power, or dependent upon his will.

Now what, in the most applauded philosopher of the most enlightened age of the world, would have been deemed worthy of his wisdom, and of his character, to say, our Saviour hath said, and upon just such an occasion as that which we have feigned.

"Then one of them, which was a lawyer, asked him a question, tempting him, and saying, Master, which is the great commandment in the law? Jesus said unto him, Thou shalt love the Lord thy God with all thy heart, and with all thy soul, and with all thy mind; this is the first and great commandment: and the second is like unto it, Thou shalt love thy neighbour as thyself: on these two commandments hang all the law and the prophets." (Matt. xxii. 35-40.)

The second precept occurs in St. Matthew (xix. 16), on another occasion similar to this; and both of them, on a third similar occasion, in Luke (x. 27). In these two latter instances the question proposed was, "What shall I do to inherit eternal life?"

Upon all these occasions I consider the words of our Saviour as expressing precisely the same thing as what I have put into the mouth of the moral philosopher. Nor do I think that it detracts much from the merit of the answer, that these precepts are extant in the Mosaic code: for his laying his finger, if I may so say, upon these precepts; his drawing them out from the rest of that voluminous institution; his stating of them, not simply amongst the number, but as the greatest and the sum of all the others; in a word, his proposing of them to his hearers for their rule and principle, was our Saviour's own.

And what our Saviour had said upon the subject appears to me to have fixed the sentiment amongst his followers.

Saint Paul has it expressly, "If there be any other commandment, it is briefly comprehended in this saying, Thou shalt love thy neighbour as thyself;" (Rom. xiii. 9.) and again, "For all the law is fulfilled in one word, even in this, Thou shalt love thy neighbour as thyself." (Gal. v. 14.)

Saint John, in like manner, "This commandment have we from him, that he who loveth God love his brother also." (1 John iv. 21.)

Saint Peter, not very differently: "Seeing that ye have purified your souls in obeying the truth through the Spirit, unto unfeigned love of the brethren, see that ye love one another with a pure heart fervently." (I Peter i, 22.)

And it is so well known as to require no citations to verify it, that this love, or charity, or, in other words, regard to the welfare of others, runs in various forms through all the preceptive parts of the apostolic writings. It is the theme of all their exhortations, that with which their morality begins and ends, from which all their details and enumerations set out, and into which they return.

And that this temper, for some time at least, descended in its purity to succeeding Christians, is attested by one of the earliest and best of the remaining writings of the apostolical fathers, the epistle of the Roman Clement. The meekness of the Christian character reigns throughout the whole of that excellent piece. The occasion called for it. It was to compose the dissensions of the church of Corinth. And the venerable hearer of the apostles does not fall short, in the display of this principle, of the finest passages of their writings. He calls to the remembrance of the Corinthian church its former character in which "ye were all of you," he tells them, "humble-minded, not boasting of anything, desiring rather to be subject than to govern, to give than to receive, being content with the portion God had dispensed to you and hearkening diligently to his word; ye were enlarged in your bowels, having his sufferings always before your eyes. Ye contended day and night for the whole brotherhood, that with compassion and a good conscience the number of his elect might be saved. Ye were sincere, and without offence towards each other. Ye bewailed every one his neighbour's sins, esteeming their defects your own." His prayer for them was for the "return of peace, long-suffering, and patience." (Ep. Clem. Rom. c. 2 & 53; Abp. Wake's Translation.) And his advice to those who might have been the occasion of difference in the society is conceived in the true spirit, and with a perfect knowledge of the Christian character: "Who is there among you that is generous? who that is compassionate? Who that has any charity? Let him say, If this sedition, this contention, and these schisms be upon my account, I am ready to depart, to go away whithersoever ye please, and do whatsoever ye shall command me; only let the flock of Christ be in peace with the elders who are set over it. He that shall do this shall get to himself a very great honour in the Lord; and there is no place but what will he ready to receive him; for the earth is the Lord's and the fullness thereof. These things they who have their conversation towards God, not to be repented of, both have done, and will always be ready to do." (Ep. Clem. Rom. c. 54; Abp. Wake's Translation.)

This sacred principle, this earnest recommendation of forbearance, lenity, and forgiveness, mixes with all the writings of that age. There are more quotations in the apostolical fathers of texts which relate to these points than of any other. Christ's sayings had struck them. "Not rendering," said Polycarp, the disciple of John, "evil for evil, or railing for railing, or striking for striking, or cursing for cursing." Again, speaking of some whose behaviour had given great offence, "Be ye moderate," says he, "on this occasion, and look not upon such as enemies, but call them back as suffering and erring members, that ye save your whole body." (Pol. Ep. ad Phil. c. 2 & 11.)

"Be ye mild at their anger," saith Ignatius, the companion of Polycarp, "humble at their boastings, to their blasphemies return your prayers, to their error your firmness in the faith; when they are cruel, be ye gentle; not endeavouring to imitate their ways, let us be their brethren in all kindness and moderation: but let us be followers of the Lord; for who was ever more unjustly used, more destitute, more despised?"

IV. A fourth quality by which the morality of the Gospel is distinguished is the exclusion of regard to fame and reputation.

"Take heed that ye do not your alms before men, to be seen of them, otherwise ye have no reward of your father which is in heaven." "When thou prayest, enter into thy closet, and when thou hast shut the door, pray to thy father which is in secret; and thy Father which seeth in secret shall reward thee openly." (Matt. vi. 1 & 6.)

And the rule, by parity of reason, is extended to all other virtues.

I do not think that either in these or in any other passage of the New Testament, the pursuit of fame is stated as a vice; it is only said that an action, to be virtuous, must be independent of it. I would also observe that it is not publicity, but ostentation, which is prohibited; not the mode, but the motive of the action, which is regulated. A good man will prefer that mode, as well as those objects of his beneficence, by which he can produce the greatest effect; and the view of this purpose may dictate sometimes publication, and sometimes concealment. Either the one or the other may be the mode of the action, according as the end to be promoted by it appears to require. But from the motive, the reputation of the deed, and the fruits and advantage of that reputation to ourselves, must be shut out, or, in whatever proportion they are not so, the action in that proportion fails of being virtuous.

This exclusion of regard to human opinion is a difference not so much in the duties to which the teachers of virtue would persuade mankind, as in the manner and topics of persuasion. And in this view the difference is great. When we set about to give advice, our lectures are full of the advantages of character, of the regard that is due to appearances and to opinion; of what the world, especially of what the good or great, will think and say; of the value of public esteem, and of the qualities by which men acquire it. Widely different from this was our Saviour's instruction; and the difference was founded upon the best reasons. For, however the care of reputation, the authority of public opinion, or even of the opinion of good men, the satisfaction of being well received and well thought of, the benefit of being known and distinguished, are topics to which we are fain to have recourse in our exhortations; the true virtue is that which discards these considerations absolutely, and which retires from them all to the single internal purpose of pleasing God. This at least was the virtue which our Saviour taught. And in teaching this, he not only confined the views of his followers to the proper measure and principle of human duty, but acted in consistency with his office as a monitor from heaven.

Next to what our Saviour taught, may be considered the manner of his teaching; which was extremely peculiar, yet, I think, precisely adapted to the peculiarity of his character and situation. His lessons did not consist of

145

disquisitions; of anything like moral essays, or like sermons, or like set treatises upon the several points which he mentioned. When he delivered a precept, it was seldom that he added any proof or argument; still more seldom that he accompanied it with what all precepts require, limitations and distinctions. His instructions were conceived in short, emphatic, sententious rules, in occasional reflections, or in round maxims. I do not think that this was a natural, or would have been a proper method for a philosopher or a moralist; or that it is a method which can be successfully imitated by us. But I contend that it was suitable to the character which Christ assumed, and to the situation in which, as a teacher, he was placed. He produced himself as a messenger from God. He put the truth of what he taught upon authority. (I say unto you, Swear not at all; I say auto you, Resist not evil; I say unto you, Love your enemies.—Matt. v. 34, 39, 44.) In the choice, therefore, of his mode of teaching, the purpose by him to be consulted was impression: because conviction, which forms the principal end of our discourses, was to arise in the minds of his followers from a different source, from their respect to his person and authority. Now, for the purpose of impression singly and exclusively, (I repeat again, that we are not here to consider the convincing of the understanding,) I know nothing which would have so great force as strong ponderous maxims, frequently urged and frequently brought back to the thoughts of the hearers. I know nothing that could in this view be said better, than "Do unto others as ye would that others should do unto you:" "The first and great commandment is, Thou shalt love the Lord thy God: and the second is like unto it, Thou shalt love thy neighbour as thyself." It must also be remembered, that our Lord's ministry, upon the supposition either of one year or three, compared with his work, was of short duration; that, within this time, he had many places to visit, various audiences to address; that his person was generally besieged by crowds of followers; that he was, sometimes, driven away from the place where he was teaching by persecution, and at other times thought fit to withdraw himself from the commotions of the populace. Under these circumstances, nothing appears to have been so practicable, or likely to be so efficacious, as leaving, wherever he came, concise lessons of duty. These circumstances at least show the necessity he was under of comprising what he delivered within a small compass. In particular, his sermon upon the mount ought always to be considered with a view to these observations. The question is not, whether a fuller, a more accurate, a more systematic, or a more argumentative discourse upon morals might not have been pronounced; but whether more could have been said in the same room better adapted to the exigencies of the hearers, or better calculated for the purpose of impression? Seen in this light, it has always appeared to me to be admirable. Dr. Lardner thought that this discourse was made up of what

Christ had said at different times, and on different occasions, several of which occasions are noticed in St Luke's narrative.

I can perceive no reason for this opinion. I believe that our Lord delivered this discourse at one time and place, in the manner related by Saint Matthew, and that he repeated the same rules and maxims at different times, as opportunity or occasion suggested; that they were often in his mouth, and were repeated to different audiences, and in various conversations.

It is incidental to this mode of moral instruction, which proceeds not by proof but upon authority, not by disquisition but by precept, that the rules will be conceived in absolute terms, leaving the application and the distinctions that attend it to the reason of the hearer. It is likewise to be expected that they will be delivered in terms by so much the more forcible and energetic, as they have to encounter natural or general propensities. It is further also to be remarked, that many of those strong instances which appear in our Lord's sermon, such as, "If any man will smite thee on the right cheek, turn to him the other also:" "If any man will sue thee at the law, and take away thy coat, let him have thy cloak also:" "Whosoever shall compel thee to go a mile, go with him twain:" though they appear in the form of specific precepts, are intended as descriptive of disposition and character. A specific compliance with the precepts would be of little value, but the disposition which they inculcate is of the highest. He who should content himself with waiting for the occasion, and with literally observing the rule when the occasion offered, would do nothing, or worse than nothing: but he who considers the character and disposition which is hereby inculcated, and places that disposition before him as the model to which he should bring his own, takes, perhaps, the best possible method of improving the benevolence, and of calming and rectifying the vices of his temper.

If it be said that this disposition is unattainable, I answer, so is all perfection: ought therefore a moralist to recommend imperfections? One excellency, however, of our Saviour's rules is, that they are either never mistaken, or never so mistaken as to do harm. I could feign a hundred cases in which the literal application of the rule, "of doing to others as we would that others should do unto us," might mislead us; but I never yet met with the man who was actually misled by it. Notwithstanding that our Lord bade his followers, "not to resist evil," and to "forgive the enemy who should trespass against them, not till seven times, but till seventy times seven," the Christian world has hitherto suffered little by too much placability or forbearance. I would repeat once more, what has already been twice remarked, that these rules were designed to regulate personal conduct from personal motives, and for this purpose alone. I think that these observations will assist us greatly in placing our Saviour's conduct as a moral teacher in a proper point of view; especially when it is considered, that to deliver moral disquisitions was no part of his design,—to teach morality at all was only a subordinate part of it; his great business being to supply what was much more wanting than lessons of morality, stronger moral sanctions, and clearer assurances of a future judgment.[2]

The parables of the New Testament are, many of them, such as would have done honour to any book in the world: I do not mean in style and diction, but in the choice of the subjects, in the structure of the narratives, in the aptness, propriety, and force of the circumstances woven into them; and in some, as that of the Good Samaritan, the Prodigal Son, the Pharisee and the Publican, in an union of pathos and simplicity, which in the best productions of human genius is the fruit only of a much exercised and well cultivated judgment.

The Lord's Prayer, for a succession of solemn thoughts, for fixing the attention upon a few great points, for suitableness to every condition, for sufficiency, for conciseness without obscurity, for the weight and real importance of its petitions, is without an equal or a rival.

From whence did these come? Whence had this man his wisdom? Was our Saviour, in fact, a well instructed philosopher, whilst he is represented to us as an illiterate peasant? Or shall we say that some early Christians of taste and education composed these pieces and ascribed them to Christ? Beside all other incredibilities in this account, I answer, with Dr. Jortin, that they could not do it. No specimens of composition which the Christians of the first century have left us authorise us to believe that they were equal to the task. And how little qualified the Jews, the countrymen and companions of Christ, were to assist him in the undertaking, may be judged of from the traditions and writings of theirs which were the nearest to that age. The whole collection of the Talmud is one continued proof into what follies they fell whenever they left their Bible; and how little capable they were of furnishing out such lessons as Christ delivered.

But there is still another view in which our Lord's discourses deserve to be considered; and that is, in their negative character,—not in what

---

[2] Some appear to require in a religious system, or in the books which profess to deliver that system, minute directions for every case and occurrence that may arise. This, say they, is necessary to render a revelation perfect, especially one which has for its object the regulation of human conduct. Now, how prolix, and yet how incomplete and unavailing, such an attempt must have been, is proved by one notable example: "The Indoo and Mussulman religions are institutes of civil law, regulating the minutest questions, both of property and of all questions which come under the cognizance of the magistrate. And to what length details of this kind are necessarily carried when once begun, may be understood from an anecdote of the Mussulman code, which we have received from the most respectable authority, that not less than seventy-five thousand traditional precepts have been promulgated." (Hamilton's translation of Hedays, or Guide.)

they did, but in what they did not, contain. Under this head the following reflections appear to me to possess some weight.

I. They exhibit no particular description of the invisible world. The future happiness of the good, and the misery of the bad, which is all we want to be assured of, is directly and positively affirmed, and is represented by metaphors and comparisons, which were plainly intended as metaphors and comparisons, and as nothing more. As to the rest, a solemn reserve is maintained. The question concerning the woman who had been married to seven brothers, "Whose shall she be on the resurrection?" was of a nature calculated to have drawn from Christ a more circumstantial account of the state of the human species in their future existence. He cuts short, however, the inquiry by an answer, which at once rebuked intruding curiosity, and was agreeable to the best apprehensions we are able to form upon the subject, viz. "That they who are accounted worthy of that resurrection, shall be as the angels of God in heaven." I lay a stress upon this reserve, because it repels the suspicion of enthusiasm: for enthusiasm is wont to expatiate upon the condition of the departed, above all other subjects, and with a wild particularity. It is moreover a topic which is always listened to with greediness. The teacher, therefore, whose principal purpose is to draw upon himself attention, is sure to be full of it. The Koran of Mahomet is half made up of it.

II. Our Lord enjoined no austerities. He not only enjoined none as absolute duties, but he recommended none as carrying men to a higher degree of Divine favour. Place Christianity, in this respect, by the side of all institutions which have been founded in the fanaticism either of their author or of his first followers: or, rather, compare in this respect Christianity, as it came from Christ, with the same religion after it fell into other hands—with the extravagant merit very soon ascribed to celibacy, solitude, voluntary poverty; with the rigours of an ascetic, and the vows of a monastic life; the hair-shirt, the watchings, the midnight prayers, the obmutescence, the gloom and mortification of religious orders, and of those who aspired to religious perfection.

III. Our Saviour uttered no impassioned devotion. There was no heat in his piety, or in the language in which he expressed it; no vehement or rapturous ejaculations, no violent urgency, in his prayers. The Lord's Prayer is a model of calm devotion. His words in the garden are unaffected expressions of a deep, indeed, but sober piety. He never appears to have been worked up into anything like that elation, or that emotion of spirits which is occasionally observed in most of those to whom the name of enthusiast can in any degree be applied. I feel a respect for Methodists, because I believe that there is to be found amongst them much sincere piety, and availing though not always well-informed Christianity: yet I never attended a meeting of theirs but I came away with the reflection, how different what I heard was from what I read! I do not mean in doctrine, with which at present I have no concern, but in manner how different from the calmness, the sobriety, the good sense, and I may add, the strength and authority of our Lord's discourses!

IV. It is very usual with the human mind to substitute forwardness and fervency in a particular cause for the merit of general and regular morality; and it is natural, and politic also, in the leader of a sect or party, to encourage such a disposition in his followers. Christ did not overlook this turn of thought; yet, though avowedly placing himself at the head of a new institution, he notices it only to condemn it. "Not every one that saith unto me, Lord, Lord, shall enter into the kingdom of heaven; but he that doeth the will of my Father which is in heaven. Many will say unto me in that day, Lord, Lord, have we not prophesied in thy name? and in thy name have we cast out devils? and in thy name done many wonderful works? And then will I profess unto you, I never knew you: depart from me, ye that work iniquity." (Matt. vii. 21, 22.) So far was the Author of Christianity from courting the attachment of his followers by any sacrifice of principle, or by a condescension to the errors which even zeal in his service might have inspired. This was a proof both of sincerity and judgment.

V. Nor, fifthly, did he fall in with any of the depraved fashions of his country, or with the natural bias of his own education. Bred up a Jew, under a religion extremely technical, in an age and amongst a people more tenacious of the ceremonies than of any other part of that religion, he delivered an institution containing less of ritual, and that more simple, than is to be found in any religion which ever prevailed amongst mankind. We have known, I do allow, examples of an enthusiasm which has swept away all external ordinances before it. But this spirit certainly did not dictate our Saviour's conduct, either in his treatment of the religion of his country, or in the formation of his own institution. In both he displayed the soundness and moderation of his judgment. He censured an overstrained scrupulousness, or perhaps an affectation of scrupulousness, about the Sabbath: but how did he censure it? not by contemning or decrying the institution itself, but by declaring that "the Sabbath was made for man, not man for the Sabbath;" that is to say, that the Sabbath was to be subordinate to its purpose, and that that purpose was the real good of those who were the subjects of the law. The same concerning the nicety of some of the Pharisees, in paying tithes of the most trifling articles, accompanied with a neglect of justice, fidelity, and mercy. He finds fault with them for misplacing their anxiety. He does not speak disrespectfully of the law of tithes, nor of their observance of it; but he assigns to each class of duties its proper station in the scale of moral importance. All this might be expected perhaps from a well-instructed, cool, and judicious philosopher, but was not to be looked for from an illiterate Jew; certainly not from an impetuous enthusiast.

VI. Nothing could be more quibbling than were the comments and expositions of the Jewish doctors at that time; nothing so puerile as their distinctions. Their evasion of the fifth commandment, their exposition of the law of oaths, are specimens of the bad taste in morals which then prevailed. Whereas, in a numerous collection of our Saviour's apophthegms, many of them referring to sundry precepts of the Jewish law, there is not to be found one example of sophistry, or of false subtlety, or of anything approaching thereunto.

VII. The national temper of the Jews was intolerant, narrow-minded, and excluding. In Jesus, on the contrary, whether we regard his lessons or his example, we see not only benevolence, but benevolence the most enlarged and comprehensive. In the parable of the Good Samaritan, the very point of the story is, that the person relieved by him was the national and religious enemy of his benefactor. Our Lord declared the equity of the Divine administration, when he told the Jews, (what, probably, they were surprised to hear,) "That many should come from the east and west, and should sit down with Abraham, Isaac, and Jacob, in the kingdom of heaven; but that the children of the kingdom should be cast into outer darkness." (Matt. viii. 11.) His reproof of the hasty zeal of his disciples, who would needs call down fire from heaven to revenge an affront put upon their Master, shows the lenity of his character, and of his religion: and his opinion of the manner in which the most unreasonable opponents ought to be treated, or at least of the manner in which they ought not to be treated. The terms in which his rebuke was conveyed deserve to be noticed:—"Ye know not what manner of spirit ye are of." (Luke ix. 55.)

VIII. Lastly, amongst the negative qualities of our religion, as it came out of the hands of its Founder and his apostles, we may reckon its complete abstraction from all views either of ecclesiastical or civil policy; or, to meet a language much in fashion with some men, from the politics either of priests or statesmen. Christ's declaration, that "his kingdom was not of this world," recorded by Saint John; his evasion of the question, whether it was lawful or not to give tribute unto Caesar, mentioned by the three other evangelists; his reply to an application that was made to him, to interpose his authority in a question of property; "Man, who made me a ruler or a judge over you?" ascribed to him by St. Luke; his declining to exercise the office of a criminal judge in the case of the woman taken in adultery, as related by John, are all intelligible significations of our Saviour's sentiments upon this head. And with respect to politics, in the usual sense of that word, or discussions concerning different forms of government, Christianity declines every question upon the subject. Whilst politicians are disputing about monarchies, aristocracies, and republics, the Gospel is alike applicable, useful, and friendly to them all; inasmuch, as, 1stly, it tends to make men virtuous, and as it is easier to govern good men than bad men under any constitution; as, 2ndly, it states obedience to government, in ordinary cases, to be not merely a submission to force, but a duty of conscience; as, 3rdly, it induces dispositions favourable to public tranquillity, a Christian's chief care being to pass quietly through this world to a better; as, 4thly, it prays for communities, and, for the governors of communities, of whatever description or denomination they be, with a solicitude and fervency proportioned to the influence which they possess upon human happiness. All which, in my opinion, is just as it should be. Had there been more to be found in Scripture of a political nature, or convertible to political purposes, the worst use would have been made of it, on whichever side it seemed to lie.

When, therefore, we consider Christ as a moral teacher (remembering that this was only a secondary part of his office; and that morality, by the nature of the subject, does not admit of discovery, properly so called)— when we consider either what he taught, or what he did not teach, either the substance or the manner of his instruction; his preference of solid to popular virtues, of a character which is commonly despised to a character which is universally extolled; his placing, in our licentious vices, the check in the right place, viz. upon the thoughts; his collecting of human duty into two well-devised rules, his repetition of these rules, the stress he laid upon them, especially in comparison with positive duties, and his fixing thereby the sentiments of his followers; his exclusion of all regard to reputation in our devotion and alms, and by parity of reason in our other virtues;—when we consider that his instructions were delivered in a form calculated for impression, the precise purpose in his situation to be consulted; and that they were illustrated by parables, the choice and structure of which would have been admired in any composition whatever;—when we observe him free from the usual symptoms of enthusiasm, heat and vehemence in devotion, austerity in institutions, and a wild particularity in the description of a future state; free also from the depravities of his age and country; without superstition amongst the most superstitious of men, yet not decrying positive distinctions or external observances, but soberly calling them to the principle of their establishment, and to their place in the scale of human duties; without sophistry or trifling, amidst teachers remarkable for nothing so much as frivolous subtleties and quibbling expositions; candid and liberal in his judgment of the rest of mankind, although belonging to a people who affected a separate claim to Divine favour, and in consequence of that opinion prone to uncharitableness, partiality, and restriction;—when we find in his religion no scheme of building up a hierarchy, or of ministering to the views of human governments;—in a word, when we compare Christianity, as it came from its Author, either with other religions, or with itself in other hands, the most reluctant understanding will be induced to acknowledge the probity, I think also the good sense, of those to whom it owes its origin; and that some regard is due to the testimony of such men, when they declare their knowledge that the religion proceeded from God; and when they appeal for the truth of their assertion, to miracles which they wrought, or which they saw.

Perhaps the qualities which we observe in the religion may be thought to prove something more. They would have been extraordinary had the religion come from any person; from the person from whom it did come, they are exceedingly so. What was Jesus in external appearance? A Jewish peasant, the son of a carpenter, living with his father and mother in a remote province of Palestine, until the time that he produced himself in his public character. He had no master to instruct or prompt him; he had read no books but the works of Moses and the prophets; he had visited no polished cities; he had received no lessons from Socrates or Plato,— nothing to form in him a taste or judgment different from that of the rest of his countrymen, and of persons of the same rank of life with himself. Supposing it to be true, which it is not, that all his points of morality might be picked out of Greek and Roman writings, they were writings which he had never seen. Supposing them to be no more than what some or other had taught in various times and places, he could not collect them together.

Who were his coadjutors in the undertaking,—the persons into whose hands the religion came after his death? A few fishermen upon the lake of Tiberias, persons just as uneducated, and, for the purpose of framing rules of morality, as unpromising as himself. Suppose the mission to be real, all this is accounted for; the unsuitableness of the authors to the production, of the characters to the undertaking, no longer surprises us: but without reality, it is very difficult to explain how such a system should proceed from such persons. Christ was not like any other carpenter; the apostles were not like any other fishermen.

But the subject is not exhausted by these observations. That portion of it which is most reducible to points of argument has been stated, and, I trust, truly. There are, however, some topics of a more diffuse nature, which yet deserve to be proposed to the reader's attention.

The character of Christ is a part of the morality of the Gospel: one strong observation upon which is, that, neither as represented by his followers, nor as attacked by his enemies, is he charged with any personal vice. This remark is as old as Origen: "Though innumerable lies and calumnies had been forged against the venerable Jesus, none had dared to charge him with an intemperance." (Or. Ep. Cels. 1. 3, num. 36, ed. Bened.) Not a reflection upon his moral character, not an imputation or suspicion of any offence against purity and chastity, appears for five hundred years after his birth. This faultlessness is more peculiar than we are apt to imagine. Some stain pollutes the morals or the morality of almost every other teacher, and of every other lawgiver.[3] Zeno the stoic, and Diogenes the cynic, fell into the foulest impurities; of which also Socrates himself was more than suspected. Solon forbade unnatural crimes to slaves. Lycurgus tolerated theft as a part of education. Plato recommended a community of women. Aristotle maintained the general right of making war upon barbarians. The elder Cato was remarkable for the ill usage of his slaves; the younger gave up the person of his wife. One loose principle is found in almost all the Pagan moralists; is distinctly, however, perceived in the writings of Plato, Xenophon, Cicero, Seneca, Epictetus; and that is, the allowing, and even the recommending to their disciples, a compliance with the religion, and with the religious rites, of every country into which they came. In speaking of the founders of new institutions we cannot forget Mahomet. His licentious transgressions of his own licentious rules; his abuse of the character which he assumed, and of the power which he had acquired, for the purposes of personal and privileged indulgence; his avowed claim of a special permission from heaven of unlimited sensuality, is known to every reader, as it is confessed by every writer of the Moslem story.

Secondly, in the histories which are left us of Jesus Christ, although very short, and although dealing in narrative, and not in observation or panegyric, we perceive, beside the absence of every appearance of vice, traces of devotion, humility, benignity, mildness, patience, prudence. I speak of traces of these qualities, because the qualities themselves are to be collected from incidents; inasmuch as the terms are never used of Christ in the Gospels, nor is any formal character of him drawn in any part of the New Testament.

Thus we see the devoutness of his mind in his frequent retirement to solitary prayer; (Matt. xiv. 23. Luke ix. 28. Matt. xxvi. 36.) in his habitual giving of thanks; (Matt. xi. 25. Mark viii. 6. John vi. 23. Luke xxii. 17.) in his reference of the beauties and operations of nature to the bounty of Providence; (Matt. vi, 26—28.) in his earnest addresses to his Father, more particularly that short but solemn one before the raising of Lazarus from the dead; (John xi. 41.) and in the deep piety of his behaviour in the garden on the last evening of his life:(Matt. xxvi. 86—47.) his humility in his constant reproof of contentions for superiority:(Mark ix. 33.) the benignity and affectionateness of his temper in his kindness to children; (Mark x. 16.) in the tears which he shed over his falling country, (Luke xix. 41.) and upon the death of his friend; (John xi. 35.) in his noticing of the widow's mite; (Mark xii. 42.) in his parables of the good Samaritan, of the ungrateful servant, and of the Pharisee and publican, of which parables no one but a man of humanity could have been the author: the

---

[3] See many instances collected by Grotius, de Veritate Christianae Religionis, in the notes to his second book, p. 116. Pocock's edition.

mildness and lenity of his character is discovered in his rebuke of the forward zeal of his disciples at the Samaritan village; (Luke ix. 55.) in his expostulation with Pilate; (John xix. 11.) in his prayer for his enemies at the moment of his suffering, (Luke xxiii. 34.) which, though it has been since very properly and frequently imitated, was then, I apprehend, new. His prudence is discerned, where prudence is most wanted, in his conduct on trying occasions, and in answers to artful questions. Of these the following are examples:—His withdrawing in various instances from the first symptoms of tumult, (Matt. xiv. 22. Luke v. 15, 16. John v. 13; vi. 15.) and with the express care, as appears from Saint Matthew, (Chap. xii. 19.) of carrying on his ministry in quietness; his declining of every species of interference with the civil affairs of the country, which disposition is manifested by his behaviour in the case of the woman caught in adultery, (John viii. 1.) and in his repulse of the application which was made to him to interpose his decision about a disputed inheritance:(Luke xii. 14.) his judicious, yet, as it should seem, unprepared answers, will be confessed in the case of the Roman tribute (Matt. xxii. 19.) in the difficulty concerning the interfering relations of a future state, as proposed to him in the instance of a woman who had married seven brethren; (Matt. xxii. 28.) and more especially in his reply to those who demanded from him an explanation of the authority by which he acted, which reply consisted in propounding a question to them, situated between the very difficulties into which they were insidiously endeavouring to draw him. (Matt. xxi. 23, et seq.)

Our Saviour's lessons, beside what has already been remarked in them, touch, and that oftentimes by very affecting representations, upon some of the most interesting topics of human duty, and of human meditation; upon the principles by which the decisions of the last day will be regulated; (Matt. xxv. 31, et seq.) upon the superior, or rather the supreme importance of religion; (Mark viii. 35. Matt. vi. 31—33. Luke xii. 4, 5, 16—21.) upon penitence, by the most pressing calls, and the most encouraging invitations; (Luke xv.) upon self-denial, (Matt. v. 29.) watchfulhess, (Mark xiii. 37. Matt. xxiv. 42; xxv. 13.) placability, (Luke xvii. 4. Matt. xviii. 33, et seq.) confidence in God, (Matt. vi. 25—30.) the value of spiritual, that is, of mental worship, (John iv. 23, 24.) the necessity of moral obedience, and the directing of that obedience to the spirit and principle of the law, instead of seeking for evasions in a technical construction of its terms. (Matt. v. 21.)

If we extend our argument to other parts of the New Testament, we may offer, as amongst the best and shortest rules of life, or, which is the same thing, descriptions of virtue, that have ever been delivered, the following passages:—

"Pure religion, and undefiled, before God and the Father, is this; to visit the fatherless and widows in their affliction, and to keep himself unspotted from the world." (James i. 27.)

"Now the end of the commandment is charity, out of a pure heart and a good conscience, and faith unfeigned." (I Tim. i. 5.)

"For the grace of God that bringeth salvation hath appeared to all men, teaching us that, denying ungodliness and worldly lusts, we should live soberly, righteously, and godly, in this present world." (Tit. ii. 11, 12.)

Enumerations of virtues and vices, and those sufficiently accurate and unquestionably just, are given by St. Paul to his converts in three several epistles. (Gal. v. 19. Col. iii. 12. 1 Cor. xiii.)

The relative duties of husbands and wives, of parents and children, of masters and servants, of Christian teachers and their flocks, of governors and their subjects, are set forth by the same writer, (Eph. v. 33; vi. 1—5. 2 Cor. vi. 6, 7. Rom. xiii.) not indeed with the copiousness, the detail, or the distinctness of a moralist who should in these days sit down to write chapters upon the subject, but with the leading rules and principles in each; and, above all, with truth and with authority.

Lastly, the whole volume of the New Testament is replete with piety; with what were almost unknown to heathen moralists, devotional virtues, the most profound veneration of the Deity, an habitual sense of his bounty and protection, a firm confidence in the final result of his counsels and dispensations, a disposition to resort upon all occasions to his mercy for the supply of human wants, for assistance in danger, for relief from pain, for the pardon of sin.

CHAPTER III.

THE CANDOUR OF THE WRITERS OF
THE NEW TESTAMENT.

I make this candour to consist in their putting down many passages, and noticing many circumstances, which no writer whatever was likely to have forged; and which no writer would have chosen to appear in his book who had been careful to present the story in the most unexceptionable form, or who had thought himself at liberty to carve and mould the particulars of that story according to his choice, or according to his judgment of the effect.

A strong and well-known example of the fairness of the evangelists offers itself in their account of Christ's resurrection, namely, in their unanimously stating that after he was risen he appeared to his disciples alone. I do not mean that they have used the exclusive word alone; but that all the instances which they have recorded of his appearance are instances of appearance to his disciples; that their reasonings upon it, and allusions to it, are confined to this supposition; and that by one of them Peter is made to say, "Him God raised up the third day, and showed him openly, not to all the people, but to witnesses chosen before of God, even to us who did eat and drink with him after he rose from the dead." (Acts x. 40, 41.) The most common understanding must have perceived that the history of the resurrection would have come with more advantage if they had related that Jesus appeared, after he was risen, to his foes as well as his friends, to the scribes and Pharisees, the Jewish council, and the Roman governor: or even if they had asserted the public appearance of Christ in general unqualified terms, without noticing, as they have done, the presence of his disciples on each occasion, and noticing it in such a manner as to lead their readers to suppose that none but disciples were present. They could have represented in one way as well as the other. And if their point had been to have their religion believed, whether true or false; if they had fabricated the story ab initio; or if they had been disposed either to have delivered their testimony as witnesses, or to have worked up their materials and information as historians, in such a manner as to render their narrative as specious and unobjectionable as they could; in a word, if they had thought of anything but of the truth of the case, as they understood and believed it; they would in their account of Christ's several appearances after his resurrection, at least have omitted this restriction. At this distance of time, the account as we have it is perhaps more credible than it would have been the other way; because this manifestation of the historians' candour is of more advantage to their testimony than the difference in the circumstances of the account would have been to the nature of the evidence. But this is an effect which the evangelists would not foresee: and I think that it was by no means the case at the time when the books were composed.

Mr. Gibbon has argued for the genuineness of the Koran, from the confessions which it contains, to the apparent disadvantage of the Mahometan cause. (Vol. ix. c. 50, note 96.) The same defence vindicates the genuineness of our Gospels, and without prejudice to the cause at all.

There are some other instances in which the evangelists honestly relate what they must have perceived would make against them.

Of this kind is John the Baptist's message preserved by Saint Matthew (xi. 2) and Saint Luke (vii. 18): "Now when John had heard in the prison the works of Christ, he sent two of his disciples, and said unto him, Art thou he that should come, or look we for another?" To confess, still more to state, that John the Baptist had his doubts concerning the character of Jesus, could not but afford a handle to cavil and objection. But truth, like honesty, neglects appearances. The same observation, perhaps, holds concerning the apostacy of Judas.[1]

John vi. 66. "From that time, many of his disciples went back, and walked no more with him." Was it the part of a writer who dealt in suppression and disguise to put down this anecdote? Or this, which Matthew has preserved (xii. 58)? "He did not many mighty works there, because of their unbelief."

Again, in the same evangelist (v. 17, 18): "Think not that I am come to destroy the law or the prophets: I am not come to destroy, but to fulfil; for, verily, I say unto you, till heaven and earth pass, one jot, or one tittle, shall in no wise pass from the law, till all be fulfilled." At the time the Gospels were written, the apparent tendency of Christ's mission was to diminish the authority of the Mosaic code, and it was so considered by the Jews themselves. It is very improbable, therefore, that, without the constraint of truth, Matthew should have ascribed a saying to Christ,

---

[1] I had once placed amongst these examples of fair concession the remarkable words of Saint Matthew in his account of Christ's appearance upon the Galilean mountain: "And when they saw him they worshipped him; but some doubted." (Chap. xxviii. 17.) I have since, however, been convinced, by what is observed concerning this passage in Dr. Townshend's Discourse (Page 177.) upon the Resurrection, that the transaction, as related by Saint Matthew, was really this: "Christ appeared first at a distance; the greater part of the company, the moment they saw him, worshipped, but some as yet, i.e. upon this first distant view of his person, doubted; whereupon Christ came up to them, and spake to them,"[*] &c.: that the doubt, therefore, was a doubt only at first for a moment, and upon his being seen at a distance, and was afterwards dispelled by his nearer approach, and by his entering into conversation with them.

[1*] Saint Matthew's words are: kai proselthon o Iesous elalesen autois [and having come toward them, Jesus spoke]. This intimates that when he first appeared it was at a distance, at least from many of the spectators. Ib. p. 197.

which, primo intuitu, militated with the judgment of the age in which his Gospel was written. Marcion thought this text so objectionable, that he altered the words, so as to invert the sense. (Lardner, Cred., vol. xv. p. 422.)

Once more (Acts xxv. 18): "They brought none accusation against him of such things as I supposed; but had certain questions against him of their own superstition, and of one Jesus which was dead, whom Paul affirmed to be alive." Nothing could be more in the character of a Roman governor than these words. But that is not precisely the point I am concerned with. A mere panegyrist, or a dishonest narrator, would not have represented his cause, or have made a great magistrate represent it, in this manner, i.e. in terms not a little disparaging, and bespeaking, on his part, much unconcern and indifference about the matter. The same observation may be repeated of the speech which is ascribed to Gallio (Acts xviii. 15): "If it be a question of words and names, and of your law, look ye to it; for I will be no judge of such matters."

Lastly, where do we discern a stronger mark of candour, or less disposition to extol and magnify, than in the conclusion of the same history? in which the evangelist, after relating that Paul, on his first arrival at Rome, preached to the Jews from morning until evening, adds, "And some believed the things which were spoken, and some believed not."

The following, I think, are passages which were very unlikely to have presented themselves to the mind of a forger or a fabulist.

Matt. xxi. 21. "Jesus answered and said unto them, Verily I say unto you, If ye have faith, and doubt not, ye shall not only do this which is done unto the fig-tree, but also, if ye shall say unto this mountain, Be thou removed, and be thou cast into the sea, it shall be done; all things whatsoever ye shall ask in prayer, believing, it shall be done." (See also chap. xvii. 20. Luke xvii. 6.) It appears to me very improbable that these words should have been put into Christ's mouth, if he had not actually spoken them. The term "faith," as here used, is perhaps rightly interpreted of confidence in that internal notice by which the apostles were admonished of their power to perform any particular miracle. And this exposition renders the sense of the text more easy. But the words undoubtedly, in their obvious construction, carry with them a difficulty which no writer would have brought upon himself officiously.

Luke ix. 59. "And he said unto another, Follow me: but he said, Lord, suffer me first to go and bury my father. Jesus said unto him, Let the dead bury their dead, but go thou and preach the kingdom of God." (See also Matt. viii. 21.) This answer, though very expressive of the transcendent importance of religious concerns, was apparently harsh and repulsive; and such as would not have been made for Christ if he had not really used it. At least some other instance would bare been chosen.

The following passage, I, for the same reason, think impossible to have been the production of artifice, or of a cold forgery:—"But I say unto you, that whosoever is angry with his brother without a cause shall be in danger of the judgment; and whosoever shall say to his brother, Raca, shall be in danger of the council; but whosoever shall say, Thou fool, shall be in danger of hell-fire (Gehennae)." Matt. v. 22. It is emphatic, cogent, and well calculated for the purpose of impression; but is inconsistent with the supposition of art or wariness on the part of the relator.

The short reply of our Lord to Mary Magdalen, after his resurrection (John xx. 16, 17), "Touch me not, for I am not yet ascended unto my Father," in my opinion must have been founded in a reference or allusion to some prior conversation, for the want of knowing which his meaning is hidden from us. This very obscurity, however, is a proof of genuineness. No one would have forged such an answer.

John vi. The whole of the conversation recorded in this chapter is in the highest degree unlikely to be fabricated, especially the part of our Saviour's reply between the fiftieth and the fifty-eighth verse. I need only put down the first sentence: "I am the living bread which came down from heaven: if any man eat of this bread he shall live for ever: and the bread that I will give him is my flesh, which I will give for the life of the world." Without calling in question the expositions that have been given of this passage, we may be permitted to say, that it labours under an obscurity, in which it is impossible to believe that any one, who made speeches for the persons of his narrative, would have voluntarily involved them. That this discourse was obscure, even at the time, is confessed by the writer who had preserved it, when he tells us, at the conclusion, that many of our Lord's disciples, when they had heard this, said, "This is a hard saying; who can hear it?"

Christ's taking of a young child, and placing it in the midst of his contentious disciples (Matt. xviii. 2), though as decisive a proof as any could be of the benignity of his temper, and very expressive of the character of the religion which he wished to inculcate, was not by any means an obvious thought. Nor am I acquainted with anything in any ancient writing which resembles it.

The account of the institution of the eucharist bears strong internal marks of genuineness. If it had been feigned, it would have been more full; it would have come nearer to the actual mode of celebrating the rite as that mode obtained very early in the Christian churches; and it would have been more formal than it is. In the forged piece called the Apostolic Constitutions, the apostles are made to enjoin many parts of the ritual which was in use in the second and third centuries, with as much particularity as a modern rubric could have done. Whereas, in the history of the Lord's Supper, as we read it in Saint Matthew's Gospel, there is not so much as the command to repeat it. This, surely, looks like undesignedness. I think also that the difficulty arising from the conciseness of Christ's expression, "This is my body," would have been avoided in a made-up story. I allow that the explication of these words given by Protestants is satisfactory; but it is deduced from a diligent comparison of the words in question with forms of expression used in Scripture, and especially by Christ upon other occasions. No writer would arbitrarily and unnecessarily have thus cast in his reader's way a difficulty which, to say the least, it required research and erudition to clear up.

Now it ought to be observed that the argument which is built upon these examples extends both to the authenticity of the books, and to the truth of the narrative; for it is improbable that the forger of a history in the name of another should have inserted such passages into it: and it is improbable, also, that the persons whose names the books hear should have fabricated such passages; or even have allowed them a place in their work, if they had not believed them to express the truth.

The following observation, therefore, of Dr. Lardner, the most candid of all advocates, and the most cautious of all inquirers, seems to be well founded:—"Christians are induced to believe the writers of the Gospel by observing the evidences of piety and probity that appear in their writings, in which there is no deceit, or artifice, or cunning, or design." "No remarks," as Dr. Beattie hath properly said, "are thrown in to anticipate objections; nothing of that caution which never fails to distinguish the testimony of those who are conscious of imposture; no endeavour to reconcile the reader's mind to what may be extraordinary in the narrative."

I beg leave to cite also another author, (Duchal, pp. 97, 98.) who has well expressed the reflection which the examples now brought forward were intended to suggest. "It doth not appear that ever it came into the mind of these writers to consider how this or the other action would appear to mankind, or what objections might be raised upon them. But without at all attending to this, they lay the facts before you, at no pains to think whether they would appear credible or not. If the reader will not believe their testimony, there is no help for it: they tell the truth and attend to nothing else. Surely this looks like sincerity, and that they published nothing to the world but that they believed themselves."

As no improper supplement to this chapter, I crave a place here for observing the extreme naturalness of some of the things related in the New Testament.

Mark ix. 23. "Jesus said unto him, If thou canst believe, all things are possible to him that believeth. And straightway the father of the child cried out, and said with tears, Lord, I believe; help thou mine unbelief." This struggle in the father's heart, between solicitude for the preservation of his child, and a kind of involuntary distrust of Christ's power to heal him, is here expressed with an air of reality which could hardly be counterfeited.

Again (Matt. xxi. 9), the eagerness of the people to introduce Christ into Jerusalem, and their demand, a short time afterwards, of his crucifixion, when he did not turn out what they expected him to be, so far from affording matter of objection, represents popular favour in exact agreement with nature and with experience, as the flux and reflux of a wave.

The rulers and Pharisees rejecting Christ, whilst many of the common people received him, was the effect which, in the then state of Jewish prejudices, I should have expected. And the reason with which they who rejected Christ's mission kept themselves in countenance, and with which also they answered the arguments of those who favoured it, is precisely the reason which such men usually give:—"Have any of the Scribes or Pharisees believed on him?" (John vii. 48.)

In our Lord's conversation at the well (John iv. 29), Christ had surprised the Samaritan woman with an allusion to a single particular in her domestic situation, "Thou hast had five husbands; and he whom thou now hast is not thy husband." The woman, soon after this, ran back to the city, and called out to her neighbours, "Come, see a man which told me all things that ever I did." This exaggeration appears to me very natural; especially in the hurried state of spirits into which the woman may be supposed to have been thrown.

The lawyer's subtilty in running a distinction upon the word neighbour, in the precept, "Thou shalt love thy neighbour as thyself," was no less natural than our Saviour's answer was decisive and satisfactory. (Luke x. 20.) The lawyer of the New Testament, it must be observed, was a Jewish divine.

The behaviour of Gallio (Acts xviii. 12-17), and of Festus (xxv. 18, 19), have been observed upon already.

The consistency of Saint Paul's character throughout the whole of his history (viz. the warmth and activity of his zeal, first against, and then for, Christianity) carries with it very much of the appearance of truth.

There are also some properties, as they may be called, observable in the Gospels; that is, circumstances separately suiting with the situation, character, and intention of their respective authors.

Saint Matthew, who was an inhabitant of Galilee, and did not join Christ's society until some time after Christ had come into Galilee to preach, has given us very little of his history prior to that period. Saint John, who had been converted before, and who wrote to supply omissions in the other Gospels, relates some remarkable particulars which had taken place before Christ left Judea, to go into Galilee. (Hartley's Observations, vol. ii. p. 103.)

Saint Matthew (xv. 1) has recorded the cavil of the Pharisees against the disciples of Jesus, for eating "with unclean hands." Saint Mark has also (vii. 1) recorded the same transaction (taken probably from Saint Matthew), but with this addition: "For the Pharisees, and all the Jews, except they wash their hands often, eat not, holding the tradition of the elders: and when they come from the market, except they wash, they eat not: and many other things there be which they have received to hold, as the washing of cups and pots, brazen vessels, and of tables." Now Saint Matthew was not only a Jew himself, but it is evident, from the whole structure of his Gospel, especially from his numerous references to the Old Testament, that he wrote for Jewish readers. The above explanation, therefore, in him, would have been unnatural, as not being wanted by the readers whom he addressed. But in Mark, who, whatever use he might make of Matthew's Gospel, intended his own narrative for a general circulation, and who himself travelled to distant countries in the service of the religion, it was properly added.

CHAPTER IV.

IDENTITY OF CHRIST'S CHARACTER.

THE argument expressed by this title I apply principally to the comparison of the first three Gospels with that of Saint John. It is known to every reader of Scripture that the passages of Christ's history preserved by Saint John are, except his passion and resurrection, for the most part different from those which are delivered by the other evangelists. And I think the ancient account of this difference to be the true one, viz., that Saint John wrote after the rest, and to supply what he thought omissions in their narratives, of which the principal were our Saviour's conferences with the Jews of Jerusalem, and his discourses to his apostles at his last supper. But what I observe in the comparison of these several accounts is, that, although actions and discourses are ascribed to Christ by Saint John in general different from what are given to him by the other evangelists, yet, under this diversity, there is a similitude of manner, which indicates that the actions and discourses proceeded from the same person. I should have laid little stress upon the repetition of actions substantially alike, or of discourses containing many of the same expressions, because that is a species of resemblance which would either belong to a true history, or might easily be imitate in a false one. Nor do I deny that a dramatic writer is able to sustain propriety and distinction of character through a great variety of separate incidents and situations. But the evangelists were not dramatic writers; nor possessed the talents of dramatic writers; nor will it, I believe, be suspected that they studied uniformity of character, or ever thought of any such thing in the person who was the subject of their histories. Such uniformity, if it exist, is on their part casual; and if there be, as I contend there is, a perceptible resemblance of manner, in passages, and between discourses, which are in themselves extremely distinct, and are delivered by historians writing without any imitation of, or reference to, one another, it affords a just presumption that these are what they profess to be, the actions and the discourses of the same real person; that the evangelists wrote from fact, and not from imagination.

The article in which I find this agreement most strong is in our Saviour's mode of teaching, and in that particular property of it which consists in his drawing of his doctrine from the occasion; or, which is nearly the same thing, raising reflections from the objects and incidents before him, or turning a particular discourse then passing into an opportunity of general instruction.

It will be my business to point out this manner in the first three evangelists; and then to inquire whether it do not appear also in several examples of Christ's discourses preserved by Saint John.

The reader will observe in the following quotations that the Italic letter contains the reflection; the common letter the incident or occasion from which it springs.

Matt. xii. 47—50. "Then they said unto him, Behold, thy mother and thy brethren stand without, desiring to speak with thee. But he answered and said unto him that told him, Who is my mother; and who are my brethren? And he stretched forth his hand towards his disciples, and said, Behold my mother and my brethren: for whosoever shall do the will of my Father which is in heaven, the same is my brother, and sister, and mother."

Matt. xvi. 5. "And when his disciples were come to the other side, they had forgotten to take bread; then Jesus said unto them, Take heed, and beware of the leaven of the Pharisees and of the Sadducees. And they reasoned among themselves, saying, It is because we have taken no bread.—How is it that ye do not understand, that I speak it not to you concerning bread, that ye shall beware of the leaven of the Pharisees and of the Sadducees? Then understood they how that he bade them not beware of the leaven of bread, but of the DOCTRINE of the Pharisees and of the Sadducees."

Matt. xv. 1, 2; 10, 11; 15—20. "Then came to Jesus scribes and Pharisees, which were of Jerusalem, saying, Why do thy disciples transgress the traditions of the elders? for they wash not their hands when they eat bread.—And he called the multitude, and said unto them, Hear and understand: Not that which goeth into the mouth defileth a man, but that which cometh out of the mouth, this defileth the man.—Then answered Peter, and said unto him, Declare unto us this parable. And Jesus said, Are ye also yet without understanding? Do ye not understand that whatsoever entereth in at the mouth goeth into the belly, and is cast out into the draught? but those things which proceed out of the mouth come forth from the heart, and they defile the man: for out of the heart proceed evil thoughts, murders, adulteries, fornications, thefts, false witness, blasphemies; these are the things which defile a man: BUT TO EAT WITH UNWASHEN HANDS DEFILETH NOT A MAN." Our Saviour, on this occasion, expatiates rather more at large than usual, and his discourse also is more divided; but the concluding sentence brings back the whole train of thought to the incident in the first verse, viz. the objurgatory question of the Pharisees, and renders it evident that the whole sprang from that circumstance.

Mark x. 13, 14, 15. "And they brought young children to him, that he should touch them; and his disciples rebuked those that brought them: but when Jesus saw it, he was much displeased, and said unto them, Suffer the little children to come unto me, and forbid them not; for of such is the kingdom of God: verily I say unto you, whosoever shall not receive the kingdom of God as a little child, he shall not enter therein."

Mark i. 16, 17. "Now as he walked by the sea of Galilee, he saw Simon and Andrew his brother casting a net into the sea, for they were fishers: and Jesus said unto them, Come ye after me, and I will make you fishers of men."

Luke xi. 27. "And it came to pass as he spake these things, a certain woman of the company lifted up her voice, and said unto him, Blessed is the womb that bare thee, and the paps which thou hast sucked: but he said, Yea, rather, blessed are they that hear the word of God and keep it."

Luke xiii. 1—3. "There were present at that season some that told him of the Galileans, whose blood Pilate had mingled with their sacrifices; and Jesus answering said unto them, Suppose ye, that these Galileans were sinners above all the Galileans, because they suffered such things? I tell you, Nay: but, except ye repent, ye shall all likewise perish."

Luke xiv. 15. "And when one of them that sat at meat with him heard these things, he said unto him, Blessed is he that shall eat bread in the kingdom of God. Then said he unto him, A certain man made a great supper, and bade many," &c. The parable is rather too long for insertion, but affords a striking instance of Christ's manner of raising a discourse from the occasion. Observe also in the same chapter two other examples of advice, drawn from the circumstances of the entertainment and the behaviour of the guests.

We will now see how this manner discovers itself in Saint John's history of Christ.

John vi. 25. "And when they had found him on the other side of the sea, they said unto him, Rabbi, when camest thou hither? Jesus answered them and said, Verily I say unto you, ye seek me not because ye saw the miracles, but because ye did eat of the loaves and were filled. Labour not for the meat which perisheth, but for that meat which endureth unto everlasting life, which the Son of man shall give unto you."

John iv. 12. "Art thou greater than our father Abraham, who gave us the well, and drank thereof himself, and his children, and his cattle? Jesus answered, and said unto her (the woman of Samaria), Whosoever drinketh of this water shall thirst again; but whosoever drinketh of the water that I shall give him, shall never thirst; but the water that I shall give him shall be in him a well of water, springing up into everlasting life."

John iv. 31. "In the mean while, his disciples prayed him, saying, Master, eat; but he said unto them, I have meat to eat that ye know not of. Therefore said the disciples one to another, Hath any man brought him aught to eat? Jesus saith unto them, My meat is to do the will of Him that sent me, and to finish his work."

John ix. 1—5. "And as Jesus passed by, he saw a man which was blind from his birth: and his disciples asked him, saying, Who did sin, this man or his parents, that he was born blind? Jesus answered, Neither hath this man sinned, nor his parents, but that the works of God should be

166

made manifest in him. I must work the works of Him that sent me while it is day; the night cometh when no man can work. As long as I am in the world, I am the light of the world."

John ix. 35—40. "Jesus heard that they had cast him (the blind man above mentioned) out: and when he had found him, he said unto him, Dost thou believe on the Son of God? And he answered and said, Who is he, Lord, that I might believe on him? And Jesus said unto him, Thou hast both seen him, and it is he that talketh with thee. And he said, Lord, I believe; and he worshipped him. And Jesus said. For judgment I am come into this world, that they which see not might see; and that they which might be made blind."

All that the reader has now to do, is to compare the series of examples taken from Saint John with the series of examples taken from the other evangelists, and to judge whether there be not a visible agreement of manner between them. In the above-quoted passages, the occasion is stated, as well as the reflection. They seem, therefore, the most proper for the purpose of our argument. A large, however, and curious collection has been made by different writers, (Newton on Daniel, p. 148, note a. Jottin, Dis., p. 218. Bishop Law's Life of Christ.) of instances in which it is extremely probable that Christ spoke in allusion to some object, or some occasion then before him, though the mention of the occasion, or of the object, be omitted in the history. I only observe that these instances are common to Saint John's Gospel with the other three.

I conclude this article by remarking, that nothing of this manner is perceptible in the speeches recorded in the Acts, or in any other but those which are attributed to Christ, and that, in truth, it was a very unlikely manner for a forger or fabulist to attempt; and a manner very difficult for any writer to execute, if he had to supply all the materials, both the incidents and the observations upon them, out of his own head. A forger or a fabulist would have made for Christ, discourses exhorting to virtue and dissuading from vice in general terms. It would never have entered into the thoughts of either, to have crowded together such a number of allusions to time, place, and other little circumstances, as occur, for instance, in the sermon on the mount, and which nothing but the actual presence of the objects could have suggested (See Bishop Law's Life of Christ).

II. There appears to me to exist an affinity between the history of Christ's placing a little child in the midst of his disciples, as related by the first three evangelists, (Matt. xviii. 1. Mark ix. 33. Luke ix. 46.) and the history of Christ's washing his disciples' feet, as given by Saint John. (Chap. xiii. 3.) In the stories themselves there is no resemblance. But the affinity which I would point out consists in these two articles: First, that both stories denote the emulation which prevailed amongst Christ's disciples, and his own care and desire to correct it; the moral of both is the same. Secondly, that both stories are specimens of the same manner of teaching, viz., by action; a mode of emblematic instruction extremely peculiar, and, in these passages, ascribed, we see, to our Saviour by the first three evangelists, and by Saint John, in instances totally unlike, and without the smallest suspicion of their borrowing from each other.

III. A singularity in Christ's language which runs through all the evangelists, and which is found in those discourses of Saint John that have nothing similar to them in the other Gospels, is the appellation of "the Son of man;" and it is in all the evangelists found under the peculiar circumstance of being applied by Christ to himself, but of never being used of him, or towards him, by any other person. It occurs seventeen times in Matthew's Gospel, twenty times in Mark's, twenty-one times in Luke's and eleven times in John's, and always with this restriction.

IV. A point of agreement in the conduct of Christ, as represented by his different historians, is that of his withdrawing himself out of the way whenever the behaviour of the multitude indicated a disposition to tumult.

Matt. xiv. 22. "And straightway Jesus constrained his disciples to get into a ship, and to go before him unto the other side, while he sent the multitude away. And when he had sent the multitude away, he went up into a mountain apart to pray."

Luke v. 15, 16. "But so much the more went there a fame abroad of him, and great multitudes came together to hear, and to be healed by him of their infirmities; and he withdrew himself into the wilderness and prayed." With these quotations compare the following from Saint John: Chap. v. 13. "And he that was healed wist not who it was, for Jesus had conveyed himself away, a multitude being in that place."

Chap. vi. 15. "When Jesus therefore perceived that they would come and take him by force, to make him a king, he departed again into a mountain himself alone."

In this last instance, Saint John gives the motive of Christ's conduct, which is left unexplained by the other evangelists, who have related the conduct itself.

V. Another, and a more singular circumstance in Christ's ministry, was the reserve which, for some time, and upon some occasions at least, he used in declaring his own character, and his leaving it to be collected from his works rather than his professions. Just reasons for this reserve have been assigned. (See Locke's Reasonableness of Christianity.) But it is not what one would have expected. We meet with it in Saint Matthew's Gospel (chap. xvi. 20): "Then charged he his disciples that they should tell no man that he was Jesus the Christ." Again, and upon a different occasion, in Saint Mark's (chap. iii. 11): "And unclean spirits, when they saw him, fell down before him, and cried, saying, Thou art the Son of God: and he straitly charged them that they should not make him known." Another instance similar to this last is recorded by Saint Luke (chap. iv.

41). What we thus find in the three evangelists, appears also in a passage of Saint John (chap. x. 24, 25): "Then came the Jews round about him, and said unto him, How long dost thou make us to doubt: If thou be the Christ, tell us plainly." The occasion here was different from any of the rest; and it was indirect. We only discover Christ's conduct through the upbraidings of his adversaries. But all this strengthens the argument. I had rather at any time surprise a coincidence in some oblique allusion than read it in broad assertions.

VI. In our Lord's commerce with his disciples, one very observable particular is the difficulty which they found in understanding him when he spoke to them of the future part of his history, especially of what related to his passion or resurrection. This difficulty produced, as was natural, a wish in them to ask for further explanation: from which, however, they appear to have been sometimes kept back by the fear of giving offence. All these circumstances are distinctly noticed by Mark and Luke, upon the occasion of his informing them (probably for the first time) that the Son of man should be delivered into the hands of men. "They understood not," the evangelists tell us, "this saying, and it was hid from them, that they perceived it not; and they feared to ask him of that saying." Luke ix. 45; Mark ix. 32. In Saint John's Gospel we have, on a different occasion, and in a different instance, the same difficulty of apprehension, the same curiosity, and the same restraint:—"A little while and ye shall not see me; and again, a little while and ye shall see me, because I go to the Father. Then said some of his disciples among themselves, What is this that he saith unto us? A little while and ye shall not see me: and again, a little while and ye shall see me: and, Because I go to the Father? They said, therefore, What is this that he saith? A little while? We cannot tell what he saith. Now Jesus knew that they were desirous to ask him, and said unto them,—" &c. John xvi. 16, et seq.

VII. The meekness of Christ during his last sufferings, which is conspicuous in the narratives of the first three evangelists, is preserved in that of Saint John under separate examples. The answer given by him, in Saint John, (Chap. xviii. 20, 21.) when the high priest asked him of his disciples and his doctrine; "I spake openly to the world: I ever taught in the synagogue, and in the temple, whither the Jews always resort; and in secret have I said nothing. Why askest thou me? ask them which heard me what I have said unto them," is very much of a piece with his reply to the armed party which seized him, as we read it in Saint Mark's Gospel, and in Saint Luke's:(Mark xiv. 48. Luke xxii. 52.) "Are you come out as against a thief, with swords and with staves to take me? I was daily with you in the temple teaching, and ye took me not." In both answers we discern the same tranquillity, the same reference to his public teaching. His mild expostulation with Pilate, on two several occasions, as related by Saint John, (Chap. xviii. 34; xix. 11.) is delivered with the same unruffled temper as that which conducted him through the last scene of his life, as described by his other evangelists. His answer, in Saint John's Gospel, to the officer who struck him with the palm of his hand, "If I have spoken evil, bear witness of the evil; but if well, why smitest thou me?" (Chap. xviii. 23.) was such an answer as might have been looked for from the person who, as he proceeded to the place of execution, bid his companions (as we are told by Saint Luke; Chap. xxiii. 28.) weep not for him, but for themselves, their posterity, and their country; and who, whilst he was suspended upon the cross, prayed for his murderers, "for they know not," said he, "what they do." The urgency also of his judges and his prosecutors to extort from him a defence to the accusation, and his unwillingness to make any (which was a peculiar circumstance), appears in Saint John's account, as well as in that of the other evangelists. (See John xix. 9. Matt. xxvii. 14. Luke xxiii. 9.)

There are, moreover, two other correspondencies between Saint John's history of the transaction and theirs, of a kind somewhat different from those which we have been now mentioning.

The first three evangelists record what is called our Saviour's agony, i.e. his devotion in the garden immediately before he was apprehended; in which narrative they all make him pray "that the cup might pass from him." This is the particular metaphor which they all ascribe to him. Saint Matthew adds, "O, my Father, if this cup may not pass away from me, except I drink it, thy will be done." (Chap, xxvi. 42.) Now Saint John does not give the scene in the garden: but when Jesus was seized, and some resistance was attempted to be made by Peter, Jesus, according to his account, checked the attempt, with this reply: "Put up thy sword into the sheath; the cup which my Father hath given me, shall I not drink it?" (Chap. xviii. 11.) This is something more than consistency—it is coincidence; because it is extremely natural that Jesus, who, before he was apprehended, had been praying his Father that "that cup might pass from him," yet with such a pious retraction of his request as to have added, "If this cup may not pass from me, thy will be done;" it was natural, I say, for the same person, when he actually was apprehended, to express the resignation to which he had already made up his thoughts, and to express it in the form of speech which he had before used, "The cup which my Father hath given me, shall I not drink it?" This is a coincidence between writers in whose narratives there is no imitation, but great diversity.

A second similar correspondency is the following: Matthew and Mark make the charge upon which our Lord was condemned to be a threat of destroying the temple; "We heard him say, I will destroy this temple made with hands, and within three days I will build another made without hands:" (Mark xiv. 58.) but they neither of them inform us upon what circumstance this calumny was founded. Saint John, in the early part of

170

the history, (Chap. ii. 19.) supplies us with this information; for he relates, that on our Lord's first journey to Jerusalem, when the Jews asked him "What sign showest thou unto us, seeing that thou doest these things? He answered, Destroy this temple, and in three days I will raise it up." This agreement could hardly arise from anything but the truth of the case. From any care or design in Saint John to make his narrative tally with the narratives of other evangelists, it certainly did not arise, for no such design appears, but the absence of it.

A strong and more general instance of agreement is the following.— The first three evangelists have related the appointment of the twelve apostles; (Matt. x. 1. Mark iii. 14. Luke vi. 12.) and have given a catalogue of their names in form. John, without ever mentioning the appointment, or giving the catalogue, supposes, throughout his whole narrative, Christ to be accompanied by a select party of disciples; the number of these to be twelve; (Chap. vi. 70.) and whenever he happens to notice any one as of that number, (Chap. xx, 24; vi. 71.) it is one included in the catalogue of the other evangelists: and the names principally occurring in the course of his history of Christ are the names extant in their list. This last agreement, which is of considerable moment, runs through every Gospel, and through every chapter of each. All this bespeaks reality.

CHAPTER V.

ORIGINALITY OF OUR SAVIOUR'S CHARACTER.

The Jews, whether right or wrong, had understood their prophecies to foretell the advent of a person who by some supernatural assistance should advance their nation to independence, and to a supreme degree of splendour and prosperity. This was the reigning opinion and expectation of the times. Now, had Jesus been an enthusiast, it is probable that his enthusiasm would have fallen in with the popular delusion, and that, while he gave himself out to be the person intended by these predictions, he would have assumed the character to which they were universally supposed to relate.

Had he been an impostor, it was his business to have flattered the prevailing hopes, because these hopes were to be the instruments of his attraction and success.

But what is better than conjectures is the fact, that all the pretended Messiahs actually did so. We learn from Josephus that there were many of these. Some of them, it is probable, might be impostors, who thought that an advantage was to be taken of the state of public opinion. Others, perhaps, were enthusiasts, whose imagination had been drawn to this particular object by the language and sentiments which prevailed around them. But whether impostors or enthusiasts, they concurred in producing themselves in the character which their countrymen looked for, that is to say, as the restorers and deliverers of the nation, in that sense in which restoration and deliverance were expected by the Jews.

Why therefore Jesus, if he was, like them, either an enthusiast or impostor, did not pursue the same conduct as they did, in framing his character and pretensions, it will be found difficult to explain. A mission, the operation and benefit of which was to take place in another life, was a thing unthought of as the subject of these prophecies. That Jesus, coming to them as their Messiah, should come under a character totally different from that in which they expected him; should deviate from the general persuasion, and deviate into pretensions absolutely singular and original—appears to be inconsistent with the imputation of enthusiasm or imposture, both which by their nature I should expect would, and both which, throughout the experience which this very subject furnishes, in fact, have followed the opinions that obtained at the time.

If it be said that Jesus, having tried the other plan, turned at length to this; I answer, that the thing is said without evidence; against evidence; that it was competent to the rest to have done the same, yet that nothing of this sort was thought of by any.

CHAPTER VI.

One argument which has been much relied upon (but not more than its just weight deserves) is the conformity of the facts occasionally mentioned or referred to in Scripture with the state of things in those times, as represented by foreign and independent accounts; which conformity proves, that the writers of the New Testament possessed a species of local knowledge which could belong only to an inhabitant of that country and to one living in that age. This argument, if well made out by examples, is very little short of proving the absolute genuineness of the writings. It carries them up to the age of the reputed authors, to an age in which it must have been difficult to impose upon the Christian public forgeries in the names of those authors, and in which there is no evidence that any forgeries were attempted. It proves, at least, that the books, whoever were the authors of them, were composed by persons living in the time and country in which these things were transacted; and consequently capable, by their situation, of being well informed of the facts which they relate. And the argument is stronger when applied to the New Testament, than it is in the case of almost any other writings, by reason of the mixed nature of the allusions which this book contains. The scene of action is not confined to a single country, but displayed in the greatest cities of the Roman empire. Allusions are made to the manners and principles of the Greeks, the Romans, and the Jews. This variety renders a forgery proportionably more difficult, especially to writers of a posterior age. A Greek or Roman Christian who lived in the second or third century would have been wanting in Jewish literature; a Jewish convert in those ages would have been equally deficient in the knowledge of Greece and Rome. (Michaelis's Introduction to the New Testament [Marsh's translation], c. ii. sect. xi.)

This, however, is an argument which depends entirely upon an induction of particulars; and as, consequently, it carries with it little force without a view of the instances upon which it is built, I have to request the reader's attention to a detail of examples, distinctly and articulately proposed. In collecting these examples I have done no more than epitomise the first volume of the first part of Dr. Lardner's Credibility of the Gospel History. And I have brought the argument within its present compass, first, by passing over some of his sections in which the accordancy appeared to me less certain, or upon subjects not sufficiently appropriate or circumstantial; secondly, by contracting every section into the fewest words possible, contenting myself for the most part with a mere apposition of passages; and, thirdly, by omitting many disquisitions, which, though learned and accurate, are not absolutely necessary to the understanding or verification of the argument.

The writer principally made use of in the inquiry is Josephus. Josephus was born at Jerusalem four years after Christ's ascension. He wrote his history of the Jewish war some time after the destruction of Jerusalem, which happened in the year of our Lord LXX, that is, thirty-seven years after the ascension; and his history of the Jews he finished in the year xciii, that is, sixty years after the ascension. At the head of each article I have referred, by figures included in brackets, to the page of Dr. Lardner's volume where the section from which the abridgment is made begins. The edition used is that of 1741.

I. [p. 14.] Matt. ii. 22. "When he (Joseph) heard that Archclaus did reign in Judea in the room of his father Herod, he was afraid to go thither: notwithstanding, being warned of God in a dream, he turned aside into the parts of Galilee."

II. In this passage it is asserted that Archclaus succeeded Herod in Judea; and it is implied that his power did not extend to Galilee. Now we learn from Josephus that Herod the Great, whose dominion included all the land of Israel, appointed Archelaus his successor in Judea, and assigned the rest of his dominions to other sons; and that this disposition was ratified, as to the main parts of it, by the Roman emperor (Ant. lib. xvi. c. 8, sect. 1.).

Saint Matthew says that Archclaus reigned, was king, in Judea. Agreeably to this, we are informed by Josephus, not only that Herod appointed Archclaus his successor in Judea, but that he also appointed him with the title of King; and the Greek verb basileuei, which the evangelist uses to denote the government and rank of Archclaus, is used likewise by Josephus (De Bell. lib. i. c. 3,3, sect. 7.).

The cruelty of Archelaus's character, which is not obscurely intimated by the evangelist, agrees with divers particulars in his history preserved by Josephus:—"In the tenth year of his government, the chief of the Jews and Samaritans, not being able to endure his cruelty and tyranny, presented complaints against him to Caesar." (Ant, lib. xii. 13, sect. 1.)

II. [p. 19.] Luke iii. 1. "In the fifteenth year of the reign of Tiberius Caesar—Herod being tetrarch of Galilee, and his brother Philip tetrarch of Iturea, and of the region of Trachonitis—the word of God came unto John."

By the will of Herod the Great, and the decree of Augustus thereupon, his two sons were appointed, one (Herod Antipus) tetrarch of Galilee and Peraea, and the other (Philip) tetrarch of Trachonitis and the neighbouring countries. (Ant. lib. xvii. c. 8, sect. 1.) We have, therefore, these two persons in the situations in which Saint Luke places them; and also, that they were in these situations in the fifteenth year of Tiberius; in other words, that they continued in possession of their territories and titles until that time, and afterwards, appears from a passage of Josephus, which relates of Herod, "that he was removed by Caligula, the successor of

Tiberius;" (Ant. lib. xviii. c. 8, sect. 2.) and of Philip, that he died in the twentieth year of Tiberius, when he had governed Trachonitis and Batanea and Gaulanitis thirty-seven years. (Ant. lib. xviii. c. 5, sect. 6.)

III. [p. 20.] Mark vi. 17. "Herod had sent forth, and laid hold upon John, and bound him in prison, for Heredias' sake, his brother Philip's wife: for he had married her." (See also Matt. xiv. 1—13; Luke iii. 19.)

With this compare Joseph. Antiq. 1. xviii. c. 6, sect. 1:—"He (Herod the tetrarch) made a visit to Herod his brother.—Here, failing in love with Herodias, the wife of the said Herod, he ventured to make her proposals of marriage."[1]

Again, Mark vi. 22. "And when the daughter of the said Herodias came in and danced."

With this also compare Joseph. Antiq. 1. xviii. c. 6, sect. 4. "Herodias was married to Herod, son of Herod the Great. They had a daughter, whose name was Salome; after whose birth Herodias, in utter violation of the laws of her country, left her husband, then living, and married Herod the tetrarch of Galilee, her husband's brother by the father's side."

IV. [p. 29.] Acts xii. 1. "Now, about that time, Herod the king stretched forth his hands, to vex certain of the church."

In the conclusion of the same chapter, Herod's death is represented to have taken place soon after this persecution. The accuracy of our historian, or, rather, the unmeditated coincidence which truth of its own accord produces, is in this instance remarkable. There was no portion of time for thirty years before, nor ever afterwards, in which there was a king at Jerusalem, a person exercising that authority in Judea, or to whom that title could be applied, except the last three years of this Herod's life, within which period the transaction recorded in the Acts is stated to have taken place. This prince was the grandson of Herod the Great. In the Acts he appears under his family-name of Herod; by Josephus he was called Agrippa. For proof that he was a king, properly so called, we have the testimony of Josephus, in full and direct terms:—"Sending for him to his palace, Caligula put a crown upon his head, and appointed him king of the tetrarchie of Philip, intending also to give him the tetrarchie of Lysanias."

---

[1] The affinity of the two accounts is unquestionable; but there is a difference in the name of Herodias's first husband, which in the evangelist is Philip; in Josephus, Herod. The difficulty, however, will not appear considerable when we recollect how common it was in those times for the same persons to bear two names. "Simon, which is called Peter; Lebbeus, whose surname is Thaddeus; Thomas, which is called Didymus; Simeon, who was called Niger; Saul, who was also called Paul." The solution is rendered likewise easier in the present case by the consideration that Herod the Great had children by seven or eight wives; that Josephus mentions three of his sons under the name of Herod; that it is nevertheless highly probable that the brothers bore some additional name by which they were distinguished from one another. Lardner, vol. ii. p. 897.

(Antiq. xviii. c. 7, sect. 10.) And that Judea was at last, but not until the last, included in his dominions, appears by a subsequent passage of the same Josephus, wherein he tells us that Claudius, by a decree, confirmed to Agrippa the dominion which Caligula had given him; adding also Judea and Samaria, in the utmost extent, as possessed by his grandfather Herod (Antiq. xix. c. 5, sect. 1.).

V. [p. 32.] Acts xii. 19—23. "And he (Herod) went down from Judea to Cesarea, and there abode. And on a set day Herod, arrayed in royal apparel, sat upon his throne, and made an oration unto them: and the people gave a shout, saying, It is the voice of a god, and not of a man; and immediately the angel of the Lord smote him, because he gave not God the glory: and he was eaten of worms, and gave up the ghost."

Joseph. Antiq. lib. xix. c. 8, sect. 2. "He went to the city of Cesarea. Here he celebrated shows in honour of Caesar. On the second day of the shows, early in the morning, he came into the theatre, dressed in a robe of silver, of most curious workmanship. The rays of the rising sun, reflected from such a splendid garb, gave him a majestic and awful appearance. They called him a god; and intreated him to be propitious to them, saying, Hitherto we have respected you as a man; but now we acknowledge you to be more than mortal. The king neither reproved these persons, nor rejected the impious flattery. Immediately after this he was seized with pains in his bowels, extremely violent at the very first. He was carried therefore with all haste to his palace. These pains continually tormenting him, he expired in five days' time."

The reader will perceive the accordancy of these accounts in various particulars. The place (Cesarea), the set day, the gorgeous dress, the acclamations of the assembly, the peculiar turn of the flattery, the reception of it, the sudden and critical incursion of the disease, are circumstances noticed in both narratives. The worms mentioned by Saint Luke are not remarked by Josephus; but the appearance of these is a symptom not unusually, I believe, attending the disease which Josephus describes, viz., violent affections of the bowels.

VI. [p. 41.] Acts xxiv. 24. "And after certain days, when Felix came with his wife Drusilla, which was a Jewess, he sent for Paul."

Joseph. Antiq. lib. xx. c. 6, sect. 1, 2. "Agrippa gave his sister Drusilla in marriage to Azizus, king of the Emesenes, when he had consented to be circumcised.—But this marriage of Drusilla with Azizus was dissolved in a short time after, in this manner:—When Felix was procurator of Judea, having had a sight of her, he was mightily taken with her.—She was induced to transgress the laws of her country, and marry Felix."

Here the public station of Felix, the name of his wife, and the singular circumstance of her religion, all appear in perfect conformity with the evangelist.

176

VII. [p. 46.] Acts xxv. 13. "And after certain days king Agrippa and Berenice came to Cesarea to salute Festus." By this passage we are in effect told that Agrippa was a king, but not of Judea; for he came to salute Festus, who at this time administered the government of that country at Cesarea.

Now, how does the history of the age correspond with this account? The Agrippa here spoken of was the son of Herod Agrippa, mentioned in the last article; but that he did not succeed to his father's kingdom, nor ever recovered Judea, which had been a part of it, we learn by the information of Josephus, who relates of him that when his father was dead Claudius intended at first to have put him immediately in possession of his father's dominions; but that, Agrippa being then but seventeen years of age, the emperor was persuaded to alter his mind, and appointed Cuspius Fadus prefect of Judea and the whole kingdom; (Antiq. xi. c. 9 ad fin.) which Fadus was succeeded by Tiberius Alexander, Cumanus, Felix, Festus. (Antiq. xx. de Bell. lib. ii.) But that, though disappointed of his father's kingdom, in which was included Judea, he was, nevertheless, rightly styled King Agrippa, and that he was in possession of considerable territories, bordering upon Judea, we gather from the same authority: for, after several successive donations of country, "Claudius, at the same time that he sent Felix to be procurator of Judea, promoted Agrippa from Chalcis to a greater kingdom, giving to him the tetrarchie which had been Philip's; and he added, moreover, the kingdom of Lysanias, and the province that had belonged to Varus." (De Bell. lib. li. c. 12 ad fin.)

Saint Paul addresses this person as a Jew: "King Agrippa, believest thou the prophets? I know that thou believest." As the son of Herod Agrippa, who is described by Josephus to have been a zealous Jew, it is reasonable to suppose that he maintained the same profession. But what is more material to remark, because it is more close and circumstantial, is, that Saint Luke, speaking of the father (Acts xii. 1—3), calls him Herod the, king, and gives an example of the exercise of his authority at Jerusalem: speaking of the son (xxv. 13), he calls him king, but not of Judea; which distinction agrees correctly with the history.

VIII. [p. 51.] Acts xiii. 6. "And when they had gone through the isle (Cyprus) to Paphos, they found a certain sorcerer, a false prophet, a Jew, whose name was Bar-jesus, which was with the deputy of the country, Sergius Paulus, a prudent man."

The word which is here translated deputy, signifies and upon this word our observation is founded. The provinces of the Roman empire were of two kinds; those belonging the emperor, in which the governor was called proprietor; those belonging to the senate, in which the governor was proconsul. And this was a regular distinction. Now it appears from Dio Cassius, (Lib. liv. ad A. U. 732.) that the province of Cyprus, which, in original distribution, was assigned to the emperor, had transferred to the senate, in exchange for some others; and after this exchange, the appropriate title of the Roman was proconsul.

Ib. xviii. 12. [p. 55.] "And when Gallio was deputy (proconsul) of Achaia."

The propriety of the title "proconsul" is in this still more critical. For the province of Achaia, after passing from the senate to the emperor, had been restored again by the emperor Claudius to the senate (and consequently its government had become proconsular) only six or seven years before the time in which this transaction is said to have taken place. (Suet. in Claud. c. xxv. Dio, lib. lxi.) And what confines with strictness the appellation to the time is, that Achaia under the following reign ceased to be a Roman province at all.

IX. [p. 152.] It appears, as well from the general constitution of a Roman province, as from what Josephus delivers concerning the state of Judea in particular, (Antiq. lib. xx. c. 8, sect. 5; c. 1, sect. 2.) that the power of life and death resided exclusively in the Roman governor; but that the Jews, nevertheless, had magistrates and a council, invested with a subordinate and municipal authority. This economy is discerned in every part of the Gospel narrative of our Saviour's crucifixion.

X. [p. 203.] Acts ix. 31. "Then had the churches rest throughout all Judea and Galilee and Samaria."

This rest synchronises with the attempt of Caligula to place his statue in the temple of Jerusalem; the threat of which outrage produced amongst the Jews a consternation that, for a season, diverted their attention from every other object. (Joseph. de Bell lib. Xi. c. 13, sect. 1, 3, 4.)

XI. [p. 218.] Acts xxi. 30. "And they took Paul, and drew him out of the temple; and forthwith the doors were shut. And as they went about to kill him, tidings came to the chief captain of the band that all Jerusalem was in an uproar. Then the chief captain came near, and took him and commanded him to be bound with two chains, and demanded who he was, and what he had done; and some cried one thing, and some another, among the multitude: and, when he could not know the certainty for the tumult, he commanded him to be carried into the castle. And when he came upon the stairs, so it was, that he was borne of the soldiers for the violence of the people."

In this quotation we have the band of Roman soldiers at Jerusalem, their office (to suppress tumults), the castle, the stairs, both, as it should seem, adjoining to the temple. Let us inquire whether we can find these particulars in any other record of that age and place.

Joseph. de. Ball. lib. v. e. 5, sect. 8. "Antonia was situated at the angle of the western and northern porticoes of the outer temple. It was built upon a rock fifty cubits high, steep on all sides.—On that side where it joined to the porticoes of the temple, there were stairs reaching to each portico, by which the guard descended; for there was always lodged here a Roman legion; and posting themselves in their armour in several places in the porticoes, they kept a watch on the people on the feast-days to prevent all disorders; for as the temple was a guard to the city, so was Antonia to the temple."

XII. [p. 224.] Acts iv. 1. "And as they spake unto the people, the priests, and the captain of the temple, and the Sadducees, came upon them." Here we have a public officer, under the title of captain of the temple, and he probably a Jew, as he accompanied the priests and Sadducees in apprehending the apostles.

Joseph. de Bell. lib. ii. c. 17, sect. 2. "And at the temple, Eleazer, the son of Ananias the high priest, a young man of a bold and resolute disposition, then captain, persuaded those who performed the sacred ministrations not to receive the gift or sacrifice of any stranger."

XIII. [p. 225.] Acts xxv. 12. "Then Festus, when he had conferred with the council, answered, Hast thou appealed unto Caesar? unto Caesar shalt thou go." That it was usual for the Roman presidents to have a council consisting of their friends, and other chief Romans in the province, appears expressly in the following passage of Cicero's oration against Verres:—"*Illud negare posses, aut nunc negabis, te, concilio tuo dimisso, viris primariis, qui in consilio C. Sacerdotis fuerant, tibique esse volebant, remotis, de re judicata judicasse?*"

XIV. [p. 235.] Acts xvi. 13. "And (at Philippi) on the Sabbath we went out of the city by a river-side, where prayer was wont to be made," or where a proseuche, oratory, or place of prayer was allowed. The particularity to be remarked is, the situation of the place where prayer was wont to be made, viz. by a river-side.

Philo, describing the conduct of the Jews of Alexandria, on a certain public occasion, relates of them, that, "early in the morning, flocking out of the gates of the city, they go to the neighbouring shores, (for the proseuchai were destroyed,) and, standing in a most pure place, they lift up their voices with one accord." (Philo in Flacc. p. 382.)

Josephus gives us a decree of the city of Halicarnassus, permitting the Jews to build oratories; a part of which decree runs thus:—"We ordain that the Jews, who are willing, men and women, do observe the Sabbaths, and perform sacred rites, according to the Jewish laws, and build oratories by the sea-side." (Joseph. Antiq. lib. xiv. c. 10, sect, 24.)

Tertullian, among other Jewish rites and customs, such as feasts, sabbaths, fasts, and unleavened bread, mentions "*orationes literales,*" that is, prayers by the river-side. (Tertull. ad Nat, lib. i. c. 13.)

XV. [p. 255.] Acts xxvi. 5. "After the most straitest sect of our religion, I lived a Pharisee."

Joseph. de Bell. lib. i. c. 5, sect. 2. "The Pharisees were reckoned the most religious of any of the Jews, and to be the most exact and skilful in explaining the laws."

In the original, there is an agreement not only in the sense but in the expression, it being the same Greek adjective which is rendered "strait" in the Acts, and "exact" in Josephus.

XVI. [p. 255.] Mark vii. 3,4. "The Pharisees and all the Jews, except they wash, eat not, holding the tradition of the elders; and many other things there be which they have received to hold."

Joseph. Antiq. lib. xiii. c. 10, sect. 6. "The Pharisees have delivered up to the people many institutions, as received from the fathers, which are not written in the law of Moses."

XVII. [p. 259.] Acts xxiii. 8. "For the Sadducees say, that there is no resurrection, neither angel, nor spirit; but the Pharisees confess both."

Joseph. de Bell. lib. ii. c. 8, sect. 14. "They (the Pharisees) believe every soul to be immortal, but that the soul of the good only passes into another body, and that the soul of the wicked is punished with eternal punishment." On the other hand (Antiq. lib. xviii.e. 1, sect. 4), "It is the opinion of the Sadducees that souls perish with the bodies."

XVIII. [p. 268.] Acts v. 17. "Then the high priest rose up, and all they that were with him (which is the sect of the Sadducees), and were filled with indignation." Saint Luke here intimates that the high priest was a Sadducee; which is a character one would not have expected to meet with in that station. This circumstance, remarkable as it is, was not however without examples.

Joseph. Antiq. lib. xiii. c. 10, sect. 6, 7. "John Hyreanus, high priest of the Jews, forsook the Pharisees upon a disgust, and joined himself to the party of the Sadducees." This high priest died one hundred and seven years before the Christian era.

Again (Antiq. lib. xx. e. 8, sect. 1), "This Ananus the younger, who, as we have said just now, had received the high priesthood, was fierce and haughty in his behaviour, and, above all men, hold and daring, and, moreover, was of the sect of the Sadducees." This high priest lived little more than twenty years after the transaction in the Acts.

XIX. [p. 282.] Luke ix. 51. "And it came to pass, when the time was come that he should be received up, he steadfastly set his face to go to Jerusalem, and sent messengers before his face. And they went, and entered into a village of the Samaritans, to make ready for him. And they did not receive him, because his face was as though he would go to Jerusalem."

Joseph. Antiq. lib. xx. c. 5, sect. 1. "It was the custom of the Galileans, who went up to the holy city at the feasts, to travel through the country of Samaria. As they were in their journey, some inhabitants of the village called Ginaea, which lies on the borders of Samaria and the great plain, falling upon them, killed a great many of them."

XX. [p. 278.] John iv. 20. "Our fathers," said the Samaritan woman, "worshipped in this mountain; and ye say, that Jerusalem is the place where men ought to worship."

Joseph. Antiq. lib. xviii. c. 5, sect. 1. "Commanding them to meet him at mount Gerizzim, which is by them (the Samaritans) esteemed the most sacred of all mountains."

XXI. [p. 312.] Matt. xxvi. 3. "Then assembled together the chief priests, and the elders of the people, unto the palace of the high priest, who was called Caiaphas." That Caiaphas was high priest, and high priest throughout the presidentship of Pontius Pilate, and consequently at this time, appears from the following account:—He was made high priest by Valerius Gratus, predecessor of Pontius Pilate, and was removed from his office by Vitellius, president of Syria, after Pilate was sent away out of the province of Judea. Josephus relates the advancement of Caiaphas to the high priesthood in this manner: "Gratus gave the high priesthood to Simon, the son of Camithus. He, having enjoyed this honour not above a year, was succeeded by Joseph, who is also called Caiaphas." (Antiq. lib. xviii. c. 2, sect. 2.) After this, Gratus went away for Rome, having been eleven years in Judea; and Pontius Pilate came thither as his successor. Of the removal of Caiaphas from his office, Josephus likewise afterwards informs us: and connects it with a circumstance which fixes the time to a date subsequent to the determination of Pilate's government—"Vitellius," he tells us; "ordered Pilate to repair to Rome: and after that, went up himself to Jerusalem, and then gave directions concerning several matters. And having done these things he took away the priesthood from the high priest Joseph, who is called Caiaphas." (Antiq. lib. xvii. c. 5, sect 3.)

XXII. (Michaelis, c. xi. sect. 11.) Acts xxiii. 4. "And they that stood by said, Revilest thou God's high priest? Then said Paul, I wist not, brethren, that he was the high priest?" Now, upon inquiry into the history of the age, it turns out that Ananias, of whom this is spoken, was, in truth, not the high priest, though he was sitting in judgment in that assumed capacity. The case was, that he had formerly holden the office, and had been deposed; that the person who succeeded him had been murdered; that another was not yet appointed to the station; and that during the vacancy, he had, of his own authority, taken upon himself the discharge of the office. (Joseph. Antiq. 1. xx. c. 5, sect. 2; c. 6, sect. 2; c. 9, sect. 2.) This singular situation of the high priesthood took place during the interval between the death of Jonathan, who was murdered by order of Felix, and the accession of Ismael, who was invested with the high priesthood by Agrippa; and precisely in this interval it happened that Saint Paul was apprehended, and brought before the Jewish council.

XXIII. [p. 323.] Matt. xxvi. 59. "Now the chief priests and elders, and all the council, sought false witness against him."

Joseph. Antiq. lib. xviii.e. 15, sect. 3, 4. "Then might be seen the high priests themselves with ashes on their heads and their breasts naked."

The agreement here consists in speaking of the high priests or chief priests (for the name in the original is the same) in the plural number, when in strictness there was only one high priest: which may be considered as a proof that the evangelists were habituated to the manner of speaking then in use, because they retain it when it is neither accurate nor just. For the sake of brevity, I have put down from Josephus only a single example of the application of this title in the plural number; but it is his usual style.

Ib. [p. 871.] Luke ill. 1. "Now in the fifteenth year of the reign of Tiberius Caesar, Pontius Pilate being governor of Juries, and Herod being tetrarch of Galilee, Annas and Caiaphas being the high priests, the word of God came unto John." There is a passage in Josephus very nearly parallel to this, and which may at least serve to vindicate the evangelist from objection, with respect to his giving the title of high priest specifically to two persons at the same time: "Quadratus sent two others of the most powerful men of the Jews, as also the high priests Jonathan and Ananias." (De Bell. lib. ix. c. 12, sect. 6.) That Annas was a person in an eminent station, and possessed an authority coordinate with, or next to, that of the high print properly so called, may he inferred from Saint John's Gospel, which in the history of Christ's crucifixion relates that "the soldiers led him away to Annas first." (xviii.13.) And this might be noticed as an example of undesigned coincidence in the two evangelists.

Again, [p. 870.] Acts iv. 6. Annas is called the high priest, though Caiaphas was in the office of the high priesthood. In like manner in Josephus, (Lib. ii. c. 20, sect. 3.) "Joseph the son of Gorion, and the high priest Ananus, were chosen to be supreme governors of all things in the city." Yet Ananus, though here called the high priest Ananus, was not then in the office of the high priesthood. The truth is, there is an indeterminateness in the use of this title in the Gospel:(Mark xiv. 53.) sometimes it is applied exclusively to the person who held the office at the time; sometimes to one or two more, who probably shared with him some of the powers or functions of the office; and sometimes to such of the priests as were eminent by their station or character; and there is the very same indeterminateness in Josephus.

XXIV. [p. 347.] John xix. 19, 20. "And Pilate wrote a title, and put it on the cross." That such was the custom of the Romans on these occasions appears from passages of Suetonius and Dio Cassius: "*Pattrem familias—canibus objecit, cure hoc titulo, Impie locutus parmularius.*" Suet. Domit. cap. x. And in Dio Cassius we have the following: "Having led him through the midst of the court or assembly, with a writing signifying the cause of his death, and afterwards crucifying him." Book liv.

Ib. "And it was written in Hebrew, Greek, and Latin." That it was also usual about this time in Jerusalem to set up advertisements in different languages, is gathered from the account which Josephus gives of an expostulatory message from Titus to the Jews when the city was almost in his hands; in which he says, Did ye not erect pillars with inscriptions on them, in the Greek and in our language, "Let no one pass beyond these bounds"?

XXV. [p. 352.] Matt. xxvii. 26. "When he had scourged Jesus, he delivered him to be crucified."

The following passages occur in Josephus:

"Being beaten, they were crucified opposite to the citadel." (P. 1247, edit. 24 Huds.)

"Whom, having first scourged with whips, he crucified." (P. 1080, edit. 45.)

"He was burnt alive, having been first beaten." (P. 1327, edit. 43.)

To which may he added one from Livy, lib. xi. c. 5. "*Pro ductique omnes, virgisqus caesi, ac securi percussi.*"

A modern example may illustrate the use we make of this instance. The preceding of a capital execution by the corporal punishment of the sufferer is a practice unknown in England, but retained, in some instances at least, as appears by the late execution of a regicide in Sweden. This circumstance, therefore, in the account of an English execution, purporting to come from an English writer, would not only bring a suspicion upon the truth of the account, but would in a considerable degree impeach its pretensions of having been written by the author whose name it bore. Whereas, the same circumstance in the account of a Swedish execution would verify the account, and support the authenticity of the book in which it was found, or, at least, would prove that the author, whoever he was, possessed the information and the knowledge which he ought to possess.

XXVI. [p. 353.] John xix. 16. "And they took Jesus, and led him away; and he bearing his cross went forth."

Plutarch, De iis qui sero puniuntur, p. 554; a Paris, 1624. "Every kind of wickedness produces its own particular torment; just as every malefactor, when he is brought forth to execution, carries his own cross."

XXVII. John xix. 32. "Then came the soldiers and brake the legs of the first, and of the other which was crucified with him."

Constantine abolished the punishment of the cross: in commending which edict, a heathen writer notices this very circumstance of breaking the legs: "*Eo pius, ut etiam vetus veterrimumque supplicium, patibulum, et cruribus suffringendis, primus removerit.*" Aur. Vict Ces. cap. xli.

XXVIII. [p. 457.] Acts iii. 1. "Now Peter and John went up together into the temple, at the hour of prayer, being the ninth hour."

Joseph. Antiq. lib xv. e. 7, sect. 8. "Twice every day, in the morning and at the ninth hour, the priests perform their, duty at the altar."

XXIX. [p. 462.] Acts xv. 21. "For Moses of old time hath, in every city, them that preach him, being read in the synagogues every Sabbath-day."

Joseph. contra Ap. 1. ii. "He (Moses) gave us the law, the most excellent of all institutions; nor did he appoint that it should be heard once only, or twice, or often, but that, laying aside all other works, we should meet together every week to hear it read, and gain a perfect understanding of it."

XXX. [p. 465.] Acts xxi. 23. "We have four men which have a vow on them; them take, and purify thyself with them that they may shave their heads."

Joseph. de Bell. 1. xi. c. 15. "It is customary for those who have been afflicted with some distemper, or have laboured under any other difficulties, to make a vow thirty days before they offer sacrifices, to abstain from wine, and shave the hair of their heads."

Ib. v. 24. "Them take, and purify thyself with them, and be at charges with them, that they may shave their heads."

Joseph. Antiq. 1. xix. c. 6. "He (Herod Agrippa) coming to Jerusalem, offered up sacrifices of thanksgiving, and omitted nothing that was prescribed by the law. For which reason he also ordered a good number of Nazarites to be shaved." We here find that it was an act of piety amongst the Jews to defray for those who were under the Nazaritic vow the expenses which attended its completion; and that the phrase was, "that they might be saved." The custom and the expression are both remarkable, and both in close conformity with the Scripture account.

XXXI. [p. 474.] 2 Cor. xi. 24. "Of the Jews, five times received I forty stripes save one."

Joseph. Antiq. iv. c. 8, sect. 21. "He that acts contrary hereto let him receive forty stripes, wanting one, from the officer."

The coincidence here is singular, because the law allowed forty stripes:—"Forty stripes he may give him and not exceed." Deut. xxv. 3. It proves that the author of the Epistle to the Corinthians was guided not by books, but by facts; because his statement agrees with the actual custom, even when that custom deviated from the written law, and from what he must have learnt by consulting the Jewish code, as set forth in the Old Testament.

XXXII. [p. 490.] Luke iii. 12. "Then came also publicans to be baptized." From this quotation, as well as from the history of Levi or Matthew (Luke v. 29), and of Zaccheus (Luke xix. 2), it appears that the publicans or tax-gatherers were, frequently at least, if not always, Jews: which, as the country was then under a Roman government, and the taxes were paid to the Romans, was a circumstance not to be expected. That it was the truth, however, of the case appears from a short passage of Josephus.

De Bell. lib. ii. c. 14, sect. 45. "But Florus not restraining these practices by his authority, the chief men of the Jews, among whom was John the publican, not knowing well what course to take, wait upon Florus and give him eight talents of silver to stop the building."

XXXIII. [p. 496.] Acts xxii. 25. "And as they bound him with thongs, Paul said unto the centurion that stood by, Is it lawful for you to scourge a man that is a Roman and uncondemned?"

"Facinus est vinciri civem Romanum; scelus verberari." Cic. in Verr.

"Caedebatur virgis, in medio foro Messanae, civis Romanus, Judices: cum interea nullus gemitus, nulla vox alia, istius miseri inter dolorem crepitumque plagarum audiebatur, nisi haec, Civis Romanus sum."

XXXIV. [p. 513] Acts xxii. 27. "Then the chief captain came, and said unto him (Paul), Tell me, Art thou a Roman? He said Yea." The circumstance to be here noticed is, that a Jew was a Roman citizen.

Joseph. Antiq. lib. xiv. c. 10, sect. 13. "Lucius Lentulna, the consul, declared, I have dismissed from the service the Jewish Roman citizens, who observe the rites of the Jewish religion at Ephesus."

Ib. ver. 28. "And the chief captain answered, with a great sum obtained

I this freedom."

Dio Cassius, lib. lx. "This privilege, which had been bought formerly at a great price, became so cheap, that it was commonly said a man might be made a Roman citizen for a few pieces of broken glass."

XXXV. [p. 521.] Acts xxviii. 16. "And when we came to Rome the centurion delivered the prisoners to the captain of the guard; but Paul was suffered to dwell by himself, with a soldier that kept him."

With which join vet. 20. "For the hope of Israel, I am bound with this chain."

"Quemadmedum cadem catean et custodiam et militem copulat; sic ista, quae tam dissimilia sunt, pariter incedunt." Seneca, Ep. v.

"Proconsul estimare solet, utrum in carcerera recipienda sit persona, an militi tradenda." Ulpian. l. i. sect. De Custod. et Exhib. Reor.

In the confinement of Agrippa by the order of Tiberius, Antonia managed that the centurion who presided over the guards, and the soldier to whom Agrippa was to be bound, might be men of mild character. (Joseph. Antiq. lib. xviii. c. 7, sect. 5.) After the accession of Caligula, Agrippa also, like Paul, was suffered to dwell, yet as a prisoner, in his own house.

XXXVI. [p. 531.] Acts xxvii. 1. "And when it was determined that we should sail into Italy, they delivered Paul, and certain other prisoners, unto one named Julius." Since not only Paul, but certain other prisoners were sent by the same ship into Italy, the text must be considered as carrying with it an intimation that the sending of persons from Judea to be tried at Rome was an ordinary practice. That in truth it was so, is made out by a variety of examples which the writings of Josephus furnish: and, amongst others, by the following, which comes near both to the time and the subject of the instance in the Acts. "Felix, for some slight offence, bound and sent to Rome several priests of his acquaintance, and very good and honest men, to answer for themselves to Caesar." Joseph. in Vit. sect. 3.

XXXVII. [p. 539.] Acts xi. 27. "And in these days came prophets from Jerusalem unto Antioch; and there stood up one of them, named Agabus, and signified by the Spirit that there should be a great dearth throughout all the world (or all the country); which came to pass in the days of Claudius Caesar."

Joseph. Antiq. 1. xx. c. 4, sect. 2. "In their time (i.e. about the fifth or sixth year of Claudius) a great dearth happened in Judea."

XXXVIII. [p. 555.] Acts xviii. 1, 2. "Because that Claudius had commanded all Jews to depart from Rome."

Suet. Gland. c. xxv. "*Judeos, impulsero Chresto assidue tumultuantes, Roma expulit.*"

XXXIX. [p. 664.] Acts v. 37. "After this man, rose up Judas of Galilee, in the days of the taxing, and drew away much people after him."

Joseph. de Bell. 1. vii. "He (viz. the person who in another place is called, by Josephus, Judas the Galilean, or Judas of Galilee) persuaded not a few to enrol themselves when Cyrenius the censor was sent into Judea."

XL. [p. 942.] Acts xxi. 38. "Art not thou that Egyptian which, before these days, madest an uproar, and leddest out into the wilderness four thousand men that were murderers?"

Joseph. de Bell. 1. ii. c. 13, sect. 5. "But the Egyptian false prophet brought a yet heavier disaster upon the Jews; for this impostor, coming into the country, and gaining the reputation of a prophet, gathered together thirty thousand men, who were deceived by him. Having brought them round out of the wilderness, up to the mount of Olives, he intended from thence to make his attack upon Jerusalem; but Felix, coming suddenly upon him with the Roman soldiers, prevented the attack.—A great number, or (as it should rather be rendered) the greatest part, of those that were with him were either slain or taken prisoners."

In these two passages, the designation of this impostor, an "Egyptian," without the proper name, "the wilderness ;" his escape, though his followers were destroyed; the time of the transaction, in the presidentship of Felix, which could not be any long time before the words in Luke are supposed to have been spoken; are circumstances of close correspondency. There is one, and only one, point of disagreement, and that is, in the number of his followers, which in the Acts are called four thousand, and by Josephus thirty thousand: but, beside that the names of

186

numbers, more than any other words, are liable to the errors of transcribers, we are in the present instance under the less concern to reconcile the evangelist with Josephus, as Josephus is not, in this point, consistent with himself. For whereas, in the passage here quoted, he calls the number thirty thousand, and tells us that the greatest part, or a great number (according as his words are rendered) of those that were with him were destroyed; in his Antiquities he represents four hundred to have been killed upon this occasion, and two hundred taken prisoners:(Lib. xx. c. 7, sect. 6.) which certainly was not the "greatest part," nor "a great part," nor "a great number," out of thirty thousand. It is probable, also, that Lysias and Josephus spoke of the expedition in its different stages: Lysias, of those who followed the Egyptian out of Jerusalem; Josephus, of all who were collected about him afterwards, from different quarters.

XLI. (Lardner's Jewish and Heathen Testimonies, vol. iii p. 21.) Acts xvii. 22. "Then Paul stood in the midst of Marshill, and said, Ye men of Athens, I perceive that in all things ye are too superstitious; for, as I passed by and beheld your devotions, I found an altar with this inscription, TO THE UNKNOWN GOD. Whom therefore ye ignorantly worship, him declare I unto you."

Diogenes Laertius, who wrote about the year 210, in his history of Epimenides, who is supposed to have flourished nearly six hundred years before Christ, relates of him the following story: that, being invited to Athens for the purpose, he delivered the city from a pestilence in this manner;—"Taking several sheep, some black, others white, he had them up to the Areopagus, and then let them go where they would, and gave orders to those who followed them, wherever any of them should lie down, to sacrifice it to the god to whom it belonged; and so the plague ceased.—Hence," says the historian, "it has come to pass, that to this present time may be found in the boroughs of the Athenians ANONYMOUS altars: a memorial of the expiation then made." (In Epimenide, l. i. segm. 110.) These altars, it may be presumed, were called anonymous because there was not the name of any particular deity inscribed upon them.

Pausanias, who wrote before the end of the second century, in his description of Athens, having mentioned an altar of Jupiter Olympius, adds, "And nigh unto it is an altar of unknown gods." (Paus. l. v. p. 412.) And in another place, he speaks "of altars of gods called unknown." (Paus. l. i. p. 4.)

Philostratus, who wrote in the beginning of the third century; records it as an observation of Apollonius Tyanseus, "That it was wise to speak well of all the gods, especially at Athens, where altars of unknown demons were erected." (Philos. Apoll. Tyan. l. vi. c. 3.)

The author of the dialogue Philoparis by many supposed to have been Lucian, who wrote about the year 170, by others some anonymous

Heathen writer of the fourth century, makes Critias swear by the unknown god of Athens; and, near time end of the dialogue, has these words, "But let us find out the unknown god at Athens, and, stretching our hands to heaven, offer to him our praises and thanksgivings." (Lucian. in Philop. tom. ii. Graev. pp. 767, 780.)

This is a very curious and a very important coincidence. It appears beyond controversy, that altars with this inscription were existing at Athens at the time when Saint Paul is alleged to have been there. It seems also (which is very worthy of observation) that this inscription was peculiar to the Athenians. There is no evidence that there were altars inscribed "to the unknown god" in any other country. Supposing the history of Saint Paul to have been a fable, how is it possible that such a writer as the author of the Acts of the Apostles was should hit upon a circumstance so extraordinary, and introduce it by an allusion so suitable to Saint Paul's office and character?

The examples here collected will be sufficient, I hope, to satisfy us that the writers of the Christian history knew something of what they were writing about. The argument is also strengthened by the following considerations:

I. That these agreements appear not only in articles of public history, but sometimes in minute, recondite, and very peculiar circumstances, in which, of all others, a forger is most likely to have been found tripping.

II. That the destruction of Jerusalem, which took place forty years after the commencement of the Christian institution, produced such a change in the state of the country, and the condition of the Jews, that a writer who was unacquainted with the circumstances of the nation before that event would find it difficult to avoid mistakes, in endeavouring to give detailed accounts of transactions connected with those circumstances, forasmuch as he could no longer have a living exemplar to copy from.

III. That there appears, in the writers of the New Testament, a knowledge of the affairs of those times which we do not find in authors of later ages. In particular, "many of the Christian writers of the second and third centuries, and of the following ages, had false notions concerning the state of Judea between the nativity of Jesus and the destruction of Jerusalem." (Lardner, part i. vol. ii. p. 960.) Therefore they could not have composed our histories.

Amidst so many conformities we are not to wonder that we meet with some difficulties. The principal of these I will put down, together with the solutions which they have received. But in doing this I must be contented with a brevity better suited to the limits of my volume than to the nature of a controversial argument. For the historical proofs of my assertions, and for the Greek criticisms upon which some of them are founded, I refer the reader to the second volume of the first part of Dr. Lardner's large work.

I. The taxing during which Jesus was born was "first made," as we read, according to our translation, in Saint Luke, "whilst Cyrenius was governor of Syria." (Chap. ii. ver. 2.) Now it turns out that Cyrenius was not governor of Syria until twelve, or at the soonest, ten years after the birth of Christ; and that a taxing census, or assessment, was made in Judea, in the beginning of his government, The charge, therefore, brought against the evangelist is, that, intending to refer to this taxing, he has misplaced the date of it by an error of ten or twelve years.

The answer to the accusation is founded in his using the word "first:"—"And this taxing was first made:" for, according to the mistake imputed to the evangelist, this word could have no signification whatever; it could have had no place in his narrative; because, let it relate to what it will, taxing, census, enrolment, or assessment, it imports that the writer had more than one of those in contemplation. It acquits him therefore of the charge: it is inconsistent with the supposition of his knowing only of the taxing in the beginning of Cyrenius's government. And if the evangelist knew (which this word proves that he did) of some other taxing beside that, it is too much, for the sake of convicting him of a mistake, to lay it down as certain that he intended to refer to that.

The sentence in Saint Luke may be construed thus: "This was the first assessment (or enrolment) of Cyrenius, governor of Syria;"[2] the words "governor of Syria" being used after the name of Cyrenius as his addition or title. And this title, belonging to him at the time of writing the account, was naturally enough subjoined to his name, though acquired after the transaction which the account describes. A modern writer who was not very exact in the choice of his expressions, in relating the affairs of the East Indies, might easily say that such a thing was done by Governor Hastings; though, in truth, the thing had been done by him before his advancement to the station from which he received the name of governor. And this, as we contend, is precisely the inaccuracy which has produced the difficulty in Saint Luke.

At any rate it appears from the form of the expression that he had two taxings or enrolments in contemplation. And if Cyrenius had been sent upon this business into Judea before he became governor of Syria (against which supposition there is no proof, but rather external evidence of an

---

[2] If the word which we render "first" be rendered "before," which it has been strongly contended that the Greek idiom shows of, the whole difficulty vanishes: for then the passage would be,—"Now this taxing was made before Cyreulus was governor of Syria;" which corresponds with the chronology. But I rather choose to argue, that however the word "first" be rendered, to give it a meaning at all, it militates with the objection. In this I think there can be no mistake.

enrolment going on about this time under some person or other [3]), then the census on all hands acknowledged to have been made by him in the beginning of his government would form a second, so as to occasion the other to be called the first.

II. Another chronological objection arises upon a date assigned in the beginning of the third chapter of Saint Luke. (Lardner, part i. vol. ii. p. 768.) "Now in the fifteenth year of the reign of Tiberius Caesar,—Jesus began to be about thirty years of age:" for, supposing Jesus to have been born as Saint Matthew and Saint Luke also himself relate, in the time of Herod, he must, according to the dates given in Josephus and by the Roman historians, have been at least thirty-one years of age in the fifteenth year of Tiberius. If he was born, as Saint Matthew's narrative intimates, one or two years before Herod's death, he would have been thirty-two or thirty-three years old at that time.

This is the difficulty: the solution turns upon an alteration in the construction of the Greek. Saint Luke's words in the original are allowed, by the general opinion of learned men, to signify, not "that Jesus began to be about thirty years of age," but "that he was about thirty years of age when he began his ministry." This construction being admitted, the adverb "about" gives us all the latitude we want, and more especially when applied, as it is in the present instance, to a decimal number; for such numbers, even without this qualifying addition, are often used in a laxer sense than is here contended for.[4]

III. Acts v. 36. "For before these days rose up Theudas, boasting himself to be somebody; to whom a number of men, about four hundred, joined themselves: who were slain; and all, as many as obeyed him, were scattered and brought to nought."

Josephus has preserved the account of an impostor of the name of Theudas, who created some disturbances, and was slain; but according to the date assigned to this man's appearance (in which, however, it is very possible that Josephus may have been mistaken), (Michaelis's Introduction to the New Testament [Marsh's translation], vol. i. p. 61.) it must have been, at the least, seven years after Gamaliel's speech, of which

---

[3] Josephus (Antiq. xvii. c. 2, sect. 6.) has this remarkable message: "When therefore the whole Jewish nation took an oath to be faithful to Caesar, and the interests of the king." This transaction corresponds in the course of the history with the time of Christ's birth. What is called a census, and which we render taxing, was delivering upon oath an account of their property. This might be accompanied with an oath of fidelity, or might be mistaken by Josephus for it.

[4] Livy, speaking of the peace which the conduct of Romulus had procured to the state, during the whole reign of his successor (Numa), has these words: "Ab illo enim profectis viribus datis tautum valuit, ut, in quaaraginta deiade annos, tutam proem haberet:" yet afterwards in the same chapter, "Romulus," he says, "septera et triginta regnavit annos. Numa tres et quadraginta." (Liv. Hist. c. i. sect. 16.)

this text is a part, was delivered. It has been replied to the objection, (Lardner, part i. vol. ii. p. 92.) that there might be two impostors of this name: and it has been observed, in order to give a general probability to the solution, that the same thing appears to have happened in other instances of the same kind. It is proved from Josephus, that there were not fewer than four persons of the name of Simon within forty years, and not fewer than three of the name of Judas within ten years, who were all leaders of insurrections: and it is likewise recorded by this historian, that upon the death of Herod the Great (which agrees very well with the time of the commotion referred to by Gamaliel, and with his manner of stating that time, "before these days") there were innumerable disturbances in Judea. (Antiq. 1. 17, c. 12. sect. 4.) Archbishop Usher was of opinion, that one of the three Judases above mentioned was Gamaliel's Theudas; (Annals, p. 797.) and that with a less variation of the name than we actually find in the Gospel, where one of the twelve apostles is called, by Luke, Judas; and by Mark, Thaddeus. (Luke vi. 16. Mark iii. 18.) Origen, however he came at his information, appears to have believed that there was an impostor of the name of Theudas before the nativity of Christ. (Orig. cont Cels. p. 44.)

IV. Matt. xxiii. 34. "Wherefore, behold I send unto you prophets, and wise men, and scribes, and some of them ye shall kill and crucify; and some of them shall ye scourge in your synagogues, and persecute them from city to city; that upon you may come all the righteous blood shed upon the earth, from the blood of righteous Abel unto the blood of Zacharias, son of Barachias, whom ye slew between the temple and the altar."

There is a Zacharias whose death is related in the second book of Chronicles,[5] in a manner which perfectly supports our Saviour's allusion. But this Zacharias was the son of Jehoiada.

There is also Zacharias the prophet; who was the son of Barachiah, and is so described in the superscription of his prophecy, but of whose death we have no account.

I have little doubt but that the first Zacharias was the person spoken of by our Saviour; and that the name of the father has been since added or changed, by some one who took it from the title of the prophecy, which happened to be better known to him than the history in the Chronicles.

---

[5] "And the Spirit of God came upon Zacharias, the son of Jehoiada the priest, which stood above the people, and mid unto them, Thus saith God, Why transgress ye the commandments of the Lord that ye cannot prosper? Because ye hive forsaken the Lord, he hath also forsaken you. And they conspired against him, and stoned him with stones, at the commandment of the king, in the court of the house of the Lord." 2 Chron. xxiv. 20, 21.

There is likewise a Zacharias, the son of Baruch, related by Josephus to have been slain in the temple a few years before the destruction of Jerusalem. It has been insinuated that the words put into our Saviour's mouth contain a reference to this transaction, and were composed by some writer who either confounded the time of the transaction with our Saviour's age, or inadvertently overlooked the anachronism.

Now, suppose it to have been so; suppose these words to have been suggested by the transaction related in Josephus, and to have been falsely ascribed to Christ; and observe what extraordinary coincidences (accidentally as it must in that case have been) attend the forger's mistake.

First, that we have a Zacharias in the book of Chronicles, whose death, and the manner of it, corresponds with the allusion.

Secondly, that although the name of this person's father be erroneously put down in the Gospel, yet we have a way of accounting for the error by showing another Zacharias in the Jewish Scriptures much better known than the former, whose patronymic was actually that which appears in the text.

Every one who thinks upon the subject will find these to be circumstances which could not have met together in a mistake which did not proceed from the circumstances themselves.

I have noticed, I think, all the difficulties of this kind. They are few: some of them admit of a clear, others of a probable solution. The reader will compare them with the number, the variety, the closeness, and the satisfactoriness, of the instances which are to be set against them; and he will remember the scantiness, in many cases, of our intelligence, and that difficulties always attend imperfect information.

CHAPTER VII.

UNDESIGNED COINCIDENCES.

Between the letters which bear the name of Saint Paul in our collection and his history in the Acts of the Apostles there exist many notes of correspondency. The simple perusal of the writings is sufficient to prove that neither the history was taken from the letters, nor the letters from the history. And the undesignedness of the agreements (which undesignedness is gathered from their latency, their minuteness, their obliquity, the suitableness of the circumstances in which they consist to the places in which those circumstances occur, and the circuitous references by which they are traced out) demonstrates that they have not been produced by meditation, or by any fraudulent contrivance. But coincidences, from which these causes are excluded, and which are too close and numerous to be accounted for by accidental concurrences of fiction, must necessarily have truth for their foundation. This argument appeared to my mind of so much value (especially for its assuming nothing beside the existence of the books), that I have pursued it through Saint Paul's thirteen epistles, in a work published by me four years ago, under the title of Horae Paulinae. I am sensible how feebly any argument which depends upon an induction of particulars is represented without examples. On which account I wished to have abridged my own volume, in the manner in which I have treated Dr. Lardner's in the preceding chapter. But, upon making the attempt, I did not find it in my power to render the articles intelligible by fewer words than I have there used. I must be content, therefore, to refer the reader to the work itself. And I would particularly invite his attention to the observations which are made in it upon the first three epistles. I persuade myself that he will find the proofs, both of agreement, and undesignedness, supplied by these epistles, sufficient to support the conclusion which is there maintained, in favour both of the genuineness of the writings and the truth of the narrative.

It remains only, in this place, to point out how the argument bears upon the general question of the Christian history.

First, Saint Paul in these letters affirms, in unequivocal terms, his own performance of miracles, and, what ought particularly to be remembered, "That miracles were the signs of an Apostle." (Rom. xv. 18, 19. 2 Cor. xii. 12.) If this testimony come from Saint Paul's own hand, it is invaluable. And that it does so, the argument before us fixes in my mind a firm assurance.

Secondly, it shows that the series of action represented in the epistles of Saint Paul was real; which alone lays a foundation for the proposition which forms the subject of the first part of our present work, viz. that the original witnesses of the Christian history devoted themselves to lives of toil, suffering, and danger, in consequence of their belief of the truth of that history, and for the sake of communicating the knowledge of it to others.

Thirdly, it proves that Luke, or whoever was the author of the Acts of the Apostles (for the argument does not depend upon the name of the author, though I know no reason for questioning it), was well acquainted with Saint Paul's history; and that he probably was, what he professes himself to be, a companion of Saint Paul's travels; which, if true, establishes, in a considerable degree, the credit even of his Gospel, because it shows that the writer, from his time, situation, and connexions, possessed opportunities of informing himself truly concerning the transactions which he relates. I have little difficulty in applying to the Gospel of Saint Luke what is proved concerning the Acts of the Apostles, considering them as two parts of the same history; for though there are instances of second parts being forgeries, I know none where the second part is genuine, and the first not so.

I will only observe, as a sequel of the argument, though not noticed in my work, the remarkable similitude between the style of Saint John's Gospel and of Saint John's Epistle. The style of Saint John's is not at all the style of Saint Paul's Epistles, though both are very singular; nor is it the style of Saint James's or of Saint Peter's Epistles: but it bears a resemblance to the style of the Gospel inscribed with Saint John's name, so far as that resemblance can be expected to appear, which is not in simple narrative, so much as in reflections, and in the representation of discourses. Writings so circumstanced prove themselves, and one another, to be genuine. This correspondency is the more valuable, as the epistle itself asserts, in Saint John's manner, indeed, but in terms sufficiently explicit, the writer's personal knowledge of Christ's history: "That which was from the beginning, which we have heard, which we have seen with our eyes, which we have looked upon, and our hands have handled, of the word of life; that which we have seen and heard, declare we unto you." (Ch. i. ver. 1—3.)Who would not desire, who perceives not the value of an account delivered by a writer so well informed as this?

CHAPTER VIII.

OF THE HISTORY OF THE RESURRECTION.

The history of the resurrection of Christ is a part of the evidence of Christianity: but I do not know whether the proper strength of this passage of the Christian history, or wherein its peculiar value, as a head of evidence, consists, be generally understood. It is not that, as a miracle, the resurrection ought to be accounted a more decisive proof of supernatural agency than other miracles are; it is not that, as it stands in the Gospels, it is better attested than some others; it is not, for either of these reasons, that more weight belongs to it than to other miracles, but for the following, viz., That it is completely certain that the apostles of Christ, and the first teachers of Christianity, asserted the fact. And this would have been certain, if the four Gospels had been lost, or never written. Every piece of Scripture recognizes the resurrection. Every epistle of every apostle, every author contemporary with the apostles, of the age immediately succeeding the apostles, every writing from that age to the present genuine or spurious, on the side of Christianity or against it, concur in representing the resurrection of Christ as an article of his history, received without doubt or disagreement by all who called themselves Christians, as alleged from the beginning by the propagators of the institution, and alleged as the centre of their testimony. Nothing, I apprehend, which a man does not himself see or hear can be more certain to him than this point. I do not mean that nothing can be more certain than that Christ rose from the dead; but that nothing can be more certain than that his apostles, and the first teachers of Christianity, gave out that he did so. In the other parts of the Gospel narrative, a question may be made, whether the things related of Christ be the very things which the apostles and first teachers of the religion delivered concerning him? And this question depends a good deal upon the evidence we possess of the genuineness, or rather perhaps of the antiquity, credit, and reception of the books. On the subject of the resurrection, no such discussion is necessary, because no such doubt can be entertained. The only points which can enter into our consideration are, whether the apostles knowingly published a falsehood, or whether they were themselves deceived; whether either of these suppositions be possible. The first, I think, is pretty generally given up. The nature of the undertaking, and of the men; the extreme unlikelihood that such men should engage in such a measure as a scheme; their personal toils, and dangers and sufferings in the cause; their appropriation of their whole time to the object; the warm and seemingly unaffected zeal and earnestness with which they profess their sincerity exempt their memory from the suspicion of imposture. The solution more deserving of notice is that which would resolve the conduct of the apostles into enthusiasm; which would class the evidence of Christ's resurrection with the numerous stories that are extant of the apparitions of dead men. There are circumstances in the narrative, as it is preserved in our histories, which destroy this comparison entirely. It was not one person but many, who saw him; they saw him not only separately but together, not only by night but by day, not at a distance but near, not once but several times; they not only saw him, but touched him, conversed with him, ate with him, examined his person to satisfy their doubts. These particulars are decisive: but they stand, I do admit, upon the credit of our records. I would answer, therefore, the insinuation of enthusiasm, by a circumstance which arises out of the nature of the thing; and the reality of which must be confessed by all who allow, what I believe is not denied, that the resurrection of Christ, whether true or false, was asserted by his disciples from the beginning; and that circumstance is, the non-production of the dead body. It is related in the history, what indeed the story of the resurrection necessarily implies, that the corpse was missing out of the sepulchre: it is related also in the history, that the Jews reported that the followers of Christ had stolen it away.[1] And this account, though loaded with great improbabilities, such as the situation of the disciples, their fears for their own safety at the time, the unlikelihood of their expecting to succeed, the difficulty of actual success,[2] and the inevitable consequence of detection and failure, was, nevertheless, the most credible account that could be given of the matter. But it proceeds entirely upon the supposition of fraud, as all the old objections did. What account can be given of the body, upon the supposition of enthusiasm? It is impossible our Lord's followers could believe that he was risen from the dead, if his corpse was lying before them. No enthusiasm ever reached to such a pitch of extravagancy as that: a spirit may be an illusion; a body is a real thing, an object of sense, in which there can be no mistake. All accounts of spectres leave the body in the grave. And although the body of Christ might be removed by fraud, and for the purposes of fraud, yet

---

[1] "And this saying," Saint Matthew writes, "is commonly reported amongst the Jews until this day" (chap. xxviii. 15). The evangelist may be thought good authority as to this point, even by those who do not admit his evidence in every other point: and this point is sufficient to prove that the body was missing. It has been rightly, I think, observed by Dr. Townshend (Dis. upon the Res. p. 126), that the story of the guards carried collusion upon the face of it:—"His disciples came by night, and stole him away while we slept." Men in their circumstances would not have made such an acknowledgment of their negligence without previous assurances of protection and impunity.

[2] "Especially at the full moon, the city full of people, many probably passing the whole night, as Jesus and his disciples had done, in the open air, the sepulchre so near the city as to be now enclosed within the walls." Priestley on the Resurr. p. 24.

without any such intention, and by sincere but deluded men (which is the representation of the apostolic character we are now examining), no such attempt could be made. The presence and the absence of the dead body are alike inconsistent with the hypothesis of enthusiasm: for if present, it must have cured their enthusiasm at once; if absent, fraud, not enthusiasm, must have carried it away.

But further, if we admit, upon the concurrent testimony of all the histories, so much of the account as states that the religion of Jesus was set up at Jerusalem, and set up with asserting, in the very place in which he had been buried, and a few days after he had been buried, his resurrection out of the grave, it is evident that, if his body could have been found, the Jews would have produced it, as the shortest and completest answer possible to the whole story. The attempt of the apostles could not have survived this refutation a moment. If we also admit, upon the authority of Saint Matthew, that the Jews were advertised of the expectation of Christ's followers, and that they had taken due precaution in consequence of this notice, and that the body was in marked and public custody, the observation receives more force still. For notwithstanding their precaution and although thus prepared and forewarned; when the story of the resurrection of Christ came forth, as it immediately did; when it was publicly asserted by his disciples, and made the ground and basis of their preaching in his name, and collecting followers to his religion, the Jews had not the body to produce; but were obliged to meet the testimony of the apostles by an answer not containing indeed any impossibility in itself, but absolutely inconsistent with the supposition of their integrity; that is, in other words, inconsistent with the supposition which would resolve their conduct into enthusiasm.

CHAPTER IX.

THE PROPAGATION OF CHRISTIANITY.

In this argument, the first consideration is the fact—in what degree, within what time, and to what extent, Christianity actually was propagated.

The accounts of the matter which can be collected from our books are as follow: A few days after Christ's disappearance out of the world, we find an assembly of disciples at Jerusalem, to the number of "about one hundred and twenty;" (Acts i. 15.) which hundred and twenty were probably a little association of believers, met together not merely as believers in Christ, but as personally connected with the apostles, and with one another. Whatever was the number of believers then in Jerusalem, we have no reason to be surprised that so small a company should assemble: for there is no proof that the followers of Christ were yet formed into a society; that the society was reduced into any order; that it was at this time even understood that a new religion (in the sense which that term conveys to us) was to be set up in the world, or how the professors of that religion were to be distinguished from the rest of mankind. The death of Christ had left, we may suppose, the generality of his disciples in great doubt, both as to what they were to do, and concerning what was to follow.

This meeting was holden, as we have already said, a few days after Christ's ascension: for ten days after that event was the day of Pentecost, when, as our history relates, (Acts ii. 1.) upon a signal display of divine agency attending the persons of the apostles, there were added to the society "about three thousand souls." (Acts ii. 41.) But here, it is not, I think, to be taken, that these three thousand were all converted by this single miracle; but rather that many who before were believers in Christ became now professors of Christianity; that is to say, when they found that a religion was to be established, a society formed and set up in the name of Christ, governed by his laws, avowing their belief in his mission, united amongst themselves, and separated from the rest of the world by visible distinctions; in pursuance of their former conviction, and by virtue of what they had heard and seen, and known of Christ's history, they publicly became members of it.

We read in the fourth chapter (verse 4) of the Acts, that soon after this, "the number of the men," i.e. the society openly professing their belief in Christ, "was about five thousand." So that here is an increase of two thousand within a very short time. And it is probable that there were many, both now and afterwards, who, although they believed in Christ, did not think it necessary to join themselves to this society; or who waited to see what was likely to become of it. Gamaliel, whose advice to the

Jewish council is recorded Acts v. 34, appears to have been of this description; perhaps Nicodemus, and perhaps also Joseph of Arimathea. This class of men, their character and their rank, are likewise pointed out by Saint John, in the twelfth chapter of his Gospel: "Nevertheless, among the chief rulers also many believed on him, but because of the Pharisees they did not confess him, lest they should be put out of the synagogue, for they loved the praise of men more than the praise of God." Persons such as these might admit the miracles of Christ, without being immediately convinced that they were under obligation to make a public profession of Christianity at the risk of all that was dear to them in life, and even of life itself.[1]

Christianity, however, proceeded to increase in Jerusalem by a progress equally rapid with its first success; for in the next chapter of our history, we read that "believers were the more added to the Lord, multitudes both of men and women." And this enlargement of the new society appears in the first verse of the succeeding chapter, wherein we are told, that "when the number of the disciples was multiplied, there arose a murmuring of the Grecians against the Hebrews because their widows were neglected;" (Acts v. 14; vi. 1) and afterwards, in the same chapter, it is declared expressly, that "the number of the disciples multiplied in Jerusalem greatly, and that a great company of the priests were obedient to the faith."

This I call the first period in the propagation of Christianity. It commences with the ascension of Christ, and extends, as may be collected from incidental notes of time, (Vide Pearson's Antiq. 1. xviii. c. 7. Benson's History of Christ, b. i. p. 148.) to something more than one year after that event. During which term, the preaching of Christianity, so far as our documents inform us, was confined to the single city of Jerusalem. And how did it succeed there? The first assembly which we meet with of

---

[1] "Beside those who professed, and those who rejected and opposed, Christianity, there were in all probability multitudes between both, neither perfect Christians nor yet unbelievers. They had a favourable opinion of the Gospel, but worldly considerations made them unwilling to own it. There were many circumstances which inclined them to think that Christianity was a divine revelation, but there were many inconveniences which attended the open profession of it; and they could not find in themselves courage enough to bear them to disoblige their friends and family, to ruin their fortunes, to lose their reputation, their liberty, and their life, for the sake of the new religion. Therefore they were willing to hope, that if they endeavoured to observe the great principles of morality which Christ had represented as the principal part, the sum and substance of religion; if they thought honourably of the Gospel; if they offered no injury to the Christians; if they did them all the services that they could safely perform, they were willing to hope that God would accept this, and that He would excuse and forgive the rest." Jortin's Dis. on the Christ. Rel. p. 91, ed. 4.

Christ's disciples, and that a few days after his removal from the world, consisted of "one hundred and twenty." About a week after this, "three thousand were added in one day;" and the number of Christians publicly baptized, and publicly associating together, was very soon increased to "five thousand." "Multitudes both of men and women continued to be added;" "disciples multiplied greatly," and "many of the Jewish priesthood as well as others, became obedient to the faith;" and this within a space of less than two years from the commencement of the institution.

By reason of a persecution raised against the church at Jerusalem, the converts were driven from that city, and dispersed throughout the regions of Judea and Samaria. (Acts viii. l.) Wherever they came, they brought their religion with them: for our historian informs us, (Acts viii. 4.) that "they that were scattered abroad went everywhere preaching the word." The effect of this preaching comes afterwards to be noticed, where the historian is led, in the course of his narrative, to observe that then (i.e. about three years posterior to this, [Benson, b. i. p. 207.]) the churches had rest throughout all Judea and Galilee and Samaria, and were edified, and walking in the fear of the Lord, and in the comfort of the Holy Ghost, were multiplied. This was the work of the second period, which comprises about four years.

Hitherto the preaching of the Gospel had been confined to Jews, to Jewish proselytes, and to Samaritans. And I cannot forbear from setting down in this place an observation of Mr. Bryant, which appears to me to be perfectly well founded;—"The Jews still remain: but how seldom is it that we can make a single proselyte! There is reason to think, that there were more converted by the apostles in one day than have since been won over in the last thousand years." (Bryant on the Truth of the Christian Religion, p. 112.) It was not yet known to the apostles that they were at liberty to propose the religion to mankind at large. That "mystery," as Saint Paul calls it, (Eph. iii. 3—6.) and as it then was, was revealed to Peter by an especial miracle. It appears to have been (Benson, book ii. p. 236.) about seven years after Christ's ascension that the Gospel was preached to the Gentiles of Cesarea. A year after this a great multitude of Gentiles were converted at Antioch in Syria. The expressions employed by the historian are these:—"A great number believed, and turned to the Lord;" "much people was added unto the Lord;" "the apostles Barnabas and Paul taught much people." (Acts xi. 21, 24, 26.) Upon Herod's death, which happened in the next year, (Benson, book ii, p. 289.) it is observed, that "the word of God grew and multiplied." (Acts xii. 24.) Three years from this time, upon the preaching of Paul at Iconium, the metropolis of Lycaonia, "a great multitude both of Jews and Greeks believed:" (Acts xiv. 1.) and afterwards, in the course of this very progress, he is represented as "making many disciples" at Derbe, a principal city in the same district. Three years (Benson's History of Christ, book iii. p. 50.)

after this, which brings us to sixteen after the ascension, the apostles wrote a public letter from Jerusalem to the Gentile converts in Antioch, Syria, and Cilicia, with which letter Paul travelled through these countries, and found the churches "established in the faith, and increasing in number daily." (Acts xvi. 5.) From Asia the apostle proceeded into Greece, where, soon after his arrival in Macedonia, we find him at Thessalonica: in which city, "some of the Jews believed, and of the devout Greeks a great multitude." (Acts xvii. 4.) We meet also here with an accidental hint of the general progress of the Christian mission, in the exclamation of the tumultuous Jews of Thessalonica, "that they who had turned the world upside down were come thither also." (Acts xvii. 6.) At Berea, the next city at which Saint Paul arrives, the historian, who was present, inform us that "many of the Jews believed." (Acts xvii. 12.) The next year and a half of Saint Paul's ministry was spent at Corinth. Of his success in that city we receive the following intimations; "that many of the Corinthians believed and were baptized;" and "that it was revealed to the Apostle by Christ, that be had much people in that city." (Acts xviii, 8—10.) Within less than a year after his departure from Corinth, and twenty-five (Benson, book iii. p, 160.) years after the ascension, Saint Paul fixed his station at Ephesus for the space of two years (Acts xix. 10.) and something more. The effect of his ministry in that city and neighbourhood drew from the historian a reflection how "mightily grew the word of God and prevailed." (Acts xix. 20.) And at the conclusion of this period we find Demetrius at the head of a party, who were alarmed by the progress of the religion, complaining, that "not only at Ephesus, but also throughout all Asia (i.e. the province of Lydia, and the country adjoining to Ephesus), this Paul hath persuaded and turned away much people." (Acts xix. 26.) Beside these accounts, there occurs, incidentally, mention of converts at Rome, Alexandria, Athens, Cyprus, Cyrene, Macedonia, Philippi.

This is the third period in the propagation of Christianity, setting off in the seventh year after the ascension, and ending at the twenty-eighth. Now, lay these three periods together, and observe how the progress of the religion by these accounts is represented. The institution, which properly began only after its Author's removal from the world, before the end of thirty years, had spread itself through Judea, Galilee, and Samaria, almost all the numerous districts of the Lesser Asia, through Greece, and the islands of the Aegean Sea, the seacoast of Africa, and had extended itself to Rome, and into Italy. At Antioch, in Syria, at Joppa, Ephesus, Corinth, Thessalonica, Berea, Iconium, Derbe, Antioch in Pisidia, at Lydda, Saron, the number of converts is intimated by the expressions, "a great number," "great multitudes," "much people." Converts are mentioned, without any designation of their number,[2] at Tyre, Cesarea, Troas, Athens, Philippi, Lystra, Damascus. During all this time Jerusalem continued not only the centre of the mission, but a principal seat of the religion; for when Saint Paul returned thither at the conclusion of the period of which we are now considering the accounts, the other apostles pointed out to him, as a reason for his compliance with their advice, "how many thousands (myriads, ten thousands) there were in that city who believed."[3]

Upon this abstract, and the writing from which it is drawn, the following observations seem material to be made:

I. That the account comes from a person who was himself concerned in a portion of what he relates, and was contemporary with the whole of it; who visited Jerusalem, and frequented the society of those who had acted, and were acting the chief parts in the transaction. I lay down this point positively; for had the ancient attestations to this valuable record been less satisfactory than they are, the unaffectedness and simplicity with which the author notes his presence upon certain occasions, and the entire absence of art and design from these notices, would have been sufficient to persuade my mind that, whoever he was, he actually lived in the times, and occupied the situation, in which he represents himself to be. When I say, "whoever he was," I do not mean to cast a doubt upon the name to which antiquity hath ascribed the Acts of the Apostles (for there is no cause, that I am acquainted with, for questioning it), but to observe that, in such a case as this, the time and situation of the author are of more importance than his name; and that these appear from the work itself, and in the most unsuspicious form.

II. That this account is a very incomplete account of the preaching and propagation of Christianity; I mean, that if what we read in the history be true, much more than what the history contains must be true also. For, although the narrative from which our information is derived has been entitled the Acts of the Apostles, it is, in fact, a history of the twelve apostles only during a short time of their continuing together at Jerusalem; and even of this period the account is very concise. The work

---

[2] Considering the extreme conciseness of many parts of the history, the silence about the number of converts is no proof of their paucity; for at Philippi, no mention whatever is made of the number, yet Saint Paul addressed an epistle to that church. The churches of Galatia, and the affairs of those churches, were considerable enough to be the subject of another letter, and of much of Saint Paul's solicitude; yet no account is preserved in the history of his success, or even of his preaching in that country, except the slight notice which these words convey:—"When they had gone throughout Phrygia, and the region of Galatia, they assayed to go into Bithynia." Acts xvi. 6.

[3] Acts xxi. 20.

afterwards consists of a few important passages of Peter's ministry, of the speech and death of Stephen, of the preaching of Philip the deacon; and the sequel of the volume, that is, two thirds of the whole, is taken up with the conversion, the travels, the discourses, and history of the new apostle, Paul; in which history, also, large portions of time are often passed over with very scanty notice.

III. That the account, so far as it goes, is for this very reason more credible. Had it been the author's design to have displayed the early progress of Christianity, he would undoubtedly have collected, or at least have set forth, accounts of the preaching of the rest of the apostles, who cannot without extreme improbability be supposed to have remained silent and inactive, or not to have met with a share of that success which attended their colleagues.

To which may be added, as an observation of the same kind,

IV. That the intimations of the number of converts, and of the success of the preaching of the apostles, come out for the most part incidentally: are drawn from the historian by the occasion, such as the murmuring of the Grecian converts; the rest from persecution; Herod's death; the sending of Barnabas to Antioch, and Barnabas calling Paul to his assistance; Paul coming to a place and finding there disciples; the clamour of the Jews; the complaint of artificers interested in the support of the popular religion; the reason assigned to induce Paul to give satisfaction to the Christians of Jerusalem. Had it not been for these occasions it is probable that no notice whatever would have been taken of the number of converts in several of the passages in which that notice now appears. All this tends to remove the suspicion of a design to exaggerate or deceive.

PARALLEL TESTIMONIES with the history are the letters of Saint Paul, and of the other apostles, which have come down to us. Those of Saint Paul are addressed to the churches of Corinth, Philippi, Thessalonica, the church of Galatia, and, if the inscription be right, of Ephesus; his ministry at all which places is recorded in the history: to the church of Colosse, or rather to the churches of Colosse and Laodicea jointly, which he had not then visited. They recognise by reference the churches of Judea, the churches of Asia, and "all the churches of the Gentiles." (Thess ii. 14.) In the Epistle to the Romans (Rom. xv. 18, 19.) the author is led to deliver a remarkable declaration concerning the extent of his preaching, its efficacy, and the cause to which he ascribes it,—"to make the Gentiles obedient by word and deed, through mighty signs and wonders, by the power of the Spirit of God; so that from Jerusalem, and round about unto Illyricum, I have fully preached the Gospel of Christ." In the epistle to the Colossians, (Col. i. 23.) we find an oblique but very strong signification of the then general state of the Christian mission, at least as it appeared to Saint Paul:—"If ye continue in the faith, grounded and settled, and be not moved away from the hope of the Gospel, which ye have heard, and which was preached to every creature which is under heaven;" which Gospel, he had reminded them near the beginning of his letter (Col. i. 6.), "was present with them, as it was in all the world." The expressions are hyperbolical; but they are hyperboles which could only be used by a writer who entertained a strong sense of the subject. The first epistle of Peter accosts the Christians dispersed throughout Pontus, Galatia, Cappadocia, Asia, and Bithynia.

It comes next to be considered how far these accounts are confirmed or followed up by other evidence.

Tacitus, in delivering a relation, which has already been laid before the reader, of the fire which happened at Rome in the tenth year of Nero (which coincides with the thirtieth year after Christ's ascension), asserts that the emperor, in order to suppress the rumours of having been himself the author of the mischief, procured the Christians to be accused. Of which Christians, thus brought into his narrative, the following is so much of the historian's account as belongs to our present purpose: "They had their denomination from Christus, who, in the reign of Tiberius, was put to death as a criminal by the procurator Pontius Pilate. This pernicious superstition, though checked for a while, broke out again, and spread not only over Judea, but reached the city also. At first they only were apprehended who confessed themselves of that sect; afterwards vast multitude were discovered by them." This testimony to the early propagation of Christianity is extremely material. It is from an historian of great reputation, living near the time; from a stranger and an enemy to the religion; and it joins immediately with the period through which the Scripture accounts extend. It establishes these points: that the religion began at Jerusalem; that it spread throughout Judea; that it had reached Rome, and not only so, but that it had there obtained a great number of converts. This was about six years after the time that Saint Paul wrote his Epistle to the Romans, and something more than two years after he arrived there himself. The converts to the religion were then so numerous at Rome, that of those who were betrayed by the information of the persons first persecuted, a great multitude (*multitudo ingens*) were discovered and seized.

It seems probable, that the temporary check which Tacitus represents Christianity to have received (*repressa in praesens*) referred to the persecution of Jerusalem which followed the death of Stephen (Acts viii.); and which, by dispersing the converts, caused the institution, in some measure, to disappear. Its second eruption at the same place, and within a short time, has much in it of the character of truth. It was the firmness and perseverance of men who knew what they relied upon.

Next in order of time, and perhaps superior in importance is the testimony of Pliny the Younger. Pliny was the Roman governor of Pontus and Bithynia, two considerable districts in the northern part of Asia

Minor. The situation in which he found his province led him to apply to the emperor (Trajan) for his direction as to the conduct he was to hold towards the Christians. The letter in which this application is contained was written not quite eighty years after Christ's ascension. The president, in this letter, states the measures he had already pursued, and then adds, as his reason for resorting to the emperor's counsel and authority, the following words:—"Suspending all judicial proceedings, I have recourse to you for advice; for it has appeared to me a matter highly deserving consideration, especially on account of the great number of persons who are in danger of suffering: for many of all ages, and of every rank, of both sexes likewise, are accused, and will be accused. Nor has the contagion of this superstition seized cities only, but the lesser towns also, and the open country. Nevertheless it seemed to me that it may be restrained and corrected. It is certain that the temples, which were almost forsaken, begin to be more frequented; and the sacred solemnities, after a long intermission, are revived. Victims, likewise, are everywhere (passim) bought up; whereas, for some time, there were few to purchase them. Whence it is easy to imagine that numbers of men might be reclaimed if pardon were granted to those that shall repent." (C. Plin. Trajano Imp. lib. x. ep. xcvii.)

It is obvious to observe, that the passage of Pliny's letter here quoted, proves, not only that the Christians in Pontus and Bithynia were now numerous, but that they had subsisted there for some considerable time. "It is certain," he says, "that the temples, which were almost forsaken (plainly ascribing this desertion of the popular worship to the prevalency of Christianity), begin to be more frequented; and the sacred solemnities, after a long intermission, are revived." There are also two clauses in the former part of the letter which indicate the same thing; one, in which he declares that he had "never been present at any trials of Christians, and therefore knew not what was the usual subject of inquiry and punishment, or how far either was wont to be urged." The second clause is the following: "Others were named by an informer, who, at first, confessed themselves Christians, and afterwards denied it; the rest said they had been Christians some three years ago, some longer, and some about twenty years." It is also apparent, that Pliny speaks of the Christians as a description of men well known to the person to whom he writes. His first sentence concerning them is, "I have never been present at the trials of Christians." This mention of the name of Christians, without any preparatory explanation, shows that it was a term familiar both to the writer of the letter and the person to whom it was addressed. Had it not been so, Pliny would naturally have begun his letter by informing the emperor that he had met with a certain set of men in the province called Christians.

Here then is a very singular evidence of the progress of the Christian religion in a short space. It was not fourscore years after the crucifixion of Jesus when Pliny wrote this letter; nor seventy years since the apostles of Jesus began to mention his name to the Gentile world. Bithynia and Pontus were at a great distance from Judea, the centre from which the religion spread; yet in these provinces Christianity had long subsisted, and Christians were now in such numbers as to lead the Roman governor to report to the emperor that they were found not only in cities, but in villages and in open countries; of all ages, of every rank and condition; that they abounded so much as to have produced a visible desertion of the temples; that beasts brought to market for victims had few purchasers; that the sacred solemnities were much neglected:—circumstances noted by Pliny for the express purpose of showing to the emperor the effect and prevalency of the new institution.

No evidence remains by which it can be proved that the Christians were more numerous in Pontus and Bithynia than in other parts of the Roman empire; nor has any reason been offered to show why they should be so. Christianity did not begin in these countries, nor near them. I do not know, therefore, that we ought to confine the description in Pliny's letter to the state of Christianity in these provinces, even if no other account of the same subject had come down to us; but, certainly, this letter may fairly be applied in aid and confirmation of the representations given of the general state of Christianity in the world, by Christian writers of that and the next succeeding age.

Justin Martyr, who wrote about thirty years after Pliny, and one hundred and six after the ascension, has these remarkable words: "There is not a nation, either of Greek or barbarian, or of any other name, even of those who wander in tribes, and live in tents, amongst whom prayers and thanksgivings are not offered to the Father and Creator of the universe by the name of the crucified Jesus." (Dial cum Tryph.) Tertullian, who comes about fifty years after Justin, appeals to the governors of the Roman empire in these terms: "We were but of yesterday, and we have filled your cities, islands, towns, and boroughs, the camp, the senate, and the forum. They (the heathen adversaries of Christianity) lament that every sex, age, and condition, and persons of every rank also, are converts to that name." (Tertull. Apol. c. 37.) I do allow that these expressions are loose, and may be called declamatory. But even declamation hath its bounds; this public boasting upon a subject which must be known to every reader was not only useless but unnatural, unless the truth of the case, in a considerable degree, corresponded with the description; at least, unless it had been both true and notorious, that great multitudes of Christians, of all ranks and orders, were to be found in most parts of the Roman empire. The same Tertullian, in another passage, by way of setting forth the extensive diffusion of Christianity, enumerates as belonging to

206

Christ, beside many other countries, the "Moors and Gaetulians of Africa, the borders of Spain, several nations of France, and parts of Britain inaccessible to the Romans, the Sarmatians, Daci, Germans, and Scythians;" (Ad Jud. c. 7.) and, which is more material than the extent of the institution, the number of Christians in the several countries in which it prevailed is thus expressed by him: "Although so great a multitude, that in almost every city we form the greater part, we pass our time modestly and in silence." (Ad Scap. c. iii.) A Clemens Alexandrinus, who preceded Tertullian by a few years, introduced a comparison between the success of Christianity and that of the most celebrated philosophical institutions: "The philosophers were confined to Greece, and to their particular retainers; but the doctrine of the Master of Christianity not remain in Judea, as philosophy did in Greece, but is throughout the whole world, in every nation, and village, and city, both of Greeks and barbarians, converting both whole houses and separate individuals, having already brought over to the truth not a few of the philosophers themselves. If the Greek philosophy he prohibited, it immediately vanishes; whereas, from the first preaching of our doctrine, kings and tyrants, governors and presidents, with their whole train, and with the populace on their side, have endeavoured with their whole might to exterminate it, yet doth it flourish more and more." (Clem. Al. Strora. lib. vi. ad fin.) Origen, who follows Tertullian at the distance of only thirty years, delivers nearly the same account: "In every part of the world," says he, "throughout all Greece, and in all other nations, there are innumerable and immense multitudes, who, having left the laws of their country, and those whom they esteemed gods, have given themselves up to the law of Moses, and the religion of Christ: and this not without the bitterest resentment from the idolaters, by whom they were frequently put to torture, and sometimes to death: and it is wonderful to observe how, in so short a time, the religion has increased, amidst punishment and death, and every kind of torture." (Orig. in Cels. lib. i.) In another passage, Origen draws the following candid comparison between the state of Christianity in his time and the condition of its more primitive ages: "By the good providence of God, the Christian religion has so flourished and increased continually that it is now preached freely without molestation, although there were a thousand obstacles to the spreading of the doctrine of Jesus in the world. But as it was the will of God that the Gentiles should have the benefit of it, all the counsels of men against the Christians were defeated: and by how much the more emperors and governors of provinces, and the people everywhere strove to depress them, so much the more have they increased and prevailed exceedingly." (Orig. cont. Cels. lib vii.)

It is well known that, within less than eighty years after this, the Roman empire became Christian under Constantine: and it is probable that Constantine declared himself on the side of the Christians because they were the powerful party: for Arnobius, who wrote immediately before Constantine's accession, speaks of "the whole world as filled with Christ's doctrine, of its diffusion throughout all countries, of an innumerable body of Christians in distant provinces, of the strange revolution of opinion of men of the greatest genius,—orators, grammarians, rhetoricians, lawyers, physicians having come over to the institution, and that also in the face of threats, executions and tortures." (Arnob. in Genres, 1. i. pp. 27, 9, 24, 42, 41. edit. Lug. Bat. 1650.)

And not more than twenty years after Constantine's entire possession of the empire, Julius Firmiens Maternus calls upon the emperors Constantius and Constans to extirpate the relics of the ancient religion; the reduced and fallen condition of which is described by our author in the following words: "*Licet adhue in quibusdam regionibus idololatriae morientia palpitont membra; tamen in eo res est, ut a Christianis omnibus terris pestiferum hoc malum funditus amputetur:*" and in another place, "*Modicum tautum superest, ut legibus vestris—extincta idololatriae pereat funesta contagio.*" (De Error. Profan. Relig. c. xxi. p. 172, quoted by Lardner, vol. viii. p. 262.) It will not be thought that we quote this writer in order to recommend his temper or his judgment, but to show the comparative state of Christianity and of Heathenism at this period. Fifty years afterwards, Jerome represents the decline of Paganism, in language which conveys the same idea of its approaching extinction: "*Solitudinem patitur et in urbe gentilitas. Dii quondam nationum, cum bubonibus et noctuis, in solis culminibus remanserunt.*" (Jer. ad Lect. ep. 5, 7.) Jerome here indulges a triumph, natural and allowable in a zealous friend of the cause, but which could only be suggested to his mind by the consent and universality with which he saw; the religion received. "But now," says he, "the passion and resurrection of Christ are celebrated in the discourses and writings of all nations. I need not mention Jews, Greeks, and Latins. The Indians, Persians, Goths, and Egyptians philosophise, and firmly believe the immortality of the soul, and future recompenses, which, before, the greatest philosophers had denied, or doubted of, or perplexed with their disputes. The fierceness of Thracians and Scythians is now softened by the gentle sound of the Gospel; and everywhere Christ is all in all." (Jer. ad Lect. ep. 8, ad Heliod.) Were, therefore, the motives of Constantine's conversion ever so problematical, the easy establishment of Christianity, and the ruin of Heathenism, under him and his immediate successors, is of itself a proof of the progress which had made in the preceding period. It may be added also, "that Maxentius, the rival of Constantine, had shown himself friendly to the Christians. Therefore of those who were contending for worldly power and empire, one actually favoured and flattered them, and another may be suspected to have joined himself to them partly from consideration of interest: so considerable were they become, under external disadvantages of all sorts." (Lardner, vol. vii. p. 380.) This at least is certain, that, throughout the whole transaction hitherto, the great seemed to follow, not to lead, the public opinion.

It may help to convey to us some notion of the extent and progress of Christianity, or rather of the character and quality of many early Christians, of their learning and their labours, to notice the number of Christian writers who flourished in these ages. Saint Jerome's catalogue contains sixty-six writers within the first three centuries, and the first six years of the fourth; and fifty-four between that time and his own, viz. A. D. 392. Jerome introduces his catalogue with the following just remonstrance:—"Let those who say the church has had no philosophers, nor eloquent and learned men, observe who and what they were who founded, established, and adorned it; let them cease to accuse our faith of rusticity, and confess their mistake." (Jer. Prol. in Lib. de Ser. Eccl.) Of these writers, several, as Justin, Irenaeus, Clement of Alexandria, Tertullian, Origen, Bardesanes, Hippolitus, Eusebius, were voluminous writers. Christian writers abounded particularly about the year 178. Alexander, bishop of Jerusalem, founded a library in that city, A.D. 212. Pamphilus, the friend of Origen, founded a library at Cesarea, A.D. 294. Public defences were also set forth, by various advocates of the religion, in the course of its first three centuries. Within one hundred years after Christ's ascension, Quadratus and Aristides, whose works, except some few fragments of the first, are lost; and, about twenty years afterwards, Justin Martyr, whose works remain, presented apologies for the Christian religion to the Roman emperors; Quadratus and Aristides to Adrian, Justin to Antoninus Pius, and a second to Marcus Antoninus. Melito, bishop of Sardis, and Apollinaris, bishop of Hierapolis, and Miltiades, men of great reputation, did the same to Marcus Antoninus, twenty years afterwards; (Euseb. Hist. lib. iv. c. 26. See also Lardner, vol. ii. p. 666.) and ten years after this, Apollonius, who suffered martyrdom under the emperor Commodus, composed an apology for his faith which he read in the senate, and which was afterwards published. (Lardner, vol. ii. p. 687.) Fourteen years after the apology of Apollonius, Tertullian addressed the work which now remains under that name to the governors of provinces in the Roman empire; and, about the same time, Minucius Felix composed a defence of the Christian religion, which is still extant; and, shortly after the conclusion of this century, copious defences of Christianity were published by Arnobius and Lactantius.

SECTION II.

REFLECTIONS UPON THE PRECEDING ACCOUNT.

In viewing the progress of Christianity, our first attention is due to the number of converts at Jerusalem, immediately after its Founder's death; because this success was a success at the time, and upon the spot, when and where the chief part of the history had been transacted.

We are, in the next place, called upon to attend to the early establishment of numerous Christian societies in Judea and Galilee; which countries had been the scene of Christ's miracles and ministry, and where the memory of what had passed, and the knowledge of what was alleged, must have yet been fresh and certain.

We are, thirdly, invited to recollect the success of the apostles and of their companions, at the several places to which they came, both within and without Judea; because it was the credit given to original witnesses, appealing for the truth of their accounts to what themselves had seen and heard. The effect also of their preaching strongly confirms the truth of what our history positively and circumstantially relates, that they were able to exhibit to their hearers supernatural attestations of their mission.

We are, lastly, to consider the subsequent growth and spread of the religion, of which we receive successive intimations, and satisfactory, though general and occasional, accounts, until its full and final establishment.

In all these several stages, the history is without a parallel for it must be observed, that we have not now been tracing the progress, and describing the prevalency, of an opinion founded upon philosophical or critical arguments, upon mere of reason, or the construction of ancient writing; (of which are the several theories which have, at different times, possession of the public mind in various departments of science and literature; and of one or other of which kind are the tenets also which divide the various sects of Christianity;) but that we speak of a system, the very basis and postulatum of which was a supernatural character ascribed to a particular person; of a doctrine, the truth whereof depends entirely upon the truth of a matter of fact then recent. "To establish a new religion, even amongst a few people, or in one single nation, is a thing in itself exceedingly difficult. To reform some corruptions which may have spread in a religion, or to make new regulations in it, is not perhaps so hard, when the main and principal part of that religion is preserved entire and unshaken; and yet this very often cannot be accomplished without an extraordinary concurrence of circumstances, and may be attempted a thousand times without success. But to introduce a new faith, a new way of thinking and acting, and to persuade many nations to quit the religion in which their ancestors have lived and died, which had been delivered down to them from time immemorial; to make them forsake and despise the deities which they had been accustomed to reverence and worship; this is a work of still greater difficulty." (Jortin's Dis. on the Christ. Rel. p. 107, 4th edit.) The resistance of education, worldly policy, and superstition, is almost invincible.

If men, in these days, be Christians in consequence of their education, in submission to authority, or in compliance with fashion, let us recollect that the very contrary of this, at the beginning, was the case. The first race of Christians, as wall as millions who succeeded them, became such in formal opposition to all these motives, to the whole power and strength of this influence. Every argument, therefore, and every instance, which sets forth the prejudice of education, and the almost irresistible effects of that prejudice (and no persons are more fond of expatiating upon this subject than deistical writers), in fact confirms the evidence of Christianity.

But, in order to judge of the argument which is drawn from the early propagation of Christianity, I know no fairer way of proceeding than to compare what we have seen on the subject with the success of Christian missions in modern ages. In the East India mission, supported by the Society for Promoting Christian Knowledge, we hear sometimes of thirty, sometimes of forty, being baptized in the course of a year, and these principally children. Of converts properly so called, that is, of adults voluntarily embracing Christianity, the number is extremely small. "Notwithstanding the labour of missionaries for upwards of two hundred years, and the establishments of different Christian nations who support them, there are not twelve thousand Indian Christians, and those almost entirely outcasts." (Sketches relating to the history, learning, and manners of the Hindoos, p. 48; quoted by Dr. Robertson, Hist. Dis. concerning Ancient India, p. 236.)

I lament as much as any man the little progress which Christianity has made in these countries, and the inconsiderable effect that has followed the labours of its missionaries; but I see in it a strong proof of the Divine origin of the religion. What had the apostles to assist them in propagating Christianity which the missionaries have not? If piety and zeal had been sufficient, I doubt not but that our missionaries possess these qualities in a high degree: for nothing except piety and zeal could engage them in the undertaking. If sanctity of life and manners was the allurement, the conduct of these men is unblameable. If the advantage of education and learning be looked to, there is not one of the modern missionaries who is not, in this respect, superior to all the apostles; and that not only absolutely, but, what is of more importance, relatively, in comparison, that is, with those amongst whom they exercise their office. If the intrinsic excellency of the religion, the perfection of its morality, the purity of its precepts, the eloquence, or tenderness, or sublimity, of various parts of its writings, were the recommendations by which it made its way, these remain the same. If the character and circumstances under which the preachers were introduced to the countries in which they taught be accounted of importance, this advantage is all on the side of the modern missionaries. They come from a country and a people to which the Indian world look up with sentiments of deference. The apostles came forth amongst the Gentiles under no other name than that of Jews, which was precisely the character they despised and derided. If it be disgraceful in India to become a Christian, it could not be much less so to be enrolled amongst those "quos, per flagitia invisos, vulgus Christianos appellabat." If the religion which they had to encounter be considered, the difference, I apprehend, will not be great. The theology of both was nearly the same: "what is supposed to be performed by the power of Jupiter, Neptune, of Aeolus, of Mars, of Venus, according to the mythology of the West, is ascribed, in the East, to the agency Agrio the god of fire, Varoon the god of oceans, Vayoo god of wind, Cama the god of love." (Baghvat Gets, p. 94, quoted by Dr. Robertson, Ind. Dis. p. 306.) The sacred rites of the Western Polytheism were gay, festive, and licentious; the rites of the public religion in the East partake of the same character, with a more avowed indecency. "In every function performed in the pagodas, as well as in every public procession, it is the office of these women (i.e. of women prepared by the Brahmins for the purpose) to dance before the idol, and to sing hymns in his praise; and it is difficult to say whether they trespass most against decency by the gestures they exhibit, or by the verses which they recite. The walls of the pagodas were covered with paintings in a style no less indelicate." (Others of the deities of the East are of an austere and gloomy character, to be propitiated by victims, sometimes by human sacrifices, and by voluntary torments of the most excruciating kind. Voyage de Gentil. vol. i. p. 244—260. Preface to the Code of Gentoo Laws, p. 57; quoted by Dr. Robertson, p. 320.)

On both sides of the comparison, the popular religion had a strong establishment. In ancient Greece and Rome it was strictly incorporated with the state. The magistrate was the priest. The highest officers of government bore the most distinguished part in the celebration of the public rites. In India, a powerful and numerous caste possesses exclusively the administration of the established worship; and are, of consequence, devoted to its service, and attached to its interest. In both, the prevailing mythology was destitute of any proper evidence: or rather, in both, the origin of the tradition is run up into ages long anterior to the existence of credible history, or of written language. The Indian chronology computes eras by millions of years, and the life of man by thousands "The Suffec Jogue, or age of purity, is said to have lasted three million two hundred thousand years; and they hold that the life of man was extended in that age to one hundred thousand years; but there is a difference amongst the Indian writers of six millions of years in the

212

computation of this era." (Voyage de Gentil. vol. i. p. 244—260. Preface to the Code of Gentoo Laws, p. 57; quoted by Dr. Robertson, p. 320.) and in these, or prior to these, is placed the history of their divinities. In both, the established superstition held the same place in the public opinion; that is to say, in both it was credited by the bulk of the people, but by the learned and philosophical part of the community either derided, or regarded by them as only fit to be upholden for the sake of its political uses.[1]

Or if it should be allowed, that the ancient heathens believed in their religion less generally than the present Indians do, I am far from thinking that this circumstance would afford any facility to the work of the apostles, above that of the modern missionaries. To me it appears, and I think it material to be remarked, that a disbelief of the established religion of their country has no tendency to dispose men for the reception of another; but that, on the contrary, it generates a settled contempt of all religious pretensions whatever. General infidelity is the hardest soil which the propagators of a new religion can have to work upon. Could a Methodist or Moravian promise himself a better chance of success with a French esprit fort, who had been accustomed to laugh at the popery of his country, than with a believing Mahometan or Hindoo? Or are our modern unbelievers in Christianity, for that reason, in danger of becoming Mahometans or Hindoos? It does not appear that the Jews, who had a body of historical evidence to offer for their religion, and who at that time

---

[1] "How absurd soever the articles of faith may be which superstition has adopted, or how unhallowed the rites which it prescribes, the former are received, in every age and country with unhesitating assent, by the great body of the people, and the latter observed with scrupulous exactness. In our reasonings concerning opinions and practices which differ widely from our own, we are extremely apt to err. Having been instructed ourselves in the principles of a religion worthy in every respect of that Divine wisdom by which they were dictated, we frequently express wonder at the credulity of nations, in embracing systems of belief which appear to us so directly repugnant to right reason; and sometimes suspect that tenets so wild and extravagant do not really gain credit with them. But experience may satisfy us, that neither our wonder nor suspicions are well founded. No article of the public religion was called in question by those people of ancient Europe with whose history we are best acquainted; and no practice which it enjoined appeared improper to them. On the other hand, every opinion that tended to diminish the reverence of men for the gods of their country, or to alienate them from their worship, excited, among the Greeks and Romans, that indignant zeal which is natural to every people attached to their religion by a firm persuasion of its truth." Ind. Dis. p. 321. That the learned Brahmins of the East are rational Theists, and secretly reject the established theory, and contemn the rites that were founded upon them, or rather consider them as contrivances to be supported for their political uses, see Dr. Robertson's Ind. Dis. p. 324-334.

undoubtedly entertained and held forth the expectation of a future state, derived any great advantage, as to the extension of their system, from the discredit into which the popular religion had fallen with many of their heathen neighbours.

We have particularly directed our observations to the state and progress of Christianity amongst the inhabitants of India: but the history of the Christian mission in other countries, where the efficacy of the mission is left solely to the conviction wrought by the preaching of strangers, presents the same idea as the Indian mission does of the feebleness and inadequacy of human means. About twenty-five years ago was published, in England, a translation from the Dutch of a History of Greenland and a relation of the mission for above thirty years carried on in that country by the Unitas Fratrum, or Moravians. Every part of that relation confirms the opinion we have stated. Nothing could surpass, or hardly equal, the zeal and patience of the missionaries. Yet their historian, in the conclusion of his narrative, could find place for no reflections more encouraging than the following:—"A person that had known the heathen, that had seen the little benefit from the great pains hitherto taken with them, and considered that one after another had abandoned all hopes of the conversion of these infidels (and some thought they would never be converted, till they saw miracles wrought as in the apostles' days, and this the Greenlanders expected and demanded of their instructors); one that considered this, I say, would not so much wonder at the past unfruitfulness of these young beginners, as at their steadfast perseverance in the midst of nothing but distress, difficulties, and impediments, internally and externally: and that they never desponded of the conversion of those poor creatures amidst all seeming impossibilities." (History of Greenland, vol. ii. p. 376.)

From the widely disproportionate effects which attend the preaching of modern missionaries of Christianity, compared with what followed the ministry of Christ and his apostles under circumstances either alike, or not so unlike as to account for the difference, a conclusion is fairly drawn in support of what our histories deliver concerning them, viz. that they possessed means of conviction which we have not; that they had proofs to appeal to which we want.

SECTION III.

OF THE RELIGION OF MAHOMET.

The only event in the history of the human species which admits of comparison with the propagation of Christianity is the success of Mahometanism. The Mahometan institution was rapid in its progress, was recent in its history, and was founded upon a supernatural or prophetic character assumed by its author. In these articles, the resemblance with Christianity is confessed. But there are points of difference which separate, we apprehend, the two cases entirely.

I. Mahomet did not found his pretensions upon miracles, properly so called; that is, upon proofs of supernatural agency capable of being known and attested by others. Christians are warranted in this. assertion by the evidence of the Koran, in which Mahomet not only does not affect the power of working miracles, but expressly disclaims it. The following passages of that book furnish direct proofs of the truth of what we allege:—"The infidels say, Unless a sign be sent down unto him from his lord, we will not believe; thou art a preacher only." (Sale's Koran, c. xiii. p. 201, ed. quarto.) Again; "Nothing hindered us from sending thee with miracles, except that the former nations have charged them with imposture." (C. xvii. p. 232.) And lastly; "They say, Unless a sign be sent down unto him from his lord, we will not believe: Answer; Signs are in the power of God alone, and I am no more than a public preacher. Is it not sufficient for them, that we have sent down unto them the book of the Koran to be read unto them?" (C. xxix. p. 328.) Beside these acknowledgments, I have observed thirteen distinct places in which Mahomet puts the objection (unless a sign, &c.) into the mouth of the unbeliever, in not one of which does he allege a miracle in reply. His answer is, "that God giveth the power of working miracles when and to whom he pleaseth;" (C. v. x. xiii. twice.) "that if he should work miracles, they would not believe;" (C. vi.) "that they had before rejected Moses, and Jesus and the Prophets, who wrought miracles;" (C. iii. xxi. xxviii.) "that the Koran itself was a miracle." (C. xvi.)

The only place in the Koran in which it can be pretended that a sensible miracle is referred to (for I do not allow the secret visitations of Gabriel, the night-journey of Mahomet to heaven, or the presence in battle of invisible hosts of angels, to deserve the name of sensible miracles) is the beginning of the fifty-fourth chapter. The words are these:—"The hour of judgment approacheth, and the moon hath been split in sunder: but if the unbelievers see a sign, they turn aside, saying, This is a powerful charm." The Mahometan expositors disagree in their interpretation of this passage; some explaining it to be mention of the splitting of the moon as one of the future signs of the approach of the day of judgment: others referring it to a miraculous appearance which had then taken place. (Vide Sale, in loc.) It seems to me not improbable, that Mahomet might have taken advantage of some extraordinary halo, or other unusual appearance of the moon, which had happened about this time; and which supplied a foundation both for this passage, and for the story which in after times had been raised out of it.

After this more than silence, after these authentic confessions of the Koran, we are not to be moved with miraculous stories related of Mahomet by Abulfeda, who wrote his life about six hundred years after his death; or which are found in the legend of Al-Jannabi, who came two hundred years later.[1] On the contrary, from comparing what Mahomet himself wrote and said with what was afterwards reported of him by his followers, the plain and fair conclusion is, that when the religion was established by conquest, then, and not till then, came out the stories of his miracles.

Now this difference alone constitutes, in my opinion, a bar to all reasoning from one case to the other. The success of a religion founded upon a miraculous history shows the credit which was given to the history; and this credit, under the circumstances in which it was given, i.e. by persons capable of knowing the truth, and interested to inquire after it, is evidence of the reality of the history, and, by consequence, of the truth of the religion. Where a miraculous history is not alleged, no part of this argument can be applied. We admit that multitudes acknowledged the pretensions of Mahomet: but, these pretensions being destitute of miraculous evidence, we know that the grounds upon which they were acknowledged could not be secure grounds of persuasion to his followers, nor their example any authority to us. Admit the whole of Mahomet's authentic history, so far as it was of a nature capable of being known or witnessed by others, to be true (which is certainly to admit all that the reception of the religion can be brought to prove), and Mahomet might still be an impostor, or enthusiast, or a union of both. Admit to be true almost any part of Christ's history, of that, I mean, which was public, and within the cognizance of his followers, and he must have come from God. Where matter of fact is not in question, where miracles are not alleged, I do not see that the progress of a religion is a better argument of its truth than the prevalency of any system of opinions in natural religion, morality, or physics, is a proof of the truth of those opinions. And we

---

[1] It does not, I think, appear, that these historians had any written accounts to appeal to more ancient than the Sonnah; which was a collection of traditions made by order of the Caliphs two hundred years after Mahomet's death. Mahomet died A.D. 632; Al-Bochari, one of the six doctors who compiled the Sonnah, was born A.D. 809; died 869. Prideaux's Life of Mahomet, p. 192, ed. 7th.

know that this sort of argument is inadmissible in any branch of philosophy what ever.

But it will be said, if one religion could make its way without miracles, why might not another? To which I reply, first, that this is not the question; the proper question is not, whether a religious institution could be set up without miracles, but whether a religion, or a change of religion, founding itself in miracles, could succeed without any reality to rest upon? I apprehend these two cases to be very different: and I apprehend Mahomet's not taking this course, to be one proof, amongst others, that the thing is difficult, if not impossible, to be accomplished: certainly it was not from an unconsciousness of the value and importance of miraculous evidence; for it is very observable, that in the same volume, and sometimes in the same chapters, in which Mahomet so repeatedly disclaims the power of working miracles himself, he is incessantly referring to the miracles of preceding prophets. One would imagine, to hear some men talk, or to read some books, that the setting up of a religion by dint of miraculous pretences was a thing of every day's experience: whereas, I believe that, except the Jewish and Christian religion, there is no tolerably well authenticated account of any such thing having been accomplished.

II. The establishment of Mahomet's religion was affected by causes which in no degree appertained to the origin of Christianity.

During the first twelve years of his mission, Mahomet had recourse only to persuasion. This is allowed. And there is sufficient reason from the effect to believe that, if he had confined himself to this mode of propagating his religion, we of the present day should never have heard either of him or it. "Three years were silently employed in the conversion of fourteen proselytes. For ten years, the religion advanced with a slow and painful progress, within the walls of Mecca. The number of proselytes in the seventh year of his mission may be estimated by the absence of eighty-three men and eighteen women, who retired to Aethiopia." (Gibbon's Hist. vol. ix. p. 244, et seq. ed. Dub.) Yet this progress, such as it was, appears to have been aided by some very important advantages which Mahomet found in his situation, in his mode of conducting his design, and in his doctrine.

1. Mahomet was the grandson of the most powerful and honourable family in Mecca; and although the early death of his father had not left him a patrimony suitable to his birth, he had, long before the commencement of his mission, repaired this deficiency by an opulent marriage. A person considerable by his wealth, of high descent, and nearly allied to the chiefs of his country, taking upon himself the character of a religious teacher, would not fail of attracting attention and followers.

2. Mahomet conducted his design, in the outset especially, with great art and prudence. He conducted it as a politician would conduct a plot. His first application was to his own family. This gained him his wife's uncle, a considerable person in Mecca, together with his cousin Ali, afterwards the celebrated Caliph, then a youth of great expectation, and even already distinguished by his attachment, impetuosity, and courage.[2] He next expressed himself to Abu Beer, a man amongst the first of the Koreish in wealth and influence. The interest and example of Abu Beer drew in five other principal persons in Mecca, whose solicitations prevailed upon five more of the same rank. This was the work of three years; during which time everything was transacted in secret. Upon the strength of these allies, and under the powerful protection of his family, who, however some of them might disapprove his enterprise, or deride his pretensions, would not suffer the orphan of their house, the relict of their favourite brother, to be insulted, Mahomet now commenced his public preaching. And the advance which he made during the nine or ten remaining years of his peaceable ministry was by no means greater than what, with these advantages, and with the additional and singular circumstance of there being no established religion at Mecca at that time to contend with, might reasonably have been expected. How soon his primitive adherents were let into the secret of his views of empire, or in what stage of his undertaking these views first opened themselves to his own mind, it is not now easy to determine. The event however was, that these, his first proselytes, all ultimately attained to riches and honours, to the command of armies, and the government of kingdoms. (Gibbon, vol. ix. p 244.)

3. The Arabs deduced their descent from Abraham through the line of Ishmael. The inhabitants of Mecca, in common probably with the other Arabian tribes, acknowledged, as I think may clearly be collected from the Koran, one supreme Deity, but had associated with him many objects of idolatrous worship. The great doctrine with which Mahomet set out was the strict and exclusive unity of God. Abraham, he told them, their illustrous ancestor; Ishmael, the father of their nation; Moses, the lawgiver of the Jews; and Jesus, the author of Christianity—had all asserted the same thing; that their followers had universally corrupted the truth, and that he was now commissioned to restore it to the world. Was it to be wondered at, that a doctrine so specious, and authorized by names,

---

[2] Of which Mr. Gibbon has preserved the following specimen: "When Mahomet called out in an assembly of his family, Who among you will be my companion, and my vizir? Ali, then only in the fourteenth year of his age, suddenly replied, O prophet I am the man;—whosoever rises against thee, I will dash out his teeth, tear out his eyes, break his legs, rip up his belly. O prophet! I will be thy vizir over them." Vol. ix. p. 215.

some or other of which were holden in the highest veneration by every description of his hearers, should, in the hands of a popular missionary, prevail to the extent in which Mahomet succeeded by his pacific ministry?

4. Of the institution which Mahomet joined with this fundamental doctrine, and of the Koran in which that institution is delivered, we discover, I think, two purposes that pervade the whole, viz., to make converts, and to make his converts soldiers. The following particulars, amongst others, may be considered as pretty evident indications of these designs:

1. When Mahomet began to preach, his address to the Jews, to the Christians, and to the Pagan Arabs, was, that the religion which he taught was no other than what had been originally their own.—"We believe in God, and that which hath been sent down unto us, and that which hath been sent down unto Abraham, and Ishmael, and Isaac, and Jacob, and the Tribes, and that which was delivered unto Moses and Jesus, and that which was delivered unto the prophets from their Lord: we make no distinction between any of them." (Sale's Koran, c. ii. p. 17.) "He hath ordained you the religion which he commanded Noah, and which we have revealed unto thee, O Mohammed, and which we commanded Abraham, and Moses, and Jesus, saying, Observe this religion, and be not divided therein." (Sale's Koran, c. xlii. p. 393.) "He hath chosen you, and hath not imposed on you any difficulty in the religion which he hath given you, the religion of your father Abraham." (Sale's Koran, c. xxii. p. 281.)

2. The author of the Koran never ceases from describing the future anguish of unbelievers, their despair, regret, penitence, and torment. It is the point which he labours above all others. And these descriptions are conceived in terms which will appear in no small degree impressive, even to the modern reader of an English translation. Doubtless they would operate with much greater force upon the minds of those to whom they were immediately directed. The terror which they seem well calculated to inspire would be to many tempers a powerful application.

3. On the other hand: his voluptuous paradise; his robes of silk, his palaces of marble, his riven, and shades, his groves and couches, his wines, his dainties; and, above all, his seventy-two virgins assigned to each of the faithful, of resplendent beauty and eternal youth—intoxicated the imaginations, and seized the passions of his Eastern followers.

4. But Mahomet's highest heaven was reserved for those who fought his battles or expended their fortunes in his cause: "Those believers who sit still at home, not having any hurt, and those who employ their fortunes and their persons for the religion of God, shall not be held equal. God hath preferred those who employ their fortunes and their persons in that cause to a degree above those who sit at home. God had indeed promised every one Paradise; but God had preferred those who fight for the faith

219

before those who sit still, by adding unto them a great reward; by degrees of honour conferred upon them from him, and by granting them forgiveness and mercy." (Sale's Koran, c. iv. p. 73.) Again; "Do ye reckon the giving drink to the pilgrims, and the visiting of the holy temple, to be actions as meritorious as those performed by him who believeth in God and the last day, and fighteth for the religion of God? They shall not be held equal with God.—They who have believed and fled their country, and employed their substance and their persons in the defence of God's true religion, shall be in the highest degree of honour with God; and these are they who shall be happy. The Lord sendeth them good tidings of mercy from him, and good will, and of gardens wherein they shall enjoy lasting pleasures. They shall continue therein for ever; for with God is a great reward." (Sale's Koran, c. ix. p. 151.) And, once more; "Verily God hath purchased of the true believers their souls and their substance, promising them the enjoyment of Paradise on condition that they fight for the cause of God: whether they slay or be slain, the promise for the same is assuredly due by the Law and the Gospel and the Koran." (Sale's Koran, c. ix. p. 164.)[3]

5. His doctrine of predestination was applicable, and was applied by him, to the same purpose of fortifying and of exalting the courage of his adherents.—"If anything of the matter had happened unto us, we had not been slain here. Answer; If ye had been in your houses, verily they would have gone forth to fight, whose slaughter was decreed, to the places where they died." (Sale's Koran, c. iii. p. 54.)

6. In warm regions, the appetite of the sexes is ardent, the passion for inebriating liquors moderate. In compliance with this distinction, although Mahomet laid a restraint upon the drinking of wine, in the use of women he allowed an almost unbounded indulgence. Four wives, with the liberty of changing them at pleasure, (Sale's Koran, c. iv. p. 63.) together with the persons of all his captives, (Gibbon, vol. ix. p. 225.) was an irresistible bribe to an Arabian warrior. "God is minded," says he, speaking of this very subject, "to make his religion light unto you; for man was created weak." How different this from the unaccommodating purity of the Gospel! How would Mahomet have succeeded with the Christian lesson in his mouth.—"Whosoever looketh upon a woman to lust after her, hath committed adultery with her already in his heart"? It must be added, that Mahomet did not venture upon the prohibition of wine till the fourth year

---

[3] "The sword," saith Mahomet, "is the key of heaven and of hell; a drop of blood shed in the cause of God, a night spent in arms, is of more avail than two months' fasting or prayer. Whosoever falls in battle, his sins are forgiven at the day of judgment; his wounds shall be resplendent as vermilion, and odoriferous as musk; and the loss of his limbs shall be supplied by the wings of angels and cherubim." Gibbon, vol. ix. p. 256.

of the Hegira, or the seventeenth of his mission, when his military successes had completely established his authority. The same observation holds of the fast of the Ramadan, (Mod. Univ. Hist. Vol. i. pp. 126 & 112.) and of the most laborious part of his institution, the pilgrimage to Mecca. (This latter, however, already prevailed amongst the Arabs, and had grown out of their excessive veneration for the Caaba. Mahomot's law, in this respect, was rather a compliance than an innovation. Sale's Prelim. Disc. p. 122.)

What has hitherto been collected from the records of the Musselman history relates to the twelve or thirteen years of Mahomet's peaceable preaching, which part alone of his life and enterprise admits of the smallest comparison with the origin of Christianity. A new scene is now unfolded. The city of Medina, distant about ten days' journey from Mecca, was at that time distracted by the hereditary contentions of two hostile tribes. These feuds were exasperated by the mutual persecutions of the Jews and Christians, and of the different Christian sects by which the city was inhabited. (Mod. Univ. Hist. Vol. i. p. 100.) The religion of Mahomet presented, in some measure, a point of union or compromise to these divided opinions. It embraced the principles which were common to them all. Each party saw in it an honourable acknowledgment of the fundamental truth of their own system. To the Pagan Arab, somewhat imbued with the sentiments and knowledge of his Jewish or Christian fellow-citizen, it offered no defensive or very improbable theology. This recommendation procured to Mahometanism a more favourable reception at Medina than its author had been able, by twelve years' painful endeavours, to obtain for it at Mecca. Yet, after all, the progress of the religion was inconsiderable. His missionary could only collect a congregation of forty persons. It was not a religious, but a political association, which ultimately introduced Mahomet into Medina. Harassed, as it should seem, and disgusted by the long continuance of factions and disputes, the inhabitants of that city saw in the admission of the prophet's authority a rest from the miseries which they had suffered, and a suppression of the violence and fury which they had learned to condemn. After an embassy, therefore, composed of believers and unbelievers, (Mod. Univ. Hist. Vol. i. p. 85.) and of persons of both tribes, with whom a treaty was concluded of strict alliance and support, Mahomet made his public entry, and was received as the sovereign of Medina.

From this time, or soon after this time, the impostor changed his language and his conduct. Having now a town at his command, where to arm his party, and to head them with security, he enters upon new counsels. He now pretends that a divine commission is given him to attack the infidels, to destroy idolatry, and to set up the true faith by the sword. (Mod. Univ. Hist. Vol. i. p. 88.) An early victory over a very superior force, achieved by conduct and bravery, established the renown of his arms, and of his personal character. (Victory of Bedr, Mod. Univ. Hist. Vol. i. p. 106.) Every year after this was marked by battles or assassinations. The nature and activity of Mahomet's future exertions may be estimated from the computation, that in the nine following years of his life he commanded his army in person in eight general engagements, (Mod. Univ. Hist. vol. i. p. 255.) and undertook, by himself or his lieutenants, fifty military enterprises.

From this time we have nothing left to account for, but that Mahomet should collect an army, that his army should conquer, and that his religion should proceed together with his conquests. The ordinary experience of human affairs leaves us little to wonder at in any of these effects: and they were likewise each assisted by peculiar facilities. From all sides, the roving Arabs crowded round the standard of religion and plunder, of freedom and victory, of arms and rapine. Beside the highly painted joys of a carnal paradise, Mahomet rewarded his followers in this world with a liberal division of the spoils, and with the persons of their female captives. (Gibbon, vol. ix. p. 255.) The condition of Arabia, occupied by small independent tribes, exposed it to the impression, and yielded to the progress of a firm and resolute army. After the reduction of his native peninsula, the weakness also of the Roman provinces on the north and the west, as well as the distracted state of the Persian empire on the east, facilitated the successful invasion of neighbouring countries. That Mahomet's conquests should carry his religion along with them will excite little surprise, when we know the conditions which he proposed to the vanquished. Death or conversion was the only choice offered to idolaters. "Strike off their heads! strike off all the ends of their fingers!(Sale's Koran, c. viii. p. 140.) kill the idolaters, wheresoever ye shall find them!" (Sale's Koran, c. ix. p. 149.) To the Jews and Christians was left the somewhat milder alternative of subjection and tribute, if they persisted in their own religion, or of an equal participation in the rights and liberties, the honours and privileges, of the faithful, if they embraced the religion of their conquerors. "Ye Christian dogs, you know your option; the Koran, the tribute, or the sword." (Gibbon, vol. ix. p. 337.) The corrupted state of Christianity in the seventh century, and the contentions of its sects, unhappily so fell in with men's care of their safety or their fortunes, as to induce many to forsake its profession. Add to all which, that Mahomet's victories not only operated by the natural effect of conquest, but that they were constantly represented, both to his friends and enemies, as divine declarations in his favour. Success was evidence. Prosperity carried with it, not only influence, but proof. "Ye have already," says he, after the battle of Bedr, "had a miracle shown you, in two armies which attacked each other; one army fought for God's true religion, but the other were infidels." (Sale's Koran, c. iii. p. 36.) Again;

"Ye slew not those who were slain at Bedr, but God slew them.—If ye desire a decision of the matter between us, now hath a decision come unto you." (Sale's Koran, c. viii. p. 141.)

Many more passages might be collected out of the Koran to the same effect; but they are unnecessary. The success of Mahometanism during this, and indeed every future period of its history, bears so little resemblance to the early propagation of Christianity, that no inference whatever can justly be drawn from it to the prejudice of the Christian argument. For what are we comparing? A Galilean peasant accompanied by a few fishermen with a conqueror at the head of his army. We compare Jesus, without force, without power, without support, without One external circumstance of attraction or influence, prevailing against the prejudices, the learning, the hierarchy, of his country; against the ancient religious opinions, the pompous religious rites, the philosophy, the wisdom, the authority, of the Roman empire, in the most polished and enlightened period of its existence,—with Mahomet making his way amongst Arabs; collecting followers in the midst of conquests and triumphs, in the darkest ages and countries of the world, and when success in arms not only operated by that command of men's wills and persons which attend prosperous undertakings, but was considered as a sure testimony of Divine approbation. That multitudes, persuaded by this argument, should join the train of a victorious chief; that still greater multitudes should, without any argument, bow down before irresistible power—is a conduct in which we cannot see much to surprise us; in which we can see nothing that resembles the causes by which the establishment of Christianity was effected.

The success, therefore, of Mahometanism stands not in the way of this important conclusion; that the propagation of Christianity, in the manner and under the circumstances in which it was propagated, is an unique in the history of the species. A Jewish peasant overthrew the religion of the world.

I have, nevertheless, placed the prevalency of the religion amongst the auxiliary arguments of its truth; because, whether it had prevailed or not, or whether its prevalency can or cannot be accounted for, the direct argument remains still. It is still true that a great number of men upon the spot, personally connected with the history and with the Author of the religion, were induced by what they heard and saw, and knew, not only to change their former opinions, but to give up their time, and sacrifice their ease, to traverse seas and kingdoms without rest and without weariness, to commit themselves to extreme dangers, to undertake incessant toils, to undergo grievous sufferings, and all this solely in consequence, and in support, of their belief of facts, which, if true, establish the truth of the religion, which, if false, they must have known to be so.

PART III.

A BRIEF CONSIDERATION OF SOME POPULAR OBJECTIONS.

CHAPTER I.

THE DISCREPANCIES BETWEEN THE SEVERAL GOSPELS.

I know not a more rash or unphilosophical conduct of the understanding, than to reject the substance of a story by reason of some diversity in the circumstances with which it is related. The usual character of human testimony is substantial truth under circumstantial variety. This is what the daily experience of courts of justice teaches. When accounts of a transaction come from the mouths of different witnesses, it is seldom that it is not possible to pick out apparent or real inconsistencies between them. These inconsistencies are studiously displayed by an adverse pleader, but oftentimes with little impression upon the minds of the judges. On the contrary, a close and minute agreement induces the suspicion of confederacy and fraud. When written histories touch upon the same scenes of action; the comparison almost always affords ground for a like reflection. Numerous, and sometimes important, variations present themselves; not seldom, also, absolute and final contradictions; yet neither one nor the other are deemed sufficient to shake the credibility of the main fact. The embassy of the Jews to deprecate the execution of Claudian's order to place his statue, in their temple, Philo places in harvest, Josephus in seed time; both contemporary writers. No reader is led by this inconsistency to doubt whether such an embassy was sent, or whether such an order was given. Our own history supplies examples of the same kind. In the account of the Marquis of Argyle's death, in the reign of Charles the Second, we have a very remarkable contradiction. Lord Clarendon relates that he was condemned to be hanged, which was performed the same day; on the contrary, Burnet, Woodrew, Heath, Echard, concur in stating that he was beheaded; and that he was condemned upon the Saturday, and executed upon the Monday. (See Biog. Britann.) Was any reader of English history ever sceptic enough to raise from hence a question whether the Marquis of Argyle was executed or not? Yet this ought to be left in uncertainty, according to the principles upon which the Christian history has sometimes been attacked. Dr. Middleton contended, that the different hours of the day assigned to the crucifixion of Christ, by John and by the other Evangelists, did not admit of the reconcilement which learned men had proposed: and then concludes the discussion with this hard remark; "We must be forced, with several of the critics, to leave the difficulty just as we found it, chargeable with all the consequences of manifest inconsistency." (Middleton's

Reflections answered by Benson, Hist. Christ. vol. iii. p. 50.) But what are these consequences? By no means the discrediting of the history as to the principal fact, by a repugnancy (even supposing that repugnancy not to be resolvable into different modes of computation) in the time of the day in which it is said to have taken place.

A great deal of the discrepancy observable in the Gospels arises from omission; from a fact or a passage of Christ's life being noticed by one writer which is unnoticed by another. Now, omission is at all times a very uncertain ground of objection. We perceive it, not only in the comparison of different writers, but even in the same writer when compared with himself. There are a great many particulars, and some of them of importance, mentioned by Josephus in his Antiquities, which, as we should have supposed, ought to have been put down by him in their place in the Jewish Wars. (Lardner, part i. vol. ii. p. 735, et seq.) Suetonius, Tacitus, Dio Cassius, have, all three, written of the reign of Tiberius. Each has mentioned many things omitted by the rest, (Lardner, part i. vol. ii. p. 743.) yet no objection is from thence taken to the respective credit of their histories. We have in our own times, if there were not something indecorous in the comparison, the life of an eminent person written by three of his friends, in which there is very great variety in the incidents selected by them; some apparent, and perhaps some real contradictions; yet without any impeachment of the substantial truth of their accounts, of the authenticity of the books, of the competent information or general fidelity of the writers.

But these discrepancies will be still more numerous, when men do not write histories, but memoirs: which is, perhaps, the true name and proper description of our Gospels: that is, when they do not undertake, nor ever meant to deliver, in order of time, a regular and complete account of all the things of importance which the person who is the subject of their history did or said; but only, out of many similar ones, to give such passages, or such actions and discourses, as offered themselves more immediately to their attention, came in the way of their inquiries, occurred to their recollection, or were suggested by their particular design at the time of writing.

This particular design may appear sometimes, but not always, nor often. Thus I think that the particular design which Saint Matthew had in view whilst he was writing the history of the resurrection was to attest the faithful performance of Christ's promise to his disciples to go before them into Galilee; because he alone, except Mark, who seems to have taken it from him, has recorded this promise, and he alone has confined his narrative to that single appearance to the disciples which fulfilled it. It was the preconcerted, the great and most public manifestation of our Lord's person. It was the thing which dwelt upon Saint Matthew's mind, and he adapted his narrative to it. But, that there is nothing in Saint

Matthew's language which negatives other appearances, or which imports that this his appearance to his disciples in Galilee, in pursuance of his promise, was his first or only appearance, is made pretty evident by Saint Mark's Gospel, which uses the same terms concerning the appearance in Galilee as Saint Matthew uses, yet itself records two other appearances prior to this: "Go your way, tell his disciples and Peter, that he goeth before you into Galilee: there shall ye see him as he said unto you" (xvi. 7). We might be apt to infer from these words, that this was the first time they were to see him; at least, we might infer it, with as much reason as we draw the inference from the same words in Matthew: the historian himself did not perceive that he was leading his readers to any such conclusion; for, in the twelfth and following verses of this chapter, he informs us of two appearances, which, by comparing the order of events, are shown to have been prior to the appearance in Galilee. "He appeared in another form unto two of them, as they walked, and went into the country; and they went and told it unto the residue, neither believed they them: afterwards he appeared unto the eleven, as they sat at meat, and upbraided them with their unbelief, because they believed not them that had seen him after he was risen."

Probably the same observation, concerning the particular design which guided the historian, may be of use in comparing many other passages of the Gospels.

CHAPTER II.

ERRONEOUS OPINIONS IMPUTED TO THE APOSTLES.

A species of candour which is shown towards every other book is sometimes refused to the Scriptures: and that is, the placing of a distinction between judgment and testimony. We do not usually question the credit of a writer, by reason of an opinion he may have delivered upon subjects unconnected with his evidence: and even upon subjects connected with his account, or mixed with it in the same discourse or writing, we naturally separate facts from opinions, testimony from observation, narrative from argument.

To apply this equitable consideration to the Christian records, much controversy and much objection has been raised concerning the quotations of the Old Testament found in the New; some of which quotations, it is said, are applied in a sense and to events apparently different from that which they bear, and from those to which they belong in the original. It is probable, to my apprehension, that many of those quotations were intended by the writers of the New Testament as nothing more than accommodations. They quoted passages of their Scripture which suited, and fell in with, the occasion before them, without always undertaking to assert that the occasion was in the view of the author of the words. Such accommodations of passages from old authors, from books especially which are in every one's hands, are common with writers of all countries; but in none, perhaps, were more to be expected than in the writings of the Jews, whose literature was almost entirely confined to their Scriptures. Those prophecies which are alleged with more solemnity, and which are accompanied with a precise declaration that they originally respected the event then related, are, I think, truly alleged. But were it otherwise; is the judgment of the writers of the New Testament, in interpreting passages of the Old, or sometimes, perhaps, in receiving established interpretations, so connected either with their veracity, or with their means of information concerning what was passing in their own times, as that a critical mistake, even were it clearly made out, should overthrow their historical credit?—Does it diminish it? Has it anything to do with it?

Another error imputed to the first Christians was the expected approach of the day of judgment. I would introduce this objection by a remark upon what appears to me a somewhat similar example. Our Saviour, speaking to Peter of John, said, "If I will that he tarry till I come, what is that to thee?"' (John xxi. 22.) These words we find had been so misconstrued, as that a report from thence "went abroad among the brethren, that that disciple should not die." Suppose that this had come down to us amongst the prevailing opinions of the early Christians, and that the particular circumstance from which the mistake sprang had been lost (which, humanly speaking, was most likely to have been the case), some, at this day, would have been ready to regard and quote the error as an impeachment of the whole Christian system. Yet with how little justice such a conclusion would have been drawn, or rather such a presumption taken up, the information which we happen to possess enables us now to perceive. To those who think that the Scriptures lead us to believe that the early Christians, and even the apostles, expected the approach of the day of judgment in their own times, the same reflection will occur as that which we have made with respect to the more partial, perhaps, and temporary, but still no less ancient, error concerning the duration of Saint John's life. It was an error, it may be likewise said, which would effectually hinder those who entertained it from acting the part of impostors.

The difficulty which attends the subject of the present chapter is contained in this question; If we once admit the fallibility of the apostolic judgment, where are we to stop, or in what can we rely upon it? To which question, as arguing with unbelievers, and as arguing for the substantial truth of the Christian history, and for that alone, it is competent to the advocate of Christianity to reply, Give me the apostles' testimony, and I do not stand in need of their judgment; give me the facts, and I have complete security for every conclusion I want.

But, although I think that it is competent to the Christian apologist to return this answer, I do not think that it is the only answer which the objection is capable of receiving. The two following cautions, founded, I apprehend, in the most reasonable distinctions, will exclude all uncertainty upon this head which can be attended with danger.

First, to separate what was the object of the apostolic mission, and declared by them to be so, from what was extraneous to it, or only incidentally connected with it. Of points clearly extraneous to the religion nothing need be said. Of points incidentally connected with it something may be added. Demoniacal possession is one of these points: concerning the reality of which, as this place will not admit the examination, nor even the production of the argument on either side of the question, it would be arrogance in me to deliver any judgment. And it is unnecessary. For what I am concerned to observe is, that even they who think it was a general, but erroneous opinion of those times; and that the writers of the New Testament, in common with other Jewish writers of that age, fell into the manner of speaking and of thinking upon the subject which then universally prevailed, need not be alarmed by the concession, as though they had anything to fear from it for the truth of Christianity. The doctrine was not what Christ brought into the world. It appears in the Christian records, incidentally and accidentally, as being the subsisting opinion of the age and country in which his ministry was exercised. It was no part of

228

the object of his revelation, to regulate men's opinions concerning the action of spiritual substances upon animal bodies. At any rate it is unconnected with testimony. If a dumb person was by a word restored to the use of his speech, it signifies little to what cause the dumbness was ascribed; and the like of every other cure wrought upon these who are said to have been possessed. The malady was real, the cure was real, whether the popular explication of the cause was well founded or not. The matter of fact, the change, so far as it was an object of sense, or of testimony, was in either case the same.

Secondly, that, in reading the apostolic writings, we distinguish between their doctrines and their arguments. Their doctrines came to them by revelation properly so called; yet in propounding these doctrines in their writings or discourses they were wont to illustrate, support, and enforce them by such analogies, arguments, and considerations as their own thoughts suggested. Thus the call of the gentiles, that is, the admission of the Gentiles to the Christian profession without a previous subjection to the law of Moses, was imported to the apostles by revelation, and was attested by the miracles which attended the Christian ministry among them. The apostles' own assurance of the matter rested upon this foundation. Nevertheless, Saint Paul, when treating of the subject, often a great variety of topics in its proof and vindication. The doctrine itself must be received: but it is not necessary, in order to defend Christianity, to defend the propriety of every comparison, or the validity of every argument, which the apostle has brought into the discussion. The same observation applies to some other instances, and is, in my opinion, very well founded; "When divine writers argue upon any point, we are always bound to believe the conclusions that their reasonings end in, as parts of divine revelation: but we are not bound to be able to make out, or even to assent to all the premises made use of by them, in their whole extent, unless it appear plainly, that they affirm the premises as expressly as they do the conclusions proved by them." (Burnets Expos. art. 6.)

229

CHAPTER III.

THE CONNEXION OF CHRISTIANITY WITH THE JEWISH HISTORY.

Undoubtedly our Saviour assumes the divine origin of the Mosaic institution: and, independently of his authority, I conceive it to be very difficult to assign any other cause for the commencement or existence of that institution; especially for the singular circumstance of the Jews adhering to the unity when every other people slid into polytheism; for their being men in religion, children in everything else; behind other nations in the arts of peace and war, superior to the most improved in their sentiments and doctrines relating to the Deity.[1]

Undoubtedly, also, our Saviour recognises the prophetic character of many of their ancient writers. So far, therefore, we are bound as Christians to go. But to make Christianity answerable, with its life, for the circumstantial truth of each separate passage of the Old Testament, the genuineness of every book, the information, fidelity, and judgment of every writer in it, is to bring, I will not say great, but unnecessary difficulties into the whole system. These books were universally read and received by the Jews of our Saviour's time. He and his apostles, in common with all other Jews, referred to them, alluded to them, used them. Yet, except where he expressly ascribes a divine authority to particular predictions, I do not know that we can strictly draw any conclusion from the books being so used and applied, beside the proof, which it unquestionably is, of their notoriety and reception at that time. In this view, our Scriptures afford a valuable testimony to those of the Jews. But the nature of this testimony ought to be understood. It is surely very different from what it is sometimes represented to be, a specific

---

[1] "In the doctrine, for example, of the unity, the eternity, the omnipotence, the omniscience, the omnipresence, the wisdom, and the goodness of God; in their opinions concerning providence, and the creation, preservation, and government of the world." Campbell on Mir. p. 207. To which we may add, in the acts of their religion not being accompanied either with cruelties or impurities: in the religion itself being free from a species of superstition which prevailed universally in the popular religions of the ancient world, and which is to be found perhaps in all religions that have their origin in human artifice and credulity, viz. fanciful connexions between certain appearances and actions, and the destiny of nations or individuals. Upon these conceits rested the whole train of auguries and auspices, which formed so much even of the serious part of the religions of Greece and Rome, and of the charms and incantations which were practised in those countries by the common people. From everything of this sort the religion of the Jews, and of the Jews alone, was free. Vide. Priestley's Lectures on the Truth of the Jewish and Christian Revelation; 1794.

ratification of each particular fact and opinion; and not only of each particular fact, but of the motives assigned for every action, together with the judgment of praise or dispraise bestowed upon them. Saint James, in his Epistle, says, "Ye have heard of the patience of Job, and have seen the end of the Lord." Notwithstanding this text, the reality of Job's history, and even the existence of such a person, have been always deemed a fair subject of inquiry and discussion amongst Christian divines. Saint James's authority is considered as good evidence of the existence of the book of Job at that time, and of its reception by the Jews; and of nothing more. Saint Paul, in his Second Epistle to Timothy, has this similitude: "Now, as Jannes and Jambres withstood Moses, so do these also resist the truth." These names are not found in the Old Testament. And it is uncertain whether Saint Paul took them from some apocryphal writing then extant, or from tradition. But no one ever imagined that Saint Paul is here asserting the authority of the writing, if it was a written account which he quoted, or making himself answerable for the authenticity of the tradition; much less that he so involves himself with either of these questions as that the credit of his own history and mission should depend upon the fact whether Jannes and Jambres withstood Moses or not. For what reason a more rigorous interpretation should be put upon other references it is difficult to know. I do not mean, that other passages of the Jewish history stand upon no better evidence than the history of Job, or of Jannes and Jambres (I think much otherwise); but I mean, that a reference in the New Testament to a passage in the Old does not so fix its authority as to exclude all inquiry into its credibility, or into the separate reasons upon which that credibility is founded; and that it is an unwarrantable as well as unsafe rule to lay down concerning the Jewish history, what was never laid down concerning any other, that either every particular of it must be true, or the whole false.

I have thought it necessary to state this point explicitly, because a fashion, revived by Voltaire, and pursued by the disciples of his school, seems to have much prevailed of late, of attacking Christianity through the sides of Judaism. Some objections of this class are founded in misconstruction, some in exaggeration; but all proceed upon a supposition, which has not been made out by argument, viz. that the attestation which the Author and first teachers of Christianity gave to the divine mission of Moses and the prophets extends to every point and portion of the Jewish history; and so extends as to make Christianity responsible, in its own credibility, for the circumstantial truth (I had almost said for the critical exactness) of every narrative contained in the Old Testament.

CHAPTER IV.

REJECTION OF CHRISTIANITY.

We acknowledge that the Christian religion, although it converted great numbers, did not produce an universal, or even a general conviction in the minds of men of the age and countries in which it appeared. And this want of a more complete and extensive success is called the rejection of the Christian history and miracles; and has been thought by some to form a strong objection to the reality of the facts which the history contains.

The matter of the objection divides itself into two parts; as it relates to the Jews, and as it relates to Heathen nations: because the minds of these two descriptions of men may have been, with respect to Christianity, under the influence of very different causes. The case of the Jews, inasmuch as our Saviour's ministry was originally addressed to them, offers itself first to our consideration.

Now upon the subject of the truth of the Christian religion; with us there is but one question, viz., whether the miracles were actually wrought? From acknowledging the miracles, we pass instantaneously to the acknowledgment of the whole. No doubt lies between the premises and the conclusion. If we believe the works of any one of them, we believe in Jesus. And this order of reasoning has become so universal and familiar that we do not readily apprehend how it could ever have been otherwise. Yet it appears to me perfectly certain, that the state of thought in the mind of a Jew of our Saviour's age was totally different from this. After allowing the reality of the miracle, he had a great deal to do to persuade himself that Jesus was the Messiah. This is clearly intimated by various passages of the Gospel history. It appears that, in the apprehension of the writers of the New Testament, the miracles did not irresistibly carry even those who saw them to the conclusion intended to be drawn from them; or so compel assent, as to leave no room for suspense, for the exercise of candour, or the effects of prejudice. And to this point, at least, the evangelists may he allowed to be good witnesses; because it is a point in which exaggeration or disguise would have been the other way. Their accounts, if they could he suspected of falsehood, would rather have magnified than diminished the effects of the miracles.

John vii. 21—31. "Jesus answered and said unto them, I have done one work, and ye all marvel.—If a man on the Sabbath-day receive circumcision, that the law of Moses should not be broken; are ye angry at me, because I have made a man every whit whole on the Sabbath-day? Judge not according to the appearance, but judge righteous judgment. Then said some of them of Jerusalem, Is not this he whom they seek to kill? But lo, he speaketh boldly, and they say nothing to him: do the rulers know indeed that this is the very Christ? Howbeit we know this man, whence he is: but when Christ cometh, no man knoweth whence he is. Then cried Jesus in the temple as he taught, saying, Ye both know me, and ye know whence I am: and I am not come of myself, but He that sent me is true, whom ye know not. But I know Him, for I am from Him, and He hath sent me. Then they sought to take him: but no man laid hands on him, because his hour was not yet come. And many of the people believed on him and said, When Christ cometh, will he do more miracles than those which this man hath done?"

This passage is very observable. It exhibits the reasoning of different sorts of persons upon the occasion of a miracle which persons of all sorts are represented to have acknowledged as real. One sort of men thought that there was something very extraordinary in all this; but that still Jesus could not be the Christ, because there was a circumstance in his appearance which militated with an opinion concerning Christ in which they had been brought up, and of the truth of which, it is probable, they had never entertained a particle of doubt, viz. That "when Christ cometh, no man knoweth whence he is." Another sort were inclined to believe him to be the Messiah. But even these did not argue as we should; did not consider the miracle as of itself decisive of the question; as what, if once allowed, excluded all further debate upon the subject; but founded their opinion upon a kind of comparative reasoning, "When Christ cometh, will he do more miracles than those which this man hath done?"

Another passage in the same evangelist, and observable for the same purpose, is that in which he relates the resurrection of Lazarus; "Jesus," he tells us (xi. 43, 44), "when he had thus spoken, cried with a loud voice, Lazarus, come forth: and he that was dead came forth, bound hand and foot with graveclothes, and his face was bound about with a napkin. Jesus saith unto them, Loose him, and let him go." One might have suspected, that at least all those who stood by the sepulchre, when Lazarus was raised, would have believed in Jesus. Yet the evangelist does not so represent it:—"Then many of the Jews which came to Mary, and had seen the things which Jesus did, believed on him; but some of them went their ways to the Pharisees, and told them what things Jesus had done." We cannot suppose that the evangelist meant by this account to leave his readers to imagine, that any of the spectators doubted about the truth of the miracle. Far from it. Unquestionably, he states the miracle to have been fully allowed; yet the persons who allowed it were, according to his representation, capable of retaining hostile sentiments towards Jesus. "Believing in Jesus" was not only to believe that he wrought miracles, but that he was the Messiah. With us there is no difference between these two things; with them there was the greatest; and the difference is apparent in this transaction. If Saint John has represented the conduct of the Jews upon this occasion truly (and why he should not I cannot tell, for it rather makes against him than for him), it shows clearly the principles upon which their judgment proceeded. Whether he has related the matter truly or not, the relation itself discovers the writer's own opinion of those principles: and that alone possesses considerable authority. In the next chapter, we have a reflection of the evangelist entirely suited to this state of the case: "But though he had done so many miracles before them, yet believed they not on him." (Chap. xii. 37.) The evangelist does not mean to impute the defect of their belief to any doubt about the miracles, but to their not perceiving, what all now sufficiently perceive, and what they would have perceived had not their understandings been governed by strong prejudices, the infallible attestation which the works of Jesus bore to the truth of his pretensions.

The ninth chapter of Saint John's Gospel contains a very circumstantial account of the cure of a blind man; a miracle submitted to all the scrutiny and examination which a sceptic could propose. If a modern unbeliever had drawn up the interrogatories, they could hardly have been more critical or searching. The account contains also a very curious conference between the Jewish rulers and the patient, in which the point for our present notice is, their resistance of the force of the miracle, and of the conclusion to which it led, after they had failed in discrediting its evidence. "We know that God spake unto Moses, but as for this fellow, we know not whence he is." That was the answer which set their minds at rest. And by the help of much prejudice, and great unwillingness to yield, it might do so. In the mind of the poor man restored to sight, which was under no such bias, and felt no such reluctance, the miracle had its natural operation. "Herein," says he, "is a marvellous thing, that ye know not from whence he is, yet he hath opened mine eyes. Now we know that God heareth not sinners: but if any man be a worshipper of God, and doeth his will, him he heareth. Since the world began, was it not heard, that any man opened the eyes of one that was born blind. If this man were not of God, he could do nothing." We do not find that the Jewish rulers had any other reply to make to this defence, than that which authority is sometimes apt to make to argument, "Dost thou teach us?"

If it shall be inquired how a turn of thought, so different from what prevails at present, should obtain currency with the ancient Jews; the answer is found in two opinions which are proved to have subsisted in that age and country. The one was their expectation of a Messiah of a kind totally contrary to what the appearance of Jesus bespoke him to be; the other, their persuasion of the agency of demons in the production of supernatural effects. These opinions are not supposed by us for the purpose of argument, but are evidently recognised in the Jewish writings as well as in ours. And it ought moreover to be considered, that in these opinions the Jews of that age had been from their infancy brought up; that they were opinions, the grounds of which they had probably few of them inquired into, and of the truth of which they entertained no doubt. And I think that these two opinions conjointly afford an explanation of their conduct. The first put them upon seeking out some excuse to themselves for not receiving Jesus in the character in which he claimed to be received; and the second supplied them with just such an excuse as they wanted. Let Jesus work what miracles he would, still the answer was in readiness, "that he wrought them by the assistance of Beelzebub." And to this answer no reply could be made, but that which our Saviour did make, by showing that the tendency of his mission was so adverse to the views with which this being was, by the objectors themselves, supposed to act, that it could not reasonably be supposed that he would assist in carrying it on. The power displayed in the miracles did not alone refute the Jewish solution, because the interposition of invisible agents being once admitted, it is impossible to ascertain the limits by which their efficiency is circumscribed. We of this day may be disposed possibly to think such opinions too absurd to have been ever seriously entertained. I am not bound to contend for the credibility of the opinions. They were at least as reasonable as the belief in witchcraft. They were opinions in which the Jews of that age had from their infancy been instructed; and those who cannot see enough in the force of this reason to account for their conduct towards our Saviour, do not sufficiently consider how such opinions may sometimes become very general in a country, and with what pertinacity, when once become so, they are for that reason alone adhered to. In the suspense which these notions and the prejudices resulting from them might occasion, the candid and docile and humble-minded would probably decide in Christ's favour; the proud and obstinate, together with the giddy and the thoughtless, almost universally against him.

This state of opinion discovers to us also the reason of what some choose to wonder at, why the Jews should reject miracles when they saw them, yet rely so much upon the tradition of them in their own history. It does not appear that it had ever entered into the minds of those who lived in the time of Moses and the prophets to ascribe their miracles to the supernatural agency of evil being. The solution was not then invented. The authority of Moses and the prophets being established, and become the foundation of the national polity and religion, it was not probable that the later Jews, brought up in a reverence for that religion, and the subjects of that polity, should apply to their history a reasoning which tended to overthrow the foundation of both.

II. The infidelity of the Gentile world, and that more especially of men of rank and learning in it, is resolvable into a principle which, in my judgment, will account for the inefficacy of any argument or any evidence whatever, viz. contempt prior to examination. The state of religion amongst the Greeks and Romans had a natural tendency to induce this disposition. Dionysius Halicarnassensis remarks, that there were six hundred different kinds of religions or sacred rites exercised at Rome. (Jortin's Remarks on Eccl. Hist. Vol. i. p. 371.) The superior classes of the community treated them all as fables. Can we wonder, then, that Christianity was included in the number, without inquiry into its separate merits, or the particular grounds of its pretensions? It might be either true or false for anything they knew about it. The religion had nothing in its character which immediately engaged their notice. It mixed with no politics. It produced no fine writers. It contained no curious speculations. When it did reach their knowledge, I doubt not but that it appeared to them a very strange system,—so unphilosophical,—dealing so little in argument and discussion, in such arguments however and discussions as they were accustomed to entertain. What is said of Jesus Christ, of his nature, office, and ministry, would be in the highest degree alien from the conceptions of their theology. The Redeemer and the destined Judge of the human race a poor young man, executed at Jerusalem with two thieves upon a cross! Still more would the language in which the Christian doctrine was delivered be dissonant and barbarous to their ears. What knew they of grace, of redemption, of justification, of the blood of Christ shed for the sins of men, of reconcilement, of mediation? Christianity was made up of points they had never thought of; of terms which they had never heard.

It was presented also to the imagination of the learned Heathen under additional disadvantage, by reason of its real, and still more of its nominal, connexion with Judaism. It shared in the obloquy and ridicule with which that people and their religion were treated by the Greeks and Romans. They regarded Jehovah himself only as the idol of the Jewish nation, and what was related of him as of a piece with what was told of the tutelar deities of other countries; nay, the Jews were in a particular manner ridiculed for being a credulous race; so that whatever reports of a miraculous nature came out of that country were looked upon by the Heathen world as false and frivolous. When they heard of Christianity, they heard of it as a quarrel amongst this people about some articles of their own superstition. Despising, therefore, as they did, the whole system, it was not probable that they would enter, with any degree of seriousness or attention, into the detail of its disputes or the merits of either side. How little they knew, and with what carelessness they judged of these matters, appears, I think, pretty plainly from an example of no less weight than that of Tacitus, who, in a grave and professed discourse upon the history of the Jews, states that they worshipped the effigy of an ass. (Tacit. Hist. lib. v. c. 2.) The passage is a proof how prone the learned men of those times were, and upon how little evidence, to heap together stories which might increase the contempt and odium in which that people was holden. The same foolish charge is also confidently repeated by Plutarch. (Sympos. lib. iv. quaest. 5.)

It is observable that all these considerations are of a nature to operate with the greatest force upon the highest ranks; upon men of education, and that order of the public from which writers are principally taken: I may add also upon the philosophical as well as the libertine character; upon the Antonines or Julian, not less than upon Nero or Domitian; and, more particularly, upon that large and polished class of men who acquiesced in the general persuasion, that all they had to do was to practise the duties of morality, and to worship the Deity more patrio; a habit of thinking, liberal as it may appear, which shuts the door against every argument for a new religion. The considerations above mentioned would acquire also strength from the prejudices which men of rank and learning universally entertain against anything that originates with the vulgar and illiterate; which prejudice is known to be as obstinate as any prejudice whatever.

Yet Christianity was still making its way: and, amidst so many impediments to its progress, so much difficulty in procuring audience and attention, its actual success is more to be wondered at, than that it should not have universally conquered scorn and indifference, fixed the levity of a voluptuous age, or, through a cloud of adverse prejudications, opened for itself a passage to the hearts and understandings of the scholars of the age.

And the cause which is here assigned for the rejection of Christianity by men of rank and learning among the Heathens, namely, a strong antecedent contempt, accounts also for their silence concerning it. If they had rejected it upon examination, they would have written about it; they would have given their reasons. Whereas, what men repudiate upon the strength of some prefixed persuasion, or from a settled contempt of the subject, of the persons who propose it, or of the manner in which it is proposed, they do not naturally write books about, or notice much in what they write upon other subjects.

The letters of the younger Pliny furnish an example of this silence, and let us, in some measure, into the cause of it. From his celebrated correspondence with Trajan, we know that the Christian religion prevailed in a very considerable degree in the province over which he presided; that it had excited his attention; that he had inquired into the matter just so much as a Roman magistrate might be expected to inquire, viz., whether the religion contained any opinions dangerous to government; but that of its doctrines, its evidences, or its books, he had not taken the trouble to inform himself with any degree of care or correctness. But although Pliny had viewed Christianity in a nearer position than most of his learned countrymen saw it in, yet he had regarded the whole with such negligence and disdain (further than as it seemed to concern his administration), that, in more than two hundred and forty letters of his which have come down to us, the subject is never once again mentioned. If, out of this number, the two letters between him and Trajan had been lost, with what confidence would the obscurity of the Christian religion have been argued from Pliny's silence about it, and with how little truth!

The name and character which Tacitus has given to Christianity, "exitiabilis superstitio" (a pernicious superstition), and by which two words he disposes of the whole question of the merits or demerits of the religion, afford a strong proof how little he knew, or concerned himself to know, about the matter. I apprehend that I shall not be contradicted, when I take upon me to assert, that no unbeliever of the present age would apply this epithet to the Christianity of the New Testament, or not allow that it was entirely unmerited. Read the instructions given by a great teacher of the religion to those very Roman converts of whom Tacitus speaks; and given also a very few years before the time of which he is speaking; and which are not, let it be observed, a collection of fine sayings brought together from different parts of a large work, but stand in one entire passage of a public letter, without the intermixture of a single thought which is frivolous or exceptionable:—"Abhor that which is evil, cleave to that which is good. Be kindly affectioned one to another, with brotherly love; in honour preferring one another; not slothful in business; fervent in spirit; serving the Lord; rejoicing in hope; patient in tribulation; continuing instant in prayer; distributing to the necessity of saints; given to hospitality. Bless them which persecute you; bless, and curse not. Rejoice with them that do rejoice, and weep with them that weep. Be of the same mind one towards another. Mind not high things, but condescend to men of low estate. Be not wise in your own conceits. Recompense to no man evil for evil. Provide things honest in the sight of all men. If it be possible, as much as lieth in you, live peaceably with all men. Avenge not yourselves, but rather give place unto wrath: for it is written, Vengeance is mine; I will repay, saith the Lord: therefore, if thine enemy hunger, feed him; if he thirst, give him drink: for, in so doing, thou shalt heap coals of fire on his head. Be not overcome of evil, but overcome evil with good.

"Let every soul be subject unto the higher powers. For there is no power but of God: the powers that be are ordained of God. Whosoever, therefore, resisteth the power, resisteth the ordinance of God: and they that resist shall receive to themselves damnation. For rulers are not a terror to good works, but to the evil. Wilt thou then not be afraid of the power? Do that which is good, and thou shalt have praise of the same: for he is the minister of God to thee for good. But if thou do that which is evil, be afraid; for he beareth not the sword in vain: for he is the minister of God, a revenger to execute wrath upon him that doeth evil. Wherefore ye must needs be subject, not only for wrath, but also for conscience' sake. For, for this cause pay ye tribute also: for they are God's ministers, attending continually upon this very thing. Render therefore to all their dues; tribute to whom tribute is due; custom to whom custom; fear to whom fear; honour to whom honour.

"Owe no man anything, but to love one another; for he that loveth another, hath fulfilled the law. For this, Thou shalt not commit adultery, Thou shalt not kill, Thou shalt not steal, Thou shalt not bear false witness, Thou shalt not covet; and if there be any other commandment, it is briefly comprehended in this saying, Thou shalt love thy neighbour as thyself. Love worketh no ill to his neighbour; therefore love is the fulfilling of the law.

"And that, knowing the time, that now it is high time to awake out of sleep; for now is our salvation nearer than when we believed. The night is far spent, the day is at hand; let us therefore cast off the works of darkness, and let us put on the armour of light. Let us walk honestly as in the day; not in rioting and drunkenness, not in chambering and wantonness, not in strife and envying." (Romans, xii. 9—xiii. 13.)

Read this, and then think of "exitiabilis superstitio!" Or, if we be not allowed, in contending with Heathen authorities, to produce our books against theirs, we may at least be permitted to confront theirs with one another. Of this "pernicious superstition" what could Pliny find to blame, when he was led, by his office, to institute something like an examination into the conduct and principles of the sect? He discovered nothing but that they were went to meet together on a stated day before it was light, and sing among themselves a hymn to Christ as a God, and to bind themselves by an oath, not to the commission of any wickedness, but, not to be guilty of theft, robbery, or adultery; never to falsify their word, nor to deny a pledge committed to them, when called upon to return it.

Upon the words of Tacitus we may build the following observations:

First; That we are well warranted in calling the view under which the learned men of that age beheld Christianity an obscure and distant view. Had Tacitus known more of Christianity, of its precepts, duties, constitution, or design, however he had discredited the story, he would have respected the principle. He would have described the religion differently, though he had rejected it. It has been very satisfactorily shown, that the "superstition" of the Christians consisted in worshipping a person unknown to the Roman calendar; and that the "perniciousness" with which they were reproached was nothing else but their opposition to the established polytheism; and this view of the matter was just such an one as might be expected to occur to a mind which held the sect in too much contempt to concern itself about the grounds and reasons of their conduct.

Secondly; We may from hence remark how little reliance can be placed upon the most acute judgments in subjects which they are pleased to despise; and which, of course, they from the first consider as unworthy to be inquired into. Had not Christianity survived to tell its own story, it must have gone down to posterity as a "pernicious superstition;" and that upon the credit of Tacitus's account, much, I doubt not, strengthened by the name of the writer, and the reputation of his sagacity.

Thirdly; That this contempt, prior to examination, is an intellectual vice, from which the greatest faculties of mind are not free. I know not, indeed, whether men of the greatest faculties of mind are not the most subject to it. Such men feel themselves seated upon an eminence. Looking down from their height upon the follies of mankind, they behold contending tenets wasting their idle strength upon one another with the common disdain of the absurdity of them all. This habit of thought, however comfortable to the mind which entertain it, or however natural to great parts, is extremely dangerous; and more apt than almost any other disposition to produce hasty and contemptuous, and, by consequence, erroneous judgments, both of persons and opinions.

Fourthly; We need not be surprised at many writers of that age not mentioning Christianity at all, when they who did mention it appear to have entirely misconceived its nature and character; and, in consequence of this misconception, to have regarded it with negligence and contempt.

To the knowledge of the greatest part of the learned heathens, the facts of the Christian history could only come by report. The books, probably, they had never looked into. The settled habit of their minds was, and long had been, an indiscriminate rejection of all reports of the kind. With these sweeping conclusions truth hath no chance. It depends upon distinction. If they would not inquire, how should they be convinced? It might be founded in truth, though they, who made no search, might not discover it.

"Men of rank and fortune, of wit and abilities, are often found, even in Christian countries, to be surprisingly ignorant of religion, and of everything that relates to it. Such were many of the heathens. Their thoughts were all fixed upon other things; upon reputation and glory, upon wealth and power, upon luxury and pleasure, upon business or learning. They thought, and they had reason to think, that the religion of their country was fable and forgery, a heap of inconsistent lies; which inclined them to suppose that other religions were no better. Hence it came to pass, that when the apostles preached the Gospel, and wrought miracles in confirmation of a doctrine every way worthy of God, many Gentiles knew little or nothing of it, and would not take the least pains to inform themselves about it. This appears plainly from ancient history." (Jortin's Disc. on the Christ. Rel. p. 66, ed. 4th.)

I think it by no means unreasonable to suppose that the heathen public, especially that part which is made up of men of rank and education, were divided into two classes; these who despised Christianity beforehand, and those who received it. In correspondency with which division of character the writers of that age would also be of two classes;

those who were silent about Christianity, and those who were Christians. "A good man, who attended sufficiently to the Christian affairs, would become a Christian; after which his testimony ceased to be pagan and became Christian." (Hartley, Obs. p. 119.)

I must also add, that I think it sufficiently proved, that the notion of magic was resorted to by the heathen adversaries of Christianity, in like manner as that of diabolical agency had before been by the Jews. Justin Martyr alleges this as his reason for arguing from prophecy rather than from miracles. Origen imputes this evasion to Celsus; Jerome to Porphyry; and Lactantius to the heathen in general. The several passages which contain these testimonies will be produced in the next chapter. It being difficult, however, to ascertain in what degree this notion prevailed, especially the superior ranks of the heathen communities, another, and think an adequate, cause has been assigned for their infidelity. It is probable that in many cases the two causes would together.

CHAPTER V.

THAT THE CHRISTIAN MIRACLES ARE NOT RECITED, OR APPEALED TO, BY EARLY CHRISTIAN WRITERS THEMSELVES SO FULLY OR FREQUENTLY AS MIGHT HAVE BEEN EXPECTED.

I shall consider this objection, first, as it applies to the letters of the apostles preserved in the New Testament; and secondly, as it applies to the remaining writings of other early Christians.

The epistles of the apostles are either hortatory or argumentative. So far as they were occupied in delivering lessons of duty, rules of public order, admonitions against certain prevailing corruptions, against vice, or any particular species of it, or in fortifying and encouraging the constancy of the disciples under the trials to which they were exposed, there appears to be no place or occasion for more of these references than we actually find.

So far as these epistles are argumentative, the nature of the argument which they handle accounts for the infrequency of these allusions. These epistles were not written to prove the truth of Christianity. The subject under consideration was not that which the miracles decided, the reality of our Lord's mission; but it was that which the miracles did not decide, the nature of his person or power, the design of his advent, its effects, and of those effects the value, kind, and extent. Still I maintain that miraculous evidence lies at the bottom of the argument. For nothing could be so preposterous as for the disciples of Jesus to dispute amongst themselves, or with others, concerning his office or character; unless they believed that he had shown, by supernatural proofs, that there was something extraordinary in both. Miraculous evidence, therefore, forming not the texture of these arguments, but the ground and substratum, if it be occasionally discerned, if it be incidentally appealed to, it is exactly so much as ought take place, supposing the history to be true.

As a further answer to the objection, that the apostolic epistles do not contain so frequent, or such direct and circumstantial recitals of miracles as might be expected, I would add, that the apostolic epistles resemble in this respect the apostolic speeches, which speeches are given by a writer who distinctly records numerous miracles wrought by these apostles themselves, and by the Founder of the institution in their presence; that it is unwarrantable to contend that the omission, or infrequency, of such recitals in the speeches of the apostles negatives the existence of the miracles, when the speeches are given in immediate conjunction with the history of those miracles: and that a conclusion which cannot be inferred from the speeches without contradicting the whole tenour of the book which contains them cannot be inferred from letters, which in this respect are similar only to the speeches.

To prove the similitude which we allege, it may be remarked, that although in Saint Luke's Gospel the apostle Peter is represented to have been present at many decisive miracles wrought by Christ; and although the second part of the same history ascribes other decisive miracles to Peter himself, particularly the cure of the lame man at the gate of the temple (Acts iii. 1), the death of Ananias and Sapphira (Acts v. 1), the cure of Aeneas (Acts ix. 34), the resurrection of Dorcas (Acts ix. 40); yet out of six speeches of Peter, preserved in the Acts, I know but two in which reference is made to the miracles wrought by Christ, and only one in which he refers to miraculous powers possessed by himself. In his speech upon the day of Pentecost, Peter addresses his audience with great solemnity thus: "Ye men of Israel, hear these words: Jesus of Nazareth, a man approved of God among you, by miracles, and wonders, and signs, which God did by him in the midst of you, as ye yourselves also know:" (Acts ii. 22.) &c. In his speech upon the conversion of Cornelius, he delivers his testimony to the miracles performed by Christ in these words: "We are witnesses of all things which he did, both in the land of the Jews and in Jerusalem." (Acts x. 39.) But in this latter speech no allusion appears to the miracles wrought by himself notwithstanding that the miracles above enumerated all preceded the time in which it was delivered. In his speech upon the election of Matthias, (Acts i. 15.) no distinct reference is made to any of the miracles of Christ's history except his resurrection. The same also may be observed of his speech upon the cure of the lame man at the of the temple; (Acts iii. 12.) the same in his speech before the Sanhedrim; (Acts iv. 8.) the same in his second apology in the presence of that assembly Stephen's long speech contains no reference whatever to miracles, though it be expressly related of him, in the book which preserves the speech, and almost immediately before the speech, "that he did great wonders and miracles among the people." (Acts vi. 8.) Again, although miracles be expressly attributed to Saint Paul in the Acts of the Apostles, first generally, as at Iconium (Acts xiv. 3), during the whole tour through the Upper Asia (xiv. 27; xv. 12), at Ephesus (xix. 11, 12); secondly, in specific instances, as the blindness of Elymas at Paphos, (Acts xiii. 11.) the cure of the cripple at Lystra, (Acts xiv. 8.) of the pythoness at Philippi, (Acts xvi. 16.) the miraculous liberation from prison in the same city, (Acts xvi. 26.) the restoration of Eutychus, (Acts xx. 10.) the predictions of his shipwreck, (Acts xxvii. 1.) the viper at Melita, the cure of Publius's father; (Acts xxvii. 8.) at all which miracles, except the first two, the historian himself was present: notwithstanding, I say, this positive ascription of miracles to St. Paul, yet in the speeches delivered by him, and given as delivered by him, in the same book in which the miracles are related, and the miraculous powers asserted, the appeals to his own miracles, or indeed to any miracles at all, are rare and incidental. In his speech at Antioch in Pisidia, (Acts xiii. 16.) there is no allusion but to the resurrection. In his discourse at Miletus, (Acts xx. 17.) none to any miracle: none in his speech before Felix; (Acts xxiv. 10.) none in his speech before Festus; (Acts xxv. 8.) except to Christ's resurrection and his own conversion.

Agreeably hereunto, in thirteen letters ascribed to Saint Paul, we have incessant references to Christ's resurrection, frequent references to his own conversion, three indubitable references to the miracles which he wrought; (Gal. iii. 5; Rom. xv. 18, 19; 2 Cor. xii. 12.) four other references to the same, less direct, yet highly probable; (1 Cor. ii. 4,5; Eph. iii. 7; Gal. ii. 8; 1 Thess. i. 8.) but more copious or circumstantial recitals we have not. The consent, therefore, between Saint Paul's speeches and letters is in this respect sufficiently exact; and the reason in both is the same, namely, that the miraculous history was all along presupposed, and that the question which occupied the speaker's and the writer's thoughts was this: whether, allowing the history of Jesus to be true, he was, upon the strength of it, to be received as the promised Messiah; and, if he was, what were the consequences, what was the object and benefit of his mission?

The general observation which has been made upon the apostolic writings, namely, that the subject of which they treated did not lead them to any direct recital of the Christian history, belongs to the writings of the apostolic fathers. The epistle of Barnabas is, in its subject and general composition, much like the epistle to the Hebrews; an allegorical application of divers passages of the Jewish history, of their law and ritual, to those parts of the Christian dispensation in which the author perceived a resemblance. The epistle of Clement was written for the sole purpose of quieting certain dissensions that had arisen amongst the members of the church of Corinth, and of reviving in their minds that temper and spirit of which their predecessors in the Gospel had left them an example. The work of Hermas is a vision; quotes neither the Old Testament nor the New, and merely falls now and then into the language and the mode of speech which the author had read in our Gospels. The epistles of Polycarp and Ignatius had for their principal object the order and discipline of the churches which they addressed. Yet, under all these circumstances of disadvantage, the great points of the Christian history are fully recognised. This hath been shown in its proper place. (Vide supra, pp. 48-51. [Part 1, Chapter 8])

There is, however, another class of writers to whom the answer above given, viz. the unsuitableness of any such appeals or references as the objection demands to the subjects of which the writings treated, does not apply; and that is the class of ancient apologists, whose declared design it was to defend Christianity, and to give the reasons of their adherence to it.

It is necessary, therefore, to inquire how the matter of the objection stands in these.

The most ancient apologist of whose works we have the smallest knowledge is Quadratus. Quadratus lived about seventy years after the ascension, and presented his apology to the Emperor Adrian. From a passage of this work, preserved in Eusebius, it appears that the author did directly and formally appeal to the miracles of Christ, and in terms as express and confident as we could desire. The passage (which has been once already stated) is as follows: "The works of our Saviour were always conspicuous, for they were real: both they that were healed, and they that were raised from the dead, were seen, not only when they were healed or raised, but for a long time afterwards; not only whilst he dwelled on this earth, but also after his departure, and for a good while after it; insomuch as that some of them have reached to our times," (Euseb. Hist. I. iv. c. 3.) Nothing can be more rational or satisfactory than this.

Justin Martyr, the next of the Christian apologists, whose work is not lost, and who followed Quadratus at the distance of about thirty years, has touched upon passages of Christ's history in so many places, that a tolerably complete account of Christ's life might be collected out of his works. In the following quotation he asserts the performance of miracles by Christ, in words as strong and positive as the language possesses: "Christ healed those who from their birth were blind, and deaf, and lame; causing, by his word, one to leap, another to hear, and a third to see; and having raised the dead, and caused them to live, he, by his works, excited attention, and induced the men of that age to know him: who, however, seeing these things done, said that it was a magical appearance, and dared to call him a magician, and a deceiver of the people." (Just. Dial. p. 258, ed. Thirlby.)

In his first apology, (Apolog. prim. p. 48, ib.) Justin expressly assigns the reason for his having recourse to the argument from prophecy, rather than alleging the miracles of the Christian history; which reason was, that the persons with whom he contended would ascribe these miracles to magic; "lest any of our opponents should say, What hinders, but that he who is called Christ by us, being a man sprung from men, performed the miracles which we attribute to him by magical art?" The suggestion of this reason meets, as I apprehend, the very point of the present objection; more especially when we find Justin followed in it by other writers of that age. Irenaeus, who came about forty years after him, notices the same evasion in the adversaries of Christianity, and replies to it by the same argument: "But if they shall say, that the Lord performed these things by an illusory appearance (phantasiodos), leading these objectors to the prophecies, we will show from them, that all things were thus predicted concerning him, and Strictly came to pass." (Iren. I. ii. c. 57.) Lactantius, who lived a century lower, delivers the same sentiment upon the same occasion: "He performed miracles;—we might have supposed him to have been a magician, as ye say, and as the Jews then supposed, if all the prophets had not with one spirit foretold that Christ should perform these very things." (Lactant. v. 3.)

But to return to the Christian apologists in their order. Tertullian:— "That person whom the Jews had vainly imagined, from the meanness of his appearance, to be a mere man, they afterwards, in consequence of the power he exerted, considered as a magician, when he, with one word, ejected devils out of the bodies of men, gave sight to the blind, cleansed the leprous, strengthened the nerves of those that had the palsy, and lastly, with one command, restored the dead to life; when he, I say, made the very elements obey him, assuaged the storms, walked upon the seas, demonstrating himself to be the Word of God." (Tertul. Apolos. p. 20; ed. Priorii, Par. 1675.)

Next in the catalogue of professed apologists we may place Origen, who, it is well known, published a formal defence of Christianity, in answer to Celsus, a heathen, who had written a discourse against it. I know no expressions by which a plainer or more positive appeal to the Christian miracles can be made, than the expressions used by Origen; "Undoubtedly we do think him to be the Christ, and the Son of God, because he healed the lame and the blind; and we are the more confirmed in this persuasion by what is written in the prophecies: 'Then shall the eyes of the blind be opened, and the ears of the deaf shall hear, and the lame man shall leap as a hart.' But that he also raised the dead, and that it is not a fiction of those who wrote the Gospels, is evident from hence, that if it had been a fiction, there would have been many recorded to be raised up, and such as had been a long time in their graves. But, it not being a fiction, few have been recorded: for instance, the daughter of the ruler of a synagogue, of whom I do not know why he said, She is not dead, but sleepeth, expressing something peculiar to her, not common to all dead persons: and the only son of a widow, on whom he had compassion, and raised him to life, after he had bid the bearers of the corpse to stop; and the third, Lazarus, who had been buried four days." This is positively to assert the miracles of Christ, and it is also to comment upon them, and that with a considerable degree of accuracy and candour.

In another passage of the same author, we meet with the old solution of magic applied to the miracles of Christ by the adversaries of the religion. "Celsus," saith Origen, "well knowing what great works may be alleged to have been done by Jesus, pretends to grant that the things related of him are true; such as healing diseases, raising the dead, feeding multitudes with a few leaves, of which large fragments were left." (Orig. cont. Cels. lib. ii. sect. 48.) And then Celsus gives, it seems, an answer to these proofs of our Lord's mission, which, as Origen understood it, resolved the phenomena into magic; for Origen begins his reply by observing, "You see that Celsus in a manner allows that there is such a thing as magic." (Lardner's Jewish and Heath. Test, vol. ii. p. 294, ed. 4to.)

It appears also from the testimony of St. Jerome, that Porphyry, the most learned and able of the heathen writers against Christianity, resorted to the same solution: "Unless," says he, speaking to Vigilantius, "according to the manner of the Gentiles and the profane, of Porphyry and Eunomius, you pretend that these are the tricks of demons." (Jerome cont. Vigil.)

This magic, these demons, this illusory appearance, this comparison with the tricks of jugglers, by which many of that age accounted so easily for the Christian miracles, and which answers the advocates of Christianity often thought it necessary to refute by arguments drawn from other topics, and particularly from prophecy (to which, it seems, these solutions did not apply), we now perceive to be gross subterfuges. That such reasons were ever seriously urged and seriously received, is only a proof what a gloss and varnish fashion can give to any opinion.

It appears, therefore, that the miracles of Christ, understood as we understand them in their literal and historical sense, were positively and precisely asserted and appealed to by the apologists for Christianity; which answers the allegation of the objection.

I am ready, however, to admit, that the ancient Christian advocates did not insist upon the miracles in argument so frequently as I should have done. It was their lot to contend with notions of magical agency, against which the mere production of the facts was not sufficient for the convincing of their adversaries: I do not know whether they themselves thought it quite decisive of the controversy. But since it is proved, I conceive with certainty, that the sparingness with which they appealed to miracles was owing neither to their ignorance nor their doubt of the facts, it is, at any rate, an objection not to the truth of the history, but to the judgment of its defenders.

CHAPTER VI.

WANT OF UNIVERSALITY IN THE KNOWLEDGE AND RECEPTION OF CHRISTIANITY, AND OF GREATER CLEARNESS IN THE EVIDENCE.

Or, a Revelation which really came from God, the proof, it has been said, would in all ages be so public and manifest, that no part of the human species would remain ignorant of it, no understanding could fail of being convinced by it.

The advocates of Christianity do not pretend that the evidence of their religion possesses these qualities. They do not deny that we can conceive it to be within the compass of divine power to have communicated to the world a higher degree of assurance, and to have given to his communication a stronger and more extensive influence. For anything we are able to discern, God could have so formed men, as to have perceived the truths of religion intuitively; or to have carried on a communication with the other world whilst they lived in this; or to have seen the individuals of the species, instead of dying, pass to heaven by a sensible translation. He could have presented a separate miracle to each man's senses. He could have established a standing miracle. He could have caused miracles to be wrought in every different age and country. These and many more methods, which we may imagine if we once give loose to our imaginations, are, so far as we can judge, all practicable.

The question therefore is, not whether Christianity possesses the highest possible degree of evidence, but whether the not having more evidence be a sufficient reason for rejecting that which we have.

Now there appears to be no fairer method of judging concerning any dispensation which is alleged to come from God, when question is made whether such a dispensation could come from God or not, than by comparing it with other things which are acknowledged to proceed from the same counsel, and to be produced by the same agency. If the dispensation in question labour under no defects but what apparently belong to other dispensations, these seeming defects do not justify us in setting aside the proofs which are offered of its authenticity, if they be otherwise entitled to credit.

Throughout that order then of nature, of which God is the author, what we find is a system of beneficence: we are seldom or never able to make out a system of optimism. I mean, that there are few cases in which, if we permit ourselves to range in possibilities, we cannot suppose something more perfect, and, more unobjectionable, than what we see. The rain which descends from heaven is confessedly amongst the contrivances of the Creator for the sustentation of the animals and vegetables which subsist upon the surface of the earth. Yet how partially: and irregularly is it supplied! How much of it falls upon sea, where it can be of no use! how often is it wanted where it would be of the greatest! What tracts of continent are rendered deserts by the scarcity of it! Or, not to speak of extreme cases, how much sometimes do inhabited countries suffer by its deficiency or delay!—We could imagine, if to imagine were our business, the matter to be otherwise regulated. We could imagine showers to fall just where and when they would do good; always seasonable, everywhere sufficient; so distributed as not to leave a field upon the face of the globe scorched by drought or even a plant withering for the lack of moisture. Yet, does the difference between the real case and the imagined case, or the seeming inferiority of the one to the other, authorise us to say, that the present disposition of the atmosphere is not amongst the productions or the designs of the Deity? Does it check the inference which we draw from the confessed beneficence of the provision? or does it make us cease to admire the contrivance? The observation which we have exemplified in the single instance of the rain of heaven may be repeated concerning most of the phenomena of nature; and the true conclusion to which it leads is this—that to inquire what the Deity might have done, could have done, or, as we even sometimes presume to speak, ought to have done, or, in hypothetical cases, would have done; and to build any propositions upon such inquiries against evidence of facts, is wholly unwarrantable. It is a mode of reasoning which will not do in natural history, which will not do in natural religion, which cannot therefore be applied with safety to revelation. It may have same foundation in certain speculative a priori ideas of the divine attributes, but it has none in experience or in analogy. The general character of the works of nature is, on the one hand, goodness both in design and effect; and, on the other hand, a liability to difficulty and to objections, if such objections be allowed, by reason of seeming incompleteness or uncertainty in attaining their end. Christianity participates of this character. The true similitude between nature and revelation consists in this—that they each bear strong marks of their original, that they each also bear appearances of irregularity and defect. A system of strict optimism may, nevertheless, be the real system in both cases. But what I contend is, that the proof is hidden from us; that we ought not to expect to perceive that in revelation which we hardly perceive in anything; that beneficence, of which, we can judge, ought to satisfy us that optimism, of which we cannot judge, ought not to be sought after. We can judge of beneficence, because it depends upon effects which we experience, and upon the relation between the means which we see acting and the ends which we see produced. We cannot judge of optimism because it necessarily implies a comparison of that which is tried with that which is not tried; of consequences which we see with others which we imagine, and concerning many of which, it is more than probable, we know nothing; concerning some that we have no notion.

If Christianity be compared with the state and progress of natural religion, the argument of the objector will gain nothing by the comparison. I remember hearing an unbeliever say that, if God had given a revelation, he would have written it in the skies. Are the truths of natural religion written in the skies, or in a language which every one reads? or is this the case with the most useful arts, or the most necessary sciences of human life? An Otaheitean or an Esquimaux knows nothing of Christianity; does he know more of the principles of deism or morality? which, notwithstanding his ignorance, are neither untrue, nor unimportant, nor uncertain. The existence of Deity is left to be collected from observations, which every man does not make, which every man, perhaps, is not capable of making. Can it be argued that God does not exist because if he did, he would let us see him, or discover himself to man kind by proofs (such as, we may think, the nature of the subject merited) which no inadvertency could miss, no prejudice withstand?

If Christianity be regarded as a providential instrument the melioration of mankind, its progress and diffusion that of other causes by which human life is improved diversity is not greater, nor the advance more slow, in than we find it to be in learning, liberty, government, laws. The Deity hath not touched the order of nature in vain. The Jewish religion produced great and permanent effects; the Christian religion hath done the same. It hath disposed the world to amendment: it hath put things in a train. It is by no means improbable that it may become universal; and that the world may continue in that stage so long as that the duration of its reign may bear a vast proportion to the time of its partial influence.

When we argue concerning Christianity, that it must necessarily be true because it is beneficial, we go, perhaps, too far on one side; and we certainly go too far on the other when we conclude that it must be false because it is not so efficacious as we could have supposed. The question of its truth is to be tried upon its proper evidence, without deferring much to this sort of argument on either side. "The evidence," as Bishop Butler hath rightly observed, "depends upon the judgment we form of human conduct, under given circumstances, of which it may be presumed that we know something; the objection stands upon the supposed conduct of the Deity, under relations with which we are not acquainted."

What would be the real effect of that overpowering evidence which our adversaries require in a revelation it is difficult foretell; at least we must speak of it as of a dispensation which we have no experience. Some consequences, however, would, it is probable, attend this economy, which do not seem to befit a revelation that proceeded from God. One is, that irresistible proof would restrain the voluntary powers too much; would not answer the purpose of trial and probation; would call for no exercise of candour, seriousness, humility, inquiry, no submission of passion, interests, and prejudices, to moral evidence and to probable truth; no habits of reflection; none of that previous desire to learn and to obey the will of God, which forms perhaps the test of the virtuous principle, and which induces men to attend, with care and reverence, to every credible intimation of that will, and to resign present advantages and present pleasures to every reasonable expectation of propitiating his favour. "Men's moral probation may be, whether they will take due care to inform themselves by impartial consideration; and, afterwards, whether they will act, as the case requires, upon the evidence which they have. And this we find by experience is often our probation in our temporal capacity." (Butler's Analogy, part ii. c. 6.)

II. These modes of communication would leave no place for the admission of internal evidence; which ought, perhaps, to bear a considerable part in the proof of every revelation, because it is a species of evidence which applies itself to the knowledge, love, and practice, of virtue, and which operates in proportion to the degree of those qualities which it finds in the person whom it addresses. Men of good dispositions, amongst Christians, are greatly affected by the impression which the Scriptures themselves make upon their minds. Their conviction is much strengthened by these impressions. And this perhaps was intended to be one effect to be produced by the religion. It is likewise true, to whatever cause we ascribe it (for I am not in this work at liberty to introduce the Christian doctrine of grace or assistance, or the Christian promise that, "if any man will do his will, he shall know of the doctrine, whether it be of God" John vii. 17.),—it is true, I say, that they who sincerely act, or sincerely endeavour to act, according to what they believe, that is, according to the just result of the probabilities, or, if you please, the possibilities in natural and revealed religion, which they themselves perceive, and according to a rational estimate of consequences, and, above all, according to the just effect of those principles of gratitude and devotion which even the view of nature generates in a well-ordered mind, seldom fail of proceeding farther. This also may have been exactly what was designed.

Whereas, may it not be said that irresistible evidence would confound all characters and all dispositions? would subvert rather than promote the true purpose of the Divine counsels; which is, not to produce obedience by a force little short of mechanical constraint, (which obedience would be regularity, not virtue, and would hardly perhaps differ from that which inanimate bodies pay to the laws impressed upon their nature), but to treat moral agents agreeably to what they are; which is done, when light and motives are of such kinds, and are imparted in such measures, that the

251

influence of them depends upon the recipients themselves? "It is not meet to govern rational free agents in via by sight and sense. It would be no trial or thanks to the most sensual wretch to forbear sinning, if heaven and hell were open to his sight. That spiritual vision and fruition is our state in patria." (Baxter's Reasons, p. 357.) There may be truth in this thought, though roughly expressed. Few things are more improbable than that we (the human species) should be the highest order of beings in the universe: that animated nature should ascend from the lowest reptile to us, and all at once stop there. If there be classes above us of rational intelligences, clearer manifestations may belong to them. This may be one of the distinctions. And it may be one to which we ourselves hereafter shall attain.

III. But may it not also be asked, whether the perfect display of a future state of existence would be compatible with the activity of civil life, and with the success of human affairs? I can easily conceive that this impression may be overdone; that it may so seize and fill the thoughts as to leave no place for the cares and offices of men's several stations, no anxiety for worldly prosperity, or even for a worldly provision, and, by consequence, no sufficient stimulus to secular industry. Of the first Christians we read, "that all that believed were together, and had all things common; and sold their possessions and goods, and parted them to all men, as every man had need; and continuing daily with one accord in the temple, and breaking bread from house to house, did eat their meat with gladness and singleness of heart" (Acts ii. 44-46.) This was extremely natural, and just what might be expected from miraculous evidence coming with full force upon the senses of mankind: but I much doubt whether, if this state of mind had been universal, or long-continued, the business of the world could have gone on. The necessary art of social life would have been little cultivated. The plough and the loom would have stood still. Agriculture, manufactures, trade, and navigation, would not, I think, have flourished, if they could have been exercised at all. Men would have addicted themselves to contemplative and ascetic lives, instead of lives of business and of useful industry. We observe that St. Paul found it necessary frequently to recall his converts to the ordinary labours and domestic duties of their condition; and to give them, in his own example, a lesson of contented application to their worldly employments.

By the manner in which the religion is now proposed, a great portion of the human species is enabled and of these multitudes of every generation are induced, to seek and effectuate their salvation through the medium of Christianity, without interruption of the prosperity or of the regular course of human affairs.

CHAPTER VII.

THE SUPPOSED EFFECTS OF CHRISTIANITY.

That a religion which under every form in which it is taught holds forth the final reward of virtue and punishment of vice, and proposes those distinctions of virtue and vice which the wisest and most cultivated part of mankind confess to be just, should not be believed, is very possible; but that, so far as it is believed, it should not produce any good, but rather a bad effect upon public happiness, is a proposition which it requires very strong evidence to render credible. Yet many have been found to contend for this paradox, and very confident appeals have been made to history and to observation for the truth of it.

In the conclusions, however, which these writers draw from what they call experience, two sources, I think, of mistake may be perceived.

One is, that they look for the influence of religion in the wrong place.

The other, that they charge Christianity with many consequences for which it is not responsible.

I. The influence of religion is not to be sought for in the councils of princes, in the debates or resolutions of popular assemblies, in the conduct of governments towards their subjects, of states and sovereigns towards one another; of conquerors at the head of their armies, or of parties intriguing for power at home (topics which alone almost occupy the attention, and fill the pages of history); but must be perceived, if perceived at all, in the silent course of private and domestic life. Nay, even there its influence may not be very obvious to observation. If it check, in some degree, personal dissoluteness, if it beget general probity in the transaction of business, if it produce soft and humane manners in the mass of the community, and occasional exertions of laborious or expensive benevolence in a individuals, it is all the effect which can offer itself to external notice. The kingdom of heaven is within us. That which the substance of the religion, its hopes and consolation, its intermixture with the thoughts by day and by night, the devotion of the heart, the control of appetite, the steady direction of will to the commands of God, is necessarily invisible. Yet these depend the virtue and the happiness of millions. This cause renders the representations of history, with respect to religion, defect and fallacious in a greater degree than they are upon any other subject. Religion operates most upon those of whom history knows the least; upon fathers and mothers their families, upon men-servants and maid-servants, upon orderly tradesman, the quiet villager, the manufacturer at his loom, the husbandman in his fields. Amongst such, its collectively may be of inestimable value, yet its effects, in mean time, little upon those who figure upon the stage of world. They may know nothing of it; they may believe nothing of it; they may be actuated by motives more impetuous than those which religion is able to excite. It cannot, be thought strange that this influence should elude the grasp and touch of public history; for what is public history but register of the successes and disappointments, the vices, the follies, and the quarrels, of those who engage in contentions power?

I will add, that much of this influence may be felt in times of public distress, and little of it in times of public wealth and security. This also increases the uncertainty of any opinions that we draw from historical representations. The influence of Christianity is commensurate with no effects which history states. We do not pretend that it has any such necessary and irresistible power over the affairs of nations as to surmount the force of other causes.

The Christian religion also acts upon public usages and institutions, by an operation which is only secondary and indirect. Christianity is not a code of civil law. It can only reach public institutions through private character. Now its influence upon private character may be considerable, yet many public usages and institutions repugnant to its principles may remain. To get rid of these, the reigning part of the community must act, and act together. But it may be long before the persons who compose this body be sufficiently touched with the Christian character to join in the suppression of practices to which they and the public have been reconciled by causes which will reconcile the human mind to anything, by habit and interest. Nevertheless, the effects of Christianity, even in this view, have been important. It has mitigated the conduct of war, and the treatment of captives. It has softened the administration of despotic, or of nominally despotic governments. It has abolished polygamy. It has restrained the licentiousness of divorces. It has put an end to the exposure of children and the immolation of slaves. It has suppressed the combats of gladiators,[1] and the impurities of religions rites. It has banished, if not unnatural vices, at least the toleration of them. It has greatly meliorated the condition of the laborious part, that is to say, of the mass of every community, by procuring for them a day of weekly rest. In all countries in which it is professed it has produced numerous establishments for the relief of sickness and poverty; and in some, a regular and general provision by law. It has triumphed over the slavery established in the Roman empire: it is contending, and I trust will one day prevail, against the worse slavery of the West Indies.

A Christian writer, (Bardesanes, ap. Euseb. Praep. Evang. vi. 10.) so early as in the second century, has testified the resistance which

---

[1] Lipsius affirms (Sat. b. i. c. 12) that the gladiatorial shows sometimes cost Europe twenty or thirty thousand lives in a month; and that not only the men, but even the women of all ranks were passionately fond of these shows. See Bishop Porteus, Sermon XIII.

Christianity made to wicked and licentious practices though established by law and by public usage:—"Neither in Parthia do the Christians, though Parthians, use polygamy; nor in Persia, though Persians, do they marry their own daughters; nor among the Bactri, or Galli, do they violate the sanctity of marriage; nor wherever they are, do they suffer themselves to be overcome by ill-constituted laws and manners."

Socrates did not destroy the idolatry of Athens, or produce the slighter revolution in the manners of his country.

But the argument to which I recur is, that the benefit of religion, being felt chiefly in the obscurity of private stations, necessarily escapes the observation of history. From the first general notification of Christianity to the present day, there have been in every age many millions, whose names were never heard of, made better by it, not only in their conduct, but in their disposition; and happier, not so much in their external circumstances, as in that which is inter praecordia, in that which alone deserves the name of happiness, the tranquillity and consolation of their thoughts. It has been since its commencement the author of happiness and virtue to millions and millions of the human race. Who is there that would not wish his son to be a Christian?

Christianity also, in every country in which it is professed, hath obtained a sensible, although not a complete influence upon the public judgment of morals. And this is very important. For without the occasional correction which public opinion receives, by referring to some fixed standard of morality, no man can foretell into what extravagances it might wander. Assassination might become as honourable as duelling: unnatural crimes be accounted as venal as fornication is wont to be accounted. In this way it is possible that many may be kept in order by Christianity who are not themselves Christians. They may be guided by the rectitude which it communicates to public opinion. Their consciences may suggest their duty truly, and they may ascribe these suggestions to a moral sense, or to the native capacity of the human intellect, when in fact they are nothing more than the public opinion, reflected from their own minds; and opinion, in a considerable degree, modified by the lessons of Christianity. "Certain it is, and this is a great deal to say, that the generality, even of the meanest and most vulgar and ignorant people, have truer and worthier notions of God more just and right apprehensions concerning his attributes and perfections, a deeper sense of the difference of good and evil, a greater regard to moral obligations, and to the plain and most necessary duties of life, and a more firm and universal expectation of a future state of rewards and punishments, than in any heathen country any considerable number of men were found to have had." (Clarke, Ev. Nat. Rel. p. 208. ed. v.)

After all, the value of Christianity is not to be appreciated by its temporal effects. The object of revelation is to influence human conduct in this life; but what is gained to happiness by that influence can only be estimated by taking in the whole of human existence. Then, as hath already been observed, there may be also great consequences of Christianity which do not belong to it as a revelation. The effects upon human salvation of the mission, of the death, of the present, of the future agency of Christ, may be universal, though the religion be not universally known.

Secondly, I assert that Christianity is charged with many consequences for which it is not responsible. I believe that religious motives have had no more to do in the formation of nine tenths of the intolerant and persecuting laws which in different countries have been established upon the subject of religion, than they have had to do in England with the making of the game-laws. These measures, although they have the Christian religion for their subject, are resolvable into a principle which Christianity certainly did not plant (and which Christianity could not universally condemn, because it is not universally wrong), which principle is no other than this, that they who are in possession of power do what they can to keep it. Christianity is answerable for no part of the mischief which has been brought upon the world by persecution, except that which has arisen from conscientious persecutors. Now these perhaps have never been either numerous or powerful. Nor is it to Christianity that even their mistake can fairly be imputed. They have been misled by an error not properly Christian or religious, but by an error in their moral philosophy. They pursued the particular, without adverting to the general consequence. Believing certain articles of faith, or a certain mode of worship, to be highly conducive, or perhaps essential, to salvation, they thought themselves bound to bring all they could, by every means, into them, and this they thought, without considering what would be the effect of such a conclusion when adopted amongst mankind as a general rule of conduct. Had there been in the New Testament, what there are in the Koran, precepts authorising coercion in the propagation of the religion, and the use of violence towards unbelievers, the case would have been different. This distinction could not have been taken, nor this defence made.

I apologise for no species nor degree of persecution, but I think that even the fact has been exaggerated. The slave-trade destroys more in a year than the Inquisition does in a hundred or perhaps hath done since its foundation.

If it be objected, as I apprehend it will be, that Christianity is chargeable with every mischief of which it has been the occasion, though not the motive; I answer that, if the malevolent passions be there, the world will never want occasions. The noxious element will always find a conductor. Any point will produce an explosion. Did the applauded intercommunity of the pagan theology preserve the peace of the Roman world? did it prevent oppressions, proscriptions, massacres, devastation? Was it bigotry that carried Alexander into the East, or brought Caesar into Gaul? Are the nations of the world into which Christianity hath not found its way, or from which it hath been banished, free from contentions? Are their contentions less ruinous and sanguinary? Is it owing to Christianity, or to the want of it, that the regions of the East, the countries inter quatuor maria, peninsula of Greece, together with a great part of the Mediterranean coast, are at this day a desert? or that the banks of the Nile, whose constantly renewed fertility is not to be impaired by neglect, or destroyed by the ravages of war, serve only for the scene of a ferocious anarchy, or the supply of unceasing hostilities? Europe itself has known no religious wars for some centuries, yet has hardly ever been without war. Are the calamities which at this day afflict it to be imputed to Christianity? Hath Poland fallen by a Christian crusade? Hath the overthrow in France of civil order and security been effected by the votaries of our religion, or by the foes? Amongst the awful lessons which the crimes and the miseries of that country afford to mankind this is one; that in order to be a persecutor it is not necessary to be a bigot: that in rage and cruelty, in mischief and destruction, fanaticism itself can be outdone by infidelity.

Finally, if war, as it is now carried on between nations produce less misery and ruin than formerly, we are indebted perhaps to Christianity for the change more than to any other cause. Viewed therefore even in its relation to this subject, it appears to have been of advantage to the world. It hath humanised the conduct of wars; it hath ceased to excite them.

The differences of opinion that have in all ages prevailed amongst Christians fall very much within the alternative which has been stated. If we possessed the disposition which Christianity labours, above all other qualities, to inculcate, these differences would do little harm. If that disposition be wanting, other causes, even were these absent, would continually rise up to call forth the malevolent passions into action. Differences of opinion, when accompanied with mutual charity, which Christianity forbids them to violate, are for the most part innocent, and for some purposes useful. They promote inquiry, discussion, and knowledge. They help to keep up an attention to religious subjects, and a concern about them, which might be apt to die away in the calm and silence of universal agreement. I do not know that it is in any degree true that the influence of religion is the greatest where there are the fewest dissenters.

CHAPTER VIII.

THE CONCLUSION

In religion, as in every other subject of human reasoning, much depends upon the order in which we dispose our inquiries. A man who takes up a system of divinity with a previous opinion that either every part must be true or the whole false, approaches the discussion with great disadvantage. No other system, which is founded upon moral evidence, would bear to be treated in the same manner. Nevertheless, in a certain degree, we are all introduced to our religious studies under this prejudication. And it cannot be avoided. The weakness of the human judgment in the early part of youth, yet its extreme susceptibility of impression, renders it necessary to furnish it with some opinions, and with some principles or other. Or indeed, without much express care, or much endeavour for this purpose, the tendency of the mind of man to assimilate itself to the habits of thinking and speaking which prevail around him, produces the same effect. That indifferency and suspense, that waiting and equilibrium of the judgment, which some require in religious matters, and which some would wish to be aimed at in the conduct of education, are impossible to be preserved. They are not given to the condition of human life.

It is a consequence of this institution that the doctrines of religion come to us before the proofs; and come to us with that mixture of explications and inferences from which no public creed is, or can be, free. And the effect which too frequently follows, from Christianity being presented to the understanding in this form, is, that when any articles, which appear as parts of it, contradict the apprehension of the persons to whom it is proposed, men of rash and confident tempers hastily and indiscriminately reject the whole. But is this to do justice, either to themselves or to the religion? The rational way of treating a subject of such acknowledged importance is, to attend, in the first place, to the general and substantial truth of its principles, and to that alone. When we once feel a foundation; when we once perceive a ground of credibility in its history; we shall proceed with safety to inquire into the interpretation of its records, and into the doctrines which have been deduced from them. Nor will it either endanger our faith, or diminish or alter our motives for obedience, if we should discover that these conclusions are formed with very different degrees of probability, and possess very different degrees of importance.

This conduct of the understanding, dictated by every rule of right reasoning, will uphold personal Christianity, even in those countries in which it is established under forms the most liable to difficulty and objection. It will also have the further effect of guarding us against the prejudices which are wont to arise in our minds to the disadvantage of religion, from observing the numerous controversies which are carried on amongst its professors; and likewise of inducing a spirit of lenity and moderation in our judgment, as well as in our treatment of those who stand, in such controversies, upon sides opposite to ours. What is clear in Christianity we shall find to be sufficient, and to be infinitely valuable; what is dubious, unnecessary to be decided, or of very subordinate importance, and what is most obscure, will teach us to bear with the opinions which others may have formed upon the same subject. We shall say to those who the most widely dissent from us, what Augustine said to the worst heretics of his age; "*Illi in vos saeviant, qui nasciunt, cum quo labore verum inveniatur, et quam difficile caveantur errores;—-qui nesciunt, cure quanta difficultate sanetur oculus interioris hominis;—qui nesciunt, quibus suspiriis et gemitibus fiat ut ex quantulacumque parte possit intelligi Deus.*". (Aug. contra. Ep. Fund. Cap. ii. n. 2,3.)

A judgment, moreover, which is once pretty well satisfied of the general truth of the religion will not only thus discriminate in its doctrines, but will possess sufficient strength to overcome the reluctance of the imagination to admit articles of faith which are attended with difficulty of apprehension, if such articles of faith appear to be truly parts of the revelation. It was to be expected beforehand, that what related to the economy and to the persons of the invisible world, which revelation profess to do, and which, if true, it actually does, should contain some points remote from our analogies, and from the comprehension of a mind which hath acquired all its ideas from sense and from experience.

It hath been my care in the preceding work to preserve the separation between evidences and doctrines as inviolable as I could; to remove from the primary question all considerations which have been unnecessarily joined with it; and to offer a defence to Christianity which every Christian might read without seeing the tenets in which he had been brought up attacked or decried: and it always afforded a satisfaction to my mind to observe that this was practicable; that few or none of our many controversies with one another affect or relate to the proofs of our religion; that the rent never descends to the foundation.

The truth of Christianity depends upon its leading facts, and upon them alone. Now of these we have evidence which ought to satisfy us, at least until it appear that mankind have ever been deceived by the same. We have some uncontested and incontestable points, to which the history of the human species hath nothing similar to offer. A Jewish peasant changed the religion of the world, and that without force, without power, without support; without one natural source or circumstance of attraction, influence, or success. Such a thing hath not happened in any other instance. The companions of this Person, after he himself had been put to death for his attempt, asserted his supernatural character, founded upon his supernatural operations: and, in testimony of the truth of their assertions, i.e. in consequence of their own belief of that truth, and in order to communicate the knowledge of it to others, voluntarily entered upon lives of toil and hardship, and, with a full experience of their danger, committed themselves to the last extremities of persecution. This hath not a parallel. More particularly, a very few days after this Person had been publicly executed, and in the very city in which he was buried, these his companions declared with one voice that his body was restored to life: that they had seen him, handled him, ate with him, conversed with him; and, in pursuance of their persuasion of the truth of what they told, preached his religion, with this strange fact as the foundation of it, in the face of those who had killed him, who were armed with the power of the country, and necessarily and naturally disposed to treat his followers as they had treated himself; and having done this upon the spot where the event took place, carried the intelligence of it abroad, in despite of difficulties and opposition, and where the nature of their errand gave them nothing to expect but derision, insult, and outrage.—This is without example. These three facts, I think, are certain, and would have been nearly so, if the Gospels had never been written. The Christian story, as to these points, hath never varied. No other hath been set up against it. Every letter, every discourse, every controversy, amongst the followers of the religion; every book written by them from the age of its commencement to the present time, in every part of the world in which it hath been professed, and with every sect into which it hath been divided (and we have letters and discourses written by contemporaries, by witnesses of the transaction, by persons themselves bearing a share in it, and other writings following that again regular succession), concur in representing these facts in this manner. A religion which now possesses the greatest part of the civilised world unquestionably sprang up at Jerusalem at this time. Some account must be given of its origin; some cause assigned for its rise. All the accounts of this origin, all the explications of this cause, whether taken from the writings of the early followers of the religion (in which, and in which perhaps alone, it could he expected that they should he distinctly unfolded), or from occasional notices in other writings of that or the adjoining age, either expressly allege the facts above stated as the means by which the religion was set up, or advert to its commencement in a manner which agrees with the supposition of these facts being true, and which testifies their operation and effects.

These prepositions alone lay a foundation for our faith; for they prove the existence of a transaction which cannot even, in its most general parts, be accounted for upon any reasonable supposition, except that of the truth of the mission. But the particulars, the detail of the miracles or miraculous pretences (for such there necessarily must have been) upon which this unexampled transaction rested, and for which these men acted and suffered as they did act and suffer, it is undoubtedly of great importance to us to know. We have this detail from the fountain-head, from the persons themselves; in accounts written by eye-witnesses of the scene, by contemporaries and companions of those who were so; not in one book but four, each containing enough for the verification of the religion, all agreeing in the fundamental parts of the history. We have the authenticity of these books established by more and stronger proofs than belong to almost any other ancient book whatever, and by proofs which widely distinguish them from any others claiming a similar authority to theirs. If there were any good reason for doubt concerning the names to which these books are ascribed (which there is not, for they were never ascribed to any other, and we have evidence not long after their publication of their bearing the names which they now bear); their antiquity, of which there is no question, their reputation and authority amongst the early disciples of the religion, of which there is as little, form a valid proof that they must, in the main at least, have agreed with what the first teachers of the religion delivered.

When we open these ancient volumes, we discover in them marks of truth, whether we consider each in itself, or collate them with one another. The writers certainly knew something of what they were writing about, for they manifest an acquaintance with local circumstances, with the history and usages of the times, which could belong only to an inhabitant of that country, living in that age. In every narrative we perceive simplicity and undesignedness; the air and the language of reality. When we compare the different narratives together, we find them so varying as to repel all suspicion of confederacy; so agreeing under this variety as to show that the accounts had one real transaction for their common foundation; often attributing different actions and discourses to the Person whose history, or rather memoirs of whose history, they profess to relate, yet actions and discourses so similar as very much to bespeak the same character: which is a coincidence that, in such writers as they were, could only be the consequence of their writing from fact, and not from imagination.

These four narratives are confined to the history of the Founder of the religion, and end with his ministry. Since, however, it is certain that the affair went on, we cannot help being anxious to know how it proceeded. This intelligence hath come down to us in a work purporting to be written by a person, himself connected with the business during the first stages of its progress, taking up the story where the former histories had left it, carrying on the narrative, oftentimes with great particularity, and throughout with the appearance of good sense,[1] information and candour;

---

[1] See Peter's speech upon curing the cripple (Acts iii. 18), the council of the apostles (xv.), Paul's discourse at Athens (xvii. 22), before Agrippa (xxvi.). I

stating all along the origin, and the only probable origin, of effects which unquestionably were produced, together with the natural consequences of situations which unquestionably did exist; and confirmed, in the substance at least of the account, by the strongest possible accession of testimony which a history can receive, original letters, written by the person who is the principal subject of the history, written upon the business to which the history relates, and during the period, or soon after the period, which the history comprises. No man can say that this all together is not a body of strong historical evidence.

When we reflect that some of those from whom the books proceeded are related to have themselves wrought miracles, to have been the subject of miracles, or of supernatural assistance in propagating the religion, we may perhaps be led to think that more credit, or a different kind of credit, is due to these accounts, than what can be claimed by merely human testimony. But this is an argument which cannot be addressed to sceptics or unbelievers. A man must be a Christian before he can receive it. The inspiration of the historical Scriptures, the nature, degree, and extent of that inspiration, are questions undoubtedly of serious discussion; but they are questions amongst Christians themselves, and not between them and others. The doctrine itself is by no means necessary to the belief of Christianity, which must, in the first instance at least, depend upon the ordinary maxim of historical credibility. (See Powell's Discourse, disc. xv. P. 245.)

In viewing the detail of miracles recorded in these books, we find every supposition negatived by which they can be resolved into fraud or delusion. They were not secret, nor momentary, nor tentative, nor ambiguous; nor performed under the sanction of authority, with the spectators on their side, or in affirmance of tenets and practices already established. We find also the evidence alleged for them, and which evidence was by great numbers received, different from that upon which other miraculous accounts rest. It was contemporary, it was published upon the spot, it continued; it involved interests and questions of the greatest magnitude; it contradicted the most fixed persuasions and prejudices of the persons to whom it was addressed; it required from those who accepted it, not a simple, indolent assent, but a change, from thenceforward, of principles and conduct, a submission to consequences the most serious and the most deterring, to loss and danger, to insult, outrage, and persecution. How such a story should be false, or, if false, how under such circumstances it should make its way, I think impossible to be explained; yet such the Christian story was, such were the

---

notice these passages, both as fraught with good sense and as free from the smallest tincture of enthusiasm.

circumstances under which it came forth, and in opposition to such difficulties did it prevail.

An event so connected with the religion, and with the fortunes, of the Jewish people, as one of their race, one born amongst them, establishing his authority and his law throughout a great portion of the civilised world, it was perhaps to be expected should be noticed in the prophetic writings of that nation; especially when this Person, together with his own mission, caused also to be acknowledged the Divine original of their institution, and by those who before had altogether rejected it. Accordingly, we perceive in these writings various intimations concurring in the person and history of Jesus, in a manner and in a degree in which passages taken from these books could not be made to concur in any person arbitrarily assumed, or in any person except him who has been the author of great changes in the affairs and opinions of mankind. Of some of these predictions the weight depends a good deal upon the concurrence. Others possess great separate strength: one in particular does this in an eminent degree. It is an entire description, manifestly directed to one character and to one scene of things; it is extant in a writing, or collection of writings, declaredly prophetic; and it applies to Christ's character, and to the circumstances of his life and death, with considerable precision, and in a way which no diversity of interpretation hath, in my opinion, been able to confound. That the advent of Christ, and the consequences of it, should not have been more distinctly revealed in the Jewish sacred books, is I think in some measure accounted for by the consideration, that for the Jews to have foreseen the fall of their institution, and that it was to merge at length into a more perfect and comprehensive dispensation, would have cooled too much, and relaxed, their zeal for it, and their adherence to it, upon which zeal and adherence the preservation in the world of any remains, for many ages, of religious truth might in a great measure depend.

Of what a revelation discloses to mankind, one, and only one, question can properly be asked—Was it of importance to mankind to know, or to be better assured of? In this question, when we turn our thoughts to the great Christian doctrine of the resurrection of the dead, and of a future judgment, no doubt can possibly be entertained. He who gives me riches or honours, does nothing; he who even gives me health, does little, in comparison with that which lays before me just grounds for expecting a restoration to life, and a day of account and retribution; which thing Christianity hath done for millions.

Other articles of the Christian faith, although of infinite importance when placed beside any other topic of human inquiry, are only the adjuncts and circumstances of this. They are, however, such as appear worthy of the original to which we ascribe them. The morality of the religion, whether taken from the precepts or the example of its Founder,

263

or from the lessons of its primitive teachers, derived, as it should seem, from what had been inculcated by their Master, is, in all its parts, wise and pure; neither adapted to vulgar prejudices, nor flattering popular notions, nor excusing established practices, but calculated, in the matter of its instruction, truly to promote human happiness; and in the form in which it was conveyed, to produce impression and effect: a morality which, let it have proceeded from any person whatever, would have been satisfactory evidence of his good sense and integrity, of the soundness of his understanding and the probity of his designs: a morality, in every view of it, much more perfect than could have been expected from the natural circumstances and character of the person who delivered it; a morality, in a word, which is, and hath been, most beneficial to mankind.

Upon the greatest, therefore, of all possible occasions, and for a purpose of inestimable value, it pleased the Deity to vouchsafe a miraculous attestation. Having done this for the institution, when this alone could fix its authority, or give to it a beginning, he committed its future progress to the natural means of human communication, and to the influence of those causes by which human conduct and human affairs are governed. The seed, being sown, was left to vegetate; the leaven, being inserted, was left to ferment; and both according to the laws of nature: laws, nevertheless, disposed and controlled by that Providence which conducts the affairs of the universe, though by an influence inscrutable, and generally undistinguishable by us. And in this, Christianity is analogous to most other provisions for happiness. The provision is made; and; being made, is left to act according to laws which, forming a part of a more general system, regulate this particular subject in common with many others.

Let the constant recurrence to our observation of contrivance, design, and wisdom, in the works of nature, once fix upon our minds the belief of a God, and after that all is easy. In the counsels of a being possessed of the power and disposition which the Creator of the universe must possess, it is not improbable that there should be a future state; it is not improbable that we should be acquainted with it. A future state rectifies everything; because, if moral agents be made, in the last event, happy or miserable, according to their conduct in the station and under the circumstances in which they are placed, it seems not very material by the operation of what causes, according to what rules, or even, if you please to call it so, by what chance or caprice these stations are assigned, or these circumstances determined. This hypothesis, therefore, solves all that objection to the divine care and goodness which the promiscuous distribution of good and evil (I do not mean in the doubtful advantages of riches and grandeur, but in the unquestionably important distinctions of health and sickness, strength and infirmity, bodily ease and pain, mental alacrity and depression) is apt on so many occasions to create. This one truth changes the nature of things; gives order to confusion; makes the moral world of a piece with the natural.

Nevertheless, a higher degree of assurance than that to which it is possible to advance this, or any argument drawn from the light of nature, was necessary, especially to overcome the shock which the imagination and the senses received from the effects and the appearances of death, and the obstruction which thence arises to the expectation of either a continued or a future existence. This difficulty, although of a nature no doubt to act very forcibly, will be found, I think, upon reflection to reside more in our habits of apprehension than in the subject: and that the giving way to it, when we have any reasonable grounds or the contrary, is rather an indulging of the imagination than anything else. Abstractedly considered, that is, considered without relation to the difference which habit, and merely habit, produces in our faculties and modes of apprehension, I do not see anything more in the resurrection of a dead man than in the conception of a child; except it be this, that the one comes into his world with a system of prior consciousness about him, which the other does not: and no person will say that he knows enough of either subject to perceive that this circumstance makes such a difference in the two cases that the one should be easy, and the other impossible; the one natural, the other not so. To the first man the succession of the species would be as incomprehensible as the resurrection of the dead is to us.

Thought is different from motion, perception from impact: the individuality of a mind is hardly consistent with the divisibility of an extended substance; or its volition, that is, its power of originating motion, with the inertness which cleaves to every portion of matter which our observation or our experiments can reach. These distinctions lead us to an immaterial principle: at least, they do this: they so negative the mechanical properties of matter, in the constitution of a sentient, still more of a rational, being, that no argument drawn from the properties can be of any great weight in opposition to other reasons, when the question respects the changes of which such: a nature is capable, or the manner in which these changes am effected. Whatever thought be, or whatever it depend upon the regular experience of sleep makes one thing concerning it certain, that it can be completely suspended, and completely restored.

If any one find it too great a strain upon his thoughts to admit the notion of a substance strictly immaterial, that is, from which extension and solidity are excluded, he can find no difficulty in allowing, that a particle as small as a particle of light, minuter than all conceivable dimensions, may just as easily be the depositary, the organ, and the vehicle of consciousness as the congeries of animal substance which forms a human body, or the human brain; that, being so, it may transfer a proper identity to whatever shall hereafter be united to it; may be safe amidst the destruction of its integuments; may connect the natural with the spiritual, the corruptible with the glorified body. If it be said that the mode and means of all this is imperceptible by our senses, it is only what is true of the most important agencies and operations. The great powers of nature are all invisible. Gravitation, electricity, magnetism, though constantly present, and constantly exerting their influence; though within us, near us, and about us; though diffused throughout all space, overspreading the surface, or penetrating the contexture, of all bodies with which we are acquainted, depend upon substances and actions which are totally concealed from our senses. The Supreme Intelligence is so himself.

But whether these or any other attempts to satisfy the imagination bear any resemblance to the truth; or whether the imagination, which, as I have said before, is the mere slave of habit, can be satisfied or not; when a future state, and the revelation of a future state is not only perfectly consistent with the attributes of the Being who governs the universe; but when it is more; when it alone removes the appearance of contrariety which attends the operations of his will towards creatures capable of comparative merit and demerit, of reward and punishment; when a strong body of historical evidence, confirmed by many internal tokens of truth and authenticity, gives us just reason to believe that such a revelation hath actually been made; we ought to set our minds at rest with the assurance, that in the resources of Creative Wisdom expedients cannot be wanted to carry into effect what the Deity hath purposed: that either a new and mighty influence will descend upon the human world to resuscitate extinguished consciousness; or that, amidst the other wonderful contrivances with which the universe abounds, and by some of which we see animal life, in many instances, assuming improved forms of existence, acquiring new organs, new perceptions, and new sources of enjoyment, provision is also made, though by methods secret to us (as all the great processes of nature are), for conducting the objects of God's moral government, through the necessary changes of their frame, to those final distinctions of happiness and misery which he hath declared to be reserved for obedience and transgression, for virtue and vice, for the use and the neglect, the right and the wrong employment of the faculties and opportunities with which he hath been pleased, severally, to intrust and to try us.

Index

www.ingramcontent.com/pod-product-compliance
Lightning Source LLC
LaVergne TN
LVHW011321080426
835513LV00006B/154